Methods in Analytical Political Theory

This is the first book to explain how to use key methods in analytical political theory. The methods discussed include contractualism, reflective equilibrium, positive political theory, thought experiments and ideological analysis. Many discussions of political theory methods describe and justify these methods with little or no discussion of their application, emphasizing 'what is' and 'why do' over 'how to'. This book covers all three. Each chapter explains what kinds of problems in political theory might require researchers to use a particular method, the basic principles behind the method being proposed, and an analysis of how to apply it, including concrete principles of good practice. The book thus summarizes methodological ideas, grouped in one place and made accessible to students, and it makes innovative contributions to research methods in analytical political theory.

D1563829

Methods in Analytical Political Theory

Edited By

Adrian Blau
King's College, London

CAMBRIDGE
UNIVERSITY PRESS

CAMBRIDGE
UNIVERSITY PRESS

University Printing House, Cambridge CB2 8BS, United Kingdom

One Liberty Plaza, 20th Floor, New York, NY 10006, USA

477 Williamstown Road, Port Melbourne, VIC 3207, Australia

4843/24, 2nd Floor, Ansari Road, Daryaganj, Delhi – 110002, India

79 Anson Road, #06–04/06, Singapore 079906

Cambridge University Press is part of the University of Cambridge.

It furthers the University's mission by disseminating knowledge in the pursuit of education, learning, and research at the highest international levels of excellence.

www.cambridge.org
Information on this title: www.cambridge.org/9781107098794
DOI: 10.1017/9781316162576

First published 2017

Printed in the United States of America by Sheridan Books, Inc.

A catalogue record for this publication is available from the British Library.

Library of Congress Cataloging-in-Publication Data
Names: Blau, Adrian, 1972– editor.
Title: Methods in analytical political theory / edited by Adrian Blau, King's College, London.
Description: New York, NY : Cambridge University Press, 2017.
Identifiers: LCCN 2016047820 | ISBN 9781107098794 (hardback)
Subjects: LCSH: Political science – Methodology. | Political science – Research – Methodology.
Classification: LCC JA71 .M4225 2017 | DDC 320.01–dc23
LC record available at https://lccn.loc.gov/2016047820

ISBN 978-1-107-09879-4 Hardback
ISBN 978-1-107-49170-0 Paperback

Contents

Contributors

Brooke Ackerly is Associate Professor in the Department of Political Science at Vanderbilt University.

Rochana Bajpai is Senior Lecturer in Politics in the Department of Politics and International Studies at SOAS.

Adrian Blau is Senior Lecturer in Politics in the Department of Political Economy at King's College London.

Kimberley Brownlee is Associate Professor of Legal and Moral Philosophy in the Department of Philosophy at the University of Warwick.

Keith Dowding is Professor of Political Science in the School of Politics and International Relations at the Australian National University.

Michael L. Frazer is Lecturer in Political and Social Theory in the School of Politics, Philosophy, Language and Communication Studies at the University of East Anglia.

Gerald Gaus is the James E. Rogers Professor of Philosophy in the Philosophy Department at the University of Arizona.

Robert E. Goodin is Distinguished Professor in the School of Philosophy at the Australian National University.

Alan Hamlin is Emeritus Professor of Political Theory in Politics, School of Social Sciences at the University of Manchester, and Senior Research Fellow in the Department of Political Economy at King's College London.

Robert Jubb is Lecturer in Political Theory in the Department of Politics and International Relations at the University of Reading.

Carl Knight is Lecturer in Political Theory in the School of Social and Political Sciences at the University of Glasgow.

Brian Kogelmann is a PhD student in the Philosophy Department at the University of Arizona.

Jonathan Leader Maynard is Departmental Lecturer in International Relations in the Department of Politics and International Relations at the University of Oxford.

Johan Olsthoorn is a post-doctoral fellow of the Research Foundation Flanders (FWO)/KU Leuven.

Jonathan Quong is Associate Professor of Philosophy in the School of Philosophy at the University of Southern California.

David Schmidtz is Kendrick Professor of Philosophy (College of Social & Behavior Sciences) and Eller Chair of Service-Dominant Logic (College of Management) at the University of Arizona.

Zofia Stemplowska is Associate Professor of Political Theory at Worcester College, Oxford.

Preface

I had the idea for this book in late 2008. The central concept has stayed the same – a 'how-to' book with practical advice in bold type. But much else has changed. I owe a great deal to early guidance from my former colleagues at the Manchester Centre for Political Theory (MANCEPT), especially Alan Hamlin, Jon Quong and Hillel Steiner. My Cambridge University Press editor, John Haslam, and my anonymous reviewers had invaluable advice about content and scope: they made this book far better.

I have greatly enjoyed working with my contributors. I wanted every chapter to give clear, concrete advice grounded in examples of good or bad practice. It was a pleasure to see this take shape and I hope our readers will benefit.

I dedicate this book to the memory of my father, Nat Blau, who passed away in 2010 after a long and productive life. He was a doctor, researcher and teacher. He would have approved of a book that seeks to be helpful, practical and well exemplified.

My father had a strong sense of our intellectual limits: for example, he sometimes said that 'if a theory explains all the facts, the theory must be wrong, because some of the facts are wrong.' This book is written not in the expectation that our arguments and tips are right, but in the hope that enough of them are right that we can advance the debate – and that readers' challenges to our arguments and tips will do so further.

This is the first book of its kind. It must not be the last.

1   Introduction: A 'How-to' Approach

Adrian Blau

1   Introduction

This is the first 'how-to' handbook in political theory. It describes different methods ('what is method X?'), justifies them ('why do method X?'), and explains what to do ('how should I do method X?'). 'How-to' guidance is our main aim. Political scientists have hundreds of such handbooks, from general overviews on research design to textbooks on specific techniques. Philosophers have dozens of handbooks on logic and critical thinking. But political theorists have no handbook on how to apply the methods we use.

Existing books on political theory methods typically describe and justify methods without much detail on implementation – 'what is' and 'why do' more than 'how to'. For example, Quentin Skinner's book on methods in the history of political thought contains relatively little prac-tical guidance (Skinner 2002: 40–2, 75–6, 79–80, 114–20). If you want to interpret texts like Skinner, you will learn more from his actual research. Similarly, there is little advice on how to implement the methods and approaches covered in the fine volume edited by Leopold and Stears (2008).

When we praise or criticize work in political theory, 'how-to' principles are often implicit. For example, if you find that some definitions are clearer than others, you have already grasped some principles of concep-tual clarity, consciously or subconsciously. But you will struggle to find much published guidance on defining terms clearly. Our book aims to make such implicit principles explicit and adds new how-to principles as well.

Much of our focus, then, is on *the logic of inference* – on how best to draw robust conclusions, on how to justify our conclusions against actual or potential critics. 'It came to me in a dream' is not typically considered good methodology in political theory. Rather better is 'I carefully distin-guished freedom and autonomy, used thought experiments to test their relative importance, and engaged with comparative political thought to see if these ideas fit non-Western cultures.' True, some scholars will disagree with methods like thought experiments, just as some social scientists reject statistical analysis or ethnography, say: healthy disciplines see disputes about methods. But there are principles of good practice in statistical analysis and ethnography for social scientists who want to use these methods, and principles of good practice in thought experiments for political theorists who want to use this method. Each chapter in this book outlines such principles.

Our book's key contribution, then, is practical guidance on what to do and what to avoid in the methods you may use in political theory. Since your methods affect your answers, how-to guidance should help.

2   What Is the 'How-to' Approach?

Each author has placed 'how-to advice' – sometimes obvious, sometimes not – in bold type. Some chapters spread the advice through the text; sometimes it is more concentrated. After reading a chapter, you can flick through it looking only at the advice in bold and remind yourself how to apply that method.

Consider the method of thought experiments, where we imagine situations that help us probe moral or political problems. Is medical experimentation on humans ethically wrong? We could try to answer this by seeing how we react to the idea of Nazis experimenting on people in concentration camps. But this particular example will probably bias us against medical experimentation. To answer the question more reliably, we should consider medical experimentation in less extreme cases, without Nazis. 'Be sensitive to possible narrative-framing biases' is Brownlee and Stemplowska's advice in the thought experiments chapter. This may seem obvious, but many published thought experiments have such biases. Learning to spot this will improve your own reasoning and help you criticize some existing arguments.

A second example comes from the textual interpretation chapter, where I write: 'indicate how confident you are in your interpretations.' We can never know for sure what Marx meant by 'class' or why Machiavelli wrote *The Prince*. If two explanations are plausible but one is better supported by the evidence, we do not help our readers by pretending that one is definitely right while the other is undeniably wrong. This advice may seem obvious, but such indications of uncertainty are not common in published research on textual interpretation.

We are not presenting a neutral handbook: all of our prescriptions are contestable. Indeed, we want them to be contested. Being explicit about how-to principles will hopefully clarify the issues, stimulate debate, and advance research in political theory.

3   Why Use a 'How-to' Approach?

There are five main reasons for a 'how-to' approach. First, and most mundane, students and academics often have to discuss methods in dissertations, PhD proposals, funding applications and so on. A better developed methods literature will help us compete with other researchers. You can explain to readers if you are using consent contractualism, fairness contractualism or rationality contractualism; conceptual analysis as resolution, extensional analysis and/or disambiguation; normative, historical, interpretive and/or critical comparative political thought; and so on.

Second, 'how-to' analysis helps us answer 'why do' questions: understanding how to apply a method can help us decide whether to use it, in at least three ways. One way is where we avoid a method because we wrongly think that it cannot be implemented. For example, realist political theory has often been criticized as overly negative, lacking a constructive programme. By showing – at last! – how to do realist political theory, Jubb's chapter in this volume strengthens the case for realism.

Another way in which 'how to' addresses 'why do' is where we wrongly think that a given approach is not how we do things and thus not what we should do. My chapter on textual interpretation partly targets historians who see philosophical analysis as something for political theorists and philosophers. But when we see how we actually interpret texts, we find that everyone does philosophical analysis: historians should thus learn how to do it well. Hamlin's chapter argues that since many of us do positive political theory without realizing it, we should recognize this, and do it better. Frazer's chapter on moral sentimentalism sees the abstract, rationalistic nature of much political theory as a fairly recent invention. Great political theorists like Hume and Smith often took sentimentalist approaches, as does Rawls in some respects: sentimentalism is not alien to political theory.

But the most important way in which 'how to' helps us answer 'why do' is where people wrongly reject a method in general due to particular applications of it: such criticisms can evaporate if we see how to apply the method better. Examples in this book include some objections to rational choice theory discussed by Kogelmann and Gaus, some challenges to reflective equilibrium answered by Knight, and some doubts about thought experiments considered by Brownlee and Stemplowska.

Third, how-to guidance helps us avoid mistakes. Olsthoorn's chapter on conceptual analysis notes that some arguments try to make normative points by definitional sleight-of-hand. It is better to define concepts more neutrally and argue for the normative position separately. Schmidtz's chapter on realistic idealism criticizes act-utilitarians for being curiously inattentive to consequences, focusing on utility maximization without considering unintended consequences. Too many political theorists, he suggests, emphasize thought experiments at the expense of empirical research, wish away the problem with overly idealized depictions of human interactions, or recommend massive state powers without considering corruption. Kogelmann and Gaus note that rational choice analysis can be undermined by not distinguishing between parametric and strategic situations.

Fourth, and closely related, how-to guidance can strengthen our arguments. Goodin's chapter gives many tips for writing and structuring papers. Brownlee and Stemplowska explain how thought experiments help us test abstract principles. Ackerly and Bajpai show comparative political theorists the value of looking beyond elites and beyond texts. Leader Maynard notes that ideological analysis may help us grasp the real-world effects of some normative principles.

Fifth, how-to analysis can help us improve methods and thus contribute to the four points just raised. This is a key aim of our book, which both summarizes good practice *and* contributes to these techniques. Knight rejects Rawls's view that the key judgements in reflective equilibrium are judgements held with confidence. Quong distinguishes three types of contractualism in terms of five dimensions of contractualism. Ackerly and Bajpai support all four types of comparative political thought, against those who want to restrict it to one type. My chapter argues that previous methodological discussions of textual interpretation have largely overlooked the principles of good practice that actually drive good research.

4   Historical Reflections

Of course, debates over methods have always been important in political theory. Plato's *Republic* can be read as highlighting the weaknesses of Socrates's method and the strengths of Plato's new method, 'dialectic' (Reeve 1988: 4–9, 21–3). Machiavelli scorns abstract Platonic theorizing: we should 'concentrate on what really happens', because a prince who follows 'theories or speculations' will 'undermine his power rather than maintain it' (Machiavelli 1988: ch. 15, 54). In other words, empirical observation gives us more guidance than theoretical conjecture about what works and what does not.

Hobbes uses as little empirical observation as possible to derive normative principles. If we get the methods right, he argues, we will all agree
about politics. The key is reason, which for Hobbes means applying
deductive logic to clearly defined concepts (Hobbes 1991: 4.4, 25–6;
4.9–13, 26–9; 5, 31–7). This shows, for example, that monarchies and
republics have the same amount of liberty (1991: 21.8–9, 149–50).
Hobbes mocks the prevailing methods of political argument, such as
quoting classical authors to support claims (1991: 5.22, 37; 25.12, 180).

Poor methods lead to insufficient authority, thinks Hobbes (1990:
2–4), or to excess authority, for Bentham and Mill (Bentham 1843: 13,
495; Mill 1989: 1.4–7, 8–12; 3.13, 66–7). All three writers dismiss
intuitionism – justifying normative claims by consulting our instincts,
feelings and non-inferential reactions to normative problems (Hobbes
1994: 6.8, 42; Bentham 1996: 2.11–16, 21–31; Mill 1989: 4.12, 84).
Rousseau disagrees: morally pure men can look inside themselves and see
what is good. Conscience is a better philosopher than reason, he writes in
Emile, and we only need reason when conscience fails us (Rousseau 1979:
book 4, 286, 289–90). This from the man who told a recently bereaved
woman that she was luckier than Rousseau: she had only lost her hus-
band, but poor Rousseau had also lost her friendship (Cranston 1997:
87–8). We are lucky that we are not as morally pure as Rousseau.

Although Rousseau defends moral intuition, his *political* arguments are
not justified by appeal to intuition. Indeed, the draft of *The Social Contract*
treats intuition as inappropriate in modern society (Rousseau 1997:
1.2.6–14, 154–7). Rousseau's political method is broadly contractarian,
alongside Hobbes, Locke, Kant, Rawls and Habermas: a normative position is justified if all specified agents do or could accept it under certain
conditions (Darwall 2003). The precise version of this idea varies markedly among these writers, but the general method is strikingly different to
that used by writers like Burke, who opposes abstract reasoning and
justifies political actions through prudence, necessity, expedience and
experience (e.g. Burke 1999: 228, 237–8, 280–1). But Burkean justification is now rare in academic political theory.

The twentieth century saw considerable innovation and progress in
methods (Wolff 2013). Many of these developments underpin the chapters in this book. Strikingly, though, much political theory still seeks what
Plato and his predecessors sought: conceptual clarity. What does
X mean? How do X and Y differ? Analysis of equality, for example, has
changed hugely in the past twenty-five years because of new distinctions –
between equality, sufficiency and priority, between deontic and telic
egalitarianism, and so on. Many people who saw themselves as favouring
equality now realize that they favour something else. This has not solved

the normative debates, but it has changed the picture and led to better answers.

This brief historical overview does not imply that good methods ensure universally accepted answers or that progress is impossible without a how-to handbook. But methods have clearly been important in political theory from the beginning, and a how-to handbook could thus bring this key issue into sharper focus and foster further development.

5   The Scope of This Book

I should briefly discuss the key terms in this book's title. I will also touch on what and whom this book has left out.

Obviously, this book's title is somewhat misleading: a more accurate title would have been *Methods, Methodologies, Techniques and Approaches in Analytical Political Theory (To The Extent That We Can and Should Distinguish Analytical and Continental Political Theory Anyway)*. But even if that fitted on the front cover, no one would read the book. Mill, criticizing the 'utter unreadableness' of the late Bentham, wrote perceptively that Bentham 'could not bear, for the sake of clearness and the reader's ease, to say, as ordinary men are content to do, a little more than the truth in one sentence, and correct it in the next' (Mill 1974: 114–15). I have said a little less than the truth in the title, and corrected it here.

I will not specify what 'methods' are, although some chapters do diverge somewhat from mainstream understandings. For Quong, contractualism is a method and not, as some people think, a substantive position like utilitarianism or deontology. My chapter on interpreting texts argues that supposedly different methods in history of political thought are not different methods: scholars have thus overlooked some core principles that apparently different methods share. My chapter is thus more about methodology (seen as the logic of inference) than methods; Frazer's chapter, in contrast, is more about an approach and its techniques than a method and methodology.

This book treats 'political theory' very broadly. In effect, we cover political philosophy, moral philosophy, normative jurisprudence, positive political theory, history of political thought and more. But we concentrate on 'analytical' political theory, not 'continental' political theory. This distinction is questionable, of course, but roughly, we can associate analytical political theory with the work of such writers as G. A. Cohen, Ronald Dworkin, Hobbes, Frances Kamm, Mill, Martha Nussbaum, John Rawls, Quentin Skinner and Jeremy Waldron, and continental political theory with the work of such writers as Theodor Adorno, Judith Butler, William Connolly, Michel Foucault, Hegel, Nietzsche,

Richard Rorty and Slavoj Žižek. There is huge variety within these camps, of course; some writers, like Jürgen Habermas and Bernard Williams, arguably fit in both camps; and not all of these names would classify themselves like this. Nor do all authors in this book.

Miller and Dagger (2003: 446–9) outline five principles of analytical political theory: (a) it is essentially separate from deep metaphysical questions about the meaning of human life, (b) it involves conceptual clarity and argumentative rigour, (c) it is normative, (d) it addresses a plurality of competing values, and (e) it 'aims to serve as the public philosophy of a society of free and equal citizens who have choices to make about how their society will be organised.'

I do not believe we need principles (d) and (e). More importantly, principle (c) only entails normative political theory, whereas this book is wider. What did Locke mean by 'man'? Why did Tocqueville write what he wrote? These questions are essentially empirical. Was Hayek a conservative? Does Arendt have a positive conception of liberty? These questions are both empirical and conceptual: we infer Hayek's and Arendt's beliefs, then compare them to criteria of conservatism and positive liberty, respectively. What is equality? Do liberty and power overlap? These questions are fundamentally conceptual. Do Hobbes's laws of nature follow necessarily from his premises? Would Rawls's principles of justice differ if we changed the motivations of people in the original position? These questions could be normative, but are in essence exercises in logic and conceptual clarity. I see no reason to exclude these questions from analytical political theory.

But ultimately, it does not matter whether you agree with this view of analytical political theory. Nor does it matter whether you see yourself in the analytical and/or continental camp, or even as something different. All that matters is whether some of this book's guidance helps you.

Although I sought a wide coverage for this book, there are gaps. We have nothing on international political theory, for example, or on how political theorists should use empirical research in history and social science. Such gaps will be criticized, and rightly so. I have some excuses here, but not for the paucity of women authors – only four out of seventeen. When I started inviting authors, it was men who tended to spring to my mind and to the minds of most of the men and women I sought advice from. Only late in the day did I see the effects of this implicit bias. Around the same time I was struck by a perceptive comment on the *Feminist Philosophers* blog, which notes that while it might seem arbitrary to invite a woman to speak at a conference just because she is a woman, it is also arbitrary that many of us tend to think of men when we are asked who the leading figures in a field are. I've tried to change my thinking and my actions after reading the *Feminist Philosophers* blog, the *Being a Woman in Philosophy* blog, and the edited book *Women in Philosophy* (Hutchison and Jenkins 2013). But this came too late to have much effect on the line-up of authors. Mea culpa.

So the range of authors is not representative; we have not covered all of political theory, or even all of analytical political theory; and the title is a bit of a lie. But what we have is still an exciting venture that seeks to do something new and important: the first book that seeks to explain how to do much of political theory.

6   Overview of This Book

Robert Goodin's short introduction on **How to Write Analytical Political Theory** offers concise, practical tips on writing clear and effective analytical political theory. Goodin gives advice on such issues as structure (e.g. organization = argument), techniques (e.g. distinctions = arguments) and the process of writing and revising (e.g. don't overreact to advice).

Kimberley Brownlee and Zofia Stemplowska's chapter on **Thought Experiments** covers imaginary scenarios such as John Rawls's original position and Nozick's experience machine. For thought experiments to be useful, the chapter argues, they must be philosophically respectable and argumentatively relevant. We need not avoid 'crazy' or 'wacky' thought experiments: indeed, if we understand how-to issues properly, we see that wacky examples can be beneficial, for example by highlighting the limits of our conceptual and argumentative structures.

Carl Knight's chapter on **Reflective Equilibrium** explains and develops John Rawls's influential approach to moral justification, by which we try to reach an accord between our principles and our judgements. Knight rejects Rawls's view that judgements should be confident: Knight prefers judgements to be considered. Knight also challenges Singer's objection that some judgements are emotive, evolutionary responses: this is something to feed into the reflective equilibrium process, rather, to see if some judgements are unreliable. Knight offers a step-by-step guide to the process of reflective equilibrium: we should list the main contending principles, test those principles with cases, revise principles, and so on. Knight exemplifies this with an example from his own work, showing how he came to support a combination of luck egalitarianism and prioritarianism.

Jonathan Quong's chapter on **Contractualism** denies that contractualism is a specific position, like utilitarianism or deontology. Rather, it is a method by which we consider what idealized agents would or could accept under certain specified constraints. Or to be precise, contractualism is a family of three methods. Consent contractualism asks what people would freely consent to, even if we cannot ask them (as when considering the coercive authority of the state). Fairness contractualism asks what is fair, even if people would not consent to it (as when card players discover during a game that a card is missing: since some players will be doing better than others, we might mistrust their actual, self-interested views about what to do). Rationality contractualism asks what is instrumentally rational for people to do, whether or not they consent, whether or not it is fair. Each type of contractualism involves different answers to five key questions, such as what agents' motives and interests are. Much confusion comes from defenders and critics not adequately distinguishing these different contractualisms.

Michael Frazer's chapter on **Moral Sentimentalism** argues against the overly rationalistic nature of most modern political theory – cold, abstract and with too many trolleys. Yet there is ample evidence that our normative judgements rest in part on emotions. Frazer thus argues that we should draw not just on reason, but also non-rational faculties of the human mind, including emotion, imagination and the imaginative sharing of emotion through sympathy or empathy. He looks to philosophers like Hume and Smith, who engaged their readers with stories and examples. Moral sentimentalists should replace technical terminology with the evocative language of everyday life. They should move from empathetic assessment of particular cases to more general principles, not vice versa. And they should beware their own biases by considering multiple perspectives: your assessment of alleged police injustice will be stronger if you have considered the perspective of the police, not just the policed.

Robert Jubb's chapter on **Realism** discusses the realist critique of ideal theory. Realists like Bernard Williams criticize Rawls and others for being overly reliant on general moral claims that neglect the distinctive character of the political. Politics should come first: realists urge political philosophers to pay more attention to how political institutions and actors produce or fail to produce a particular set of goods in response to a particular set of problems, and to consider how this should constrain their theorizing. Jubb disagrees with Williams that only liberalism can adequately answer our basic legitimation demands: various solutions are possible, and realists should not fall into the trap of themselves being overly moralistic by appealing to values whose contestation is actually a key part of the problem. Realists should also engage with particular political circumstances, developing a finer sense of real political possibilities and motivations.

David Schmidtz's chapter on **Realistic Idealism** also criticizes Rawls for starting with justice. The first virtue of social institutions, rather, is to enable peaceful cooperation. Schmidtz's criticisms of ideal theory are different to Jubb's but complementary. Schmidtz criticizes ideal theorists who assume away the problems they try to solve. An ideal solution is one that works with actual agents, not one that would work with idealized people: we should focus not on a kingdom of ends, but a kingdom of players. While the political theorist's job is to some extent to say how the world should be in the grand scheme of things, actual governance is the art of compromise in a world that is not a blank canvas. Realistic idealists should thus focus less on abstract thought experiments and engage more with history, political economy and empirical insights about the behaviour of actual human beings.

Johan Olsthoorn's chapter on **Conceptual Analysis** starts, as one would expect, with careful conceptual analysis of 'conceptual analysis'. Olsthoorn distinguishes between concepts and terms, between concepts and conceptions, between principles and criteria of application, between different types of concepts and between different types of conceptual analysis. He offers advice on defining and naming concepts, and on comparing/contrasting interpretations of concepts advanced by different writers. Olsthoorn also highlights the limitations of what conceptual analysis can contribute to normative argument. While conceptual analysis helps us clarify ideas, make distinctions, and keep separate ideas apart, disagreements over competing normative ideas are not usually resolvable by conceptual analysis alone.

Alan Hamlin's chapter on **Positive Political Theory** treats positive political theory as a kind of model, like a map of the London Underground – abstracting, simplifying and idealizing aspects of the real world in order to highlight and systematize key features of a process, institution or argument. For example, in considering whether voting should be compulsory, we might make assumptions about low turnout leading to unequal turnout, leading to differential policy impact and so on. Being clear about such assumptions, even if not in the published version of an analysis, can help us think through the relevant steps. In particular, we can use 'sensitivity analysis' to test the relative importance of various factors, changing one factor at a time to see how it affects our conclusions. Would compulsory voting be more or less desirable if, say, unequal turnout did not affect policy? Since many of us do this kind of thing informally, Hamlin recommends that we should learn to do it well.

Brian Kogelmann and Gerald Gaus's chapter on **Rational Choice Theory** explains why political theorists should take rational choice theory seriously, whether as a central feature of their work (e.g. game-theoretic approaches to morality) or to help with other issues (e.g. democratic theorists interested in institutional design). Part of the chapter involves explaining core features of rational choice theory, such as the relational nature of preferences, assumptions such as transitivity and the idea of Nash equilibria. The chapter deflects common criticisms of rational choice theory, such as the objection that people aren't rational, or the view that rational choice theory isn't sufficiently predictive. Normatively, Kogelmann and Gaus discuss applications of rational choice theory in contractarian arguments about what people would agree to. Importantly, such deliberations need not exclude considerations of morality or fairness. Still, we should be careful not to overstate what rational choice theory can offer normative analysis, the chapter argues.

My chapter on **Interpreting Texts** challenges the dominant categorization of interpretive approaches, e.g. contextualism, rational reconstruction, Marxism and Straussianism. These categories have their uses, but are problematic. For example, contextualism, or the 'Cambridge School' approach, is not best seen as a method. The focus should be on evidence. Contextualists need textual, contextual, motivational and philosophical evidence – as do all of us, ideally. Likewise, 'reconstruction' is not a technique just for philosophers, but is something we all do to resolve ambiguities and gaps in communication. Unfortunately, the emphasis on different approaches means that methodologists have not outlined core principles of good practice that apply to all of us (and that already underpin much research). My chapter collates those principles.

Brooke Ackerly and Rochana Bajpai's chapter on **Comparative Political Thought** sees two key features in comparative political thought (CPT): an emphasis on bringing African, Chinese, Indian, Islamic and Latin American ethical-political thought to Western audiences, and an effort to make political theory more relevant by combining it with political science, anthropology and history. Ackerly and Bajpai's stance is pluralist, in contrast to the restrictive scope of some CPT scholars. Four main types of CPT are identified: normative-analytic, historical, interpretive and critical. These are not necessarily alternatives: scholars may want to 'triangulate' different approaches. Ackerly and Bajpai thus stress the value of a question-driven approach: we should not be too wedded to a particular approach, but should let the problem guide our methods and tools.

Jonathan Leader Maynard's chapter on **Ideological Analysis** considers how the study of real-world systems of political ideas enhances analytical political theory, including normative political theory. For example, normative theorists can use ideological analysis to reveal the problematic ideologies that some institutions generate, and vice versa, and can probe the background ideological assumptions behind normative arguments. In terms of analysing ideologies themselves, the highly interdisciplinary nature of ideological analysis makes a cross-disciplinary approach desirable. Leader Maynard shows how to uncover the content of ideologies, how to explain ideological attachment and how to analyse the effects of ideologies. He encourages us not to see ideologies in pejorative terms, as many have; ideologies are simply the normative and factual ideas that shape our under- standings and actions. There is no such thing as 'beyond ideology'.

Robert Goodin and Keith Dowding's short piece on **How to Do a Political Theory PhD** gives advice on how to choose a PhD topic/problem, and how considering why other scholars are wrong helps one develop answers. Goodin and Dowding encourage PhD students to break down the thesis into manageable chunks, but to be flexible: struc- ture and arguments often change. Planning ahead is especially important for PhD students considering academic careers: thinking about publica- tions early on will help.

7   How Do the Chapters Fit Together?

Which chapters complement or compete with each other? I would say – some would disagree – that reflective equilibrium (Knight) is fundamen- tal to normative political theory, even if we all fall short of the ideal to greater or lesser extents. Within reflective equilibrium, we can use thought experiments (Brownlee and Stemplowska), contractualism (Quong), moral sentimentalism (Frazer), realism (Jubb) and realistic idealism (Schmidtz). Contractualism typically involves thought experi- ments, but moral sentimentalism, realism and realistic individualism all oppose some uses of thought experiments, without necessarily rejecting them entirely. Realists and realistic idealists may have qualms about some contractualist arguments.

Also fundamental is conceptual analysis (Olsthoorn). Everyone uses concepts: they are the building blocks of clear thinking, even for primarily non-normative political theorists.

Positive political theory (Hamlin) is more widespread within political theory than one may think: we all make assumptions about connections between different aspects of processes, institutions and arguments. Rational choice theory (Kogelmann and Gaus) is a subset of positive political theory.

Interpreting texts (Blau) is not just for people studying history of political thought: we can easily misread Rawls, for example, by dipping in and quoting ideas out of context. Textual interpretation is particularly important for comparative political thought (Ackerly and Bajpai) and ideological analysis (Leader Maynard). But both of these latter chapters discuss aspects of textual interpretation that range far beyond what my chapter covers – and both chapters have important lessons for normative political theorists using reflective equilibrium, thought experiments, contractualism, moral sentimentalism, realism, realistic idealism and conceptual analysis.

Finally, the short chapters at the start and end of this book, on how to do analytical political theory (Goodin) and how to do a political theory PhD (Goodin and Dowding), will help everyone, especially PhD students, in some core skills of political theory and of scholarly practice more generally.

8   Conclusion: General Lessons from this Book

Some useful general principles can be discerned in this book. One is that **distinctions are vital.** This is equally true in political science, where comparison is seen as essential. (As in the old joke: 'Who first discovered water?' 'I don't know, but it wasn't a fish.') Arguably we cannot even think without comparison and distinction; certainly we cannot think clearly. Much political theory is thus about making distinctions and showing how they affect our conclusions – for example, that the positive/negative liberty distinction excludes important types of liberty, or that some criticisms of 'liberalism' do not weaken all types of liberalism.

Distinctions, unsurprisingly, play a key part in this book. At the most general level, some chapters will introduce entirely new ideas. I suspect that for many readers this will include Frazer's chapter on moral sentimentalism and Hamlin's on positive political theory: simply being exposed to these ideas, seeing a distinction that one had not been aware of, will attract some readers to those methods. More specific distinctions include Quong's typology of three forms of contractualism, Olsthoorn's account of different types of conceptual analysis and Kogelmann and Gaus's distinction between the use of rational choice theory for explanatory, predictive or normative ends, and in parametric or strategic situations. But every chapter does something like this: it is what political theorists and philosophers do.

However, **distinctions can constrain.** Thus Ackerly and Bajpai enjoin readers not to see their four types of comparative political thought as alternatives, while I criticize the distinctions that dominate current methodological thinking about textual interpretation. Of course, many of this book's distinctions will be superseded in time.

Political theorists may need to engage with empirical research, as argued by Jubb, Schmidtz, Ackerly and Bajpai and Leader Maynard. Meanwhile, **we may already be using some methods without realizing it, so we should learn to use them well**, as argued by Brownlee and Stemplowska, Frazer, Hamlin and me, and implicitly by Knight and by Olsthoorn. This is one reason why **we should have a broad methods training in political theory**. Another reason is that it may suggest that **we might not be using a method or approach that would in fact help us.** Brownlee and Stemplowska's argument that good thought experiments are equivalent to valid philosophical arguments should make some sceptics more open to thought experiments. Kogelmann and Gaus encourage political theorists to engage with rational choice theory. Ackerly and Bajpai want normative theorists to broaden their horizons by engaging with comparative political thought. Leader Maynard encourages normative theorists to conduct ideological analysis on their own ideas. Goodin's enjoinder to engage with continental political theory is something this book does not, alas, deliver on (Ackerly and Bajpai's chapter being a partial exception). My chapter suggests that historians often shut themselves off from philosophical readings of texts. Frazer reminds us that the rhetorical norms of political theory are recent inventions: perhaps we have wrongly avoided sentimentalist approaches. Indeed, every chapter, explicitly or implicitly, justifies its method – and every chapter, explicitly or implicitly, shows that **we may not always be using current approaches as well as we could.** That is of course this book's main message.

Research should ideally be problem-driven, emphasize Ackerly and Bajpai. We should pick methods that best suit the problem at hand rather than picking problems that 'our' method can answer. But in practice, some scholars simply do see themselves as exponents of a particular method or approach (e.g. rational choice, textual interpretation, ideological analysis) and rarely have difficulty finding problems. Indeed, collective progress might even be greater if problem-driven scholars build on the insights of method-driven experts, just as social scientists benefit from having quantitative social scientists wedded to a particular statistical technique or ethnographers skilled at collecting detailed anthropological data.

This means that **the ideal type of research is not ideal for everyone and would not be ideal if everyone did it.** Academia works best when we study what we love and when there is rigorous and robust discussion of whether there are gaps or under-emphases in our collective focus. People might then change their approach or newcomers can correct these lapses.

Contrast this view with John Dunn's 'contempt' for political scientists who do empirical research without considering norms: 'an adult and civically responsible human being' would not study politics like this (1996: 30–1). Dunn is right that we need more integration of empirical and normative research. But we do not need or want *everyone* to do this: normative researchers may need to draw on empirical research involving meticulous case studies or exhaustive statistical number-crunching conducted by scholars with no taste for normative analysis and no skill in doing it. And those narrow empirical political scientists may in turn depend on even narrower methodological research by political scientists who are not even interested in empirical research but merely the methodology of case studies or of statistical analysis.

So, when Skinner is criticized for overlooking social and religious contexts, or when Rawls is criticized for overlooking institutional details, this might merely be a criticism of such oversights, not a recommendation that Skinner and Rawls should actually have done such research. Let Skinner be Skinner: why make him start new research projects in social or religious history when authorities in social and religious history can do that themselves, building on Skinner's expertise, filling in his gaps, and seeing how his conclusions would differ? Let Rawls be Rawls: why make one of the world's great political philosophers learn political science when *we* can add that to his philosophizing while he concentrates on doing what he does best? Of course it could be that Skinner or Rawls could spend a few weeks reading up on other people's research, and that this would change their conclusions; but we should not forget that the individual and the collective ideal are not always identical.

So, we probably want a diversity of approaches – methods-driven and problem-driven research, specialist and pluralist research. We want people who see deeply and people who see widely. So, **political theorists should play to their strengths** while recognizing the inevitable limitations of any approach, narrow or wide, and while being aware that political theory is a collective enterprise where we all stand on each other's shoulders, so to speak.

I want to finish with some brief comments on how methodology of political theory benefits you, and most importantly, with some meta-reflections on how to *do* methodology of political theory. There are two main benefits of thinking about political theory methods. First, **good methods can improve your arguments** – the central aim of this book. Second, and less obvious, **methodological reflection can give you extra publications**, e.g. a journal article early in a PhD, or a spin-off article from a substantive project. This helps your academic career, gives you a wider audience than you might otherwise get and lets you potentially make a significant contribution to the discipline.

But be careful of writing highly abstract methodological analyses. If this book convinces you of anything, it is hopefully that **methodological publications should ideally be practical and well exemplified**, by showing what practical guidelines follow from one's methodological principles and by illustrating how these ideas have been or should be implemented. Jubb's chapter is significant partly because realist political theory is often very negative: its practical implications have been hard to grasp. My own chapter reflects my feeling that little methodological discussion in the history of political thought has actually helped me to interpret ambiguous passages in texts or to resolve apparent contradictions between different parts of the same text. Indeed, every chapter has sought to show the value of a practical and well-exemplified approach to methods in political theory.

This suggests that **studying methodology should also be practical and well exemplified.** If using this book to teach methods, one could for example set students a chapter to read *and* a substantive application (good or bad) of the relevant method. This encourages students to think through the methodological issues and apply them to a substantive issue or study – which can in turn help us think through the methodological issues.

So, **methodological insights often come from substantive research.** Although methodological developments can happen at a very theoretical level, or by borrowing from methods in other fields, often one simply reflects on actual research in political theory and makes inferences about what is done well or less well. We hope that by reflecting on our methodological recommendations, and by reflecting on actual research in political theory, **you can contribute to the continuing development of methods in analytical political theory.** That is the spirit in which we have written this book.

Acknowledgements

For comments and criticisms on earlier versions of this chapter, I thank Kimberley Brownlee, Alan Hamlin, and my anonymous Cambridge University Press reviewers.

References

Bentham, Jeremy, 1843. *The Works of Jeremy Bentham*, volume III, ed. John Bowring. Edinburgh: William Tait.

Bentham, Jeremy, 1996. *An Introduction to the Principles of Morals and Legislation*, ed. J. H. Burns and H. L. A. Hart. Oxford: Clarendon Press.

Burke, Edmund, 1999. *Select Works of Edmund Burke: Volume 1*. Indianapolis, IN: Liberty Fund.

Cranston, Maurice, 1997. *The Solitary Self: Jean-Jacques Rousseau in Exile and Adversity*. University of Chicago Press.

Darwall, Stephen, 2003. 'Introduction', in Stephen Darwall, ed., *Contractarianism, Contractualism*. Oxford: Blackwell, 1–8.

Dunn, John, 1996. *The History of Political Theory and Other Essays*. Cambridge University Press.

Hobbes, Thomas, 1990. *Behemoth or The Long Parliament*, ed. Ferdinand Tönnies. University of Chicago Press.

Hobbes, Thomas, 1991. *Leviathan*, ed. Richard Tuck. Cambridge University Press.

Hobbes, Thomas, 1994. *The Elements of Law*, in *Human Nature and De Corpore Politico*, ed. J. C. A. Gaskin. Oxford University Press.

Hutchinson, Katrina, and Fiona Jenkins, eds., 2013. *Women in Philosophy: What Needs to Change?* Oxford University Press.

Leopold, David, and Marc Stears, eds., 2008. *Political Theory: Methods and Approaches*. Oxford University Press.

Machiavelli, Niccolò, 1988. *The Prince*, ed. Quentin Skinner and Russell Price. Cambridge University Press.

Mill, J. S., 1974. *Essays on Ethics, Religion and Society*, ed. J. M. Robson. University of Toronto Press.

Mill, J. S., 1989. *On Liberty and Other Writings*, ed. Stefan Collini. Cambridge University Press.

Miller, David, and Richard Dagger, 2003. 'Utilitarianism and beyond: contemporary analytical political theory', in Terence Ball and Richard Bellamy, eds., *The Cambridge History of Twentieth-Century Political Thought*. Cambridge University Press, 446–69.

Reeve, C. D. C., 1988. *Philosopher-Kings: The Argument of Plato's Republic*. Princeton, NJ: Princeton University Press.

Rousseau, Jean-Jacques, 1979. *Emile or On Education*, ed. Allan Bloom. New York: Basic Books.

Rousseau, Jean-Jacques, 1997. *The Social Contract and Other Later Political Writings*, ed. Victor Gourevitch. Cambridge University Press.

Skinner, Quentin, 2002. *Visions of Politics. Volume I: Regarding Method*. Cambridge University Press.

Wolff, Jonathan, 2013. 'Analytic political philosophy', in Michael Beaney, ed., *The Oxford Handbook of the History of Analytic Philosophy*. Oxford University Press, 795–822.

2 How to Write Analytical Political Theory

Robert E. Goodin

1) **Show your work.** When you are thinking through a problem, you naturally start by thinking up some plausible line, then considering things that might be wrong with that, and often rejecting what was superficially a promising line. Instead of just erasing all of that as a 'mistake' or 'false start', write it all out (the original idea, why it was tempting, why it is wrong). That's what counts as argument in analytical philosophy.

2) **Clean kill/clear clutter.** Once you've identified your main argument, clear away superfluous clutter that doesn't speak to that argument directly. KISS ('Keep It Simple, Stupid.'). Remember, 'clear' is the highest term of praise in analytical philosophy.

3) **Organization = argument.** Use the structure of the paper to show the structure of the argument, wherever possible. If you've got several separate arguments, or complex sub-arguments, put them into new (sub) sections whenever you can. Let the structure of section breaks do a lot of work for you.

4) **Layer.** Once you have a nice clear main line of argument, feel free to add layers of texture within subsections.

5) **Revise, revise, revise.** Leave it in the bottom drawer for a month (maybe while it's out for comment) and come back to it and revise again. It's surprising what you'll see upon revisiting it with a fresh eye.

6) **Let weight on the page be proportional to the weight the proposition bears in your argument.** If something is important, signal clearly that fact ('And here's the crucial point: ... '). If it's important, go on about it at appropriate length, even at the risk of redundancy and just rephrasing the same point in other words.

7) **Distinctions = arguments.** Simply pointing out a distinction – drawing attention to the fact that this is different from that (with which it might naively be confused or conflated) – is the most typical way of making arguments in analytic philosophy.

8) **Introduce key devices early.** Where there is some important distinction or device that you're going to need later, particularly at multiple points in the paper, it can be a good idea to introduce it early. If it's important, and you want people to notice it, don't just sneak up on it

without warning, and leave some important point buried somewhere in the middle of the paper where it might get overlooked.

9) **Intuition pumps require care**. The grandest ambition of analytic philosophy is to get support for some proposition about which we feel less confident by showing that it follows from some other proposition in which we're more certain. (Think of Descartes, tracing everything ultimately back to the proposition of which he felt most certain, 'Cogito ergo sum.') The way that in practice plays out in applied moral philosophy is via 'intuition pumps', examples (often contrived, artificial) about which we have a strong intuitive response; and then assimilate other cases of interest to those. The strategy often misfires, for various reasons. One is that the cases described are 'crazy', atypical of real life and not ones around which our intuitions have been honed – so our intuitive responses to them are not to be trusted. Another classic way that strategy misfires is that the analogy to real-world cases is flawed in some way.

10) **Horses for courses.** Analytic philosophy is not the only mode. There are clear cases in which, and audiences for which, you should write in a more lugubrious and less clipped mode. Sometimes pure random free association is a good way of generating ideas that, stepping back from which, you can then clean up and put into proper analytical order.[1] Letting continental philosophy wash over you can sometimes be useful, in just that way.

11) **Getting started.** A good way to start a new project is to compile a whole jumble of dot-points and short paragraphs containing random ideas that you might include in a paper. Then look across them all to see if there's some 'story' you can draw out of those (drawing out some of them, throwing away others, typically).

12) **Ask around.** Both before writing and after, don't hesitate to send things to colleagues who might give you good background information, advice or comments. But do exercise quality control: people who are not very good give you advice that's not very good. (Sometimes you have to circulate papers to such people out of courtesy, of course: just remember, 'not all comments are created equal'.)

13) **Feel free to ignore advice, even good advice.** Don't overreact to advice. You can make a paper a lot worse by revising it too much – by trying to take on board all advice you get on it. This obviously might happen when you try to be too accommodating, taking on board points that don't really fit just to be nice to someone who has gone to the trouble to comment. But it can happen too when you revise to take into account points that you agree are genuinely good and important points – even so,

---

[1] This is what James G. March (1976: 76–81) celebrates as 'the technology of foolishness'.

the revisions can sometimes pull the paper all out of shape. If they're really important, you might want to rewrite the whole paper (or whole section of the paper) afresh. But often retrofitting them to the existing structure just doesn't work.

14) **Placement.** Every paper has a 'natural home'. It's just a case of matchmaking, knowing the personality of a journal and whether this paper would be a good fit.

Acknowledgements

These notes grew out of discussions with Chiara Lepora during our time together at the National Institutes of Health, 2009–10.

Reference

March, James, 1976. 'The technology of foolishness', in James March and Johan Olsen, eds., *Ambiguity and Choice in Organizations*. Bergen: Universitetsforlaget, 69–81.

3   Thought Experiments

Kimberley Brownlee and Zofia Stemplowska

1   Introduction

A thought experiment is, in one sense, just what its name suggests – an experiment in thinking. But it is thinking of a distinctive, imaginative kind that offers a potentially powerful investigative and analytic tool in mathematics, science, and philosophy. In science, thought experiments are a well-accepted, uncontroversial mechanism for testing hypotheses, and in mathematics, they are one of the principal tools for valid reasoning. They can build and destroy arguments (Brown 1986). In negative terms, they can (1) expose a contradiction, (2) undermine a key premise, (3) reveal a conflation of concepts or principles, or (4) highlight the counterintuitive implications of an argument. In positive terms, they can (1) demonstrate the consistency or coherence of a set of principles/concepts, (2) highlight congruities and similarities between different claims, (3) reveal the scope of the application of a given principle, and (4) bring forth intuitions not previously considered, amongst other things.

In philosophy, some thought experiments are highly influential, even famous. In moral and political theory, famous examples include the following:

1. Philippa Foot's/Judith Jarvis Thomson's **Trolley Problem**: A runaway trolley is hurtling towards five people who are working on the railroad track up ahead. The driver can either continue onto the track ahead, thereby killing the five, or steer onto a second track off to the side on which only one man is working, thereby killing the one. Is it permissible to turn the trolley? (Foot 2002: 23; Thomson 1985: 1395).

This thought experiment serves various purposes. Some argue, for example, that it is permissible to turn the trolley because the negative duty not to kill the five outweighs the negative duty not to kill the one. This experiment is discussed in a variety of political theory contexts, including in just war theory on the legitimacy of defensive harm.

2. Philippa Foot's/Judith Jarvis Thomson's **Trolley Problem and Transplant Case**: A doctor can save the lives of five dying patients by killing one healthy person and giving her organs to the five. If it is permissible to turn the trolley, is it also permissible to kill the one to save the five? (Foot 2002: 24; Thomson 1985: 1396).

This thought experiment also serves various purposes. Some thinkers argue, for example, that unlike the trolley problem, it is impermissible to kill the one healthy person in the transplant case because the positive duty to save the five outweighs the negative duty not to kill the one.

3. G. A. Cohen's **Camping Trip**: Suppose that a group of friends goes camping together. The campers could either contribute according to their abilities and resources, with the expert fisher going fishing and the skilled forager finding apples, and so on. Alternatively, they could each assert their rights over their own equipment and talents and use them to bargain with the other members of the camping group. Is it better to base a camping trip on the principles of market exchange and private ownership or on the socialist principles of collective ownership and planned mutual giving? (Cohen 2009: 3ff.).

Cohen uses this thought experiment as his starting point to challenge the idea that socialism is infeasible and counterintuitive, and to consider whether societies are relevantly distinct from camping trips, or whether societies that cultivate the mechanisms to harness human generosity could be governed by socialist principles.

4. John Rawls's **Original Position**: We are asked to put ourselves in the position of free and equal persons collectively deciding on and committing to a set of principles of justice for society. To ensure our impartiality as deliberators, we engage in this process behind a 'veil of ignorance' that shields us from the knowledge about who we will be in the society and what advantages and disadvantages we will have. What principles would we choose? (Rawls 1971).

This thought experiment is used to offer support for a liberal-egalitarian conception of *justice*.

5. Robert Nozick's **Experience Machine**: Suppose that you could put yourself into an experience machine for the rest of your life, which would give you all the experiences you find enjoyable and valuable without your knowing, once you were in the machine, that these experiences were not real. Would entering the machine be a good choice from the point of view of well-being? Would it give you all that mattered? (Nozick 1974: 42–5).

This thought experiment is used to challenge the claim that the realm of value is exhausted by hedonistic pleasure. Nozick argues that the realm of value and well-being is not exhausted by the pleasure of 'experiences'; we care about whether our experiences are real.

6. Robert Nozick's **Utility Monster**: Suppose there is a person who gets enormously greater gains in utility from any sacrifice of others than those others lose in utility through their own sacrifice. Is it morally required or morally permissible to sacrifice these persons for the sake of the monster's greater utility? (Nozick 1974: 41).

This thought experiment is used to challenge the intuitiveness of hedonistic utilitarianism.

7. **Ticking Bomb**: Suppose that you are an investigator who has a suspect in custody who you know has planted a bomb somewhere in your city. The bomb will soon explode. Suppose also that torturing this person will give you the information you need to locate and neutralize the bomb. Is it either morally permissible or required to torture the person in custody? (adapted from Walzer 1973: 166-7).

This thought experiment is used to gauge the permissibility of torture. (See the Appendix for other examples of thought experiments.)

Unlike in mathematics and science, in political theory and in philosophy in general, the use of thought experiments is a matter of lively controversy. Two especially pressing objections against their use are the following:

1. The Objection of Bias: Thought experiments both invite systematic bias and entrench existing biases.
2. The Objection of Inherent Ambiguity: Thought experiments often are inherently ambiguous, leading to inescapably opaque judgements.

These objections are troubling because they challenge the very possibility of making logically and philosophically respectable use of thought experiments. Neither objection is forceful in its general form because, if it were, it would impugn the less controversial use of thought experiments in mathematics and science and not just philosophy. These two objections, however, may be thought to target the use of thought experiments in sub-disciplines of philosophy such as political theory and moral theory where thought experiments are deployed not only for conceptual and logical purposes, but also for normative and evaluative purposes. Using thought experiments in political and moral theory in particular may seem suspect because such thought experiments abstract away from and idealize real-life cases or even invent fantastical scenarios, but nonetheless purport to guide real-life behaviour.

The use of thought experiments in political and moral theory is also subject to further, less weighty objections. First, such thought experiments are said to be in poor taste since they often involve fantastic scenarios of suffering, death, and cruelty that trivialize that suffering.

(Ironically, thought experiments of the past were also criticized as too trivial: see Winch 1965: 199–200.) Second, they are said to impoverish our understanding of urgent problems, as they are devoid of rich social context (O'Neill 1986: 12, 20–1; but note that O'Neill herself does not attribute this feature to thought experiments in general, only in some contexts within political and moral theory). Third, thought experiments, such as the Ticking Bomb, are said to misrepresent the vast majority of relevant real-life cases and thus create the false impression that the world is simpler and more manageable than it is. These latter three objections can be set aside, however, because their force, while somewhat doubtful, could be granted without abandoning the practice of thought experiments in political and moral theory. They seem to invite theorists to engage in careful and tactful delineation of thought experiments rather than to abandon them altogether.

The main purpose of this chapter is to provide a guide for the use of thought experiments in political theory (although what we say holds more generally for normative theory). As part of that objective, we aim to refute the Objection of Bias and the Objection of Inherent Ambiguity against thought experiments in this area. A further, related purpose of this chapter is to flesh out positively the distinctive argumentative value that thought experiments have in normative theory. We begin by distinguishing the concept of a *thought experiment* from things with which it is sometimes conflated, namely, introspective *psychological experiments* and other argumentative tools that appeal to the workings of the imagination such as *descriptive hypothetical examples* (Section 2). We then respond to the Objection of Bias and the Objection of Inherent Ambiguity, first by articulating and defending a set of necessary, formal conditions for formulating well-posed thought experiments in normative theory (Section 3), and second by showing that these conditions do not preclude the use of thought experiments that involve practical impossibilities or imaginatively opaque components (Section 4). We conclude by highlighting the key 'how-to' instructions for designing thought experiments in political and moral theory (Section 5).

2   Definitions

Thought experiments have been characterized variously as devices 'of the imagination used to investigate the nature of things' (Brown and Fehige 2014), picturesque arguments (Norton 1996: 334), purely mental procedures that aim to reveal something about the relationship between two or more variables (Sorensen 1992: 186, 205), and judgements about what would be the case if the particular state of affairs described in some imaginary scenario were actual (Gendler 1998: 398). Our conception of *thought experiments* in normative theory is as follows:

A *thought experiment* is a multi-step process that involves (1) the mental visualization of some specific scenario for the purpose of (2) answering a further, more general, and at least partly mental-state-independent question about reality.[1]

The reference here to 'mental visualization' highlights the imaginative quality of thought experiments. They are not purely abstract or formal operations of thought. Rather, they are operations of thought structured to invite visualization. This does not mean that, by their nature, thought experiments cannot intelligibly and profitably deploy concepts that defy visualization, such as a square circle, a world with different laws of nature, or an episode of giving birth to oneself. Rather, the point in highlighting the visual quality of thought experiments is to note that they are not carried out purely at the level of abstract principle, but instead 'invoke particulars irrelevant to the generality of the conclusion' (Norton 1996: 336) to be drawn from their use.

2.1   Descriptive Hypothetical Examples versus Thought Experiments

The reference to 'mental visualization' should not obscure the fact that thought experiments are only a subset of a broader category of hypothetical scenarios that involve visualization and imagination. A second subset of that category is *descriptive hypothetical examples*, which, unlike thought experiments, neither test nor contribute an independent step to a chain of reasoning. Purely descriptive hypothetical examples, such as 'I have in mind here someone like Anna Karenina,' or 'God is an example of a perfect being,' or 'Annette is a person who is so poor that her cupboard is bare,' are elucidatory not argumentative. Descriptive hypotheticals and thought experiments have different functions. The former set the parameters of the type of problem under consideration and/or clarify the concepts at issue. The latter either are independent argumentative moves' or they test, and hence support or undermine, argumentative moves.

Although we shall not examine descriptive hypothetical examples in what follows, it is worth noting two features of them in relation to thought experiments. First, descriptive hypotheticals can be proto-thought experiments, that is, sometimes they can be easily developed

---

[1] We do not mean to settle the debate between expressivists/non-cognitivists on the one hand and cognitivists on the other. Even if normative judgements are ultimately entirely a matter of affective states (and hence are not mental-state-independent), we mean to signal that thought experiments aim to provide answers that at least appear to be partly mental-state-independent.

into thought experiments. For instance, once we begin to describe Annette's situation to specify the type of poverty we wish to examine, we can also use that description to test the acceptability of various responses to her plight. Hence, we might ask: 'Would we be prepared to leave someone so impoverished to struggle on her own?' Our initial description of Annette's impoverishment is not a thought experiment, but it opens up the prospect of posing questions about how to treat Annette.

Second, unlike thought experiments, descriptive hypotheticals can assume what they are meant to illustrate. This would be a fatal problem for a thought experiment as part of a chain of reasoning, but not for a descriptive hypothetical as an elucidatory device. We return to this in Section 3.1.1.

2.2   Psychological Experiments versus Thought Experiments

The second part of our conception of a *thought experiment* – that its function is to answer a further, more general, and at least partly mental-state-independent question about reality – allows us to distinguish thought experiments from *introspective psychological experiments* (or 'psychological experiments' for short) (Unger 1982: 117, Sorensen 1992: 67, Brown 2014). The latter are mental procedures that aim simply to predict or to reveal to us our psychological/mental states. A psychological experiment asks such things as: 'Can you make yourself believe that you are an oyster?', 'Can we imagine what it is like to be a bat?', 'Putting aside whether it is permissible, would we actually be able to bring ourselves to turn the trolley?', or 'How would you feel if your child were killed?' Psychological experiments are a distinctive kind of mental experiment in which the generation of a given mental state is precisely and uniquely what is being tested. For instance, when you ask someone whether, in circumstance C, she would fear an attacker enough to kill him, your aim is to ascertain through this test what her mental state is likely to be in such circumstances (or at least what she thinks it is likely to be). By contrast, when you ask an accountant what is 1,236 divided by 3, ascertaining her mental state is not normally the object of the 'experiment' (unless you wish to find out how she will react). The object of the experiment is to get at some feature of the world – the answer 412 – that is independent of her mental state.

The commonly asserted claim that thought experiments, such as the ones outlined above, generate strong intuitions invites confusion between thought experiments and psychological experiments because it can be read to imply that all that thought experiments are meant to test are affective (psychological) states. But the confusion between thought experiments and psychological experiments may also have a deeper source in that some thought experiments necessarily include psychological experiments as a preliminary step in order to reach further conclusions. This occurs when (and because) the variables that a given thought experiment examines include or depend on psychological states, usually ones involving emotions (i.e. affective states). For example, take the following thought experiment:

Attacker: Suppose that we see a person being attacked. And suppose that we are morally required to call the police when we see a person being lethally attacked. If the police cannot arrive in time, are we also morally required ourselves to kill the attacker (assuming that our action will not threaten the institution of policing)?

In order to engage with this thought experiment, it may be necessary amongst other things to run a psychological experiment by asking ourselves if we would be able to bring ourselves to kill the attacker. (Would you?) We might want to ask this question if, say, we accept that 'ought implies psychological can'; i.e., if we were psychologically unable to bring ourselves to kill the attacker, then, if ought implies psychological can, we would not be morally required to do so. Nonetheless, although this psychological experiment is part of Attacker, that thought experiment is not exhausted by the performance of the psychological experiment since the thought experiment requires us in addition to reach a *judgement* about a moral requirement. That is, it requires us to reach a judgement about what is morally required of us in this kind of case (and that judgement is, on standard objective conceptions of morality, at least partly independent of our beliefs as the agent).

Given that psychological experiments in political and moral theory usually test affective states, one rough and ready way to distinguish thought experiments from psychological experiments in this area is to think of thought experiments as answering 'What is your moral judgement?' and psychological experiments as answering 'How would you feel?'[2] We stress the distinction between thought experiments and psychological experiments for several reasons. First, it allows us to explain the nature of the intuitions that thought experiments are designed to elicit. Simply put, unlike most psychological experiments, thought experiments are not intended to elicit raw, unreflective intuitions or brute reactions. Their results can and often should be the fruit of reflection (see Knight's chapter

---

[2] One might worry that an expressivist or non-cognitivist would reject this as a false distinction. But a sufficiently sophisticated version of non-cognitivism presumably accepts that, even if moral judgement is ultimately a matter of affective states, there is nonetheless a plausible distinction to be drawn between raw affective states and 'gardened' or reflective ones.

on reflective equilibrium in this volume). Second, it has implications for the way in which data gathered through thought experiments can enter into normative reasoning. If what matters in thought experiments are not (or not exclusively) raw affective states, then there is more room for rational debate over the appropriate response to a given thought experiment.

2.3   *Simple Thought Experiments versus Complex Thought Experiments*

Within the category of *thought experiments*, there are some important distinctions to be drawn. The first is between simple and complex thought experiments. A simple thought experiment, such as the Trolley Problem, considers a single scenario. In political and moral theory, simple thought experiments tend to raise questions of whether some action is morally wrong, permissible, or obligatory, or whether some state of affairs is fair, equal, just, good, and so on. For instance, the Trolley Problem raises the question of whether it is permissible to turn the trolley and divert the harm from the five to the one. Oftentimes, the theorist's intuitive, though not unreflective response to such thought experiments is taken to be *evidence* for or against the hypothesis being tested in the thought experiment (e.g. that turning the trolley is morally permissible/required).

By contrast, a complex thought experiment, such as the combination of the Trolley Problem and Transplant Case, considers two or more scenarios in relation to each other.[3] This complex experiment – Trolley Problem and Transplant Case – contrasts (the simple thought experiment) Trolley Problem with (the simple thought experiment) Transplant Case. It aims to establish whether our normative answers in the one case align with our answers in the other case. In political theory, complex thought experiments serve various negative and positive argumentative purposes, such as exposing a disanalogy or confirming an analogy, undermining or affirming a hypothesis, revealing a conflation of concepts or principles, and bringing to light unacknowledged intuitions.

This distinction between simple and complex thought experiments is significant because some simple thought experiments need not satisfy the condition of validity (see Section 3.1.2) that applies to all complex thought experiments.

2.4   *Contingency, Necessity, and Imaginability*

The final distinctions to highlight within the category of *thought experiments* relate to their degree of practical possibility and of imaginative clarity.

---

[3] Paradigmatically, complex thought experiments involve pairwise comparisons.

Thought experiments can be more or less practically possible. The category of *hypothetical* is a continuum that includes both the likely and probable though non-actual at one end, and the extremely unlikely and even the impossible at the other end. The former can be described as *contingently hypothetical* (e.g. 'Imagine that you are walking by a pond and spot a drowning child'). Such hypotheticals can be structured around actual events, such as rescue boat operators in New Orleans after Hurricane Katrina having to choose between rescuing the five adults on one rooftop or the three children on another, but they remain hypothetical in that they abstract away from the real case. One reason to construct contingently hypothetical thought experiments even when real-world cases are readily available is that often the mention of a real-world example invites protracted discussion of the facts, which can distract from the problem at hand.

At the other end of the continuum lie thought experiments that can be described as *necessarily hypothetical* (e.g. 'Imagine a spear flying towards the edge of the universe') or at least *necessarily hypothetical for us here and now* (e.g. 'Imagine a society that has eliminated poverty'). Thought experiments that fall closer to this latter end of the spectrum are controversial to some because they depart significantly from our lived, everyday reality. Being necessarily hypothetical in either of the two senses just noted is one way in which a normative-theory thought experiment may be said to be 'wacky'.

Another way in which a normative-theory thought experiment may be 'wacky' is in being *imaginatively opaque*. Robert Nozick's Utility Monster involves an imaginatively opaque being since his, her, or its pleasure in sacrificing others must be of a fantastic quality to outweigh the acute suffering of all of those who are sacrificed. As ordinary creatures with ordinary abilities for happiness, we are unable to imagine the kind of fantastic happiness that such a being would have to feel in order to outweigh the suffering it caused to those it sacrificed (Parfit 1986: 389).

These two senses (and sources) of wackiness – necessary hypotheticality and imaginative opacity – can overlap but are conceptually distinct, since some cases of practical impossibility, such as my jumping 100 feet in the air, are nonetheless readily imaginable, while some cases of imaginative opacity, such as the experiences of sleepwalking and of insanity, are nonetheless readily practically possible and indeed actual. Commonly cited examples of wacky thought experiments include Rawls's Original Position, Nozick's Experience Machine, and Nozick's Utility Monster. Since imaginatively opaque and necessarily hypothetical thought experiments invite the most controversy in normative theory, they will be the main focus of our defence of thought experiments in Section 4.

3   Necessary Conditions for Well-Posed Thought Experiments

What would a well-posed thought experiment in political theory look like? In this section, we outline and defend two necessary conditions for well-posed thought experiments in normative theory: philosophical respectability (Section 3.1) and argumentative relevance (Section 3.2). In broad terms, these conditions of well-posed thought experiments apply outside of normative theory, but they are particularly salient to normative theory. Although both conditions apply to both simple and complex thought experiments, the first condition places different constraints on each type of thought experiment.

These conditions are a non-exhaustive set in the sense that there are further conditions that any good argument must meet (e.g. clarity), which we do not mention, as we wish to focus on what is special to thought experiments in particular. We believe that thought experiments that satisfy these conditions will be genuinely well-posed provided they do not fall foul of conditions that apply more generally to philosophical investigation.

3.1   Philosophical Respectability

This condition has two distinct dimensions, the first of which is non-question-beggingness (Section 3.1.1), which applies straightforwardly to both simple and complex thought experiments. The second dimension, validity, applies to all complex thought experiments and to some simple ones (Section 3.1.2).

3.1.1   Non-Question-Beggingness   Thought experiments should not assume an answer to the question they pose. So, when formulating thought experiments, one cannot assume that it is permissible to torture the bomb planter in order to argue that it is permissible to torture him.

Of course, it is not always obvious when answers are being assumed and questions are being begged. Consider Wittgenstein on the ontology of moral judgements:

Suppose one of you were an omniscient person and therefore knew all the movements of all the bodies in the world dead or alive and that he also knew all the states of mind of all human beings that ever lived, and suppose this man wrote all he knew in a big book, then this book would contain the whole description of the world; and what I want to say is, that this book would contain nothing that we would call an *ethical* judgment or anything that would logically imply such a judgment. (Wittgenstein 1965: 6)

Wittgenstein's scenario presupposes that there are no facts in the world of the kind that he aims to deny and hence his hypothetical does not test the claim that this is the case. Any other conclusion about the book's content would be contradictory. This would be a fatal problem for a thought experiment testing whether ethical judgements are facts. However, the example would be acceptable as a descriptive hypothetical that merely aims to elucidate what Wittgenstein means by *facts*.

3.1.2   Validity   When we first pose a thought experiment to ourselves, we should pose it as an open question, in the way that all of the thought experiments presented thus far have been posed. However, the question hopefully gives rise to answers, that is, the results of the thought experiment. Results are broadly of two types. First, they may simply consist in answers about what is morally required, permissible, etc. (e.g. it is impermissible to kill one to save five in the Transplant Case). Second, they may consist in such answers together with a further hypothesis about why this is the correct answer (e.g. because harming is worse than not aiding). Simple thought experiments allow but do not require the researcher to propose the hypothesis. All complex thought experiments, however, necessarily contain at least an implicit hypothesis about what does the work in one of the simple thought experiments; the next simple thought experiment is then added precisely in order to test that hypothesis (see later in this chapter for more on this).

Where a thought experiment contains or generates a hypothesis explaining our intuitive reactions to the scenarios involved, the thought experiment can be 'translated' into an argument (See also Norton 1996). That argument must satisfy the condition of validity. In other words, the argument should not involve logically fallacious reasoning. Of course, what constitutes fallacious reasoning is a matter of some debate. The point is simply that thought experiments that contain and generate hypotheses can and should be held to the same standards of valid reasoning as conventional arguments, whatever those standards may be. Inability to translate such thought experiments into a valid argument would indicate that we are unsure either of what the experiment is supposed to test or of whether it presupposes what it is meant to reveal.

An example of a thought experiment that satisfies the validity condition is the following from Peter Singer.

The Pond and the Envelope: Imagine that you are walking by a shallow and isolated pond in which you spot a drowning child. You can easily save the child. Must you save the child? Imagine next that you receive a letter from a charity such as Oxfam asking you for a donation that you can easily make, to save a child (or, likely, many children) abroad. If you accepted that you must save the child in the pond case, must you also save the child(ren) in the envelope case? (Singer 1972: 231–2)

The thought experiment is used to show, amongst other things, that it makes no moral difference whether the person we can help is a neighbour's child ten yards away or a foreigner whose name we shall never know 10,000 miles away.

Assume that, following Singer, you answer all questions in the affirmative. Once we form an intuitive affirmative response to the questions, this thought experiment can be readily translated into a valid, conventional argument as follows:

P1: We can easily save the child in the pond.
P2: We have a duty to save the child in the pond.
P3: The best explanation for P2 is that we have a duty to save others when we can do so at little cost to ourselves.
C1 (THE HYPOTHESIS): We have a duty to save others when we can do so at little cost to ourselves.
P4: We can send money to Oxfam at little cost to ourselves.
P5: We can save others by sending money to Oxfam.
C2: We have a duty to send money to Oxfam.

The condition of validity is satisfied here since the argument into which the complex thought experiment is translated tracks what the thought experiment was intending to test or establish and satisfies the criteria for a valid argument. More generally, of course, Singer would want us to see the argument not only as valid, but also as sound: he would want us to accept that there is no relevant difference between the Pond and the Envelope scenarios in that both require the same moral response and both are explained by the same general principle (the hypothesis: C1).

A thought experiment that does not satisfy the condition of validity is the following:

A Sibling and a Stranger: Imagine that your sibling contracts malaria and can be saved only if you agree to finance expensive medical treatment involving a helicopter ride. You can finance it, albeit it will cost you a lot and you won't be able to go on holiday for a few years. Must you do it? Imagine next that your sibling is healthy, but you can finance similar life-saving medical treatment for a stranger. If you accepted that you must save your sibling, must you not also save the stranger?

This thought experiment can be readily translated into a fallacious argument:

P1: We can save our sibling at high cost to ourselves.
P2: We have a duty to save our sibling.
P3: The best explanation for why we have a duty to save our sibling is because this is our sibling.
C1 (THE HYPOTHESIS): We have a duty to save our sibling even when this involves a high cost to ourselves.
P4: Saving strangers would involve high costs.
P5: The costs of saving the strangers would be identical to those of saving our sibling.
C2: We have a duty to save strangers even when this involves a high cost to ourselves.

This argument is invalid because, even were the premises all true, the conclusion need not be true: it does not follow from the fact that we have a duty to save a sibling at high cost to ourselves that we necessarily have a duty to do other things that are equally costly.

The condition of philosophical respectability has the virtue of demystifying the status of thought experiments. If thought experiments can be represented as conventional arguments that meet the standards of valid reasoning, then it is unsurprising that they can act as solutions to philosophical problems. As we argued, this is the case with all complex thought experiments and with at least some simple thought experiments. To be genuinely well-posed, however, thought experiments should also be analytically useful to us and not corrupt our reflections. This is addressed by the second condition, the condition of argumentative relevance.

3.2 Argumentative Relevance

Thought experiments should be designed in such a way that we can focus on the relevant aspects of the scenario. We do not want our intuitive answers to respond to features of the scenario that are not part of the test and that thereby pollute it. For example, when testing a given hypothesis (such as a hypothesis about how we ought to treat strangers), it is necessary not to construct scenarios that more plausibly test an alternative hypothesis (such as a hypothesis about how we ought to treat our siblings), as we cannot assume that they will elicit the same answers. For instance, the Sibling and the Stranger could be translated into a valid argument that fails to meet this condition:

P1: We can save our sibling at high cost to ourselves.
P2′: The best explanation for why we have a duty to save our sibling is because we have a duty to save others even at a high cost to ourselves.
C1′ (THE HYPOTHESIS): We have a duty to save others even when this involves high cost to ourselves.
P3: Saving strangers would involve high costs.
P4: The costs of saving the strangers would be identical to those of saving the sibling.
C2: We have a duty to save strangers even at a high cost to ourselves.

The argument is valid, but ridiculous: P2′ misidentifies the principle to be derived from considering the case of the sibling. Similarly, looking at a simple thought experiment, if, in the Transplant Case, we forbid the doctor to kill the one person to save the five on the grounds that a doctor may never kill, then we are not testing what the experiment is meant to test, which, among other things, is whether there is a normatively significant difference between killing and letting die (see likewise Rivera-Lopez 2005). By prohibiting the doctor from killing, we block the relevant test, as we allow her status as a doctor to infect our reflection on the scenario.

All in all, if we want to use our thought experiments as *evidence* for or against a given hypothesis (premise), we need to make sure that the results of the experiment actually support or challenge the argumentative move in question. The key question is whether it is possible to make this condition of testing the relevant hypothesis more concrete beyond prohibiting obvious shifts in focus. We argue that the condition of argumentative relevance translates into two weak constraints on the design of thought experiments. The first requires that the experiment allow for rudimentary alternatives (the Rudimentary Alternatives Constraint). The second requires that the experiment not encourage narrative-framing bias (the Moderate Narrative-Framing Constraint). These two weak constraints can be contrasted with more demanding variants, which we reject.

3.2.1   Rudimentary Alternatives Constraint   When we assume the absence of some (believed) necessary feature of the world, we should stipulate at least a rudimentary alternative. The aim here is to eliminate the bias that may come from continuing to assume that the feature still obtains. For example, an ancient philosopher who believes that objects can only move by *willing* to move should not run a thought experiment like the following:

Unwilling Rock: Assume that a large rock is not willing to move, but still moves. Is the rock to blame when it kills someone?

The ancient philosopher who holds that willing is a necessary condition for moving should not run this thought experiment – without some extra stipulations – because he is pre-committed to the view that the object that moved must have been willing to move. He should stipulate instead a rudimentary alternative for *how* the object moved; for example, the object moved because it fell just like a human being might fall if pushed by a gust of wind.

Unwilling Rock 2: Assume that a large rock is not willing to move, but still moves, pushed by a gust of wind (against its will). Is the rock to blame when it kills someone?

Although we endorse the Rudimentary Alternatives Constraint, we reject the more demanding Fleshed-Out Alternatives Constraint, which holds that allowed alternatives must be fully fleshed out and rendered comprehensible to us given what we know about the world (Wilkes 1988: 43ff.). Returning to the ancient philosopher, unlike the Rudimentary Alternatives Constraint, the Fleshed-Out Alternatives Constraint would require him to explain *how* a large, heavy rock can be pushed by a gust of wind. We acknowledge that a fully fleshed-out alternative would protect us from certain biases, but the protection is too restrictive. It is implausible to hold that we really need a fleshed-out, clear statement of the alternative to the ruled-out feature of the scenario, in order to prevent the ruled-out feature from determining our conclusions.

All in all, then, we accept that unconscious bias is real bias. But the possibility of bias is not a reason to abandon theorizing that might be subject to it. It is a reason to guard against it within the parameters of the case. We think that the Rudimentary Alternatives Constraint allows us to do so.

3.2.2 Moderate Narrative-Framing Constraint We also support, more tentatively, the Moderate Narrative-Framing Constraint that guards against thought experiments that encourage narrative-framing bias. For instance, a thought experiment that draws its scenario from a well-known novel, event, film, genre, cultural myth, or icon can bring with it considerable narrative baggage in that the context of its creation has its own purposes that might subordinate or undermine clear reflection on the scenario as a thought experiment. The problem is best explained with the use of an example that we owe to Roy Sorensen (1992: 264; see also Parfit

1986: 199–200; Coleman 2000: 58–60). Consider teleportation. Since it is almost exclusively encountered in the context of sci-fi adventures such as Star Trek and Harry Potter, its context makes demands of narrative unity on our reading of teleportation scenarios. As viewers, we want to believe, for the sake of the story, that it is the same person who is teleported rather than a new person who is created by the process, and this may infect the philosophical use we seek to make of teleportation scenarios.

Sorensen goes on to suggest less plausibly that Nozick's Experience Machine also may be systematically distorted for a similar reason, namely, that we approach this thought experiment as a story about someone entering an Experience Machine and we find the possibility of such a story so unbearably boring that we reject it as a legitimate prospect. But Sorensen's position on this is implausible. There is no putative demand of narrative unity about Experience Machines that necessitates that an Experience Machine scenario be irretrievably boring. We can rewrite this kind of scenario as an exciting, *Matrix*-style adventure that eliminates the supposed anti-boredom bias. Our rewriting may introduce a pro-excitement bias in favour of the adventure, but that suggests that we need only find a middle-of-the-road description of the Experience Machine experience.

The same is true presumably for most thought experiments. Narrative bias need not hopelessly infect thought experiment scenarios provided that we are attentive to the structure of the scenario and to the narrative assumptions that it can imply. Thus, for example, when we involve the Nazis to make a point against the permissibility of medical experimentation, we should be careful not to appeal just to the horrors that the mention of Nazis invokes.

By endorsing the Moderate Narrative-Framing Constraint in this form, we reject the more demanding Extreme Narrative-Framing Constraint that requires thought experiments to be 'maximally conservative' and lie exclusively within the realm of *contingent hypotheticals* and never that of *necessary hypotheticals*, the spectrum of which we discussed in Section 1 (see Haggqvist 1996: 147; Rivera-Lopez 2005). The central idea behind maximal conservatism is that experiments that require us to depart from standard circumstances that we would encounter in our world will not track our reactions to the features of the case *as set out in the experiment*, but will instead track our reactions to the standard features of a case *encountered in the actual world*. For example, when asked to assess whether to kill one to save five in the Transplant Case, we will ultimately not be able to take on board the stipulation that the alternative deaths really are certitudes, since in our common experience we may hope that the five would still have a chance of surviving since we never know for certain. This alleged limitation of our mental abilities calls into doubt the usefulness, or even the possibility, of wacky thought experiments such as necessary hypotheticals.

But, while the problem of polluted intuitions is genuine, the assumption underlying the postulate of maximal conservatism is mistaken. The postulate rests on the wrong-footed assumption that we are likely to reach better judgements when we operate within a familiar, real-life context than when we operate within an unfamiliar context. But this is not generally true. We might be better able to react only to the variables that the thought experiment is meant to test when the case is set in the context that we do not normally encounter and are not familiar with, just as a non-native English speaker might be quicker than a native speaker to spot certain linguistic patterns in English, or a person unfamiliar with a given family's dynamics might be quicker than family members are to spot instances of mental abuse and exploitation. A radically unfamiliar context may well make us more attentive to the features of the scenario that matter precisely because we are less likely to smuggle in additional assumptions.

That said, we do not deny the potential legitimacy of the worry about narrative bias. A thought experiment that asks us to assume a hateful baby or a saintly Mafioso might be hard to execute correctly. Similarly, we might also worry in relation to the ticking-bomb thought experiment that it asks us to assume what is very hard to imagine, namely that the torturer will be exceptionally well informed and never tempted to abuse his power. However, thought experiments are processes that we can approach slowly and reflectively, thereby guarding against possible biases. If such biases occur, this does not rule out the use of thought experiments, but rather requires us to redesign them, especially as similar, if not greater, biases are likely to plague actual, real-world scenarios.

4   Why Wacky Thought Experiments Can Be Well-Posed

We reject the possibility that a bar on wackiness is one condition of a well-posed thought experiment. In this section, we explain why.

The 'wackiness' of thought experiments can be disambiguated into the two main categories noted in Sections 1 and 2: *imaginative opacity* and *necessary hypotheticality*, including *necessary hypotheticality for us here and now*. We hold that neither of these dimensions of wackiness bars thought experiments from being well-posed. Before we consider imaginative opacity or necessary hypotheticality, we need to address an objection that applies not only to these dimensions of wackiness, but also to something that is not at all wacky: contingent hypotheticality.

4.1   Contingently Hypothetical Thought Experiments

Some critics seem to hold that we can conduct respectable normative theory without thought experiments. Such critics maintain that it does not matter that a given theory or principle would lead to counterintuitive recommendations when checked against a hypothetical scenario because all we need to know is whether our principles will serve us in our *actual* world (e.g. Hare 1981: 135 and chapter 8 passim; for discussion, see Carson 1993). The suggestion is that all that matters in normative theory is whether our principles perform well in the actual world, and not how well they cope with non-actual situations.

Against this view, we offer two arguments. First, the performance of our principles in actual scenarios is not all that matters in normative theory. Frequently, normative principles are put forward as explanations of *why* a given course of action is right or wrong. Call such principles *explanatory principles*. Explanatory principles must be more abstract than the principles that bear on a given actual situation if they are to explain our judgements in that situation. For instance, it is wrong to kill five patients in order to harvest their organs to save one patient because it is wrong to kill in order to save. Since such explanatory principles are more general than the situations that call for them in the actual world, they must be testable against all situations to which they could, in principle, apply. This means that they also stand or fall by their performance in hypothetical situations. This is one reason that political theorists often need to consider counterexamples, and rely on hypothetical scenarios to expand their range, in order to challenge abstract principles.

Second, even if we are not seeking explanatory principles, but merely principles that will serve us well with the problem at hand, thought experiments offer us a way of trying to resolve disagreement on which principles these are. All else being equal, it should count in favour of a principle that it holds across a wider range of scenarios (just as it counts in favour of a theory that it applies to a wider range of problems). So, thought experiments are important in normative theory because they can help us break ties.

These responses might be taken to suggest that normative theories (call them applied theories) would not need thought experiments if they did not seek explanatory principles or were not challenged by other theories. But even this suggestion should be resisted. That is, even applied theories that carry support need a method to discern whether the considerations brought to bear on a given problem (to reach an all-things-considered judgement) are relevant from the moral point of view. For example, we need to ask whether it is relevant to consider such things as 'this is my house,' or 'this is extremely demanding,' or 'she is a woman,' or 'it's repellent,' or 'I would not do it myself.' Thought experiments offer an efficient way of testing the salience of such considerations (which is not to say that such testing would amount to a proof. On the fact that thought experiments alone do not deliver transparent data, see Kagan 1988).

4.2   Imaginative Opacity

Turning to imaginative opacity, this dimension of wackiness raises the following worry (Cooper 2005: 328–47; Parfit 1986: 389; Wilkes 1988: 15ff). Imaginatively opaque thought experiments fail to have an adequate imaginative grip, and hence they pose 'what if?' questions that the experimenter cannot answer. The reason that the experimenter cannot answer those questions may be that she has no knowledge of the laws that govern the behaviour of the entity she is imagining. Or she may have knowledge of the laws relevant for predicting that behaviour in the actual world (e.g. the process of human birth), but those laws do not apply in the hypothetical scenario (e.g. giving birth to oneself). The fact that the experimenter cannot answer these questions is said to negate whatever argumentative value the thought experiment might have.

At least two replies can be made to this objection. First, ruling out the use of imaginatively opaque thought experiments would be unduly prohibitive. It would rule out the use of thought experiments that expose certain paradoxes. For instance, it would rule out the use of a thought experiment used to show that causal paradoxes would emerge if one could go back in time and kill one's father. But the opacity of the experiment does not stop us from pointing out the potential paradoxes.

Second, it is not clear that being able to imagine all aspects of a given case is essential to run the thought experiment. For example, we (the authors of this chapter) cannot fully conceive of a being that is both a dog *and* able to talk, but we can still ask whether such a dog would count as a person. Likewise, we cannot imagine a utility monster that derives almost boundless pleasure from the suffering of others, but we can ask whether such a being would be right to make others suffer. Recall that thought experiments are not 'run' (simply) to establish how we (the experimenters) would *feel*, but to establish what we may plausibly *think*, and hence we may not require a full character brief in the way that actors would if they were required to play a given part and to react 'in character'.

4.3   Necessary Hypotheticals

The worry that we do not understand the laws that govern some imaginatively opaque cases resurfaces in a form that applies also to necessarily hypothetical thought experiments. The worry takes the form of a dilemma:

Thought experiments are useless because we either cannot set them up properly or cannot derive any credible conclusions from them. That is, either we are assuming a world similar to ours, in which case we cannot set up a wacky thought experiment at all (e.g. in a world similar to ours, dogs are not as intelligent as persons; there is no teleporting; etc.), or we are assuming a world that is radically different from ours, in which case we cannot know what to say about *this world*. (See Raz 1986: 419–20; Mulhall 2002: 16–18.)

Why can we apparently not know what to say about this world? The answer relates to 'semantic holism' (see Sorensen 1992: 282–4). The idea is that *our* concepts developed to track *our* world, rather than the wacky worlds that we set up in our experiments, and wacky worlds cannot plausibly capture our real-life concepts. For instance, suppose that half of the standard tests that we use to determine whether a piece of copper wire is electrified give us a positive answer and half of the tests give us a negative answer. What should we say about this piece of copper wire? The answer, according to Nowell-Smith, should be: 'I simply do not know what I should say' (1954: 240; quoted in Sorensen 1992: 283). Now consider a wacky, normative-theory thought experiment (inspired by Roger Crisp's Beverly Hills Case; Crisp 2003: 755).

Rich and Superrich: Imagine a world in which there are only rich and superrich. Is the inequality that holds between the rich and the superrich unfair or otherwise problematic?

The answer, according to a critic of wacky thought experiments, is 'I simply do not know' since our concepts developed to deal with entirely different cases and they are of no use in radically reimagined worlds. To give an analogy, paint colours developed to paint the British landscape are of little use in painting the African landscape, given the very different light of the two environments.

However, this objection rests on a mistake. It assumes that thought experiments ask us what we *would* say if our concepts were developed to accommodate the wacky cases as standard. But this is not what thought experiments ask us to do. They ask us, instead, to judge how our current, familiar concepts behave when exposed to new situations. To see this, first return to the paint analogy. The thought here is that we are not asked to use the British paints to paint the African landscape; we are asked instead to use the African light to rule, say, on whether two identical-looking British colours really are identical. When we cannot easily tell if the colours are the same against the British light, we may benefit from examining them under the African light. We examine the value of equality by asking if we still value equality in such a context. If not, then we have reason to suspect that what matters to us in our ordinary context is not simply equality, but absolute levels of deprivation.

Second, consider another illustration of the application of our ordinary concepts to new situations. In Rich and Superrich, we do not ask what we would think if we were living in such a privileged society. Instead, we ask whether we consider the inequality present in that privileged society too unfair by our own, current standards. Pointing out that in a world with only the rich and the superrich, no one would care about equality (and that they may not even have a sense that they are unequal) is irrelevant to the question of whether we now see the inequality as problematic. (There is a wrinkle here. We may have a conception of *unfair inequality* according to which inequality is only unfair if the people subject to it consider it unfair; if this is so then, indeed, we may be unable to tell whether unfair inequality characterizes the hypothetical scenario, but that is not because the thought experiment is hypothetical and wacky, but because we do not have the relevant empirical data about the people we are investigating.)

To conclude this section, we want to emphasize that wacky thought experiments are not, in fact, used solely to advance academic debates, which some might consider esoteric in any case. Testing how our familiar concepts behave when exposed to new situations is a common, undisputed, and powerful strategy in many fields, including one closely aligned with normative theory, namely, law. It is routine practice in law schools to hold moot courts revolving around wild and wonderful cases so as to train law students in the application of key legal concepts. And the application of such legal concepts as *theft* and *property* is viewed as no less legitimate when the parties are Martians stealing magic from Venusians. Moreover, in broad terms, real court cases are exercises in thought experimenting since both ordinary court procedures and norms of due process necessarily yield an abstracted and idealized presentation of the facts of the case.

Ultimately, wacky thought experiments are not undermined by our inability either to imagine all of their elements or to anticipate how the concepts we are exploring would evolve in hypothesized worlds.

5   **Conclusion: How to Design Good Thought Experiments in Political Theory**

This discussion has identified several conditions for good thought experiments. We conclude here by presenting these conditions as a set of 'how-to' instructions for the design of good thought experiments in normative theory:

1. We may stumble across thought experiments in film and novels; and life itself can generate situations that can be thought through as thought experiments. But, usually the impetus for designing them is that we want to test some premise in our argument/some hypothesis about a plausible principle or value. If so, **the most fundamental question you should pose is this: what exactly would you like your thought experiment to test (i.e. to undermine or to support)?**

2. **Ensure that the thought experiment is relevant to what is being tested** (see Section 3.2). **Try to design the simplest experiment** in the sense of having the most parsimonious story (to avoid introducing distorting elements), but do not worry if the story is also wacky in the sense of being fantastical. (Our defence of wacky thought experiments is meant to set your imagination free.)

3. **If your thought experiment involves a denial of a standard feature of the world (e.g. you deny that the police are uncertain whether they caught the right guy), hypothesize, even roughly, how this can be** – what alternative feature of the world is present. (See Section 3.2.1.)

4. **Be sensitive to possible narrative-framing biases**, that is, to the structure of the scenario and to the narrative assumptions it can imply. (See Section 3.2.2.)

5. **Consider whether any imaginatively opaque elements of the thought experiment need to be made imaginatively clear** in order for the thought experiment to function as intended. (See Section 4.2.)

6. When constructing a necessary hypothetical, **consider whether the selected 'foreign context' best serves to illuminate the features of our ordinary concepts and/or principles that are under consideration.** (See Section 4.3.)

7. **Ensure that none of the features of the experiment already assumes what is to be tested.** (See Section 3.1.1.)

8. **Ensure that the thought experiment, together with the hypothesis it is meant to support or deny, translates into a valid argument.** (See Section 3.1.2.)

Appendix: Further Examples of Thought Experiments

1. Judith Jarvis Thomson's **Famous Violinist**: A healthy person awakes in a hospital to find that, unbeknownst to her, she has been connected by her kidneys to a famous violinist. The famous violinist will die unless she remains connected to him for the next nine months, just as a foetus will die unless it remains 'connected' for nine months to the pregnant woman carrying it. Is the healthy person morally obligated to remain in the hospital with the violinist for nine months? (Thomson 1971: 48–9).

The thought experiment is used to challenge the impermissibility of abortion.

2. Judith Jarvis Thomson's **Loop Trolley**: The two tracks in the Trolley Problem split, but then circle back to form a loop. Diverting the trolley onto the track with the one person will cause the trolley to hit the one and thereby prevent the trolley from continuing around the loop to hit the five. Is it permissible to turn the trolley away from the track with the five and onto the track with the one? (Thomson 1985: 1402–3).

This thought experiment is used to show that, like in the Transplant Case, turning the trolley uses the one person merely as a means.

3. Judith Jarvis Thomson's **Fat Man on the Bridge**: The runaway trolley of the Trolley Problem cannot be stopped by diverting it, but can be stopped by pushing a fat man off a bridge onto the track in front of the trolley, resulting in his death. Is it permissible to push the fat man? (Thomson 1985: 1409).

This thought experiment is used to show that pushing the fat man uses him merely as a means and infringes his right not to be so treated.

4. Bernard Williams's **Jim and the Indians**: A jungle explorer, Jim, comes across a colonialist, Pedro, who has twenty aboriginal people lined up before a firing squad. Pedro offers Jim the 'privilege' of killing one and letting the rest go free. Jim can either refuse the offer, in which case all twenty people will be killed, or he can accept the offer and kill only one of them himself. What should Jim do and how should he feel about his choice? (Williams 1973: 98–100).

This thought experiment is used to question the thought that a plausible moral theory must be consequentialist. Focusing only on the lives lost, it seems that Jim must kill the one; but Williams argues that morality is not only about good and bad states of affairs.

5. Robert Nozick's **Wilt Chamberlain**: Suppose that basketball player Wilt Chamberlain attracts huge crowds to his games. He signs a contract with a team whereby he receives twenty-five cents for every home game ticket sold. During one season, a million people come to his games and happily drop twenty-five cents into

a special box for him, thinking it well worth it. He earns $250,000 this way, a much larger sum than the average income. Is he entitled to keep all of it?

This thought experiment is used to show that people's exercises of personal freedom, such as choosing to pay twenty-five cents to go to Chamberlain's games, will disrupt a patterned principle of distributive justice, such as the principle that everyone should have equal resources.

Acknowledgements

We thank Adrian Blau, Cécile Fabre, Fay Niker, Jonathan Quong, Victor Tadros, and Lea Ypi for their very helpful feedback on this chapter. We also thank Fay Niker for her research assistance. We thank the participants of the Oxford Political Theory Seminar (June 2010) and the Manchester Centre for Political Theory Seminar (October 2010) for their comments.

References

Brown, James Robert, 1986. 'Thought experiments in the scientific revolution', *International Studies in the Philosophy of Science* 1: 1–15.

Brown, James Robert, and Fehige, Yiftach, 2014. 'Thought experiments', in Edward Zalta (ed.), *The Stanford Encyclopedia of Philosophy* (Spring 2016 Edition). https://plato.stanford.edu/archives/spr2016/entries/thought-experiment/.

Carson, Tom, 1993. 'Hare on utilitarianism and intuitive morality', *Erkenntnis* 39: 305–31.

Cohen, G. A., 2009. *Why Not Socialism?* Princeton, NJ: Princeton University Press.

Coleman, Stephen, 2000. 'Thought experiments and personal identity', *Philosophical Studies* 98: 53–69.

Cooper, Rachel, 2005. 'Thought experiments', *Metaphilosophy* 36: 328–47.

Crisp, Roger, 2003. 'Equality, Priority, and Compassion', *Ethics* 113: 745–63.

Foot, Philippa, 2002. 'The problem of abortion and the doctrine of double effect', in *Virtues and Vices and Other Essays in Moral Philosophy*. Oxford: Clarendon Press, 19–32.

Gendler, Tamar Szabó, 1998. 'Galileo and the indispensability of scientific thought experiment', *British Journal for the Philosophy of Science* 49: 397–424.

Haggqvist, Sören, 1996. *Thought Experiments in Philosophy*. Stockholm: Almqvist & Wiksell International.

Hare, R. M., 1981. *Moral Thinking*. Oxford University Press.

Kagan, Shelly, 1988. 'The Additive Fallacy', *Ethics* 99: 5–31.

Martin, C. B., 1958. 'Identity and exact similarity', *Analysis* 18: 83–7.

Mulhall, Stephen, 2002. 'Fearful thoughts', *The London Review of Books* 24 (16): 16–18.

Norton, John, 1996. 'Are thought experiments just what you thought?', *Canadian Journal of Philosophy* 26: 333–66.

Nowell-Smith, P. H., 1954. *Ethics*. London: Penguin Books.

Nozick, Robert, 1974. *Anarchy, State, and Utopia*. Oxford: Blackwell.

O'Neill, Onora, 1986. 'The power of example', *Philosophy* 61 (235): 5–29.

Parfit, Derek, 1986. *Reasons and Persons*. Oxford University Press.

Putnam, Hilary, 1975. 'The meaning of "meaning"', in Keith Gunderson (ed.), *Language, Mind, and Knowledge*. Minneapolis: University of Minnesota Press, 131–93.

Rawls, John, 1971. *A Theory of Justice*. Cambridge, MA: Harvard University Press.

Raz, Joseph, 1986. *The Morality of Freedom*. Oxford University Press

Rivera-Lopez, Eduardo, 2005. 'Use and misuse of examples in normative ethics', *The Journal of Value Inquiry* 39: 115–25.

Singer, Peter, 1972. 'Famine, affluence, and morality', *Philosophy and Public Affairs* 1: 229–43.

Sorensen, Roy, 1992. *Thought Experiments*. Oxford University Press.

Thomson, Judith Jarvis, 1971. 'A defense of abortion', *Philosophy and Public Affairs* 1: 47–66.

Thomson, Judith Jarvis, 1985. 'The trolley problem', *Yale Law Journal* 94: 1395–1415.

Unger, Peter, 1982. 'Toward a Psychology of Common Sense', *American Philosophical Quarterly* 19: 117–129.

Walzer, Michael, 1973, 'The problem of dirty hands', *Philosophy and Public Affairs* 2: 160–80.

Williams, Bernard, 1960. 'Bodily continuity and personal identity', *Analysis* 20: 117–20.

Williams, Bernard, 1973. 'A critique of utilitarianism', in J. J. C. Smart and Bernard Williams (eds.), *Utilitarianism: For and Against*. Cambridge University Press, 75–150.

Wilkes, Kathleen, 1988. *Real People: Personal Identity without Thought Experiments*. Oxford: Clarendon Press.

Winch, Peter, 1965. 'The universalizability of moral judgments', *The Monist* 49: 196–214.

Wittgenstein, Ludwig, 1965. 'A lecture on ethics', *The Philosophical Review* 74: 3–12.

4   Reflective Equilibrium

Carl Knight

1   Introduction

The method of reflective equilibrium focuses on the relationship between *principles* and *judgments*. Principles are relatively general rules for comprehending the area of enquiry. Judgments are our intuitions or commitments, 'at all levels of generality' (Rawls 1975: 8), regarding the subject matter. The basic idea of reflective equilibrium is to bring principles and judgments into accord. This can be achieved by revising the principles and/or the judgments. For instance, if I am considering the principle that it is always wrong to lie, but have the judgment that it would not be wrong to lie in order to save a life, I can reach equilibrium by revising either the principle or the judgment.

Reflective equilibrium is the most widely used methodology in contemporary moral and political philosophy (Sinnott-Armstrong et al. 2010: 246; Varner 2012: 11). It has even been suggested that it is 'the only defensible method' (Scanlon 2003: 149). Its popularity is undoubtedly strongly influenced by John Rawls's use of it in his seminal *A Theory of Justice*, published in 1971.[1] However, the method precedes this, and extends to other fields. For instance, Nelson Goodman wrote regarding induction that '[t]he process of justification is the delicate one of making mutual adjustments between rules and accepted inferences; and in the agreement reached lies the only justification needed for either' (Goodman 1965: 64). Some fields, by contrast, do not seem as amenable to the method of reflective equilibrium. Within linguistics, for instance, native speakers' judgments of grammaticality cannot generally be replaced as moral judgments can (Daniels 1996: ch. 4). Although most writers treat reflective equilibrium as unproblematic within empirical sciences (Daniels 1996: 31–3; Cummins 1998; Welch 2014: 4; see also McDermott 2008), adjustment of empirical judgments also seems to be

---

[1] Jo Wolff (2013: 808) notes that, of the papers collected in the first two series of *Politics, Philosophy, and Society*, Rawls's was unique in aiming to defend a substantive position, and in deploying a distinctive methodology to positive effect.

subject to stronger constraints than those that apply to moral judgments (see Singer 2005: 345).

Indeed, here there seems to be a significant difference between normative political theory and empirical political science. A normative political theorist who, to her surprise, finds that a confidently held moral judgment conflicts with an otherwise compelling principle (or set of principles) is free to reject that judgment precisely because it conflicts with the favoured principle. But it would be quite improper for a confidently held empirical judgment to be abandoned simply because it turned out not to fit with the investigator's pet hypothesis. Full reflective equilibrium, with judgments adjusted at will just as principles are, is primarily the reserve of normative political theory. It is with normative political theory that this chapter will be concerned.

I first look at normative political judgments (Section 2) before considering the role of principles, arguments, devices of representation and background theory in wide reflective equilibrium (Section 3). I then consider two of the main challenges to the method (Section 4), and show how to use it to deliberate about substantive political principles (Section 5). I conclude with an extended example of the method in action (Section 6).

2   Judgments

The starting point for reflective equilibrium is our judgments. We cannot, however, use just any judgments. For instance, judgments made 'in the heat of the moment' would not be a reliable basis for equilibrium. *Considered* judgments are what we need. These are 'those judgments in which our moral capacities are most likely to be displayed without distortion' (Rawls 1999: 42).

Most writers, including Rawls (1999: 42), suppose that, in order to count as considered, judgments should be held with *confidence*. Indeed, Rawls often uses 'convictions' as a synonym for 'judgments' (Rawls 1975: 8; 2005: 24, 26, 28, 151, 156). This 'confidence constraint' seems to me quite gratuitous (Knight 2006: 207–8). If I have the firm conviction that the state should protect its citizens from terrorism, and also believe, less firmly, that individuals have a right to privacy, a right to not be subject to pre-trial detention beyond a certain duration and a right to a public trial, the confidence constraint would seem to require that my numerous but less firmly held concerns about individual rights be set aside. But this is to give free reign to the one firm conviction, with the upshot that the principle(s) arrived at in reflective equilibrium will allow almost any breach of civil rights in the name of public protection. This is in contradiction of the majority of the judgments I hold and (most likely) my overall view.

Undoubtedly, a firmly held judgment should generally carry more weight in our deliberations than a less firmly held one. But reflective equilibrium *automatically* does that, as we are presumably more likely to give up our less firmly held judgments in the face of opposing judgments or principles. If we do not, that is because it turns out that the less firmly held judgments had something going for them. Maybe they individually or collectively capture something that, on reflection, we consider important. Thus, I think we should reject the confidence constraint.

A different constraint has sometimes been assumed, including in my earlier work (Knight 2006: 207). This specifies that our considered judgments do not display errors of reasoning, such as logical inconsistencies or empirical errors. Some writers go further, suggesting that we should disregard judgments that we do not have evidence for, as they are not epistemic assets (Gaus 1996: 86; Kelly and McGrath 2010: 347–4). Should we, then, endorse an 'epistemic constraint', requiring that only justified or warranted judgments, or (more minimally) only those that lack errors, are admitted to the reflective equilibrium procedure?

Though this may seem like simple common sense, I doubt it. Consider first the stronger version of the constraint, which requires justification or warrant for a judgment. Evidence can be rather thin on the ground when we are dealing even with firmly held judgments. If I consider some political judgment that I hold very firmly, such as the judgment that no fellow citizen should avoidably starve, it is hard to point to anything that can really count as evidence for that belief in the relevant sense. I might point out that my compatriot will suffer pain, reduced capability and eventually death, but these *empirical* facts alone cannot really be evidence for the *normative* judgment I am making. It seems that, in a case like this, the judgment itself is foundational. My judgment seems pre-theoretically plausible to me, and that is sufficient to grant it 'independent credibility' (Hooker 2012: 23). This does not mean that it has any weight in my final principles, but it is enough for it to be granted admission to the reflective equilibrium process. It is there that the credentials of our judgments are really tested, by seeing how well they fit with our other judgments and the most plausible principles, in light of the most compelling arguments we can muster.

What then of the less demanding version of the epistemic constraint, which requires merely the absence of outright error? Surely we can reject some judgments as clearly erroneous. But even this constraint might be thought to be excessively demanding in that it goes beyond providing 'conditions favorable for deliberation and judgment in general' (Rawls

1999: 42) and actually limits the admissible content of judgments. Furthermore, exactly what qualifies as an error of reasoning and what qualifies as an empirical error is controversial. We could consider these issues in piecemeal fashion prior to entering reflective equilibrium. But this is counterproductive as we have no way of knowing whether these isolated speculations will be consistent with the most plausible overall position. We should instead consider these issues holistically, as pieces in the jigsaw that is the coherent view of the conceptual terrain that we aim to arrive at in reflective equilibrium. (Specifically, these issues are settled through consideration of relevant background theories – see Section 3.) Reflective equilibrium eschews the essentialist notion 'that we can determine the nature of certain facets of these inquiries in advance of the inquiries themselves, and that nothing that comes about in inquiry will change those facets' (Walden 2013: 255). The epistemic constraint, even in its minimal form, seems to put the cart before the horse, and should be discarded. Considered judgments are just those made in 'conditions favorable for deliberation and judgment in general'.

3 Wide Reflective Equilibrium

Suppose that you have arrived at your set of considered judgments. You might first use these to reach *narrow* reflective equilibrium, in which 'one is to be presented with only those descriptions which more or less match one's existing judgments except for minor discrepancies' (Rawls 1999: 43; see also Rawls 2005: 8 n. 8). Narrow reflective equilibrium is in essence an effort to systematize an agent's pretheoretical views. As such, it has limited epistemic value. Were someone to ask you what justification you have for your principles, you do not have much of a reply. To be sure, the narrow reflective equilibrium principles might be an improvement from your perspective on the bare intuitions you started out with. But you can hardly say that your principles are well justified where they are just a direct expression of your pre-theoretical intuitions.

The more interesting version of the method is *wide* reflective equilibrium. Rawls describes this in very demanding terms: 'one is to be presented with all possible descriptions to which one might plausibly conform one's judgments together with all relevant philosophical arguments' (Rawls 1999: 43). So for wide reflective equilibrium to be reached, you must consider all principles (and combinations of principles) that you might accept. As one way in which you may conform your judgments to principles is to change your judgments, this means that you must consider every principle in every combination with every other principle!

Unsurprisingly, Rawls does not attempt to fully satisfy this unachievable standard, resolving in *A Theory of Justice* to compare only his own 'principles and arguments with a few other familiar views' (Rawls 1999: 43). For all practical purposes, it will undoubtedly be necessary to narrow our equilibrium in this way. Nevertheless, I think there is great value in keeping in mind that wide reflective equilibrium is an *ideal*. It sets the bar high. Though the theorist will inevitably only consider a few principles, this is not because that is all the method of reflective equilibrium requires for a full justification to be provided. It should always be kept in mind that consideration of more principles would provide a fuller justification. Furthermore, if we have to cut corners, we should do so in the way least harmful to the strength of the final justification. This means, for example, ensuring that we at least consider the most compelling rival principles, rather than satisfying ourselves with seeing off straw men.

Reflective equilibrium can be interpreted as providing an ecumenical answer to a long-standing problem in epistemology. The ordinary way of justifying beliefs is *inferential* and *linear*: belief A justifies belief B, which justifies belief C, and so on. The problem here is rather obvious. As the chain of inference cannot go on infinitely, it seems that *none* of our beliefs will be justified. There are two ways out of this infinite justificatory regress. *Foundationalism* denies that all justification is inferential – for example, A might be justified by something other than another belief. *Coherentism* denies that all justification is linear – for example, C might be justified by A (Brink 1989: 109). A large majority of writers see reflective equilibrium as a coherentist method (Brink 1989: 134; Daniels 1996: 60–1; Tersman 2008: 398–400; Maffetone 2010: 142–5), while a few see it as foundationalist (DePaul 1986; Ebertz 1993). In my view it clearly contains elements of both approaches. Foundationalism can be seen to be present as I would, according to the method, be justified in favouring one possible coherent set of principles and considered judgments to another purely because the former coincides with my actual considered judgments. Coherentism cannot explain this, as each set is identical as regards coherentist non-linear justificatory chains. But coherentism is evidently also present, as the method says that the fact that some judgment (or principle) coheres with the rest of our beliefs counts in its favour.

As I have mentioned, Rawls requires not only that principles be considered, but relevant arguments as well. We could reach equilibrium without arguments, but coherence among beliefs that have not been subjected to serious scrutiny would be of limited justificatory value. This introduces several new complexities. First, there are arguments that directly support or undermine judgments and principles. For instance, when contemplating utilitarianism, the objection that

Table 4.1: *Elements of wide reflective equilibrium*

Element	Scope	Role	Examples
Judgments	Specific or general	Primary subject of equilibrium	Racial discrimination is wrong; all individuals have equal moral worth.
Principles	General	Primary subject of equilibrium	The difference principle; equal moral worth principle
Direct arguments	Specific	Argumentation	Rawls's intuitive argument; the levelling down objection
Devices of representation	General	Argumentation	The original position; the ideal observer
Background theories	General	Argumentation	Theories of the person; social theory

utilitarianism seems in some circumstances to permit slavery or knowing punishment of the innocent should be considered (Varner 2012: 11). Second, there are structures for framing our deliberations that go beyond single arguments, which Rawls terms 'devices of representation' (Rawls 2005: 23–8). These typically provide special circumstances for principle selection, with the parameters of those circumstances set by the theorist's judgments regarding what is reasonable or rational. Rawls's original position is the best known example within analytical political philosophy. There are many more examples in contemporary work (Ackerman 1980; Gauthier 1986; Dworkin 2000: ch. 2) and, arguably, older social contract theory (Hobbes, Locke) and ideal observer theory (Hume, Smith). Finally, there are 'background theories' (Daniels 1996: 22–3), which are drawn on by both the direct arguments and the devices of representation, and themselves tested for intuitive appeal. For instance, if a theory of the separateness of persons were found compelling, it might be used to undermine certain principles, as Rawls (1999: 23–4) seems to argue is true of utilitarianism. The various elements of wide reflective equilibrium are summarized in Table 4.1.

In practice, it may not always be easy to distinguish the different elements, and it is not absolutely essential to do so. For instance, the table gives an example of a principle (equal moral worth principle) that is more or less a restatement of a judgment (all individuals have equal moral worth). As judgments and principles, qua judgments and principles, do not receive privileged epistemic status – '[o]ur "intuitions" are simply opinions: our philosophical theories are the same' (Lewis 1983: x; see also Freeman 2007: 33; Mandle 2009: 171–2) – there is no problem with the boundaries between them being fuzzy or overlapping.[2] Judgments and principles are only distinguished here as this is a familiar and often helpful way of arranging our thoughts. Likewise, and as indicated in the table, the direct arguments, devices of representation and background theories are really just subsets of one big category of 'argumentation'. They do not need to be systematically separated as none has priority over any other. Some of the argumentation elements may even be absent in the creation of particular equilibria; for instance, the extended example in Section 6 does not refer to device of representation.

4   Challenges

As the most widespread approach to theory selection in moral and political philosophy, the method of reflective equilibrium has faced its share of critical attention. In this section I consider a couple of the more significant challenges.

A common complaint with the method is that it relies entirely on the quality of the judgments that form a central part of the equilibrium (Brandt 1979: 20; Williamson 2007: 244–6). Advocates of the method typically build their examples around highly plausible judgments, such as Rawls' convictions about the wrongness of religious intolerance and racial subordination. But if someone starts with implausible or even repugnant judgments, there is, critics claim, nothing to stop the method from generating implausible conclusions. The point is put clearly by Thomas Kelly and Sarah McGrath (2010: 346–7):

> It is a good objection to a method if it turns out that impeccably following that method could lead one to views that are *unreasonable*. It follows from this that if beginning from all and only one's considered judgments, and from there achieving wide reflective equilibrium without making any 'downstream' mistakes, is sufficient for impeccably executing the method of reflective equilibrium, then the method is not correct. The problem is that something might very well qualify as a considered judgment, when that notion is understood in anything like the way it is understood in the broadly Rawlsian tradition, and yet be utterly lacking in rational credibility.

This is illustrated with the observation that there is nothing to stop '[o]ne is morally required to occasionally kill randomly' from counting as

---

[2] Welch even defends a radical version of reflective equilibrium in which 'there are no considered judgments to consider' (Welch 2014: 14).

a considered judgment. Kelly and McGrath therefore conclude that reflective equilibrium is an inadequate method.

This critique seems to be misdirected in several respects. First, Kelly and McGrath focus on considered judgments to such a degree that reflective equilibrium proper falls out of their picture entirely. They seem to take it as given that the final set of principles will simply be direct expressions of the initial considered judgments. While that may be more or less true of narrow reflective equilibrium, it is unlikely to be true of wide reflective equilibrium. Sustained consideration of competing principles, supporting arguments, devices of representation and background theories is extremely likely to expunge judgments that are 'utterly lacking in rational credibility',[3] in which case the alleged problem does not arise.

Second, it is not clear that we have actually been shown a case in which 'impeccably following' the method of reflective equilibrium 'lead[s] one to views that are unreasonable'. In Kelly and McGrath's example, the random killing judgment is held *initially*. So it is not the case that the method 'leads' anyone to this judgment. Rather, they had the judgment to begin with. If there is a complaint to be had here, it is with the life history that has resulted in such an absurd judgment being formed.

Finally, I doubt that it actually is 'a good objection to a method if it turns out that impeccably following that method could lead one to views that are unreasonable'. Kelly and McGrath (2010: 327–8) support this claim with the following example:

Suppose that, prior to embarking upon the systematic study of fruit flies, one held various baseless opinions about their nature. If one then devoted oneself to the study of fruit flies, and impeccably followed the best scientific procedures we have for arriving at accurate views about their nature, we would expect those earlier baseless opinions to be filtered out or corrected at some stage in the inquiry. In the unlikely event that some of those opinions were among the views that one held after ... impeccably following our best scientific methods, then, we submit, those beliefs would no longer be unreasonable ones to hold.

The conclusion may seem plausible here on account of misleading features of the case. In particular, the 'baseless opinions' are so sparsely described that we have no way of grasping whether they might be held reasonably or not. To really test the central underlying claim here that application of the scientific method, unlike reflective equilibrium, removes unreasonable beliefs, we should adjust the scientific baseless opinions, so that they are as vivid as their moral counterpart – the judgment that '[o]ne is morally required to occasionally kill randomly'.

[3] Kelly and McGrath seem to concede a similar point regarding empirical sciences – see the lengthy quote given two paragraphs later.

So suppose that the baseless beliefs about fruit flies are the following: fruit flies originate from specific acts of divine creation; these acts occurred within the past 10,000 years and are described in scripture; it is a matter of religious duty to disregard all countervailing evidence regarding the origins of fruit flies. I think it highly plausible that these views are unreasonable, and that 'devot[ing] oneself to the study of fruit flies, and impeccably follow[ing] the best scientific procedures we have for arriving at accurate views about their nature' does not stop these views from being unreasonable. The lesson to draw from this is that neither the method of reflective equilibrium nor the scientific method is *guaranteed* to rid people of unreasonable beliefs. But that doesn't change the fact that both are more likely than alternatives to provide individuals with reasonable beliefs, by exposing them to the most compelling evidence available in their respective fields.

This leads us to the second challenge. Several writers have claimed not that reflective equilibrium struggles with implausible idiosyncratic judgments, like the random killing judgment, but with the fact that our judgments are systematically undermined (Brandt 1979: 21–2; Hare 1981: 12). Peter Singer emphasizes that our moral judgments have largely arisen through an evolutionary process. For example, the commonsense idea that we have stronger duties towards relatives can be explained on the basis that the corresponding genes 'are more likely to survive and spread among social mammals than genes that do not lead to preferences for one's relatives that are typically proportional to the proximity of the relationship' (Singer 2005: 334; see also Singer 1974). It is no surprise, then, that brain scans suggest that our moral judgments often do not seem to be informed by reason, but are rather an immediate emotional response (Singer 2005: 339–42). Individuals will stick to their judgment even where they end up rejecting the reasons they initially give for it (Singer 2005: 337–8). This modern scientific understanding of 'how we make moral judgments casts serious doubt on the method of reflective equilibrium', according to Singer (2005: 348):

There is little point in constructing a moral theory designed to match considered moral judgments that themselves stem from our evolved responses to the situations in which we and our ancestors lived during the period of our evolution as social mammals, primates, and finally, human beings. We should, with our current powers of reasoning and our rapidly changing circumstances, be able to do better than that.

Suppose, for the sake of argument, that the evolutionary picture that Singer paints is correct. I would not see this as a threat to the method of reflective equilibrium. Singer is, in effect, presenting a background theory that should be considered when an individual is undergoing reflective equilibrium.[4] If the background theory is compelling, as I suspect it might be, that may cause individuals to treat their moral judgments differently, taking care to consider whether a judgment might amount to an evolved emotional response that should be set aside.

Singer (2005: 347) anticipates a response along these lines, and replies as follows:

Admittedly, it is possible to interpret the model of reflective equilibrium so that it takes into account any grounds for objecting to our intuitions, including those that I have put forward. Norman Daniels has argued persuasively for this 'wide' interpretation of reflective equilibrium. If the interpretation is truly wide enough to countenance the rejection of all our ordinary moral beliefs, then I have no objection to it. The price for avoiding the inbuilt conservatism of the narrow interpretation, however, is that reflective equilibrium ceases to be a distinctive method of doing normative ethics. Where previously there was a contrast between the method of reflective equilibrium and 'foundationalist' attempts to build an ethical system outward from some indubitable starting point, now foundational-ism simply becomes the limiting case of a wide reflective equilibrium.

Here Singer claims that reflective equilibrium would have to rely not just on the moderate, revisable foundationalism referred to earlier, but rather on a stronger 'special foundationalism' (Harman 2003: 415) that identi-fies certain ethical truths as unchallengeable. Were that true, it would certainly be the case that reflective equilibrium had been stripped of its distinctive features (in particular, mutual adjustment of judgments and principles). But it is not true. Singer says that the interpretation should be 'truly wide enough to countenance the rejection of all our ordinary moral beliefs'. Reflective equilibrium is this wide (Sandberg and Juth 2011: 222). However, Singer's conclusion implicitly assumes that countenan-cing the rejection of ordinary moral beliefs will result in (1) their whole-sale rejection and (2) the adoption of some mysterious 'indubitable starting point', rather than a set of revised moral beliefs subject to reflec-tive equilibrium's usual ongoing epistemic tests. Both of these assump-tions are quite gratuitous. A more likely result of considering Singer's background theory is a reduction in the weight we are willing to assign to judgments that have a vividly personal quality, such as judgments favour-ing family members or judgments assigning special opprobrium to harms inflicted in a direct physical way, as these are likely to have evolutionary origins (Tersman 2008: 397–8). There may be a corresponding increase in the weight we are willing to assign to universal or impartial judgments,

---

[4] Singer later seems to make this concession; see de Lazari-Radek and Singer (2012: 29–31).

which have less (or possibly no) evolutionary baggage. Reforming our judgments in this way would not mean that 'the "data" that a sound moral theory is supposed to match have become so changeable that they can play, at best, a minor role in determining the final shape of the normative moral theory' (Singer 2005: 349). On the contrary, shifting judgments play a full role as part of a 'dynamic dialectical process' (Brink 2014: 688).

5   How to Use the Method of Reflective Equilibrium

In this section I suggest some steps in the process of reflective equilibrium.

The first step in reaching equilibrium is making considered judgments on the topic at hand. These are what I take to be the requirements for considered judgments (Rawls 1999: 42):

1) *No upset, fright, tiredness, or intoxication.* This may seem obvious, but there are plenty of cases where political theorists do their work when subject to personal distress, or to a deadline, or late at night, or (so I hear) over a glass of wine or two.

2) *No conflicts of interest.* Individual political theorists often would gain more under one set of principles than another. Even though there is effectively no chance that the principles are going to be put into effect, there may still be a psychological effect. This is actually a rather hard problem to get around – surely we cannot prohibit work on social justice, on the basis that any principle would be likely to have effects on theorists' incomes. Perhaps the best we can do is be aware of our possible subconscious biases, and exercise particular caution when rejecting principles that do not serve our self-interest.

3) *The ability to reach the correct decision.* This requires at least minimal standards of competency. It would be possible to reach a reflective equilibrium about a topic within political theory that one had never read anything about, but it is unlikely to have much epistemic value (see Scanlon 2014: 82).[5]

---

[5] It might be objected that this requirement seems incompatible with my rejection of the 'epistemic constraint' in Section 2. This objection misses the importance of the distinction between constraints on the *contents* of judgments (such as the epistemic constraint) and constraints on the *circumstances* of judgments. The former type of constraint is otiose, as what it attempts to do (for instance, justification) is done more thoroughly by wide reflective equilibrium. The latter type of constraint is essential as its functions cannot be replicated by wide reflective equilibrium proper. For instance, a logical impossibility should be cleared from our judgments once we consider relevant background theory, provided we are reasoning in favourable circumstances. But the effects of unfavourable circumstances, such as being drunk or ignorant of relevant political theory, will not be cleared by reflective equilibrium, as the epistemic value of the process is fatally undercut

4) *The desire to reach the correct decision.* The individual must be motivated to arrive at justified principles. People (almost?) invariably come to political theory with a set of preconceived ideas about politics. This is fine provided that the individual is open-minded, willing to alter his or her views in response to arguments. The fact that one is on record defending a position should be no barrier to rejecting that position, even where this might prove inconvenient or embarrassing.[6]

In short, the first step is to make sure that you undertake the process of reflective equilibrium in the Rawlsian 'conditions favorable for deliberation and judgment in general'. **The conditions established in the first step must be maintained throughout the process.**

The second step is to draw up a list of the main contending principles on whatever topic you are considering. If you can think of any compelling new principles, these should also be added to the list. There is no specific number of principles that you should aim for, but as a general rule and time permitting, more is better. Remember that, while it is usually impractical in a work of political theory of 5,000 or 10,000 words to discuss a large number of principles, there is no 'word limit' when it comes to considering principles prior to or during the actual writing process. Even if you only discuss two or three principles in detail in the final product, you may have considered and rejected many more during the process of reaching equilibrium. Presumably Rawls himself did – in the 'Presentation of Alternatives' section of *A Theory of Justice* he names more than a dozen 'conceptions of justice', several of them containing multiple principles and one of them the extremely open-ended 'list of prima facie principles (as appropriate)' (Rawls 1999: 107). While it would not be usual to provide such a lengthy list in writing, it is often useful to mention in passing your reasons for rejecting some of the principles that do not receive full discussion.

The third step is to begin reflective equilibrium in earnest. You go through each principle, checking its prescriptions against your judgments. Ask yourself: what are the central cases for my topic? And what are the hard cases for this principle? The literature is, of course, an invaluable resource for finding such cases, but you will also come up with your own. **Consider whether you can accept the implications of the principle in each of these cases.** It may be that initially

---

by our adverse physical condition or inability to draw on relevant arguments, principles and theories.

[6] A fifth step would be to expose oneself to a wide and representative range of non-philosophical experiences, in order to offset formative biases. While I am attracted to this proposal, it does go beyond the method of reflective equilibrium as usually conceived; DePaul (1993) treats it as part of the separate 'method of balance of refinement'.

the principle seems to have an unacceptable implication, but that on reflection you are willing to revise your judgment. This may particularly be the case where the principle is compelling in other cases. It may seem to *explain* why we think what we do in those cases, and *extend* in an appealing way to further, previously unconsidered cases. If you can accept a principle's implications, either right away or on reflection, then it would seem that this principle is worthy of further consideration. If you cannot, you may set aside the principle for now, taking a note of the specific problems it faces. Repeat this procedure for each principle.

The fourth step is to bring in devices of representation and background theories (for example, the original position and a theory of the separateness of persons, respectively). The most important devices of representation and background theories relevant to the topic should be considered, with particular devices and theories chosen on the basis of our judgments, which may themselves be revised during the process, even in response to normative principles. It may be that you can find a device of representation that seems, at least on reflection, to capture reasonable constraints on theory selection. It may even be that you have more confidence in it than you have in any principle. For instance, I personally find the difference principle less plausible than the original position from which Rawls controversially (Hare 1975: 102–7; Harsanyi 1975) derives it. In such cases, you may decide to focus on the principles chosen from the circumstances specified by the judgment-endorsed device, though you are still free to directly check the chosen principles against considered judgments (Mandle 2009: 40). Background theories have a similar, though less dramatic role, guiding principle selection but not outright replacing direct reference to judgments. Plausible background theories are used at this point to assess principles, with a particular focus on the principles found appealing in stage three. Devices of representation are also tested by background theories. For instance, if we accepted Sandel's (1982: ch. 1) claim that the original position assumes that the self is prior to values, we might reject that device of representation as incompatible with our favoured non-moral background theory even if it were compatible with our normative judgments (Gaus 1996: 105).

Having considered principles, devices of representation and background theories, **the fifth step is to review this process. Now you know the specific challenges faced by the various principles, are there any revisions to these principles worth considering? Or do any entirely new principles now come to mind?** If so, the third and fourth steps should be repeated for these principles. If new or revised principles keep arising, many iterations of the third and fourth steps may be necessary. The same repetition applies where revised or new devices of representation and background theories arise. Likewise, if you have *not* found any principles that you find acceptable in their implications, the third and fourth steps should be repeated. It may, however, be acceptable to limit the level of repetition due to time constraints. We do not all have months or years of philosophical contemplation available to us! If all the steps are followed, the method will yield dividends even if the fifth step is attenuated, as may be necessary if writing a student essay, for example.

The sixth step is to establish priority rules. This applies only where you have accepted multiple principles that may come into conflict with each other. Where you have such principles you need to consider cases of conflict, and decide how much importance each principle has in it. It may be that one principle seems so important that it should have absolute or 'lexical' priority over another. Alternatively, the principles may seem to have similar importance, in which case some kind of weighting should be decided. It could even be found that there are 'incompatible but equally justified overall accounts of the subject, thus supporting a kind of pluralism about the subject' (Scanlon 2014: 78–9).

The seventh step is the conclusion of the process, insofar as it has one. By this point you should have found agreement between principles and judgments – or otherwise concluded that this is impossible as there are no acceptable principles! Either way, **your findings are only ever provisional, and should be considered permanently open to revision.**

6   An Example

I will now work through an example of reflective equilibrium on the topic of distributive justice, using the aforementioned step-by-step guide and my own considered judgments. I can obviously give only the scantest indication of my reasoning here, summarizing years of work in a few paragraphs. It is likely, furthermore, that the reader will disagree with me at numerous points. The example should nevertheless illustrate one way of reaching reflective equilibrium.

The first step is to make sure that my judgments are considered. As I write this, it is 9.32 am, I had a good night's sleep, I am aware of the danger of conflicts of interest when discussing the societal allocation of goods and am willing to counteract any resulting bias, and I have the motivation and desire to reach the correct decision. So it seems that, right now, I am making my judgments in suitable conditions. But as this test must be taken each time you use the method of reflective equilibrium, it must be repeated many times – indeed, many thousands of times in my case!

For the second step I have to draw up a list of the main principles within this topic. Here's my list:
- The principle of utility
- Rawls's two principles of justice
- Equality of outcome
- Luck egalitarian principles (Arneson 1989; Cohen 1989)
- Democratic egalitarian principles (Anderson 1999)
- The principle of priority (Parfit 2000)
- The principle of sufficiency (Frankfurt 1987)
- Right libertarian principles (Nozick 1974: ch. 7)
- Left libertarian principles (Steiner 1994)
- The benefiting principle (Butt 2007)
- The principle of need
- The principle of desert
- Communitarian principles (Sandel 1982)
- Contractarian principles (Gauthier 1986)
- Egoist principles

The list is eclectic, and by design – the point at this stage is to avoid missing anything important, not to construct the most elegant inventory possible. Even so, other people's lists would no doubt contain additional principles.

With the third step I begin the reflective process by testing the principles and judgments against each other. Many principles can be set aside quite quickly. I find nothing of merit in 'free for all' egoist principles, and view the results of contractarian principles for people with low bargaining power as utterly unacceptable, for instance. I do, by contrast, feel the pull of the principle of sufficiency, as I am very concerned by those who are very badly off in absolute terms. But I do not accept its implication that those who are just below the threshold of 'having enough' get absolute priority over those marginally above the threshold, who are only slightly better off (Arneson 2006: 28). I therefore conclude that the principle of priority better accommodates my concern with the absolutely badly off. Similarly, I am attracted to equality of outcome and democratic equality, as I am also concerned about inequality. But I am unhappy with democratic equality's implication that large unchosen inequalities do not matter as long as individuals have equal social standing, and equality of outcome's implication that, where some squander their equal share of resources, for instance by deliberately developing 'expensive tastes' (Dworkin 2000: 48–59), they should be 'compensated' to restore equality, at society's expense. I find that luck egalitarianism, which avoids such problems, fits with my judgments here better, but it has its own apparently objectionable implication that those who make bad choices that leave them in severe disadvantage will be 'abandoned' (Anderson 1999: 295–6). Outcome egalitarianism has no such implication. So at the end of the third stage I have a provisional endorsement of prioritarianism, and an interest in egalitarianism that I am not yet convinced is well expressed in any principle.

The fourth step sees the introduction of background theories (I set aside devices of representation). I will mention only one line of thought here, to illustrate how background theories might help us arbitrate between political principles. Some critics of luck egalitarianism have claimed (1) that it assumes that metaphysical libertarianism (the theory that free, non-causally determined human action is possible) is true, and (2) that metaphysical libertarianism is false (Scheffler 2003: 17–19). Were this true, I would have a background theory-based reason to reject luck egalitarianism in favour of outcome egalitarianism or democratic equality. However, on reflection I find reasons for rejecting both claims. While (2) is possible, we do not have adequate grounds for assuming this to be the case; political theorists would do better to proceed under the assumption that any of the main theories of free will (including sceptical views such as hard determinism) might be correct (call this the 'thin theory'). Regarding (1), the standard Arneson-Cohen construal of luck egalitarianism does not after all assume any theory of free will, but is instead responsive to the morals and metaphysics of responsibility, in the sense that what counts as 'chosen' (and therefore as potential justification for inequality) depends on the best philosophical account. If metaphysical libertarianism is false, this just means that one way in which choice might arise cannot actually happen. Luck egalitarianism would even be compatible with there being no way for true choice to arise. In that case, no inequality would be justified, a point that mitigates the 'abandonment objection' to luck egalitarianism mentioned in the previous paragraph (Knight 2015: 132–4). So luck egalitarianism is in fact admirably responsive to what I take as the most plausible background theory about free will, which is the thin theory (Knight 2009: ch. 5). Outcome egalitarianism and democratic equality are not responsive in this way, however, as they make the same prescriptions whether metaphysical libertarianism is true or hard determinism is true. This seems a significant flaw to me as, in my judgment, where a person has prima facie brought some hardship upon herself, we have more reason to assist her if her action were not a true exercise of free will, and less reason to assist her if her action were a true exercise of free will. As luck egalitarianism seems to accommodate the most plausible background theory better than rival egalitarian theories, I accept it as part of my wide reflective equilibrium.

For simplicity, I leave aside the fifth step. This brings us to the sixth step. I have found luck egalitarianism and prioritarianism to be in accord with my judgments. Now we need to decide on a rule to regulate conflicts between these principles. It seems that neither the 'eliminate involuntary disadvantage' (Cohen 1989: 916) goal of luck egalitarianism, nor prioritarianism's concern with increasing absolute advantage (in particular, that of the worst off), should be assigned lexical priority, as I would be willing to give up a small improvement in either of these dimensions for a large improvement in the other. So my conception of justice is a version of 'responsibility-catering prioritarianism' (Arneson 1999; see also Knight 2009: ch. 6), where luck egalitarianism and prioritarianism are balanced against each other. Exactly what weighting, however, to give each of these principles is a rather tricky question, to be tested through considering a large number of cases, which I cannot do here.

Suppose, though, that I find a favoured weighting, and reach the seventh and final step. Even then I cannot assume that weighting, or even the selection of principles, to be settled for all time, as we can reconsider any aspect of the process at any point. As Rawls (2005: 97) cautions, '[t]he struggle for reflective equilibrium continues indefinitely.'

References

Ackerman, Bruce, 1980. *Social Justice in the Liberal State*. New Haven, CT: Yale University Press.

Anderson, Elizabeth, 1999. 'What is the point of equality?', *Ethics* 109, 287–337.

Arneson, Richard, 1989. 'Equality and equal opportunity for welfare', *Philosophical Studies* 56, 77–93.

Arneson, Richard, 1999. 'Equality of opportunity for welfare defended and recanted', *Journal of Political Philosophy*, 7, 488–97.

Arneson, Richard, 2006. 'Distributive justice and basic capability equality', in Alexander Kaufman, ed., *Capabilities Equality*. Abingdon: Routledge, 17–43.

Brandt, Richard, 1979. *A Theory of the Good and the Right*. Oxford University Press.

Brink, David, 1989. *Moral Realism and the Foundations of Ethics*. Cambridge University Press.

Brink, David, 2014. 'Principles and intuitions in ethics', *Ethics* 124, 665–95.

Butt, Daniel, 2007. 'On benefiting from injustice', *Canadian Journal of Philosophy* 37, 129–52.

Cohen, G. A., 1989. 'On the currency of egalitarian justice', *Ethics* 99, 906–44.

Cummins, Robert, 1998. 'Reflection on reflective equilibrium', in Michael DePaul and William Ramsey, eds., *Rethinking Intuition*. Lanham, MD: Rowman and Littlefield, 113–28.

Daniels, Norman, 1996. *Justice and Justification*. Cambridge University Press.

DePaul, Michael, 1986. 'Reflective equilibrium and foundationalism', *American Philosophical Quarterly* 23, 59–69.

DePaul, Michael, 1993. *Balance and Refinement: Beyond Coherence Methods of Moral Inquiry*. London: Routledge.

Dworkin, Ronald, 2000. *Sovereign Virtue: The Theory and Practice of Equality*. Cambridge, MA: Harvard University Press.

Ebertz, Roger, 1993. 'Is reflective equilibrium a coherentist model?', *Canadian Journal of Philosophy* 23, 193–214.

Frankfurt, Harry, 1987. 'Equality as a moral ideal', *Ethics* 98, 21–43.

Freeman, Samuel, 2007. *Rawls*. Abingdon: Routledge.

Gaus, Gerald, 1996. *Justificatory Liberalism*. Oxford University Press.

Gauthier, David, 1986. *Morals by Agreement*. Oxford University Press.

Goodman, Nelson, 1965. *Fact, Fiction, and Forecast*. Indianapolis, IN: Bobbs-Merrill.

Hare, R. M., 1975. 'Rawls' theory of justice', in Norman Daniels, ed., *Reading Rawls*. Oxford: Blackwell, 81–107.

Hare, R. M., 1981. *Moral Thinking: Its Levels, Method, and Point*. Oxford University Press.

Harman, Gilbert, 2003. 'Three trends in moral and political philosophy', *Journal of Value Inquiry* 37, 415–25.

Harsanyi, John, 1975. 'Can the maximin principle serve as a basis for morality?', *American Political Science Review* 69, 594–606.

Hooker, Brad, 2012. 'Theory vs anti-theory in ethics', in Ulrike Heuer and Gerald Lang, eds., *Luck, Value, and Commitment: Themes from the Moral Philosophy of Bernard Williams*. Oxford University Press, 19–40.

Kelly, Thomas and McGrath, Sarah, 2010. 'Is reflective equilibrium enough?', *Philosophical Perspectives* 24, 325–59.

Knight, Carl, 2006. 'The method of reflective equilibrium', *Philosophical Papers* 35, 209–25.

Knight, Carl, 2009. *Luck Egalitarianism: Equality, Responsibility, and Justice*. Edinburgh University Press.

Knight, Carl, 2015. 'Abandoning the abandonment objection: luck egalitarian arguments for public insurance', *Res Publica* 21, 119–35.

de Lazari-Radek, Katarzyna and Singer, Peter, 2012. 'The objectivity of ethics and the unity of practical reason', *Ethics* 123, 9–31.

Lewis, David, 1983. *Philosophical Papers*, volume 1. Oxford University Press.

Maffetone, Sebastiano, 2010. *Rawls: An Introduction*. Cambridge: Polity.

Mandle, Jon, 2009. *Rawls's A Theory of Justice: An Introduction*. Cambridge University Press.

McDermott, Daniel, 2008. 'Analytical political philosophy', in David Leopold and Marc Stears, eds., *Political Theory: Methods and Approaches*. Oxford University Press, 11–28.

Nozick, Robert, 1974. *Anarchy, State and Utopia*. Oxford: Blackwell.

Parfit, David, 2000. 'Equality or priority?', in Matthew Clayton and Andrew Williams, eds., *The Ideal of Equality*. Basingstoke: Palgrave, 81–125.

Rawls, John, 1975. 'The independence of moral theory', *Proceedings and Addresses of the American Philosophical Association* 48, 5–22.

Rawls, John, 1999. *A Theory of Justice*, revised edition. Oxford University Press.

Rawls, John, 2005. *Political Liberalism*, expanded edition. New York: Columbia University Press.

Sandberg, Joakim and Juth, Niklas., 2011. 'Ethics and intuitions: a reply to Singer', *Journal of Ethics* 15, 209–26.

Sandel, Michael, 1982. *Liberalism and the Limits of Justice*. Cambridge University Press.

Scanlon, T. M., 2003. 'Rawls on justification', in Samuel Freeman, ed., *The Cambridge Companion to Rawls*. Cambridge University Press, 139–67.

Scanlon, T. M., 2014. *Being Realistic about Reasons*. Oxford University Press.

Scheffler, Samuel, 2003. 'What is egalitarianism?', *Philosophy and Public Affairs* 31, 5–39.

Singer, Peter, 1974. 'Sidgwick and reflective equilibrium', *The Monist* 58, 490–517.

Singer, Peter, 2005. 'Ethics and intuitions', *Journal of Ethics* 9, 331–52.

Sinnott-Armstrong, Walter, Young, Liane and Cushman, Fiery, 2010. 'Moral intuitions', in John Doris and The Moral Psychology Research Group, eds., *The Moral Psychology Handbook*. Oxford University Press, 246–72.

Steiner, Hillel, 1994. *An Essay on Rights*. Oxford: Blackwell.

Tersman, Folke, 2008. 'The reliability of moral intuitions', *Australasian Journal of Philosophy* 86, 389–405.

Varner, Gary, 2012. *Personhood, Ethics, and Animal Cognition*. Oxford University Press.

Walden, Kenneth, 2013. 'In defense of reflective equilibrium', *Philosophical Studies* 166, 243–56.

Welch, John, 2014. *Moral Strata: Another Approach to Reflective Equilibrium*. Dordrecht: Springer.

Williamson, Timothy, 2007. *The Philosophy of Philosophy*. Oxford: Blackwell.

Wolff, Jonathan, 2013. 'Analytic political philosophy', in Michael Beaney, ed., *The Oxford Handbook of the History of Analytic Philosophy*. Oxford University Press, 795–822.

5   Contractualism

Jonathan Quong

1   Introduction

Are you a contractualist? People sometimes ask this question in the same way you might ask someone, are you Muslim or are you a Utilitarian? They ask as if contractualism is a deep substantive commitment – as if it's an exclusive doctrine that competes with other normative theories. I believe that this way of thinking about contractualism is flawed. Contractualism is a method or a tool, not a first-order moral theory. Asking a philosopher if she is a contractualist is thus a bit like asking a carpenter if she is a 'Hammerist', that is, someone who uses a hammer to the exclusion of all other tools of the trade.

For the purposes of this chapter, I will assume that contractualism is a method used to answer some first-order normative question in moral or political philosophy, according to which we should consider what a group of idealized agents would or could accept under certain specified constraints. I will refer to the idealized agents as the *contractors*, and I will refer to the general choice situation in which they are placed as the *contractual scenario*. Obviously many different forms of contractualism are possible since different assumptions can be made regarding who the contractors should represent, how they should be idealized, what question they should be tasked to answer, what constraints they should face, and what alternatives they should confront in the event of non-agreement.

In this chapter I defend three main claims. First, like any good tool or method, contractualism is a helpful way to tackle some problems, but not others. Second, there are very different types of contractualism, and these different types are designed to address different normative questions. Finally, and relatedly, work in moral and political philosophy sometimes goes wrong due to the failure to carefully distinguish these different forms of contractualism.

The remainder of this chapter is organized as follows. Section 2 argues that we can usefully distinguish three different forms of contractualism: *consent contractualism, fairness contractualism*, and *rationality contractualism*.

Section 3 considers how contractual scenarios should be designed in light of the particular question we're trying to address. Section 4 identifies some ways contractualism can be misused. Section 5 concludes by summarizing this chapter's central claims.

2   Why Contractualism?

Why ask what suitably situated contractors would or could accept? Why not just ask what real people do in fact accept?

It's not always possible to ask the relevant people what they would accept. Sometimes this is because we are deciding whether to surprise someone, whether to reveal information to someone, or whether to lie to someone. Seeking the person's consent would make it impossible to surprise the person, avoid giving the person the information, or lie to the person. Other times the problem is that the relevant people don't currently exist: we cannot directly talk to past or future generations.

Even when we can communicate with the relevant people, we may have good reasons to disregard the answers they will provide. If the question that interests us is what P would agree to if she were perfectly rational, then asking the real P, who is far from perfectly rational, is not a good way to answer the question. Similarly, we might want to know what political principle persons would accept if everyone had exactly equal bargaining power. Because real people do not have exactly equal bargaining power, we cannot pose our question directly. We might also have good reasons to ask what persons would accept if they had somewhat different aims or motives – for example, what moral rules people would accept if they did not already have various firm beliefs about rightness and wrongness, or what political rules people would accept if they all shared a few particular ideals, but diverged in many other ways.

In sum, it may be either impossible or undesirable to ask what real people would accept. Under these conditions contractualism may be an appropriate method for tackling certain moral or political questions. But when exactly is it an appropriate method for doing so? What questions is contractualism well suited to help us answer?

To begin, contractualism can be a useful way of trying to understand whether some presumptively wrongful act or rule, ϕ, is in fact permissible or legitimate when we think that permissibility or legitimacy depends on whether persons would freely *consent* to ϕ if they could. For example, it is presumptively wrong to cut someone open and operate on him without his consent, but if the person freely consents to the surgery, the consent typically renders the surgery permissible. But sometimes we cannot obtain the person's consent, and yet there are powerful reasons to proceed with the surgery: an unconscious man on the road needs immediate medical attention, but obtaining his actual consent isn't possible. In cases like this, it might seem that we should ask whether we believe this person *would* consent to the emergency treatment, and if the answer is yes, this is sufficient to render the surgery permissible.

There are also situations involving larger numbers of people that may have a similar structure. For example, it is presumptively wrong to coerce others to obey commands (at least where the commands are not independent requirements of justice), unless those subject to the coercion consent to the relevant authority. But this is how the state behaves: it coerces citizens to obey a large number of commands, many of which are not independent requirements of justice, and yet most citizens do not consent to the authority of their state, nor do most citizens have a realistic opportunity to freely give or withhold their consent. Some have thus suggested that the way to vindicate at least some of the modern state's coercive authority is to consider whether suitably situated contractors would consent to its authority.

These cases share the following structure. It is presumptively wrong to do something, ϕ, to a person or group of persons unless those people freely consent to it. But in circumstances C, there seem to be good reasons to ϕ, and yet obtaining the actual consent of the relevant people is not possible. When faced with a problem of this kind, asking whether suitably situated contractors would consent might be a helpful way of deciding whether it is permissible to ϕ. I will call the version of contractualism that is designed to address this problem *consent contractualism*.

Contractualism might also be invoked, however, for other reasons. Suppose, for example, we are playing a low-stakes game of poker, and in the middle of the game, we realize that the seven of clubs has been missing from the deck the entire time (Dworkin 1973: 501). A question now arises: what should be done? Should we treat the results of the game thus far as legitimate, or should we declare the results of the game so far to be void and begin again, with each player being returned to his or her initial allocation of chips? Asking the current players what they think is fairest might not be a reliable way of answering this question, since their answers are likely to be influenced by their self-interest, by how many chips they have already won or lost. Contractualism seems like a natural way to approach the problem. To decide what the fairest rule would be, we ask what suitably situated contractors – for instance, contractors who do not have a self-interested reason to prefer a particular outcome – would all accept.

Of course, everyone in philosophy is familiar with the most famous version of this model: Rawls's use of the original position and the veil of ignorance as a method for determining the best principles of justice to regulate the distribution of the burdens and benefits of social cooperation amongst citizens (Rawls 1999: 102–68). We can call this *fairness contractualism*. We can also envisage a more general version of fairness contractualism, where the contractual device is used to determine what would be morally right or permissible in a given context, and not merely what would be fair (Scanlon 1998). Although such versions of contractualism are concerned with more than fairness, they can without too much distortion be included as variants of fairness contractualism since they share the same basic structure: the contractual device is designed to reflect some of our existing moral judgements in order to help us answer further moral questions about what is fair or right.

Although fairness contractualism and consent contractualism are often conflated, they differ in several important respects. First, the aim of fairness contractualism is not to determine whether some presumptively wrongful act or rule is morally permissible. The aim is rather to determine what fairness requires in a given context. A rule may be fair, and yet it may be impermissible to impose the rule without the actual consent of the persons involved. Conversely, it may be permissible to perform acts or impose rules on others even when doing so does not meet some standard of fairness. Fairness is thus neither necessary nor sufficient to settle questions about permissibility. Second, unlike consent contractualism, the success of fairness contractualism does not depend on how closely the contractors approximate the real persons they represent. The aim of fairness contractualism is not to establish, as far as is possible, whether some real people would consent to a given rule or policy. The aim is rather to model a contractual scenario such that it is guaranteed to produce a fair agreement. The contractors may thus depart radically from their real-world counterparts, and so it may often be true that we cannot infer anything about the consent or the will of real persons from the consent of contractors. But this is no objection to fairness contractualism, since the aim is not to accurately model or represent the consent or will of particular real persons, but rather to model a perfectly fair contractual scenario.

Sometimes, however, the question that interests us is neither the consent of real people, nor what people would accept under perfectly fair conditions. Instead, sometimes we want to understand what real people would all accept if they were perfectly rational, either in the narrow instrumental sense of choosing the most effective means to pursue their self-interest, or in the broader sense of making the most rational choice in light of all their beliefs and commitments. Suppose, for example, there's an isolated town with just one large employer: OmniCorp. Everyone who works for OmniCorp is required to contribute to a compulsory insurance scheme that provides a certain level of medical coverage in the event of serious illness or injury. We might ask many different questions about this compulsory insurance scheme, but one question is whether the scheme is one that all the employees would accept if they were self-interested and instrumentally rational. If the scheme cannot be defended on the basis that it is in everyone's self-interest, then it will have to be defended on other grounds. But if the scheme is in everyone's self-interest, then (depending on our broader moral theory) it may be irrelevant that the people in the town lack alternative employment options, and so have no realistic choice but to 'consent' to OmniCorp's insurance scheme.

This example is, in certain key respects, a small-scale version of the political situation in which many citizens find themselves. Many citizens have no realistic opportunity to refuse the package of burdens and benefits the state offers, and so they cannot meaningfully consent to it. But we can ask whether the package the state offers is prudentially rational for citizens to accept. For example, can some citizens plausibly complain that, were it possible, they would have been able to bargain for better terms prior to leaving the state of nature and entering civil society? Some political philosophers, most notably Thomas Hobbes and David Gauthier, focus on questions of this kind – on determining whether the moral or political rules that govern our lives can be partly or entirely vindicated by establishing that they are terms that would be rational for each person to accept even if each was self-interested (Gauthier 1987; Hobbes 1996). A closely related, but broader, question pursued by some contractualists is this: what moral or political rules would each person have sufficient reason to accept in light of all her beliefs and commitments (Gaus 2011)? We can call all forms of contractualism designed to consider what people would accept if they were rational, either in a narrow self-interested sense, or in some broader sense, *rationality contractualism.*[1]

Rationality contractualism differs from consent contractualism in at least two important respects. First, the aim is not to use a contractual device to ascertain whether real people would in fact consent to some rule or policy. Rather, the aim is to ascertain whether they rationally ought to accept some rule or policy given certain aims. In focusing on what would be rational, this form of contractualism deliberately sets aside various things – allegedly independent moral commitments, ignorance, and irrationality – that might influence real people's decisions. Second, rationality contractualism need not focus on acts or rules that are presumptively

---

[1] Some refer to the narrow self-interested form of rationality contractualism as *contractarianism* and contrast it with the *contractualism* of Rawls and Scanlon.

wrongful absent individual consent. Rationality contractualism can take as its focus any act, policy, or set of institutions.

Rationality contractualism also clearly differs from fairness contractualism. Unlike fairness contractualism, rationality contractualism is not an effort to model our ideas about fairness. What people would accept under perfectly fair conditions may depart dramatically from what it would be rational for them to accept given their actual circumstances and given some particular set of aims.

3   Designing Contractualism

Having identified three of the main reasons to use contractualism, we can consider in greater detail how contractualist scenarios should be designed to best address a given problem. It will be helpful to distinguish five key questions.

i. *Constituency*: Who do the contractors represent?
ii. *Primary Question*: What question do the contractors confront?
iii. *Motives and Interests*: What are the motives and interests of the contractors?
iv. *Information*: How much information should be provided to the contractors?
v. *Non-agreement*: What will happen to each contractor in the event of non-agreement?

These are not the only questions that matter in designing a model of contractualism, but they are central questions that heavily shape how the model will work and what it can achieve. Let's now consider how each of these questions might be addressed from the perspective of the different forms of contractualism.

3.1   Consent Contractualism

Consent contractualism aims to address cases that have the following structure: it is presumptively wrong to do something, ϕ, to a person or group of persons unless those people freely consent, but in circumstances C, there seem to be powerful reasons to ϕ, and yet obtaining the actual consent of the relevant people in C is not possible.

The *constituency* of consent contractualism is thus usually not difficult to determine: every real person who would have a presumptive veto against ϕ must be represented in the contractual scenario. Suppose, for example, the question is this: may the state take action now to avert a significant environmental disaster, if the consequence of doing so is that a particular group of people who are currently five years old or younger will suffer a greatly increased chance of being killed prematurely by radiation poisoning forty years from now?[2] If you believe it is presumptively wrong to take action that will greatly increase a person's chances of being killed prematurely by radiation poisoning, then consent contractualism might be well situated to address this case, since the people whose consent is of normative significance are currently too young to be consulted.

Next, let's consider the *primary question* contractors confront. As theorists, we want to know if imposing ϕ is morally permissible, or at least whether doing so would infringe the rights of those on whom ϕ is imposed. But this isn't the question the contractors are tasked to answer. They are not asked: is imposing ϕ permissible or an infringement of your rights? We don't pose this question to the contractors since the contractors would then need to have in hand the relevant moral answer that we're seeking to find via the contractual device. Instead we ask the contractors a different question: would you agree to the imposition of ϕ? If all the contractors can agree, then we might infer that the real people they represent would consent if they were in a position to do so. Of course, whether the contractors agree to the imposition of ϕ will depend on further features of the contractual scenario.

In consent contractualism, it's typically important that the *motives and interests* of the contractors mirror, as closely as possible, the motives and interests of the real people the contractors are meant to represent. In these cases, consent contractualism is used as a proxy for real consent, but this won't be plausible if the motives and interests of contractors depart too dramatically from those of the real persons they represent.

There are, however, several worries about this strategy. First, sometimes it's not possible to know much about the motives and interests of the real people in question. But this need not be an insurmountable problem. We can often make plausible general assumptions about the interests and motives of people about whom we don't otherwise know very much. We can assume, for example, that people strongly prefer not to die prematurely, and that, other things being equal, they prefer to have a greater range of legal liberties. If the consent of the parties turns only on these sorts of general interests – ones that can be safely assumed – then it may not matter that we lack detailed information about the motives and interests of the real people.

---

[2] In this example the identity of future persons is not what is at issue. Whether contractualism can also be used to address the so-called non-identity problem (where the choice of policy will affect the identity of the future persons) is a further question. For an example where contractualism is used in this way, see Reiman (2007).

A different worry, however, is that the real people whose consent matters may have morally repugnant motives or interests. Shouldn't we prevent contractors from having repugnant aims or interests to ensure the contractual device does not yield clearly unjust or immoral results? For example, it is presumptively wrong to gently pinch a person, P, on the arm, but many things can render this act permissible even if P does not consent. Suppose doing so is the only way to save twenty children from being burned alive. It's circumstances like this, I take it, that motivate the worry about excluding certain wrongful motives or interests from the contractual scenario: we don't want a contractor to be able to withhold consent in this case because she's spectacularly self-interested or a racist.

But cases like this don't pose a problem. Under these conditions, P is morally required to suffer the pinch – she cannot rightfully refuse, and so her consent (or lack of it) is irrelevant. A case like this is thus not one where the act is presumptively wrongful without P's consent. In cases where the act or rule really is presumptively wrong without the consent of P, the content of P's particular reasons for withholding consent are typically irrelevant. For example, it's wrong to force P to attend a religious service for paternalistic reasons unless P consents. P may withhold consent for morally relevant reasons (e.g. she doesn't believe in God) or for morally pernicious reasons (e.g. she is a racist and doesn't want to attend a religious service with members of some racial group); either way, P's lack of consent is decisive. Provided consent contractualism addresses only those cases where a proposed act or rule is presumptively wrongful without the consent of some person or group, then there is no need to apply moral restrictions to the motives or interests of the contractors.

We can now turn to a different question: how much *information* should the contractors be given? The answer is, as much as is needed to ensure the contractors' decision accurately reflects the wills of the real people they represent. We want to know what real people would accept if they were confronted with a certain decision, and so contractors should be given all the information that bears on the decision, where relevance is determined by appeal to the motives and interests of the persons in question. If we want to know whether Albert would consent to the imposition of ϕ, and we believe that Albert's choice would be influenced by whether some fact, F, obtains, then the contractor representing Albert should know whether F obtains when making the choice on Albert's behalf. Doing so ensures the contractor's choice is more likely to accurately reflect Albert's will.

This, however, is perfectly compatible with using consent contractualism in cases where the relevant decision is one where we don't have access to all the relevant facts. Suppose, for example, we want to know whether an unconscious patient would consent to an emergency procedure that has a 5 per cent risk of death, or whether she would opt against the procedure, in which case there is a 95 per cent chance she will suffer permanent paralysis of her upper body. In cases like this it's clearly acceptable if the contractors know only the probabilities. After all, this is all the information we have, and what we want to know is how the real person would choose given the probabilities, not how she would choose if she knew the outcome.

Finally, we can turn to the issue of *non-agreement* in consent contractualism. If contractors are being asked whether they can accept the imposition of φ, clearly a crucial feature of their decision will be information regarding what will happen in the event that φ is not imposed. Other things being equal, the worse the non-agreement point is for a given contractor, the more likely she is to accept the imposition of φ. As we did when considering how much information the contractors should be given, we should be guided by the aim of ensuring that the choice made by each contractor reflects the will of the real person being represented as closely as possible. Thus, as a general rule, the non-agreement point should be designed to accurately reflect what would happen to someone in the event that φ is not imposed.

In some simple cases, the non-agreement point is clear. For example, in the case just presented, if the doctor does not proceed with the surgery, then no surgery is performed, and the patient faces a 95 per cent chance of paralysis. In other cases, however, determining the non-agreement point is more difficult. For example, suppose the question being posed is whether citizens would consent to the coercive authority of the state if given the choice. What should we assume is the non-agreement point? Many philosophers have adopted some version of the state of nature as the non-agreement point, but accounts of the state of nature vary wildly from Hobbesian to Rousseauian.

The problem runs deeper than the mere fact that philosophers disagree about what a state of nature might look like. Real citizens in contemporary liberal democratic societies do not face the stark choice that some philosophers ask their contractors to make: live in a state of nature or under the authority of a state. Thus, even if we had a clear picture regarding what the state of nature might look like, we should be wary of inferring anything about the will or consent of real citizens from the hypothetical consent of contractors confronting the huge question of whether the state is preferable to the state of nature. Given the aims of consent contractualism, it's preferable to focus on questions that can be answered by confronting the contractors with roughly the same options as those faced by the real persons they represent.

3.2   *Fairness Contractualism*

In fairness contractualism, the aim is to situate contractors in such a way that the choice of a rule or set of rules, R, to govern a situation gives us good reason to believe that R is fair, just, or morally correct (I will focus on fairness, for simplicity). Given this aim, let's consider our five main questions.

First, who should be included in the *constituency* of fairness contractualism? Suppose, for example, we are using fairness contractualism to determine the fairest principles for regulating the distribution of certain resources. Who should the contractors represent? One initially tempting answer is that they should represent everyone who is affected by the rules that will regulate the distribution of resources. But this may not always be correct. Suppose you and I work together to achieve some common goal, and we must decide how to distribute the burdens and benefits between us. There may be others who are affected by the choice of principles (e.g. my aunt will get a more generous Christmas present if one set of principles is selected), but this seems irrelevant to what constitutes a fair distribution of our collective efforts: my aunt shouldn't be represented in the contractual scenario. There is nothing in the logic of contractualism itself that dictates the constituency of persons who ought to be represented within a model of fairness contractualism. The appropriate constituency for any model of fairness contractualism must be determined by independent ideas regarding who has the standing to be wronged or treated unfairly by some proposed rules regulating conduct or the distribution of advantages. Sometimes we may have good reason to believe that everyone affected by a proposed principle has the standing to be wronged or unfairly treated, and thus we will want all affected persons to be represented. Other times, we may have reason to believe that only those who qualify as participants in some scheme, or only those who are subject to the authority of the rules, have the requisite standing.

Second, what is the *primary question* the contractors are asked to address? As with consent contractualism, we do not pose contractors the same question we, as theorists, are trying to answer. If we simply ask contractors what fairness requires, then the contractual device is no longer doing any helpful work – we would be directly asking ourselves what fairness requires, and simply putting the answer in the mouth of an imagined contractor. Instead, we ask contractors what rules regulating some domain they would all accept if they were either entirely, or at least partially, self-interested. The further features of the contractual scenario are then meant to ensure that the resulting agreement captures what fairness requires. A sceptic may wonder, of course, why we should bother with the contractualist device here. Why not consider the question directly? I want to set aside this objection for now, but I address it in Section 4.4.

Let's move on to the *motives and interests* of contractors in fairness contractualism. Contractors must be partly driven by self-interest, at least in the broad sense described earlier. That is, they must have their own distinct plans that they wish to pursue. They will thus be motivated to prefer rules that are more likely to advance their plans. But fairness contractualism can also allow the motives and interests of contractors to depart quite radically from the real-world persons that they represent. The reason is simple: fairness contractualism does not aspire to accurately reflect the will or prudential rationality of real people. Instead the aim is to design a contractual scenario in such a way that whatever emerges as a decision is guaranteed to constitute a just or fair decision. One way to achieve this result is to stipulate that contractors are, in addition to being self-interested, partly motivated by a desire to justify themselves to others, and thus will only reject proposals on reasonable grounds, where 'reasonable' is a partly moralized notion, one that requires contractors to take due account of the interests and status of others affected by a proposed rule or its rejection (see Scanlon 1998: 189–247).

There are two important and related objections to attributing to the contractors moral motives that constrain the pursuit of their self-interest. First, sceptics complain that the appeal to what contractors could reasonably reject will leave the results of the contractual device radically indeterminate. The problem is that the ordinary or everyday notion of reasonableness is indeterminate or contested. Of course, there are some attitudes and behaviours that we can all agree are unreasonable, for example, viewing oneself as exempt from general moral rules that everyone else must follow, or behaving as if one's claims to resources or advantages carry greater weight than those of similarly situated others. But the cases in which we agree are too few to yield a precise account of the concept, such that it can be reliably deployed to evaluate whether the exercise of a veto is reasonable or unreasonable. Suppose, for example, the question is whether those who fare worst under some distributive scheme, D1, can reasonably reject D1 in favour of D2, where they would be marginally better off, but everyone else would be significantly worse off than under D1, though still better off than the worst off. The ordinary sense of reasonableness does not provide an obvious answer to this question, or to countless other questions where different considerations appear to pull in different directions. If the notion of the reasonable is so imprecise, our contractual device will be of no use for reaching determinate results in most cases. This objection need not be limited to

Scanlon's use of the notion of reasonableness. The objection will apply to any version of contractualism that attributes a moral motive to the contractors, without clearly specifying how the motive constrains the decisions contractors will make.

One way to defuse this objection is to give the moralized motive very specific content. We could, for example, specify that what it means to be reasonable is that one will only veto proposals when there is an alternative proposal that is anonymously Pareto superior, that is, one where no social position is worse off, and at least one position is better off. Offering such a specific account of what reasonableness requires in terms of exercising one's veto would defuse the charge of indeterminacy.

But this solution invites another, perhaps even more serious objection, namely, that the contractual device is now redundant. There's no longer any need to consider what contractors might accept to help understand what fairness requires: we already know what fairness requires – the anonymous Pareto principle – and we've simply told contractors that they may only veto proposals that violate this principle. Sceptics thus argue that models of contractualism that impute moral motives to the contractors face a dilemma: either the stipulated moral motive is too vague or imprecise to deliver determinate results, or else the motive is so clearly defined that it renders the contractual device entirely unnecessary.

As with many alleged dilemmas, one response is a Goldilocks solution: identify a moral motivation that is sufficiently clear so as to make determinate results possible, without being so precisely defined that it amounts to giving contractors the exact answer the contractual device is meant to help us uncover. Whether this happy medium is possible is a crucial question for anyone who uses a contractual device that attributes some moral motives to the contractors.

An alternative solution is to restrict the *information* available to contractors instead of imbuing them with moral motives. Rawls offers the most influential version of this approach. Contractors are placed behind a veil of ignorance, and are thus unaware of any specific information about the plan of life, sex, race, or social or economic position of the person they represent. By depriving contractors of any specific information about the person they represent, each contractor is forced to consider how proposed rules will affect every possible social position. The resulting agreement is one that will therefore be fair, since each person's interests will have been fully taken into account without allowing any person to unreasonably veto proposals.

Although this approach may avoid some of the worries raised by imputing moral motives to the contractors, it is not without its own difficulties.

I won't attempt a survey of the many objections that have been pressed against Rawls's use of the veil of ignorance. Instead, I want to consider how much information should be excluded from what the contractors know when designing a contractual scenario in which contractors are purely self-interested.

The answer to this question might, at first glance, seem very straightforward. We should exclude any information that would give a contractor an incentive to veto proposals for what we deem morally irrelevant reasons. For example, if contractors knew the race of the person they represent, they would be inclined to veto proposals that fail to discriminate in favour of members of their racial group. Since we don't believe race is a morally relevant basis for allocating resources, we prevent contractors from having this information. But things aren't so simple. Suppose we did allow each contractor to know the race of the person she represents. This won't yield a morally problematic result, where some people are given a greater share of resources merely on account of race, because any proposal to benefit a particular racial group will be vetoed by contractors representing people from other races. The only proposals that look capable of evading a veto are those that disregard race as a relevant consideration for the distribution of resources – any proposal that takes race into account will be vetoed by at least one contractor. The rationale for excluding information such as a person's race thus cannot be that this is the *only* way to avoid principles that wrongly allow race to serve as a basis for the distribution of advantages and disadvantages.

You might protest that allowing contractors to know the race of the person they represent will still prove problematic because it will lead to a null set, that is, the contractors will be unable to agree on anything. Even if racist proposals will be successfully vetoed, won't non-racist policies also be vetoed by contractors who will only consent to policies that give priority to the racial group of the person they represent? Once contractors have some specific information about which policies would be guaranteed to maximally benefit the person they represent, won't they refuse to consent to anything less?

This problem can be avoided if the *non-agreement* point for each contractor is less attractive than some of the proposals being considered. Suppose, for example, contractors are asked to choose amongst potential principles of distributive justice, and they know that if they cannot agree on any proposed principles, the non-agreement point is roughly like the Hobbesian state of nature. Faced with this option, contractors will readily accept a principle of justice that ignores race as a basis for distribution even if the contractors know the race of the person they represent and are purely self-interested. Of course each contractor would prefer a principle of justice that favours his own race, but each knows the others can veto any such principle, and each is strongly motivated to reach some agreement to avoid the Hobbesian state of nature. The underappreciated point is this: imposing a thick Rawlsian veil of ignorance is not necessary to avoid the sort of partiality and prejudice that is incompatible with fairness, even when contractors are strictly self-interested. Principles that unfairly favour a particular race, gender, or religion can be avoided with a combination of contractors' vetoes and a non-agreement point that is equally unappealing for all the contractors.

Some critics have complained that fairness contractualism cannot simply stipulate a non-agreement point that is sufficiently bad that contractors will prefer at least one of the proposals being considered. These critics suggest that genuine contractualism depends on showing that the agreed principles will be mutually beneficial, where the 'benefit' must be measured according to a benchmark of how well off the real people being represented could expect to be in the event of non-agreement (Cohen 1995: 225; Nozick 1974: 192–7). We cannot simply stipulate that all contractors face the same very unappealing non-agreement point. This stipulation will, in many cases, be false – for example, sometimes some subset of the real people being represented will do better in the event of non-agreement than they would under some fair set of distributive principles. If so, argue the critics, then the would-be contractualist must admit her contractualism is a sham in the sense that it fails to deliver mutually advantageous principles.

But this objection misunderstands the aims of fairness contractualism (Quong 2007: 77–82). As I've already emphasized, fairness contractualism, properly construed, doesn't aspire to track the wills of real people, nor does it purport to establish that the principles selected are instrumentally rational for real people given their current aims. The goal is rather to construct a scenario where self-interested agents must come to an agreement regarding a rule or set of rules, but the scenario is designed in such a way that the agreement that emerges is guaranteed to be fair. In this version of contractualism, nothing turns on showing that some real person would benefit from the agreement relative to the status quo or relative to a realistic non-agreement point.

Let's return to our earlier observation that depriving the contractors of all specific information about the persons they represent is inessential to ensuring that the principles remain untainted by prejudice or wrongful partiality. If this is true, why does Rawls impose a thick veil of ignorance on the contractors? I think the answer to this question is, at least in part, because doing so is a better heuristic for taking up the perspective of others. Asking 'what rules would I choose to regulate this domain if

I didn't know which person I would be?' is a powerful way of forcing oneself to empathetically take up each person's perspective. But asking, 'what rules would a group of self-interested contractors choose to regulate this domain if they were precluded by each other's vetoes from favouring selfish or unduly partial principles, but were still sufficiently motivated to come to an agreement?' is less likely to trigger the same taking up of others' perspectives. There are also other reasons to impose a thick veil of ignorance. Doing so is a way of representing what Rawls takes as fundamental to the freedom and equality of persons or citizens: a capacity for a sense of justice and a capacity for a conception of the good. But this, though important in Rawls's theory, is not essential to the more general idea of fairness contractualism.

In sum, there are several ways that a contractual scenario can be designed to try and ensure that the agreement that emerges is fair: (i) a moral motive can be directly imputed to the contractors, (ii) the contractors can be deprived of any specific information about the persons they represent, or (iii) a non-agreement point can be stipulated that is sufficiently bad such that the contractors will be motivated to arrive at an agreement and avoid insisting on proposals that others are certain to veto.

Finally, it's worth emphasizing that while Rawls and Scanlon use the contractual device to develop theories of justice or interpersonal morality, fairness contractualism can be used to pursue more modest objectives, for example, deciding what rules should regulate some specific project amongst neighbours, or how the costs created by an unintended factory accident should be distributed amongst the relevant agents.

3.3   Rationality Contractualism

Finally, let's consider our five questions from the perspective of rationality contractualism, whose aim is to determine what people would all accept if they were rational, either in the sense of most effectively pursuing their self-interest, or else in the broader sense of choosing the best option in light of all their aims and commitments. Because it has been so influential in political philosophy, I will focus mostly on the narrower self-interested form of rationality contractualism, but we shouldn't lose sight of the fact that rationality contractualism needn't be construed in this narrower way.

First, what is the *constituency* of the contractual scenario? The answer to this question can vary. We may, like Gauthier, be interested in a very broad question – determining which set of moral rules is instrumentally rational for everyone to follow – in which case the constituency will include all (or almost all) persons. But we might be interested in a much narrower question, for example: is it instrumentally rational for self-interested agents in a particular neighbourhood to accept the authority of law enforcement officials in their city? Clearly, the constituency of rationality contractualism can be broad or narrow – it all depends on whose rationality is of interest to the theorist.

Second, what is the *primary question* that contractors are given? Again the answer to this question will vary depending on our more specific objectives. But the question will usually take one of two forms. Either we are interested in whether the status quo is rationally acceptable to persons given what would most likely occur in the absence of the status quo. Or else the theorist has a more open-ended question in mind, for example, what rule or set of rules to regulate some domain would people all agree to if they were instrumentally rational, regardless of what the status quo happens to be? This more open-ended question, as we'll see later, creates a particular challenge regarding the non-agreement point.

Third, in the most influential versions of rationality contractualism, the *motives and interests* of the contractors are always self-interested. To borrow Rawls's term, the contractors are mutually disinterested: they take no interest in the plans of others – their goal is simply to advance their own aims. Can the contractors have, as one of their general aims, to act in accordance with moral or political rules? If the theorist's wider objective is to uncover whether some alleged moral or political rule conflicts or is congruent with individuals' rational self-interest, then contractors clearly cannot include conformity with the rule among their aims, since this makes the answer to the theorist's question trivial. But this doesn't mean that rationality contractualism precludes contractors from having morally motivated aims. Many people's central life plans are shaped by moral convictions: a belief that one ought to act as God commands, or that one ought to do as much as possible to alleviate human suffering. These are clearly morally motivated aims, and the broader forms of rationality contractualism allow contractors to have such objectives, but within the model, they will be treated as on a par with any other interests a contractor might have, for example, the self-interested pursuit of wealth or power.

Apart from these constraints, the aims of the contractors should mirror those of the persons they represent, though again, how closely the aims of the contractors should mirror those of the persons they represent will depend on the theorist's objective. The theorist may be interested in taking people roughly as they are – that is, in taking people's particular aims or interests as given. The objective is then to uncover how people with those particular aims would choose if they were instrumentally rational. But rationality contractualism need not take people exactly as they are. Instead, the theorist might wish to 'clean up' people's existing aims and interests – correcting for obvious inconsistencies, and discarding those plans individuals have formed that are instrumental to achieve one objective, but that are not the most effective means of pursuing a more fundamental objective. There are varying degrees to which the contractors can be idealized in this way. A moderate form of idealization might seek to eliminate only obvious inconsistencies and clearly fallacious inferences made by real persons, while leaving all the person's central commitments untouched.[3] More radical forms of idealization are possible, however. In principle, all of a person's plans or beliefs, apart from her final ends, could be subject to revision.

How much *information* should be given to the contractors? There are two main approaches to this question. On the one hand, the theorist may want to know what would be instrumentally rational for persons given the evidence available to them, even if that evidence does not include all the relevant facts. For example, there are important questions regarding what it is instrumentally rational to do given that we do not know how long we are going to live, or whether we will be afflicted by illness or injury in the future. Some governments require citizens to participate in compulsory forms of collective insurance, and we may wish to know whether rational, self-interested contractors representing all citizens would agree to such schemes. But sometimes, as theorists, we want to know what rational and self-interested agents would do if they had access to all the facts. For example, we might want to know exactly what employment contracts an employer and employee would accept if each party knew exactly what its alternatives were. It is often valuable to know how fully informed and rational contractors would act, even if their real-world counterparts are neither fully informed nor fully rational.

Finally, how does rationality contractualism handle the issue of the *non-agreement* point? Because the aim is often to understand what bargain or agreement self-interested agents would reach, it's typically crucial that the non-agreement point be specified by reference to how well-off persons would actually be in the absence of agreement. In this way rationality contractualism differs sharply from fairness contractualism. In the latter, the non-agreement point can be stipulated in any way the theorist chooses if doing so serves the goal of making the resulting agreement fair. But stipulating unrealistic non-agreements points will defeat the central purpose of most forms of rationality contractualism, namely, discovering what it would be rational for some group of people to accept given the actual alternatives. Of course, we can stipulate an unrealistic or false non-

[3] For a detailed account of moderate idealization, see Gaus (2011: 276–91).

agreement point, and ask what is rational for contractors to do in light of this unrealistic non-agreement point, but the reasons to pursue this strategy (setting aside the aims of fairness contractualism) are unclear.

4   How Not to Use Contractualism

The preceding section focused on how a theorist might design a contractualist scenario, depending on her more particular objectives. In this section I turn to consider a few of the ways in which contractualism might be misused.

4.1   Contractualism as an Account of the Fundamental Basis of Wrongness or Injustice

If utilitarianism is true, it provides the fundamental and complete explanation of wrongness and injustice. Some view contractualism as competing with utilitarianism in this sense – as offering a fundamental and complete approach to injustice or moral wrongness. I think this misdescribes the point of contractualism.

First, it should be clear that neither consent contractualism nor rationality contractualism can plausibly be presented as fundamental accounts of moral wrongness or injustice. These versions of contractualism are intended only to help us answer very specific questions about what people would, or rationally should, accept under certain circumstances.

Second, even fairness contractualism (in any of its guises) does not provide a fundamental explanation of what makes some act or rule morally wrong or unjust. It is rather a useful tool to help us better understand some moral or political puzzle in certain contexts, a tool that can help us see an answer that we might previously have been unable to see, and also a tool that enables us to organize some of our moral or political ideals in a more systematic framework. But fairness contractualism does not compete with utilitarianism as an account of the fundamental basis of moral wrongness or injustice. Whenever some act, ϕ, is correctly judged to be wrong, utilitarianism tells us that the fundamental basis of ϕ's wrongness is that it fails to maximize utility. Contractualists should not respond by saying that the fundamental basis of ϕ's wrongness is that ϕ-ing would be prohibited by the relevant contractualist procedure. Rather, they should follow Scanlon and agree that what *makes* some act wrong or unjust will be the more specific features of the act, for example, that it causes gratuitous suffering. Scanlon presents his moral contractualism as an account of what wrongness *is*. It is an account of the property that all wrong acts share, namely, that they would be disallowed by a principle that suitably situated contractors could not reasonably reject (Scanlon 1998: 13, 391). But this property isn't what ultimately makes something wrong.

I suggest that models of fairness contractualism are analogous to maps of the physical terrain.[4] We choose the map that seems to do the best job making sense of the physical terrain given our current and independently formed beliefs. Even if the map we have chosen turns out to be accurate in every respect – and even if we subsequently adjust some of our pre-existing convictions about distances or locations in light of the map's explanatory power – it is not the map itself that makes it true that the mountain to the west is 500 miles away. Fairness contractualism is, in this sense, like a map. We use our existing beliefs about fairness to construct a map or theory that provides a more complete picture of what fairness (or justice or rightness) requires.

4.2   Contractualism Where It Doesn't Belong

A closely related mistake is the use of contractualism to handle moral or political problems to which it isn't suited. Consider, for example, the following difficult question: when, if ever, is it morally permissible to kill innocent people for the sake of achieving some greater good? To bring things into sharper focus, consider the standard trolley case, where a runaway trolley is going to kill five innocent people trapped on the main tracks unless the trolley is diverted on to a sidetrack, where it will instead only kill one innocent person. Is it permissible to turn the trolley, and, if so, why? Contractualism is not a useful tool for addressing questions like this.[5]

You might think this sort of problem looks ripe for consent contractualism: if we could establish that the one person on the sidetrack would consent to the turning of the trolley, this might explain why it's permissible to do something to him that is presumptively wrongful. Of course the one person on the sidetrack will likely refuse consent if he knows doing so entails his death, but perhaps the point is that he would consent ex ante, from behind a veil of ignorance that prevents him from knowing whether he will be a member of the five on the main track, or the one on the sidetrack.

But this explanation does not accurately capture why it is permissible (assuming it is) to turn the trolley. What makes it permissible to turn the

---

[4] The final four sentences in this paragraph are taken, with slight modification, from Quong (in press).
[5] For a related discussion of contractualism as applied to this case, see Thomson (1990: 181–95).

trolley is not that the one person would have consented ex ante from behind a veil of ignorance, but rather the fact that turning the trolley can avert a sufficiently great harm. The 'consent' of the one person is only achieved by placing that person behind a veil of ignorance that deprives the person from the most important piece of information relevant to the decision, namely, that turning the trolley involves killing him for the benefit of others. The consent obtained in this way is too far removed from the interests and will of the actual person to carry the required normative weight.

Perhaps this simply shows that the type of contractualism best suited to handle these cases is not consent contractualism, but rather fairness contractualism. The point, one might argue, is that under suitably fair conditions (i.e. behind a veil of ignorance) all six people would agree that the trolley should be turned, and so this establishes that turning the trolley is the fair and thus permissible course of action.

There are several serious problems with this view. First, in these cases the central question is what it is permissible to do, and at most, what fairness contractualism could tell us is what would constitute a fair distribution of some harm. But the fact that distributing harm in one way is fairer than the alternative is *not sufficient* to conclude that imposing the harm in this way is permissible. From behind a veil of ignorance, six people might also agree that a surgeon should cut up a healthy patient and distribute his organs to five other patients who are dying and in need of organ transplants to survive, but hardly anyone thinks this is a permissible course of action. Second, an act being fair is *not necessary* to establish its permissibility. Suppose, for example, the runaway trolley can be turned either to a sidetrack to the left, where it will kill your spouse, or to a sidetrack to the right, where it will an innocent stranger. Many will agree you are permitted to turn the trolley to the right (you don't have to flip a coin), but this is not a fair distribution since the person on the right is given no chance to avoid being killed. Finally, cases such as these are not analogous to standard problems of distributive justice where fairness contractualism is often deployed. In cases like the one being considered, each person cannot share in the burdens and benefits. Rather, some people will be forced to bear all the burdens while others reap all the benefits. Though this may be the right thing to do in certain circumstances, it's not plausible to say that the burdens and benefits have been fairly distributed.

4.3   Conflating Different Types of Contractualism

One of my central claims in this chapter is that there are different types of contractualism, and that they are designed to address very different questions. A significant problem in political philosophy, I believe, is the failure to recognize this fact. Proponents and critics of contractualism are both to blame for this state of affairs.

Consider, for example, the most influential version of contractualism in our field. Rawls presents his aim as being to uncover the principles of justice appropriate to regulate social cooperation for mutual advantage among free and equal persons (Rawls 1999: 109, 456). His repeated references to mutual benefit and mutual advantage have led a number of his critics to interpret his theory as, at least in part, an account of what rational self-interested bargainers would accept. The critics then point out that Rawls's defence of his two principles of justice as fairness, in particular the difference principle, cannot be reconciled with the view that his principles are also mutually advantageous. A political society regulated by the difference principle may not, these critics plausibly argue, be advantageous for many people who might be better off under a less egalitarian regime (Barry 1989b: 241–54; Cohen 1995: 224–6).

I believe these critics misunderstand Rawls's theory: his theory is best understood as a pure version of fairness contractualism, and the statements about mutual advantage do not refer to mutual advantage in the sense familiar from rationality contractualism (Quong 2007: 77–82). But the general point the critics make is sound: fairness contractualism cannot be combined with rationality contractualism, at least where the aim is to uncover what it would be rational for self-interested agents to accept. A great deal of confusion in political philosophy is created by a failure among those who use contractualism to be clear about the role the contractualist device is designed to play.

A similar type of confusion can arise when we fail to distinguish between consent contractualism and fairness contractualism. Suppose a theorist argues that some presumptively wrong act, ϕ, may permissibly be performed because suitably situated contractors, representing those persons who would be presumptively wronged, would consent. The success of this argument depends crucially on the contractual scenario being designed in such a way that it approximates as closely as possible the will of the real people in question. If the scenario doesn't do this – for example, if the contractors are given very different aims or interests from those of the real people they represent, or if they are placed behind a thick veil of ignorance – then critics may rightly argue that the 'consent' obtained is too far removed from the will of the relevant real people.[6] This, recall, is one of the problems with an attempt to use contractualism to explain why it is permissible to turn a runaway trolley away from five people and towards one person.

I don't wish to defend the extreme thesis that hybrid models of contractualism are always unsuccessful. One reason to develop a hybrid model would be if one's wider metaethical or normative beliefs entail an identity (or at least extensional equivalence) between the different questions associated with different forms of contractualism. For example, if one independently believed that moral rules must be co-extensive with individual self-interest, then the distinction between rationality contractualism and fairness contractualism collapses. Similarly, if one had independent reasons to believe that social morality is whatever set of rules real persons (suitably idealized) have sufficient instrumental reasons to endorse, then the distinction between a version of fairness contractualism and an expansive version of rationality contractualism blurs. But as a general methodological principle, we do better to carefully distinguish the different varieties of contractualism.

4.4   Too Much or Too Little Content

A question theorists must confront when designing models of fairness contractualism is this: how much normative content can be 'front-loaded' into the model?

On the one hand, there is a risk of assuming so much specific normative content that the contractualist device no longer seems necessary. We begin with all the detailed moral content we might have hoped to get out of the contractualist procedure. Suppose the question we wish to answer with our contractual device is this: what is the fairest principle to regulate the distribution of income and wealth amongst citizens? What we must not do is stipulate that the contractors are motivated to reject any principles apart from some specific principle of distributive justice. Doing this begs the question: we simply stipulate the answer to the question we are allegedly investigating.

Brian Barry memorably accuses Rawls of making this mistake in his initial attempt to explain why contractors in the original position would favour a principle requiring saving for future generations. In reaching this conclusion, Rawls assumes that the contractors care about the well-being of those in the next generation. This, Barry scornfully says, is 'like

---

[6] Though it is sometimes the critic who bears responsibility for the mistake of conflating the two forms of contractualism. See Sandel (1982).

a conjurer putting a rabbit in a hat, taking it out again and expecting a round of applause' (Barry 1989a: 505).

Although it is crucial to avoid begging the question, this doesn't mean that it is a mistake to build a good deal of normative content into the design of the contractual scenario. Indeed, doing so is essential. In order to design a contractual scenario where we can be confident that the agreement amongst the contractors is guaranteed to reflect what fairness requires, we must already have in hand some independent ideas about fairness. The contractual device offers a way of modelling and systematizing our existing convictions about fairness. The hope is that we can begin with those convictions about which we are most confident and settled, and use them to design a contractual scenario that will help us reach answers about issues where we are uncertain.

Most of us believe, for example, that: persons are moral equals – no person's interests matter more than anyone else's; that harms imposed on one person cannot simply be outweighed by benefits conferred on others (the separateness of persons); and that sex, race, or social class are not legitimate reasons to discriminate amongst persons. So we take these convictions, among others, and represent them in the contractual scenario. We can represent the moral equality of persons by ensuring that the relative bargaining powers of the contractors is equalized. We can represent the separateness of persons by giving each contractor a veto. And we might represent the irrelevance of sex, race, and social class by placing parties behind a veil of ignorance. These are all ways in which a great deal of normative content can be built in to the contractual scenario. But this needn't be problematic, provided that we don't use, as one of our considered convictions to shape the design of the contractual device, a particular answer to the question that the contractual device is meant to answer.

Of course even if we do not assume a precise answer to the question that the contractual device is intended to answer, there is still a sense in which the answer on which the contractors converge should be entailed or be inescapable given the normative design of the contractual scenario. Some worry that this reveals the contractual device is a trick or sham. But this objection is puzzling. As with any valid argument, the conclusion should follow from the premises. Few people allege that valid syllogisms are a sham because the conclusion must follow given the premises. There is no reason to suppose this complaint has greater force when applied to contractualism.

Perhaps the objection is not that contractualism is a trick or sham, but rather that it's an unnecessary device. If the agreement the contractors reach is inescapable given the normative assumptions we use to design the contractual scenario, we should dispense with the contractual device and simply present our argument as a series of premises leading to a conclusion.

But this objection to contractualism is almost as puzzling. First, there are often several ways an argument can be presented, and I doubt there are decisive general reasons to favour one mode of presentation over another regardless of the context. Second, contractualism is not simply a method by which an argument is presented. It's also a tool we can use to help us see an answer we couldn't see before. Just like a well-designed telescope allows us to see things we might not otherwise be able to see, the process of imagining oneself behind the veil of ignorance, or imagining what self-interested bargainers might accept under certain constraints, can be a powerful heuristic. Finally, contractualism can be more than a way of presenting an argument or a heuristic; it can also function as a theoretical framework. That is, once we have designed a contractual device that we are confident has successfully helped us answer a particular question, we can use the device to answer further questions, provided those questions are sufficiently similar to our original enquiry. The more explanatory power a particular form of contractualism seems to have with regard to a normative domain, the more we can justifiably be confident that it offers a useful framework for answering similar questions in that domain. We may even, as Rawls suggests, sometimes choose to revise our existing beliefs in light of the general explanatory success of the contractualist model.

5 Summary: How to Use Contractualism

In closing, what follows is a list of some of this chapter's main claims, presented as a set of 'how-to' recommendations for using contractualism in moral and political theory.

1) **Be clear about the nature of your question.** The nature of your question will dictate which type of contractualism (consent, fairness, rationality) you need to use.
2) **Do not conflate different types of contractualism.** The aims of consent, fairness, and rationality contractualism are sufficiently distinct that they typically cannot all be successfully pursued within a single model.
3) Having identified the type of contractualism you need, **design your model of contractualism with the following five questions in mind**:

   i. *Constituency*: Who do the contractors represent?

   ii. *Primary Question*: What question do the contractors confront?

   iii. *Motives and Interests*: What are the motives and interests of the contractors?

   iv. *Information*: How much information should be provided to the contractors?

   v. *Non-agreement*: What will happen to each contractor in the event of non-agreement?

4) **Contractualism cannot provide an account of the fundamental basis of moral wrongness or injustice.** It is a model or framework for organizing moral ideas.

5) **Contractualism cannot be used to solve all moral or political problems.** It is, for example, ill-suited to helping answer questions about so-called lesser evil justifications.

6) **Models of fairness contractualism are redundant when too much normative content is assumed** – when the answer being sought is assumed in the design of the model. But **models of fairness contractualism can also fail when too little moral content is built in**. Moral conclusions cannot be derived from a model unless the model accurately reflects a sufficient set of prior moral convictions.

Acknowledgements

I am very grateful to Adrian Blau and Rebecca Stone for comments on earlier versions of this chapter.

References

Barry, Brian, 1989a. *Democracy, Power, and Justice*. Clarendon Press.

Barry, Brian, 1989b. *Theories of Justice: A Treatise on Social Justice, Vol. I*. University of California Press.

Cohen, G. A., 1995. *Self-Ownership, Freedom, and Equality*. Cambridge University Press.

Dworkin, Ronald, 1973. 'The original position', *The University of Chicago Law Review* 40: 500–33.

Gaus, Gerald, 2011. *The Order of Public Reason: A Theory of Freedom and Morality in a Diverse and Bounded World*. Cambridge University Press.

Gauthier, David, 1987. *Morals by Agreement*. Oxford University Press.

Hobbes, Thomas, 1996. *Leviathan*, ed. Richard Tuck. Cambridge University Press.

Nozick, Robert, 1974. *Anarchy, State, and Utopia*. Basic Books.

Quong, Jonathan, 2007. 'Contractualism, reciprocity, and egalitarian justice', *Politics, Philosophy, & Economics* 6, 75–105.

Quong, Jonathan (in press). 'Consequentialism, deontology, and distributive justice', in Serena Olsaretti, ed., *The Oxford Handbook of Distributive Justice*. Oxford University Press.

Rawls, John, 1999. *A Theory of Justice: Revised Edition*. Oxford University Press.

Reiman, Jeffrey, 2007. 'Being fair to future people: the non-identity problem in the original position', *Philosophy & Public Affairs* 35: 69–92.

Sandel, Michael, 1982. *Liberalism and the Limits of Justice*. Cambridge University Press.

Scanlon, T. M., 1998. *What We Owe to Each Other*. Belknap Press.

Thomson, Judith Jarvis, 1990. *The Realm of Rights*. Harvard University Press.

6 Moral Sentimentalism

Michael L. Frazer

1 Introduction

Scholars across a variety of disciplines have come to believe that eighteenth-century luminaries such as David Hume and Adam Smith were correct to see our normative judgements as *sentiments* – that is, as integrating both affective and cognitive elements, both emotions and beliefs.

There are several ways to defend this thesis (Frazer 2013: 21–4). Psychologists, neuroscientists, and other social scientists have gathered considerable evidence that normative judgements depend on emotions (e.g. Damasio 1994; Marcus et al. 2000; Haidt 2001; Westen 2007). Philosophers have then explored the deeper implications of these empirical discoveries (e.g. Nichols 2004; Prinz 2007). Normative ethicists and political theorists have argued that emotional engagements ought to be appreciated as positive features of our ethical and political lives (e.g. Walzer 2004; Hall 2005; Krause 2008; Frazer 2010; Slote 2010). During the first half of the twentieth century, many analytic metaethicists even argued that the very concept of affectless evaluation is incoherent (Ayer 1936: 102–19; Stevenson 1944). Under a particularly strong version of this metaethical view – often defended under such names as emotivism, non-cognitivism or expressivism – moral judgements consist only of emotion, and contain no cognitive content whatsoever. Among metaethicists today, moderate, qualified, hybrid or 'neosentimentalist' views are more popular (e.g. Gibbard 1990; D'Arms and Jacobson 2000).

Given the long-standing centrality of emotion in analytic metaethics, it is surprising that sentimentalism is only now gaining a foothold in Anglo-American political theory. Some might see this as evidence of the irrelevance of metaethics to politics. Even though the view that metaethics is normatively neutral has not been popular for nearly half a century (Gewirth 1968, 1970; Solomon 1970), the view that normative political theory ought to be metaethically neutral is still widespread. Following Rawls (1996: 12–15), metaethics is often classified alongside religion, metaphysics, and even comprehensive theories of normative ethics as an inappropriate starting point for political theorizing in a democratic society characterized by a broad diversity of competing worldviews.

Yet although there may be good reasons to try to build our political theories on as non-controversial a philosophical foundation as possible, our views about the necessary or proper form of normative judgements will inevitably shape the techniques we use to try to form better ones. The main implications of metaethics for political theory are thus likely to be methodological rather than substantive. Most important for our present purposes, the standard tools of analytic political theory discussed elsewhere in this volume, which are designed to help us formulate sound and valid arguments rather than to hone our emotional sensitivity, typically fail to speak to our sentiments.

The tension between the aspiration to make the standard methods of analytic political theory metaethically neutral and the likelihood that their appeal depends on some form of moral cognitivism can be felt throughout the present volume. In Chapter 3 for example, Brownlee and Stemplowska argue that 'what matters in thought experiments are not (or not exclusively) raw affective states'. Despite appearances to the contrary, they claim that this view is compatible with a 'sophisticated version of non-cognitivism', one that 'accepts that, even if moral judgement is ultimately a matter of affective states, there is nonetheless a plausible distinction to be drawn between raw affective states and "gardened" or reflective ones'. And it is true that sophisticated sentimentalists have rarely thought that one ought to follow one's immediate moral feelings, but instead must undertake a process of reflective self-correction in which all one's moral sentiments are progressively put under the test of their own evaluative scrutiny (Frazer 2010).

Later in their chapter, however, Brownlee and Stemplowska defend the permissibility of what they call 'imaginatively opaque' thought experiments – scenarios in which it is impossible to engage empathetically with the impossible situations in which the protagonists find themselves – on the grounds that 'experiments are not "run" (simply) to establish how we (the experimenters) would *feel*, but to establish what we may plausibly *think*'. Purely cognitive consideration of characters with whom empathy is impossible may allow for the formation of proper normative judgements if evaluation is a matter of pure reason, but this imaginative opacity will prevent proper judgement under most sentimentalist theories.

If the standard methods of analytic normative theory are indeed less attractive under a sentimentalist theory than they are under a cognitivist one, then the committed sentimentalist is left with at least three options. First, one might maintain that normative evaluation cannot be a legitimate part of philosophy. Early-twentieth-century emotivists believed that only analytic methods qualified as philosophical, and that these methods could never vindicate normative claims. Of course, considerations of professional survival make this option rather unattractive to normative theorists today. Fortunately for us, in the second half of the twentieth century normative moral and political philosophy came to establish themselves as important subfields in even the most analytic philosophy departments.

Second, the standard techniques of analytic normative theory could be reinterpreted in ways that make them a better fit with sentimentalism. Even if most analytic philosophers believe that they are only in the business of constructing sound and valid arguments, they may nonetheless succeed in improving their readers' normative judgements by encouraging psychologically holistic self-scrutiny, sparking empathy with other's emotional experiences, and increasing sensitivity to the affectively salient features of collective life. I have argued elsewhere that Rawls (1999) succeeds in engaging our moral sentiments in exactly these ways, and that his theory of justice is far more sentimentalist than Rawls himself ever acknowledges (Frazer 2007). Many of the most successful pieces of moral and political philosophy operate similarly; just think of the emotional power of Singer (1972) equating a nearby child drowning in a mud puddle with one dying from famine in Bangladesh. Yet since most affective effects of analytic philosophy are unintended by-products of its usual methods, this alternative is unsuited for a chapter designed to provide a guide to the intentional practice of sentimentalist theory.

Only sentimentalists who are willing to violate the conventions of contemporary philosophy will deliberately seek to evoke moral sentiments in their readers. As such, my focus here will be on a third alternative available to sentimentalists, who can make common cause with all those seeking to bring a greater diversity of methods and approaches to the practice of Anglo-American political theory.

Once we accept that political theory can be more than a matter of applied logic, we can consciously develop techniques designed to spark psychologically holistic reflection in our readers. Section 2 of this chapter will discuss the implications that sentimentalism should and should not have for our approach to normative political theory. Section 3 defends the permissibility of this theoretical approach against possible objections. Section 4 concludes by drawing on the work of Hume and Smith to provide concrete advice about how to apply sentimentalist techniques successfully.

2   Sentimentalist Theory and Impassioned Practice

This is hardly the place to provide a full defence of sentimentalism on empirical, normative or conceptual grounds. Instead, let us assume, for the sake of argument, that sentimentalism in some form is true, or at least more plausible than the available alternatives. The obvious methodological response would seem to be an impassioned form of normative argumentation. Nussbaum, for one, suggests that conducting sentimentalist theory dispassionately gives the appearance of a 'peculiar sort of self-contradiction between form and thesis'. Consider, she suggests, an article that

> argues that the emotions are essential and central in our efforts to gain understanding on any important ethical matter; and yet it is written in a style that expresses only intellectual activity and strongly suggests that only this activity matters for the reader in his or her attempts to understand. There might have been some interesting reason for writing this way; but usually, in cases of this kind, the whole issue had just not arisen. Such articles were written as they were because that was the way philosophy was being written, and sometimes because an emotive or literary style would have evoked criticism, or even ridicule. (Nussbaum 1990: 21)

Nussbaum's argument would seem to suggest that there is at least a *pro tanto* reason for those convinced of the truth of moral sentimentalism to adopt different approaches to philosophical argumentation than those their cognitivist colleagues espouse, one stemming from the desire to avoid contradiction between form and content. In order to avoid such contradictions, it can be argued that diverse philosophical positions require different investigative methods and modes of expression (Stewart 2013: 1–12, 159–70).

In fact, however, there is neither any logical entailment nor a strong empirical correlation between a commitment to moral sentimentalism and the adoption of a distinctively impassioned approach. Sentimentalists often draw a distinction between the proper practice of philosophy and the proper practice of everyday reflection, maintaining that it is not appropriate for philosophers to express or evoke moral sentiments, but only to discover the truth about them. As a result, one might argue that while first-order practical reflection is and ought to be impassioned, second-order philosophical investigation into the nature of this first-order reflection should not be.

There is considerable precedent for this sort of unemotional analysis of human emotion. While ancient philosophers may have disagreed about the proper place of passion in moral life, most agreed that the study of emotion was an important part of the philosophical enterprise, such as in the fields of rhetoric and poetics. Yet Aristotle's *Rhetoric* and *Poetics* are as dry as anything else in his corpus. Aristotle carefully examines the evocation of human emotion while failing to evoke any significant feelings in the reader (with the possible exception, depending on one's predilections, of intellectual excitement or boredom). The same dispassion can be found in the study of emotion by most experimental psychologists and sentimentalist metaethicists today. Hume is therefore guilty of no inconsistency when he insists in the *Treatise* that, when it comes to practical decision-making, 'reason is and ought only to be the slave of the passions' (2000a: 2.3.3.4, 226), while also complaining that too often in philosophy 'it is not reason, which carries the prize, but eloquence' (2000a: Intro.2, 3).

At the conclusion of the *Treatise*, however, Hume makes clear that 'were it proper in such a subject to bribe the reader's assent, or employ anything but solid argument', his seemingly dry anatomy of the moral sentiments is in fact 'abundantly supplied with topics to engage the affections' (2000a: 3.3.6.3, 394). In his later writings, Hume lost this reticence about engaging readers' affects, and used a wide variety of literary techniques in the attempt to do so (Frazer 2015).

Hume came to see that, if his readers fail to feel affective approbation for the moral sentiments that he is analysing, his normative defence of these sentiments becomes merely descriptive. Since all evaluation contains an affective component, sentimentalist theory cannot be consistently normative without being impassioned. While there is no necessary connection between sentimentalism as such and the practice of impassioned theorizing, the conjunction of sentimentalism with a commitment to practising normative evaluation does require emotion.

If sentimentalists abide by the standard methods of analytic philosophy, they will only evoke affective approbation and disapprobation unintentionally, if at all. Their work may end up merely descriptive. Even worse, it might actually weaken our moral sentiments. Hume is deeply concerned that any moral sentiment can 'with facility, be refined away ... in sifting and scrutinizing it, by every captious rule of logic, in every light or position, in which it may be placed' (Hume 1985: 482). To be sure, Hume holds that those who tamp down their moral sentiments in this way are indulging in a 'false philosophy', but even accurate philosophy may have similar results.

Although the minute moral distinctions that casuists draw are often unobjectionable when considered individually, the very process of coldly drawing distinction after distinction seems to desensitize both casuists and their audience to the properly affective features of moral life. Anyone who has ever sat through a dispassionate – or even downright cheerful – discussion by analytic ethicists of scenarios involving running over people with trolleys and resorting to cannibalism on lifeboats has to worry that standard analytic methods can have precisely this effect. Nor is this problem a new one: Seneca also objected to the logic-chopping playfulness of the ethicists of his own day. 'It makes one ashamed', he writes, 'that men of our advanced years should turn a thing as serious as this into a game' (Seneca 2004: 97).

3   Objections to Impassioned Philosophy

Before we can discuss practical techniques for successfully evoking moral sentiments in our readers, we have to address the argument that this is not an appropriate goal to pursue in the first place. I will focus on two important objections to the practice of impassioned philosophy: the objection from disciplinary distinctions, and the objection against manipulation.

3.1   The Objection from Disciplinary Distinctions

There is a remarkable degree of methodological conservatism in most academic disciplines. The most common criticism of anyone violating local conventions is that their work is not 'real': not 'real philosophy' or 'real political theory'. If research resembles work done outside the academy rather than in an adjacent discipline, it may not even qualify as 'real scholarship'.

While the professional norms of each discipline may seem self-justifying to most of their practitioners, Applebaum (2000) observes that what creates an ethical justification for abiding by the duties of a particular profession is the importance of that profession for one's larger society. If a particular vocation serves no justifiable purpose, then the internal rules of that profession are not a legitimate branch of any larger ethical system. We're all better off without professional gladiators and professional torturers. The question is therefore whether the reigning standards of a given profession – such as the methodological norms of an academic discipline – aid in the achievement of a genuinely valuable social purpose.

The methodological standards governing analytic philosophy are less than a century old. The idea of philosophy as a distinct discipline is slightly older. In the eighteenth century and earlier, philosophy was simply the search for general, nomothetic truth. As such, it included much of what we now call 'science', but still excluded activities that have something other than general truth as their aim – such as persuasive oratory and idiographic narrative, whether factual or fictional.

The principle that the search for general truth precludes the evocation of emotion has long had its defenders. Recall the young Hume's view that when discussing 'such a subject', it is inappropriate to 'employ anything but solid argument'.

Later, Smith contrasts three types of writing: narrative, didactic and rhetorical. Didactic discourse, of which philosophical writing is the paradigm, 'proposes to put before us the arguments on both sides of the question in their true light, giving each its proper degree of influence, and has it in view to persuade no farther than the arguments themselves appear convincing'. By contrast, rhetorical discourse 'endeavors by all means to persuade us, and for this purpose it magnifies the arguments on the one side and diminishes or conceals that might be brought' on the other. The goal of a didactic discourse is primarily instruction, and only secondarily persuasion; the goal of rhetoric is persuasion and 'instruction is considered only so far as it is subservient to persuasion, and no farther' (Smith 1985: 12, i.149–150, 62).

Although the line between rhetorical and didactic compositions is sharply drawn, the line between didactic and narrative writing is blurrier. This is most evident in the genre of history, a form of narrative writing that incorporates significant didactic elements. The didactic power of historical and other factual narratives, moreover, suggests a sort of hybrid genre in which an author establishes 'certain principles' that are 'confirmed by examples' (Smith 1985: 17 ii.17, 90–1). This hybrid approach is particularly well-suited for what Smith calls 'the practical sciences of politics and morality or ethics', which he complains 'have of late been treated too much in a speculative manner' (Smith 1985: i.102, 41).

If ethics and politics are treated too speculatively – that is, only in terms of nomothetic principles rather than in terms of concrete events in the lives of particular human beings – our moral sentiments may be blocked. 'When a philosopher contemplates characters and manners in his closet', Hume protests, 'the general abstract view of the objects leaves the mind so cold and unmoved, that the sentiments of nature have no room to play, and he scarce feels the difference between vice and virtue'. A historian, by contrast, 'places the objects in their true point of view', and hence develops 'a lively sentiment of blame and praise' (Hume 1985: 568). In all of his post-*Treatise* writings, Hume is therefore careful to illustrate every moral and political point with concrete examples. Hume usually takes his examples from history and the classics; Smith tends to prefer everyday experiences that his readers will recognize from their own lives.

Interdisciplinarity has thus been a hallmark of moral sentimentalism from its beginning (Frazer Forthcoming). Moral sentiments are unlikely to be evoked effectively when one strictly follows the norms of didactic, speculative eighteenth-century philosophy, let alone the norms of analytic philosophy in the twenty-first century. As such, sentimentalists can make common cause with those practising what is now called realist or non-ideal theory, overcoming the barriers between political philosophy and social science (see Jubb, Chapter 7 in this volume).

Much of the empirical work realists cite today is the sort of nomothetic social science that still qualifies as philosophy in the eighteenth-century sense, the kind of 'general facts about human society' that Rawls allows to the otherwise ignorant agents in the original position (Rawls 1999: 116). In order to integrate narrative and didactic elements in the manner Hume and Smith advocated, sentimentalists are more likely to draw on idiographic work in history and ethnography. They are particularly likely to be drawn to the work of social scientists who favour interpretive rather than causal explanations of human behaviour. In the interpretive tradition, tracing others' narratives allows us to identify their motivations, values and worldviews, hence achieving empathetic understanding, what Weber (1978: 7–8) calls *Verstehen*. Although Weber believed that *Verstehen* is compatible with a commitment to value-neutrality, sentimentalists seek such empathetic understanding insofar as it allows for accurate, affectively laden normative judgements.

There is a growing awareness in the social sciences that accurate accounts of particular incidents can serve as what Thacher (2006) calls 'normative case studies'. A 'phronetic' social science of the sort Flyvbjerg (2001) advocated considers such cases in order to help us develop the skills of ethical judgement required to guide public decision-making for the better. It is a friendly amendment to this agenda to understand the ethical skills being developed to consist largely in emotional, empathetic sensitivity.

In addition to joining forces with those seeking to challenge the division between normative theory and social science, sentimentalists may also ally themselves with those opposed to the division between philosophy and the rest of the humanities – especially the movement that Danto (1985: 63) calls 'philosophy as/and/of literature'. To be sure, turning from factual to fictional narratives poses the danger that fictions will be designed manipulatively, artificially evoking inappropriate moral sentiments. While the particular challenges that a sentimentalist faces when drawing on imaginative literature will be discussed later in this chapter, this worry suggests a second objection to the sentimentalist approach. Even if it is acceptable to challenge reigning disciplinary distinctions, one might still worry that it is unacceptable to evoke moral sentiments in one's readers because doing so is manipulative.

3.2   The Objection Against Manipulation

Recall Hume's contention that evoking moral sentiments is an attempt to 'bribe the reader's assent' (Section 2). On this view, evoking a reader's sentiments might itself be ethically objectionable – a deformation of the appropriate relationship between an author and a reader, just as bribery is a deformation of the proper relationship between a citizen and an official. This moral objection holds regardless of an author's disciplinary identity, or lack thereof.

Bentham was later to sharpen the point still further, arguing that what Hume said was merely bribery is in fact 'a cloak, and pretense, and alignment, to despotism'. Emotionally evocative literary effects are but 'so many contrivances for avoiding the obligation of appealing to any external standard, and for prevailing upon the reader to accept of the author's sentiment or opinion as a reason for itself' (Bentham 1962: 2:14, 8–9).

Bentham foreshadows the hostility to evoking emotion that we find in more recent liberal theories. Darwall (1995: 74) interprets Bentham as regarding an obligation to provide public justification 'as a necessary condition of *liberal* public moral debate. When people make a moral claim on others, he suggests, but are unwilling to offer a reason for doing so that others could be expected to accept without already sharing those moral views, this is implicitly coercive.' The contrast here is between the power of an authoritarian demagogue – for whom emotionally manipulative propaganda is just another means of control, no different in this respect from the secret police – and the non-coercive exchange of reasons among equals in democratic discourse.

There is, however, a regrettable slippage in this argument between the idea that public justification requires the provision of public reasons (in the sense of grounds for justification which you expect the entire community to share) and that it requires reasoning (in the sense of collective reliance on the rational faculty alone). As recent sentimentalist political theorists have pointed out, an important implication of moral sentimentalism is that our reasons – whether individual and private or public and shared – cannot come from reason alone (Krause 2008; Frazer 2010; Kingston 2011). Shared reasons imply the existence of shared feelings; this is why sympathy or empathy, the faculties by which emotions are communicated from one person to another, are so important in most versions of sentimentalism (but see Prinz 2011). It is no more despotic, coercive or manipulative for members of a political community to share emotions with one another than it is for them to provide rational arguments to one another.

Recent philosophers have struggled to provide a precise account of what constitutes manipulation, but there is a general consensus that evoking emotion is neither necessary nor sufficient for manipulation to occur. Most see manipulation as influence that is at best indifferent to whether its target adheres to the relevant standards of good judgement (Coons and Weber 2014: 11–14). This raises the question of whether these relevant standards are objectively binding or are grounded in the subjective commitments of the manipulator, the target, or both. Regardless, if all the parties involved are committed sentimentalists – and if they are objectively correct in being so – then the ideals in question will call for feeling proper emotions. This is not to say that morally unacceptable forms of interpersonal manipulation are impossible among sentimentalists, but that they are just as likely to involve sophistic argumentation as they are to involve the artificial evocation of affect.

4   Techniques for Impassioned Philosophy

Simply establishing that it is permissible to evoke moral sentiments in our readers would be of little value were it impossible for us ever do so successfully. Fortunately, this sentimentalist goal is eminently achievable. Admittedly, evoking emotion is an art rather than a science, and using the techniques described below is neither necessary nor sufficient for impassioned philosophy. It is not necessary because, as has already been mentioned, analytic philosophers often end up evoking moral sentiments without intending to do so. It is not sufficient because, if not practised with the right degree of philosophical and literary artistry, these techniques cannot be guaranteed to succeed.

4.1   Write Interesting Stories

As is now already evident, the best format for impassioned, sentimentalist normative theory is a genre combining both idiographic and nomothetic elements, both particular narratives and general philosophy. The most important thing sentimentalists should keep in mind when writing a story is that it should be interesting, both in the sense that we use the term 'interesting' today and in its original meaning, still dominant in the eighteenth century, of involving or engaging our interests.

The antiquated and the current uses of 'interesting' are closely connected. As Vermeule (2010: 41) observes, engaging our empathy with another human mind is a sure-fire way to hold our attention. **Sentimentalist theory should be filled with interesting stories, ones in which we sympathetically engage with the characters,**

allowing their needs and interests to become our own. Without this engagement with another's interests, we are likely to find ourselves left both cold and bored.

Livy, for example, interests us because 'we enter into all the concerns of the parties and are almost as much affected with them as if we ourselves had been concerned in them' (Smith 1985: 17, ii.27, 95–6). Via sympathy, their interests become our own. Livy and Tacitus lead us 'so far into the sentiments and mind of the actors that they are some of the most striking and interesting passages to be met with in any history' (Smith 1985: 20, ii.67, 113).

Well-written history is always interesting in this way, as are philosophical, didactic writings that make frequent use of well-written narratives. This is probably one of the reasons historians and ethnographers still regularly find an audience among the educated reading public, while philosophers who are not also storytellers rarely do so.

4.2   Show, Don't Tell

Manipulative rhetoricians often succeed in arousing moral sentiments in their audiences, but they do so in ways very different from those writing in the mode that Hume and Smith advocate. The author of a well-written historical narrative, Smith points out, 'may excite grief or compassion but only by narrating facts which excite those feelings; whereas the orator heightens every incident and pretends at least to be deeply affected by them himself' (Smith 1985: 18, ii.38, 101). A good historian 'acts as if he were an impartial narrator of the facts' (Smith 1985: 7, i.82–3, 35), and 'exclamations in his own person would not suit with the impartiality he is to maintain and the design he is to have in view of narrating facts as they are without magnifying or diminishing them' (ibid., 18, ii.40, 101).

The best writers in other genres, including the hybrid genre that is most appropriate for sentimentalist political theory, typically share the historian's characteristic 'modesty' in this regard. **When detailing their narratives, sentimentalists should refrain from telling their readers how to feel, letting their stories speak for themselves.**

Smith and Hume were both, like many of their time, admirers of the essayist Joseph Addison. While previous print moralists would harangue their readers with moral exhortation, following the model of the church sermon, Addison prefers to 'deliver his sentiments in the least assuming manner; and this would incline him rather to narrate what he had seen and heard than to deliver his opinions in his own person' (Smith 1985: 10, i.128, 53). Addison's authorial persona, like Smith's ideal moral judge, is an impartial spectator – 'Mr. Spectator', as Addison calls him – who simply tells it like he sees it. The immense popularity and influence of Addison's *Spectator* is evidence of the power of such straightforward writing.

It is a striking fact of human psychology that this modest approach can arouse even greater emotional reactions than those aroused by direct appeals. Smith argues that it is a 'general rule that when we mean to affect the reader deeply we must have recourse to the indirect method of description, relating the effects the transaction produced both on the actors and the spectators' (Smith 1985: 16, ii.7, 86–7). Creative writers are taught the rule 'show, don't tell', not to establish impartiality or to avoid manipulation, but simply to maximize emotional impact. The fact that the same technique is the best way to achieve these two very different objectives is a happy coincidence of human psychology.

4.3   Focus on Particulars, then Generalize

While analytic theorists often try to deduce particular conclusions from general moral principles, Smith insists that the general rules of morality should only be derived inductively. Specifically, they are to be 'formed, by finding from experience, that all actions of a certain kind, or circum-stanced in a certain manner, are approved or disapproved of' (Smith 1984: III.4.8, 159). **Sentimentalists should begin with empathetic consideration of particulars, only then attempting to extrapolate from these cases to more general principles, rather than vice versa.** When a general principle is stated in the abstract, we are unlikely to have any emotional reaction. When, however, it is inductively derived from a series of cases, each one of which evoked our moral sentiments, it can carry with it the force of the cases that serve as its foundation.

Even within a particular normative case study, the reader's attention is best focused on the subjective experiences of particular individuals. Smith says Tacitus is a particularly good example of an author who focuses on 'internal' micro-level phenomena rather than 'external' macro-level ones. When Tacitus fixes our attention on the psyche of a single individual, our sympathies are 'as it were concentrated, and become greatly stronger than when separated and distracted by the affecting circumstances that befell the several persons involved in a common calamity' (Smith 1985: 20, ii.66, 113).

Once we understand the individual experience of a certain event, we can then generalize to the effects of that event on relevantly similar others. It is then the empathetic understanding of particular experiences that allows us to inductively derive general principles about similar cases from the full range of human life.

It is also the empathetic understanding that each person in a statistic represents an entire subjective world of experience that can prevent large numbers from having their usual morally distorting effects. Bertrand Russell is alleged to have said that 'the mark of a civilized man is the capacity to read a column of numbers and weep', but as Vermeule (2010: 33) observes, 'on this view, none of us is really civilized'. After we have empathetically experienced the suffering of a single individual, however, learning that a troublingly large number of others have experienced something similar can have a profound emotional effect. When we are discussing global poverty, for example, we must never forget that we are discussing the lives of millions of real human beings, each of which could be recounted with the novelistic detail of the stories in Boo's (2012) account of a single Mumbai slum.

Guenther's (2013) phenomenological study of solitary confinement is a good model for how to combine Boo's focus on individual experiences with the pursuit of general philosophical conclusions. Guenther helps us understand that the experience of years of forced isolation is the phenomenological equivalent of death. Cut off from all others, a prisoner ceases to have the inescapably social experiences that are the markers of living humanity. When we empathetically feel the horror of such living death, we understand the cruelty of subjecting even a single individual to it. We can then extrapolate to the full moral significance of subjecting thousands upon thousands of prisoners to such an experience throughout a nation's penal system. We are then also able to begin establishing normative principles about the importance of social interaction to human life more generally.

4.4   Consider Multiple Perspectives

Whenever we seek to generalize from the subjective experience of a single individual, there is a danger that our generalization will fail to capture the experiences of others. If our chosen individual is not typical, then our generalization may prove misleading. Although we lack the imaginative and emotional resources to engage empathetically with a statistically representative sample of any large population, we can make a concerted effort to find counterexamples to any general theses, and then give the individuals involved in these counter-cases our full empathetic consideration. If the most likely potential counterexamples turn out to have experiences relevantly similar to those we have already considered, this provides important evidence in favour of our general hypothesis. Those wishing to question our generalization are always free to suggest other counterexamples.

In many politically important cases, however, generalizations that hold true with regard to the subjective experiences of all individuals involved are neither possible nor desirable. Politics typically involves conflict between competing interests and worldviews. **When groups with radically different experiences of a given situation are in conflict with each other, it is appropriate to consider the perspectives of representative members of each of the conflicting groups.** The ideal moral judge, Smith famously argues, is an impartial spectator; in cases where we are naturally biased in favour of one party in a conflict, our moral sentiments will be improved if we try to overcome our initial partiality.

Smith argues that, when observing a conflict, an impartial spectator must attempt to achieve what he calls 'divided sympathy' (Smith 1984: I. ii.3.1, 34). We have to consider the experiences of those on both sides of the conflict empathetically, and try to form sensitive evaluations of each of them in turn. Doing so cannot involve a single narrative with a single protagonist, but multiple, *Rashomon*-style narratives of a given case in which the perspective of each party is given due consideration.

Academics tend to come from the political left (Gross 2013), and typically have an inclination to side with those whom they see as oppressed. But Smith warns us against this instinct, and urges us to consider the perspective of both the alleged victim and the alleged oppressor in any potential case of injustice. What our initial reaction tells us is cruel or unjust may, with greater empathetic consideration of all the parties involved, turn out to have been motivated by laudable moral sentiments, such as a commitment to the common good (Smith 1984: II.ii.3.8, 88–9). Neither the perspective of the powerful nor that of the powerless should be privileged. We may ultimately conclude that some current practice – modern policing, for example – is indeed oppressive, but doing so impartially requires that we consider the point of view of the police (as in Fassin 2013) as well as the policed (as in Goffman 2014).

4.5   Use Psychologically Realistic Fiction

Sentimentalist normative argumentation requires piling narrative upon narrative, but narratives are an expensive resource. All consideration of narratives is emotionally and imaginatively draining – especially when contrasted with the ease with which a clever undergraduate can construct sound and valid arguments. Any adequate narrative will demand more space than is typically possible in a journal article. And some kinds of narrative are also expensive to source, requiring years of ethnographic fieldwork or archival exploration. This raises the question of whether the narratives that sentimentalists use must be drawn from the careful, fact-

checked work of historians, ethnographers and journalists, or can they just be made up – whether by theorists themselves or by professional writers of fiction?

Hume himself took a clear stand against creative writing. While poets 'can paint virtue in the most charming colours', their undisciplined imaginations often lead them to 'become advocates for vice'. By contrast, 'historians have been, almost without exception, the true friends of virtue, and have always represented it in its proper colours' (Hume 1985: 567). While it would be wrong to conclude that historians, ethnographers and journalists have never been guilty of emotionally manipulating their readers through the use of one-sided, unrealistic or even wholly fabricated narratives, when they have done so they have been violating the norms of their respective professions. Creative writers are not held accountable to reality in this way.

Those defending fiction under the rubric of 'philosophy as/and/of literature' find their inspiration in Aristotle, who maintains that 'poetry is more philosophical and more elevated [that is, of greater ethical import] than history, since poetry relates more of the universal, while history relates particulars.' While history recounts 'actual events', poetry recounts 'the kinds of things that might occur ... the kinds of things which it suits a certain kind of person to say or do, in terms of probability or necessity' (Aristotle 1995: 1451b, 59–61). Sentimentalists are likely to value fiction most highly in terms of its ability to trace what Nussbaum (1995: 5) calls 'the effect of circumstances on the emotions and the inner world' and its unparalleled efficacy in promoting 'identification and sympathy in the reader'.

Just as fiction can describe 'the kinds of things that might occur', however, it can also describe the kinds of things that could never occur. **Fiction need not be realistic in all its details to be useful to sentimentalists, but if it is to show us anything real about the moral sentiments, then characters' inner worlds must be realistic, even if the outer worlds that surround them are not.** It is fine to fill a fictional case with dragons, spaceships, experience machines and baroque trolley systems, as long as we can empathize with the three-dimensional characters trying to navigate these bizarre circumstances. In order not to distort our moral sentiments, however, writers must avoid flat characters like demonic villains and angelic heroes. The presence of such impossible people is a warning sign that readers are being manipulated.

The problem here is that, while it is always possible to check the accuracy of a factual narrative, there is no objective test for the psychological realism of a fictional narrative. All we can rely on is our own power to recognize and empathize with what we appreciate as plausibly human states of mind. For example, it seems psychologically realistic to most readers that the protagonist of Thomson's (1971) famous thought experiment about abortion would deeply resent being attached to an ailing violinist for nine months. Since no one has actually experienced this particular procedure, however, there is no way to check how it actually makes someone feel.

With their preference for high culture over low, academics tend to assume that great literature is more likely to be psychologically realistic than popular fiction or their own amateur storytelling. Philosophers have a particular liking for recent, philosophically-informed high fiction, such as the works of Milan Kundera, J. M. Coetzee, and David Foster Wallace. Nineteenth-century novels are also popular, from those by Jane Austen at the beginning of the century to those by Henry James at the end (the latter no doubt a favourite, at least in part, thanks to the reflected philosophical prestige from brother William).

All of these are wonderful sources for narratives, to be sure, but literary genius is by no means necessary for the purpose of sentimentalist normative argumentation. Smith's own homely stories throughout *The Theory of Moral Sentiments* – think, for example, of the unfortunate tale of the poor man's son (Smith 1984: IV.i.8, 181) – are all highly realistic examples of the kinds of effects that circumstances can have on our inner life, but none rise to the level of great literature. Thomson's is a more recent example of a successful philosopher-written narrative, as is Williams's (1981: 18) more realistic story of the spouse-rescuer with 'one thought too many'. While it is important not to underestimate the literary gifts of Smith, Williams, or Thomson, theorists without the creative genius of Kundera or James might nonetheless hope to craft serviceable fictions of this calibre.

4.6   Write in Simple, Ordinary Language

Good writers, in any genre, share sentiments with their readers. The central thesis of Smith's *Lectures on Rhetoric and Belles Lettres* is that 'when the sentiment of the speaker is expressed in a neat, clear, plain and clever manner, and the passion or affection he is possessed of and intends, by sympathy, to communicate to his hearer is plainly and cleverly hit off, then and then only the expression has all the force and beauty that language can give it' (Smith 1985: 6, i.v.56, 25). The *Lectures* is by and large a how-to guide designed to help Smith's students achieve this goal. Sentimentalists today would still be well advised to follow his stylistic suggestions.

A recurring theme in Smith's lectures is the contrast between the straightforward lucidity of Jonathan Swift and the opaque floridity of the third Earl of Shaftesbury. Shaftesbury, Smith explains, fell prey to a mistake to which we are all vulnerable. 'The idea we form of a good style is almost contrary to that which we commonly hear,' Smith explains. 'Hence it is that we conceive the further one's style is removed from the common manner . . . it is so much the nearer to the purity and perfection we have in view' (Smith 1985: 8, i.103, 42). This belief is, of course, mistaken. **In order to evoke sentiments in their readers effectively, writers should use a style of prose continuous with the ordinary language that is the normal vehicle of emotional communication in everyday life.**

Academics today would never be attracted to the aristocratic excesses of Shaftesbury's antiquated mode of writing. Instead of aping the baroque floridity of aristocratic oratory, most philosophers now seek to gain prestige by aping the dry, technical style that predominates in high-status STEM fields. Yet there are a number of ways in which these seemingly opposed modes of artificial communication are surprisingly similar. For example, the tempo of normal speech varies considerably with the matter being discussed, but both artificial modes maintain a constant rhythm even when 'this uniform and regular cadence is not at all proper' (Smith 1985: 5, i.50, 22). Both artificial modes make everyone sound the same, whereas in natural communication 'when all other circumstances are alike the character of the author must make the style different' (Smith 1985: 8, i.97, 40). The list could be continued; in each case, artificial styles prevent emotional reactions in readers while everyday language encourages them.

Perhaps the most common way of distinguishing artificial modes of communication from ordinary speech is through the use of foreign terms. Greek or Latin words and phrases – and, even worse, Latin grammatical structures – lend an unearned air of authority to English prose, but at the price of turning it into something that is not quite English. Bad writing, both in Smith's day and our own, often has 'a great deal of the air of translations from another language' (Smith 1985: 2, i.10, 7).

Smith argues that the words we use 'should be natives . . . of the language we speak in'. As always, this rule is justified in terms of the best means of evoking sentiments in our readers. 'Foreigners', Smith explains, 'though they may signify the same thing, never convey the idea with such strength as those [words that] we are acquainted with' (Smith 1985: 2, i.1, 3). Just think of the effects of choosing a word like '*ressentiment*' over 'resentment'. The gain in prestige is hardly worth the loss of evocative force. To be sure, Smith admits that foreign words 'may be naturalized by time and be as familiar to us as those which are originally our own, and may then be used with great freedom' (Smith 1985: 2, i.1, 3). Only then can these words connect with everyday life and the speech found within it, and hence carry the emotional force of these associations with lived experience.

If a neologism is needed, it should be constructed from one or more terms found in everyday English. Smith praises Greek philosophers for using only words found in their own language even when coining new terms of art (Smith 1985: 2, i.4, 4). In later centuries, German authors made use of a similar practice. Contrast Freud's *das Es, das Ich* and *das Über-Ich,* to his English translator's id, ego, and superego.

The effect of all of these recommendations will be to narrow the gulf between political theory and all other forms of discourse, both elite and popular. This loss of disciplinary distinctiveness, however, is to be celebrated rather than mourned. For one thing, it is likely to increase the impact of political theory outside the academy. Lay readers are happy to learn from academics, but only if these academics are willing to speak in the interesting, unavoidably impassioned language of normal human life. To be sure, public intellectuals are often excoriated for failing to produce 'real scholarship', but we have already seen that this accusation should carry no ethical weight.

'Be a philosopher', Hume famously urges us, 'but amidst all your philosophy be still a man' (Hume 2000b: 1.6, 7). Since academics must, unavoidably, remain human beings, we should not be ashamed that the same sort of impassioned argumentation that is persuasive among the general population is also the best form of argumentation available to us.

References

Applebaum, Arthur, 2000. *Ethics for Adversaries: The Morality of Roles in Public and Professional Life*. Princeton, NJ: Princeton University Press.
Aristotle, 1995. *Poetics*, ed. and tr. Stephen Halliwell. Cambridge, MA: Harvard University Press.
Ayer, A. J., 1936. *Language, Truth and Logic*. New York: Dover Publications.
Bentham, Jeremy, 1962. 'Introduction to the principles of morals and legislation', in J. Bowring., ed., *The Works of Jeremy Bentham*. New York: Russell & Russell.
Boo, Katherine, 2012. *Behind the Beautiful Forevers: Life, Death and Hope in a Mumbai Undercity*. New York: Random House.
Box, M. A., 1990. *The Suasive Art of David Hume*. Princeton, NJ: Princeton University Press.

Coons, Christian and Michael Weber, 2014. 'Introduction: investigating the core concept and its moral status', in Christian Coons and Michael Weber, eds., *Manipulation: Theory and Practice*. Oxford University Press, 1–16.

Damasio, Antonio, 1994. *Descartes' Error: Emotion, Reason and the Human Brain*. New York: G. P. Putnam's Sons.

Danto, Arthur, 1985. 'Philosophy as/and/of literature', in John Rajchman and Cornel West, eds., *Post-analytic Philosophy*. New York: Columbia University Press.

D'Arms, Justin and Daniel Jacobson, 2000. 'Sentiment and value', *Ethics* 110, 722–48.

Darwall, Stephen, 1995. 'Hume and the invention of utilitarianism', in M A. Stewart and John Wright, eds., *Hume and Hume's Connexions*. State College: Pennsylvania State University Press, 58–82.

Fassin, Didier, 2013. *Enforcing Order: An Ethnography of Urban Policing*. Malden, MA: Polity Press.

Flyvbjerg, Bent, 2001. *Making Social Science Matter*. Cambridge University Press.

Frazer, Michael, 2007. 'John Rawls: between two enlightenments', *Political Theory* 35, 756–80.

Frazer, Michael, 2010. *The Enlightenment of Sympathy: Justice and the Moral Sentiments in the Eighteenth Century and Today*. Oxford University Press.

Frazer, Michael, 2013. 'Sentimentalism without relativism' in James Fleming, ed., *NOMOS LIII: Passions and Emotions*. New York University Press, 19–37.

Frazer, Michael, 2015. 'Anatomist and painter: Hume's struggles as a sentimental stylist', in Heather Kerr, David Lemmings and Robert Phiddian, eds., *Passions, Sympathy and Print Culture: Public Opinion and Emotional Authenticity in Eighteenth-Century Britain*. New York: Palgrave Macmillan.

Frazer, Michael, Forthcoming. 'Interdisciplinary before the disciplines: sentimentalism and the science of man', in R. Debes and Karsten Stueber, eds., *Taking Ethical Sentimentalism Seriously*. Cambridge University Press.

Gewirth, Alan, 1968. 'Meta-ethics and normative ethics', *Mind* 69, 187–205.

Gewirth, Alan, 1970. 'Metaethics and moral neutrality', *Ethics* 78, 214–25.

Gibbard, Allan, 1990. *Wise Choices, Apt Feelings: A Theory of Normative Judgment*. Cambridge, MA: Harvard University Press.

Goffman, Alice, 2014. *On the Run: Fugitive Life in an American City*. Chicago, IL: University of Chicago Press.

Gross, Neil, 2013. *Why Are Professors Liberal and Why Do Conservatives Care?* Cambridge, MA: Harvard University Press.

Guenther, Lisa, 2013. *Solitary Confinement: Social Death and Its Afterlives*. Minneapolis: University of Minnesota Press.

Haidt, Jonathan, 2001. 'The emotional dog and its rational tail: a social intuitionist approach to moral judgment', *Psychological Review* 108, 814–34.

Hall, Cheryl, 2005. *The Trouble with Passion: Political Theory Beyond the Reign of Reason*. New York: Routledge.

Hume, David, 1985. *Essays, Moral, Political, and Literary*, ed. Eugene F. Miller. Revised Edition. Indianapolis, IN: Liberty Fund.

Hume, David, 2000a. *A Treatise of Human Nature*, eds. David Fate Norton and Mary Norton. Oxford University Press.

Hume, David, 2000b. *An Enquiry Concerning Human Understanding*, ed. Tom Beauchamp. Oxford University Press.

Kingston, Rebecca, 2011. *Public Passion: Rethinking the Grounds for Political Justice*. Montreal: McGill-Queen's University Press.

Krause, Sharon, 2008. *Civil Passions: Moral Sentiment and Democratic Deliberation*. Princeton, NJ: Princeton University Press.

Marcus, George, Russell Neuman and Michael Mackuen, 2000. *Affective Intelligence and Political Judgment*. University of Chicago Press.

Nichols, Shaun, 2004. *Sentimental Rules: On the Natural Foundations of Moral Judgment*. Oxford University Press.

Nussbaum, Martha, 1990. *Love's Knowledge: Essays on Philosophy and Literature*. Oxford University Press.

Nussbaum, Martha, 1995. *Poetic Justice. The Literary Imagination and Public Life*. Boston, MA: Beacon Press.

Prinz, Jesse, 2007. *The Emotional Construction of Morals*. Oxford University Press.

Prinz, Jesse, 2011. 'Is empathy necessary for morality?', in Amy Coplan and Peter Goldie, eds., *Empathy: Philosophical and Psychological Perspectives*. Oxford University Press, 211–29.

Rawls, John, 1996. *Political Liberalism*. Revised Paperback Edition. New York: Columbia University Press.

Rawls, John, 1999. *A Theory of Justice*. Revised Edition. Cambridge, MA: The Belknap Press of Harvard University Press.

Seneca, 2004. *Letters from a Stoic: Epistulae Morales ad Lucilium*, tr. Robin Campbell. New York: Penguin Classics.

Singer, Peter, 1972. 'Famine, affluence, and morality', *Philosophy and Public Affairs* 1, 229–43.

Slote, Michael, 2010. *Moral Sentimentalism*. Oxford University Press.

Smith, Adam, 1984. *The Theory of Moral Sentiments*, eds. A. L. Macfie and D. D Raphael. Indianapolis, IN: Liberty Fund.

Smith, Adam, 1985. *Lectures on Rhetoric and Belles Lettres*, ed. J. C. Bryce. Indianapolis, IN: Liberty Fund.

Solomon, R. C, 1970. 'Normative and meta-ethics', *Philosophy and Phenomenological Research* 31, 97–107.

Stevenson, Charles, 1944. *Ethics and Language*. New Haven, CT: Yale University Press.

Stewart, John, 2013. *The Unity of Content and Form in Philosophical Writing: The Perils of Conformity*. New York: Bloomsbury.

Thacher, David, 2006. 'The normative case study', *American Journal of Sociology* 111, 1631–76.

Thomson, Judith Jarvis, 1971. 'A defense of abortion', *Philosophy and Public Affairs* 1, 47–66.

Vermeule, Blakey, 2010. *Why Do We Care about Literary Characters?* Baltimore, MD: Johns Hopkins University Press.

Walzer, Michael, 2004. *Politics and Passion: Toward a More Egalitarian Liberalism.* New Haven, CT: Yale University Press.

Weber, Max, 1978. *Economy and Society,* eds. Guenther Roth and Claus Wittich. Berkeley: University of California Press.

Westen, Drew, 2007. *The Political Brain: The Role of Emotion in Deciding the Fate of the Nation.* New York: Public Affairs.

Williams, Bernard, 1981. *Moral Luck.* Cambridge University Press.

7   Realism

Robert Jubb

1   Introduction

Contemporary normative analytical political theory tends to think of itself as continuous with or at least an application of moral philosophy. For example, in the Introduction to his *Political Philosophy: A Beginner's Guide for Students and Politicians*, Adam Swift describes the discipline he is introducing as asking 'what the state should do', explaining that this means asking 'what moral principles should govern the way it treats its citizens' (Swift 2014: 5). Similarly, in the Introduction to his *Contemporary Political Philosophy*, Will Kymlicka says that 'there is a fundamental continuity between moral and political philosophy' (Kymlicka 2002: 5). This is because Robert Nozick was right to claim that moral philosophy sets the limits to what 'persons may and may not do to one another' including 'through the apparatus of a state' (Kymlicka 2002: 5). Nor is this only a feature of purportedly introductory texts. Cecile Fabre's *Cosmopolitan War* sees its attempt to articulate to integrate cosmopolitan principles of distributive justice and just war theory as uncomplicatedly an enquiry in 'applied ethics' (Fabre 2012: 3). Equally, the very first sentence of Thomas Christiano's *The Constitution of Equality: Democratic Authority and Its Limits* introduces its investigation into democratic authority by asking what 'the moral foundations of democracy and liberal rights' are (Christiano 2008: 1).

Realism rejects this understanding of how normative political theory should operate. This 'moralist' or 'ethics first' approach to normative political theory is, realists claim, fundamentally mistaken. The precise description of moralism's sins varies from realist theorist to realist theorist, but as realism's reaction against moralism grows in strength, various themes have emerged. This chapter treats Bernard Williams's 'Realism and moralism in political theory' as an archetypical piece of realism, using it to suggest that realists share a common commitment to the idea that politics is the contextually specific management of conflicts generated by our inability to order our lives together around an agreed set of complete moral values. It then goes on to try to demonstrate how that understanding of politics constrains normative political theorizing. Realists have not typically been very eager to move beyond critiques of moralism by engaging in first-order theorizing themselves. Although I discuss some reasons why this may be, I nonetheless explore how realism might structure our thinking about egalitarian political commitments. In the course of doing so, I provide a series of guidelines a piece of political theorizing should follow if it is to remain realist.

Section 2 discusses Williams and his realism. Section 3 provides a set of guidelines for realist political theorizing by considering a realist case for political egalitarianism. Section 4 summarizes the guidelines from the previous section and includes a warning about the possibility of genuinely political theorizing.

2   Bernard Williams's Exemplary Realism

The current realist movement in political theory seems to have begun to take off with the posthumous publication of a series of papers by the British philosopher Bernard Williams. His collection, *In the Beginning Was the Deed*, and particularly its first paper, 'Realism and moralism in political theory' (hereafter RMPT), gave new and powerful voice to an often long-held dissatisfaction with the dominant forms of political theory in the Anglophone world (Williams 2005a, 2005b). Although in many ways, Williams was there merely reiterating concerns he had previously publicly aired, often in more polished forms, RMPT served as a focus around which a range of complaints could coalesce. It has, for example, around five times the number of citations as his last major article, which, although it does not use the terms 'realism' and 'moralism', is in effect an attempt to develop a realist theory of liberty by taking into account various political constraints (Williams 2005c)[1]. According to William Galston's influential survey article, we even owe Williams the term 'realism' as a way of grouping together those dissatisfied with the way the 'high liberalism' of Rawls and Dworkin ignores the centrality of conflict and instability to political questions (Galston 2010: 386, 385). If we are to group together theorists as different as John Dunn and Bonnie Honig, Chantal Mouffe and Mark Philp, then it is to Williams we must look. It is then with Williams and RMPT that I will start.

---

[1] See https://scholar.google.co.uk/scholar?cites=10056158126568575885&as_sdt=2005&sciodt=0,5&hl=en and https://scholar.google.co.uk/scholar?cites=3956932321022311105&as_sdt=2005&sciodt=0,5&hl=en.

RMPT begins with a distinction between two different ways of thinking about the relation of 'morality to political practice' (RMPT: 1). While an enactment model of that relation surveys society 'to see how it may be made better' and so makes politics 'the instrument of the moral', a structural model is instead concerned with 'the moral conditions of co-existence under power' and so emphasizes 'constraints ... on what politics can rightfully do' (RMPT: 1–2). While utilitarianism is a paradigmatic case of the former, Rawls's theory exemplifies the latter (RMPT: 1). Despite the important differences that Williams identifies between the enactment and the structural model, they share a commitment to 'the priority of the moral over the political' and so make political theory 'something like applied morality' (RMPT: 2). Williams goes on to contrast this 'political moralism' with 'political realism', 'which gives a greater autonomy to distinctively political thought' (RMPT: 2–3).

Giving greater autonomy to distinctively political thought involves focusing on what Williams calls 'the first political question' of 'securing of order, protection, safety, trust and the conditions of cooperation' (RMPT: 3). This Hobbesian question is first not in the sense that it can be solved and then ignored, but instead in the sense that its being and remaining solved is a condition of posing, never mind solving, any other political questions (RMPT: 3). For Williams, groups that do not attempt to answer the first political question for themselves and their members do not have politics. If order is not being created out of division in a way that in some sense at least hopes to avert recognizably Hobbesian bads, politics is simply not going on. Similarly, an activity or system of thought is only political if it is circumscribed by a need to contain conflict among those at whom it is aimed. As Williams puts it in the context of a discussion of the relation between the Spartans and the Helots, the 'situation of one lot of people terrorizing another lot of people is not per se a political situation; it is rather the situation which the existence of the political is in the first place supposed to alleviate' (RMPT: 5). However we want to characterize the undesirability of Hobbesian bads – and there will surely be a range of ways to describe what is wrong with them – politics is what goes on when we seek to avert them through coercive orders.

Williams goes on to draw various further consequences from this understanding of politics. He offers the idea of the basic legitimation demand, which requires that some justification of claims to political authority is offered to all those who are subject to it (RMPT: 4). After all, the situation of the Spartans and the Helots is just one of any number of examples that demonstrate that political power can contribute to the problem of our absolute vulnerability to violence rather than offer a solution to it. As Williams puts it, '*something* has to be said to explain . . . what the difference is between the solution and the problem', to explain why the exercise of political power should not be treated simply as an illegitimate attempt at domination (RMPT: 5). The basic legitimation demand is the demand for that something. If it is a moral demand, 'it does not represent a morality which is prior to politics' (RMPT: 5). Instead, the basic legitimation demand follows from 'there being such a thing as politics', from aiming to answer the first political question, from showing that attempted solutions are not in fact 'part of the problem' (RMPT: 5).

Williams further claims that under contemporary conditions, only liberalism can adequately answer the basic legitimation demand (RMPT: 7–8). This has not always been the case, but liberals have managed to raise 'expectations of what a state can do', adopted 'more demanding standards of what counts as a threat to people's vital interests', and expanded the range of ways in which supposed justifications can come to seem like mere rationalizations (RMPT: 7). Answers to the basic legitimation demand must always be historically variable in this sense: they must 'make sense' of what they legitimate as 'an intelligible order of authority' to those to whom it must be legitimated (RMPT: 10). The universalist tendencies of political moralism that invite us to imagine ourselves 'as Kant at the court of King Arthur' may offer us a genuine possibility, but it is not a productive one (RMPT: 10). Performing that thought experiment will not help us 'to understand anything' about societies distant from ours in time and space, except perhaps that they are distant not only in time and space (RMPT: 10). It is only when we think about our own society and those it interacts with that what makes sense as an intelligible order of authority becomes normative rather than a 'category of historical understanding' (RMPT: 11).

Political moralism fails in terms of this understanding of politics. By starting with a moralized and philosophical conception of the person, it puts itself in a position from which it is impossible to give adequate normative guidance about when Hobbes's first political question has been answered. A liberal conception of the person is the product and not the justificatory foundation of the liberal political institutions we live under now. Treating it as the foundation makes it impossible to provide an explanation of those institutions or why we have them now and others, elsewhere or at other times, do or did not (RMPT: 8–9). Further, because political moralism sees politics as the application of moral philosophy to political problems, it does not understand how to deal with political disagreement. It 'naturally construes conflictual political thought in society in terms of rival elaborations of a moral text' and so sees its opponents as 'simply mistaken' instead of fellow democratic political actors whose deeply held commitments are at stake in political decisions (RMPT: 12, 13).

Realism in general shares both RMPT's hostility to much contemporary political philosophy and its diagnosis of its problems. The survey articles by Galston and by Rossi and Sleat offer four features characteristic of realism's rejection of what it sees as the moralism dominant in contemporary political philosophy (Galston 2010: 408; Rossi and Sleat 2014: 691–4). Although their lists do not overlap perfectly, there is an understandable degree of similarity. For example, Galston begins his list by claiming that realism involves taking 'politics seriously as a particular field of human endeavour' and that this means holding that 'civil order is the *sine qua non* for every other political good' (Galston 2010: 408). In turn, Rossi and Sleat first stress the importance for realists of the 'broadly Hobbesian thought ... that if ethics could effectively regulate behaviour in political communities as it does amongst (say) friends and acquaintances, we would not require politics' (Rossi and Sleat 2014: 691). In both cases, this mandates an attention to 'the specific conditions under which political decisions are taken and agents act' (Rossi and Sleat 2014: 694), whether that be in terms of a focus on institutions and a more developed moral psychology or on the history of our moral commitments and the tragic choices that political actors may find it impossible to avoid (Galston 2010: 408; Rossi and Sleat 2014: 691–4).

Many of the elements in terms of which Galston and Rossi and Sleat define realism are present in RMPT. RMPT is hostile to much contemporary political philosophy and theory on the grounds that it is not properly political in one sense or another. Williams's discussion understands politics in terms of the provision of order for agents whose interests and ideals conflict in a way that otherwise might well make it impossible for them to coexist. In stressing the importance of conflict to political thinking, Williams here also insists on the importance of context. The universalist tendencies of contemporary political philosophy and theory are part of what prevent it from addressing real political situations, which always involve actual political actors with particular disagreements. Those disagreements and the resources the situation makes available to resolve them need to be properly understood if anything helpful is going to be said about them. This will mean appreciating how we came to find ourselves here, with these conflicts and these means of defusing and controlling them. The history and specificity of our situation need to be understood so that we can grasp the limits on what we can do.

Although Williams expresses scepticism about what he sees as Habermas's project to show that 'the concept of modern law harbours the democratic ideal' in RMPT (16), he acknowledges that the discussion in RMPT occurs at 'a very high level of generality' and so does not contain any concrete positive claims of the sort he criticizes Habermas for making (15). In that sense, despite being the best known of Williams's realist pieces, there is not really any firm advice about how to do realist political theory or philosophy in RMPT. Even elsewhere, when for example Williams is discussing the particular political value of liberty, although he is eager to tell us how not to judge whether someone really does have a complaint in liberty, there is little positive theorizing. We are told that competition is not, for us here and now, the ground of a complaint that liberty has been lost but that one's position in a social structure can be, and that because of our disenchantment, liberty is more important to us than many of our forebears, all at roughly this level of generality (Williams 2005c: 91, 95). Nor is Williams unusual here. Self-identified realists have been much more interested in diagnosing problems with contemporary political philosophy than replacing the positive theorizing they criticize.

Part of the reluctance to be more forthcoming here is undoubtedly the importance Williams and other realists give to political action. Even if the title were chosen by Williams's editor and widow, it is obviously no accident that the posthumous collection containing RMPT is called *In the Beginning Was the Deed*. Williams treats that dictum from Goethe's *Faust* as a reminder that politics is about action and so will often escape our attempts to model or predict it because of the way its participants' acts will transform it, including by creating the conditions of their own success. As well as quoting it in RMPT, Williams uses Goethe's dictum as the title for another of the pieces in the posthumous collection (RMPT: 14; Williams 2005d). However, unless realists think that political theory or philosophy is a necessarily impossible activity, it must be capable of at least sometimes meeting those conditions. Indeed, Williams's own career, which involved sitting on a number of Royal Commissions and contributing to the British Labour Party's Commission on Social Justice, suggests that he felt that political theory and philosophy could address concrete political questions without falling victim to the pathologies of moralism. By in part drawing on some of Williams's own work on equality, the remainder of this piece will try to illustrate how that might be done.

3   **Working through a Case: Legitimacy and a Realistic Egalitarianism**

Williams insisted that only a liberal state could be legitimate under the conditions of modernity (see for example RMPT: 7–8). It is this, and the arguments this might give us for commitments to relatively high levels of material equality, that will serve as examples to demonstrate how to do positive realist political theorizing. The first task here is to understand why Williams thought that liberalism was the only way of legitimating a state in modernity. Although political situations must involve the management of conflict between agents whose commitments and interests cannot all be satisfied, for realists they are never exhausted by that characterization. Responding to a political situation then will have to mean responding to its particularities. **Realists must rely on an interpretation of a political situation that captures its specificities;** otherwise, they will be guilty of the universalism and the associated failure to address real political agents for which they criticize moralists.

Williams believed that modernity required liberalism because it had raised expectations of what the state could do while undermining the ease with which hierarchies can be justified (see for example RMPT: 7). The idea that modernity involves the triumph of rationality over mystical and supernatural explanations is a persistent theme throughout Williams's work, from 'The idea of equality' (hereafter IoE) in 1962 to *Truth and Truthfulness* in 2002 (Williams 2005e: 105; 2002: 231). If hierarchies of rank of the sort liberals tend to reject are not to depend on brute coercion, they must rely on seeming 'foreordained and inevitable' and so are 'undermined' by growth of their members' 'reflective consciousness', especially about the way that such hierarchies tend to enculturate their members (IoE: 105). If a modern political order was to be justified then, for Williams, it had to be justified to Weberian disenchanted agents. **A realist theory of a political good like legitimacy must be fitted to the particular political situation in which it is to be invoked.**[2]

Of course, Williams's interpretation of our situation now and around here is hardly uncontested. One might think of Alasdair MacIntyre's insistence that something roughly like the processes that undermined Williams's 'supposedly contented hierarchical societies of the past' were a disaster for reflective moral understanding analogous to the destruction of science as a practice of investigation and understanding (MacIntyre

---

[2] There is in this sense a link between practice-dependence and realism. See Sangiovanni (2008) for a definition of practice-dependence and Jubb (2016) for discussion of the relation between the two.

1981: 1–2; Williams 2011: 181). If modernity has left us with 'fragments of a conceptual scheme' stripped of the 'contexts from which their significance derived' in the place where integrated notions of the good life ought to be, then Williams's support for liberalism will seem, at best, acquiescence in a cultural catastrophe of an unimaginably vast scale (MacIntyre 1981: 2, 3). MacIntyre's stance here is at least in tension with realism because of the way in which it refuses to deal with the agents with which it understands itself as being faced. For MacIntyre, we are doomed by the complete disintegration of the traditional authorities that made possible the Thomist virtues we need for decent lives. How does that diagnosis of our problems tell us to structure our lives together? It must absolutely reject not just those institutions and their associated historical and sociological forms but with them, us.

In this sense, **a realist political theory must be based on an interpretation of our political situation that refuses both the related consolations of utopian hope and unremitting despair.** MacIntyre believes that modernity makes it impossible for us to live decent lives. He combines utopianism with despair by claiming that unless we undo all the history of at least the past three centuries, we are doomed to live fractured, empty lives. The rejection of everything there is prompts the search for something beyond it. This is not to say that such interpretations or even the commitments for which they serve as foundations are incorrect or inappropriate. It is instead to point out that if any really achievable social order destroys all but the most minimal human values, then it is hard to understand the point or even the possibility of 'securing order, protection, safety, trust, and the conditions of cooperation' (RMPT: 3). There will be no political values for distinctively political thought to articulate. Whether they are conservative or radical, realists must be able to say something that can make sense of the value of politics as an activity. The temptation to slip into moralist condemnation needs to be resisted.

Emphasizing this may cast some doubt on the credentials of some self-proclaimed realists, at least if they intend their realism to involve 'distinctively political thought' in Williams's sense (RMPT: 3). Raymond Geuss, for example, not only sees himself operating in the tradition of critical theory typified by Theodor Adorno; he criticizes Williams for 'paddling about in the tepid and slimy puddle created by Locke, J. S. Mill and Isaiah Berlin' rather than adopting Adorno's rejection of both the 'self-serving "liberalism" of the Anglo-American political world and the brutal practices of "really-existing socialism"' (Geuss 2012: 150). He also sees himself as a realist; his *Philosophy and Real Politics* is a relentless attack on behalf of realism against what he calls 'ethics-first' political philosophy (see for example Geuss 2008: 9). However, anyone taking their lead from

Adorno may find themselves too pessimistic about our historical and political situation to be able to do justice to what we can achieve through politics.

Adorno argued that while 'social freedom is inseparable from enlightened thought,' '[t]he only kind of thinking that is sufficiently hard to shatter myths is ultimately self-destructive' (Adorno and Horkheimer 1979: xiii, 4). If as a result our civilization is in fact a kind of 'barbarism', its social orders will presumably be little more than 'one lot of people terrorizing another lot of people' in more and less open ways (Adorno and Horkheimer 1979: xi; RMPT, 3). That will make it difficult to understand how, for example, Williams's first political question could be answered satisfactorily. Geuss may then not be a realist, at least in the sense I am using here. Following Adorno, he insists both that living a decent life is impossible within the 'repressive, duplicitous and alienated' social forms of late capitalist modernity and that it is impossible for us realistically 'to envisage any fundamental change in our world we could bring about by our own efforts' (Geuss 2012: 154, 160). If our historical and political situation means that our lives cannot avoid being 'radically defective', an 'impossible situation', then we will struggle to find, let alone implement or grasp the value of, ways of living together that do not betray all our hopes (Geuss 2012: 154).

There are ways to reject Williams's account of modernity that do not see it as made up of ideas that are 'misshapen, brittle, riven with cracks ... and very ill-suited to each other', and so under which it is impossible to live coherently (Geuss 2001: 9). We might, for example, question whether Williams can be right about liberalism being the only way that a modern political order can make sense to its members. One does not have to subscribe to claims about the superiority of alleged Asian values to see that various states in East Asia seem to be accepted by most of their citizens yet are neither liberal nor underdeveloped compared to the North Atlantic democracies Williams presumably had in mind when equating liberalism and modernity. There are problems too for Williams's claim even in Europe, where we might assume it would be most apt given its association with the Enlightenment and its supposedly demystifying aftermath. Many European states, most obviously those of the former Warsaw Pact, have been and in some cases remain modern and illiberal without obviously failing to give a broadly acceptable account of themselves to their citizens, even in the medium term. Even if modernity is disenchanted, it seems that there are a variety of ways of responding to that disenchantment. **The interpretation of the relevant political situation on which a realist relies must not generate obviously**

implausible implications, as Bernard Williams's does if he is taken to be discussing modernity in general.

Rawls is often the target of realists' attack on moralism. He exemplifies one of Williams's two forms of moralism, while Galston begins his survey of realism by rightly describing it as a 'countermovement' to the 'high liberalism' championed by Rawls and Dworkin. However, in his later works, Rawls drew a distinction between political and comprehensive theories and defended the political credentials of his own work (Rawls 2005). Part of this involved situating his theorizing 'in the special nature of democratic political culture as marked by reasonable pluralism' (Rawls 2005: xxi). That culture has its roots in 'the doctrine of free faith' developed in the aftermath of the Reformation that rejects the idea that 'social unity and concord requires agreement on a general and comprehensive religious, philosophical, or moral doctrine' that might otherwise have seemed natural in a world of 'salvationist, creedal, and expansionist religions' (Rawls 2005: xxv). These conditions do not characterize all twentieth-century European societies, let alone all societies that might be described as modern, as for example Rawls's references to the Weimar Republic's loss of confidence in a 'decent liberal parliamentary regime' show he was well aware (Rawls 2005: lix). In that sense, not only do Rawls and realists share concerns about treating political philosophy as a branch of ethics, but Rawls is in fact clearer than Williams is about the relatively restricted scope of the interpretation of the political situation on which his principles rely.

Realist disagreement with Rawls should not focus on his alleged failure to address properly political questions, since his later theory is in fact explicitly arranged around addressing a particular, historically situated form of disagreement, but on the tools with which he chooses to address them. The problem with Rawls's theory is not that it ignores Hobbes's question, but that it treats it as soluble through appeals to an ideal of free and equal citizenship (see for example Rawls 2005: xxv). Rawls is wrong to think that philosophical abstraction can by itself offer a way of dealing with 'deep political conflicts' like those between Lincoln and his opponents over slavery, because those conflicts are obviously not only philosophical disagreements (Rawls 2005: 44, 45). Rawls's understanding of the dilemmas of modern democratic life is inadequate because it ignores both the role of material interests in our political life and the cognitive and motivational limits of philosophical reasoning. When Rawls developed his theory, in the long period of Keynesian growth after World War II, there were real political movements that officially had plausible hopes for something like what he prescribed. Although in that sense, his views are not pejoratively utopian, his inadequate understanding of the dilemmas of modern democratic life means they are not realist. Those political movements did not draw on philosophical ideals to draw together and motivate their supporters, but on shared experiences of hardship and solidarity built up in the course of struggles against it. **Realists must acknowledge the importance of material interests and ideological and charismatic appeals, especially compared to philosophical reasoning, when theorizing political goods to fit particular political situations**.

Rawls's and Williams's interpretations of modernity illustrate two errors to which interpretations of a political situation may fall victim. Complacency about the generality of an interpretation or about the motivational and cognitive power of philosophy is not realistic. However, we can avoid both of those problems by marrying Rawls's cultural and geographical circumspection to Williams's emphasis on disenchantment. Such an interpretation of modernity will neither apply beyond the societies with which both theorists were familiar nor end up depending on the power of reason alone. This leaves us with a roughly liberal principle of transparency, which, rather than requiring a system capable of being endorsed by all 'in light of principles and ideals acceptable to their common human reason', builds on Williams's idea of the 'human point of view' (Rawls 2005: 137; IoE, 103).

The human point of view is a perspective that, when considering someone's else's life, 'is concerned primarily with what it is *for that person* to live that life and do those actions' (IoE: 103). It asks us to 'respect and try to understand other people's consciousness of their own activities', whether they manage to do what they hoped and how they feel about failures they suffer (IoE: 103). The human point of view can become a demand for transparency and rule out, Williams claims, markedly unequal societies because of the frustrations and resentments they will predictably generate. Once the idea that societies are human creations spreads, those frustrations and resentments can no longer be justified because they will no longer seem inevitable (IoE, 105). If relations between members of those societies are not to be conducted on the basis of brute force or systematic deception, neither of which can be acceptable from the human point of view, then hierarchies cannot be too steep or pervasive (IoE: 104–5). If the hierarchies are too steep or pervasive, then the social and political order that sustains them will seem too unsympathetic to the 'intentions and purposes' of those at the wrong end of those hierarchies (IoE: 103). The terms on which that sympathy operates will need to be thinner, to assume less about the commitments of those whom it is for, than the terms on which it operated in 'supposedly contented hierarchical societies of the past' (see for example Williams 2005f). It will be unable to take for granted the set of commitments we all supposedly shared in those societies. Those are gone, along with metaphysical or supernatural explanations that sustained the idea that the associated hierarchies were unavoidable. Still, that sympathy will need to be there if the political order is to 'make sense' to its members, to avoid failing to meet the basic legitimation demand for at least those particularly disadvantaged by it.

In understanding what this account of legitimacy in North Atlantic democracies might judge acceptable, we should look to real political motivations. These need not be drawn directly from reality, as long as it is clear that they have some real-world counterparts (see for example Jubb 2015a). **Our accounts of political legitimacy or any other political good must be for actually existing agents, and we can best check that there is a constituency that they address by showing that they can capture and give form to political demands that animate actual agents.** If we were to develop an account of a political good that could not be seen as an articulation of a hope or resentment that drives a stance towards a political order real people actually adopt, then that failure would count strongly against the account being genuinely realist. For example, connecting an interpretation of Williams's minimally egalitarian account of legitimacy to the resentments that seem to have motivated the most widespread civil unrest in the United Kingdom in recent decades strengthens that account by showing that it could well make sense of those real political demands (see Jubb 2015b). A series of interviews conducted with hundreds of self-identified rioters found a 'pervasive sense of injustice' (Lewis et al. 2011: 24). Barely half of the rioters felt British, compared to more than 90 per cent of Britons on average, understandably given that they felt victimized by the police and excluded from a culture of consumption by their poverty (Lewis et al. 2011: 28, 19). These interviews seem to show then that a realist egalitarianism focusing on the systematic frustration of the hopes and expectations of the least advantaged speaks to real political motivations.

Realism does not just demand that political goods are for actual agents. Actual agents may of course make demands that are not properly political and so realists will have to temper and limit them. Indeed, the intense moralism of much democratic political debate, which is for example often captivated both on the left and the right by nostalgia for supposedly lost forms of ethical community, may be a serious problem for realists. Even if that moralism can be contained within the boundaries of the properly political for now, there is presumably always a risk that dissatisfaction with the inevitable compromises of political life will break through those limits and put various political goods at risk. **Descriptions of political goods meant for moralistic publics will have to explain in terms**

they can understand why they must satisfy themselves with less moral unity than they would like. In this sense, realist political theory needs to draw not just on an interpretation of a political situation, but also on an interpretation that is capable of being publicly stated and accepted without, for example, undermining itself. If an account of legitimacy shows a population they share less than they thought, it may prevent them from sharing even that.

This is just one of a number of risks that realist pieces of theorizing face as a result of the constraints imposed by the need to remain political. The most obvious of these is that the theorizing itself relies on controversial moral values. Realist political theorizing would be moralistic in this sense if it relied on value claims that, if they were acceptable to the constituency the theory addresses, would eliminate its political problems. Politics is in part constituted by our disagreement on values around which to order our shared institutions. Consequently, **realist political theory must not appeal to values or interpretations of values whose controversy is, at least as far as its interpretation of the relevant political situation is concerned, a defining feature of that situation**.

For example, if we were to try to articulate an egalitarian theory of legitimacy along the lines suggested by Williams's idea of the human point of view, we would need to avoid basing its appeal on an ideal of the good of living as equals. While perhaps there have been some communities where such an ideal could exert enough power over most of its members to distinguish between legitimate and illegitimate rule, our society is not one. It is too divided to demonstrate the acceptability of its massively coercive, structuring power by appealing to the idea that relations of equality are central to a good life. Even if that ideal seems attractive in the abstract, its acceptability in general will not decide how it should be weighed against other ideals when it inevitably conflicts with them. A solidaristic society may be all well and good for many citizens, but only as long as it does not suppress individuality, undermine individual responsibility, respect for one's traditions or any number of other ideals.

Instead, an egalitarian theory of legitimacy must be based on a less demanding account of the value of equality. Rather than requiring citizens to accept not just a moral ideal, but a particular ranking of that ideal against other competing ideals, some more minimal explanation of the value of equality and its connection to an entitlement to rule is needed. For Williams, one of the virtues of Judith Shklar's liberalism of fear was that it tried to address 'everybody' by drawing on 'the only certainly universal materials of politics ... power, powerlessness, fear, cruelty' (Williams 2005g: 59). As Shklar herself understood, the liberalism of fear's emphasis on minimizing our exposure to cruelty could be turned against hierarchy because of the way that abuses of power 'are apt to burden the poor and weak most heavily' (Shklar 1989: 28). Inequality often brings domination and humiliation in its wake, and so the importance of equality could be explained by trying to avoid those harms. Domination and humiliation count as harms in terms of many plausible ideals, and so understanding the value of equality through the value of avoiding them would minimize conflict between that value and others. Since generating and sustaining domination and humiliation seems to make power relations illegitimate, it would also connect answering the basic legitimacy demand with meeting various egalitarian requirements. **The values to which a realist political theory appeals must be minimal in the sense that they can expect to be accepted as playing whatever role is necessary by at least most members of the society to which they must 'make sense'.**

It is not enough to be able to say that, for example, inequality causes domination and humiliation. **Insofar as an explanation of what matters about a particular value depends on claims about how it links to other values, those claims have to be substantiated by an empirically sensitive account of how social and political life actually operates.** For example, G. A. Cohen claims that market interactions are 'typically' motivated by 'some mixture of greed and fear' in that other participants in markets 'are predominantly seen as possible sources of enrichment, and threats to one's success' (Cohen 2009: 40). This is supposed to contrast with and so help explain the value of an alternative motivation of community, which values reciprocal service (Cohen 2009: 39–45). It is, though, straightforwardly false that market interactions are predominantly structured around greed and fear. The norms of basic honesty and respect for property rights on which a functioning market depends could not survive if we all saw each other primarily as ruthless exploiters desperately hiding our vulnerabilities from each other to avoid them being taken advantage of. Cohen's account of the value of community is discredited by the obviously inadequate picture of human interactions on which it partly depends. In contrast, linking equality with avoiding domination and humiliation seems to have some empirical support. Work in social epidemiology like that of Michael Marmot, Richard Wilkinson and Kate Pickett suggests that inequalities tend to ossify into status hierarchies that dominate and humiliate those at the wrong end of them (Marmot 2004; Wilkinson and Pickett 2009).

4   A Summary and a Warning

At this point, we can summarize the guidelines for which I have so far argued and which together seem to me define realism, at least when contrasted to moralism in something like Bernard Williams's sense.

1. **A realist account of a political value must be based on an interpretation of the political situation in which the value is to be realized.**
2. **That interpretation of the situation must be plausible, not least in avoiding both relentless despair and utopian hope.**
3. **The value being theorized must be one that agents can be expected to respect as the theory requires without becoming moral saints.**
4. **Actual agents should also be able to see something of their expectations or aspirations in the theory that is being offered for their political situation, even if they may have more expansive hopes than it makes room for.**
5. **That theory should not rely on controversial interpretations or rankings of values, but try to make use of the evaluative and normative material the situation presents.**
6. **When connections are drawn between different normative or evaluative claims, as they will have to be, these connections must be based on plausible theories of and claims about how human life actually operates.**

These guidelines distinguish realism from moralism. Moralism is universalist and uninterested in the details of particular situations. Swift, Kymlicka, Fabre and Christiano are all engaged in ahistorical projects of justification in the works from which I quoted in the Introduction to this chapter. Nor do they see it as problematic to criticize individuals or the world for failing to live up to ideals in which they or it obviously have little or no interest. Few actually existing states meet or look likely to meet Christiano's demanding criteria for democratic legitimacy, for example (see e.g. Christiano 2008: 260–1). Certainly his own polity, the United States of America, is a very long way from meeting those criteria. Nor is it clear that those criteria, or those that Swift, Kymlicka and Fabre endorse in their books, relate to real political aspirations held by those outside the academy. Finally, the four do not seem to feel a need to show that the values they theorize can be integrated into a realistic picture of how human social and political life actually operates.

Following the directions I have given should make a realist theory of a particular political value adequate for a particular situation at a comparatively general level. There will be nothing about the theory itself that prevents it from making sense of the value of whichever political projects it favours to those for whom it favours them. Still, being in principle able to articulate a given political value to and for a particular group of people does not mean that the articulation will satisfy or be accepted by those people. Nor does it mean that they will actually be able to organize themselves into a collective capable of achieving whatever it demands or hopes. To move beyond generic and towards what we could call full realism, a theory should not just eliminate barriers to providing an account of a particular political value to those in a particular political situation. **A realist political theory should also show that its political projects can capture and hold the allegiance of people against the rival political projects that are bound to challenge them, and that the supporters who can be attracted can collectively put them into practice**.

This will mean understanding the political, social and economic dynamics operating in particular societies. For example, an egalitarian realist theory of legitimacy seems to face at least three related questions raised by the requirement that it show not only how it is generically, but also fully, concretely realist (see Jubb 2015b for more detail on these challenges for a realist egalitarianism). If a realist theory of legitimacy is to sensibly demand that states restrict their levels of inequality or risk becoming illegitimate, it needs to show, first, that enforcing limits on inequality will not, as a matter of fact, undermine various other values. After all, for example, equality is often associated with societies and groups that tend to repress difference, and so we might find that however desirable equality is in theory, in practice there is no way of achieving it that does not compromise too many of our other commitments. Second, it must be politically possible to fulfil the demands of an egalitarian realist theory of legitimacy. If supporters of higher levels of equality cannot dominate the political scene, or if their dominance would inevitably bring about economic collapse caused by, say, capital flight, then we will have to change our attitudes. Either we will have to understand ourselves differently, as needing a different kind of explanation of what our states must do for us, or, alternatively, we will have to see our state as an alien, dominating force for at least some of its members. Third, we need to have a reasonable expectation that a constituency can be united around the indignities of inequality, and that they will not seek to deal with the frustrations associated with inequality in other ways. Otherwise, it would not be clear how the theory answered a real rather than imagined problem.

Political theorists are often unlikely to be able to meet these requirements. Indeed, even scholars with empirical expertise may not often be able to meet them given the unpredictability of political life. In this sense, political realism's emphasis on politics as a distinctive sphere of life limits the role of scholars, especially given the importance of action in that understanding of politics. The deliberately modest understanding of political theorists as 'democratic underlabourers' offered by Adam Swift and Stuart White, for example, seems in fact inappropriate and over-ambitious (Swift and White 2008: 54). The problem is not primarily, as Swift and White worry, that offering philosophical arguments will bypass the proper democratic process (Swift and White 2008: 55). It is instead that philosophical arguments are dangerously unsuited to political pro-blems. Nor will positivist empirical theories of political processes often be any better off. Politics shapes the problems with which it has to deal by shaping the agents, both individual and collective, whose motivations and dispositions create its problems. A theory of politics capable of under-standing all the processes relevant to its own applicability would be too complex for humans to understand, and of course itself a tool that, were it understood, it would have to include in its assessment of the relevant dynamics.

Political theories are in this sense necessarily incomplete. Politics is a sphere of judgement instead of scientific understanding, which will be vindicated by the acts it recommends having the intended effects and so after the fact, once the situation has been changed. No political theory can show completely that it captures and deals appropriately with a particular political situation, and so no political theory can be fully realistic. Like judgements, though, political theories can be better and worse. Realists believe that working with the guidelines they provide will at least make them more likely to avoid failing by not being about politics at all.

Acknowledgements

I sent earlier drafts of this to Ed Hall, Enzo Rossi, Paul Sagar, Matt Sleat and Patrick Tomlin, all of whom were kind enough to send very helpful comments. Adrian Blau's editorial suggestions also substan-tially improved the piece. I am grateful to all of them, and even more so to Adrian for asking me to contribute to this volume in the first place.

References

Adorno, Theodor and Horkheimer, Max, 1979. *The Dialectic of Enlightenment*. London: Verso.
Christiano, Thomas, 2008. *The Constitution of Equality*. Oxford University Press.

Cohen, G. A., 2009. *Why Not Socialism?* Princeton, NJ: Princeton University Press.

Fabre, Cecile, 2012. *Cosmopolitan War*. Oxford University Press.

Galston, William, 2010. 'Realism in political theory', *European Journal of Political Theory* 9: 385–411.

Geuss, Raymond, 2001. *History and Illusion in Politics*. Cambridge University Press.

Geuss, Raymond, 2008. *Philosophy and Real Politics*. Princeton, NJ: Princeton University Press.

Geuss, Raymond, 2012. 'Did Williams do ethics?', *Arion* 19: 141–62.

Jubb, Robert, 2015a. Playing Kant at the court of King Arthur', *Political Studies* 63: 919–34.

Jubb, Robert, 2015b. 'The real value of equality', *The Journal of Politics* 77: 679–691.

Jubb, Robert, 2016. '"Recover it from the facts as we know them": practice-dependence's predecessors', *Journal of Moral Philosophy* 13(1): 77–99.

Kymlicka, Will, 2002. *Contemporary Political Philosophy: An Introduction*. Second Edition. Oxford University Press.

Lewis, Paul, Tim Newburn, Matthew Taylor, Catriona Mcgillivray, Aster Greenhill, Harold Frayman and Rob Proctor, 2011. *Reading the Riots: Investigating England's Summer of Disorder*. London: The London School of Economics and Political Science and The Guardian.

MacIntyre, Alasdair. 1981 *After Virtue: A Study in Moral Theory*. Notre Dame, IN: University of Notre Dame Press.

Marmot, Michael, 2004. *Status Syndrome: How Your Social Standing Directly Affects Your Health*. London: Bloomsbury.

Rawls, John. 2005. *Political Liberalism*. 2nd edition. New York: Columbia University Press.

Rossi, Enzo and Matt Sleat, 2014. 'Realism in normative political theory', *Philosophy Compass* 9/10: 689–701.

Sangiovanni, Andrea, 2008. 'Justice and the priority of politics to morality', *Journal of Political Philosophy* 16: 137–64.

Shklar, Judith. 1989. 'The liberalism of fear', in Nancy Rosenblum, ed., *Liberalism and the Moral Life*. Cambridge, MA: Harvard University Press. 21–38.

Swift, Adam, 2014. *Political Philosophy: A Beginner's Guide for Students and Politicians*. Cambridge: Polity.

Swift, Adam and Stuart White, 2008. 'Political theory, social science, and real politics', in David Leopold and Marc Stears, eds., *Political Theory: Methods and Approaches*. Oxford University Press, 49–69.

Wilkinson, Richard and Kate Pickett, 2009. *The Spirit Level*. London: Allen Lane.

Williams, Bernard, 1997. 'Forward to basics', in J. Franklin, ed., *Equality*. London: Institute for Public Policy Research, 47–57.

Williams, Bernard, 2002. *Truth and Truthfulness*. Princeton, NJ: Princeton University Press.

Williams, Bernard, 2005a. *In the Beginning Was the Deed*. Princeton, NJ: Princeton University Press.

Williams, Bernard, 2005b. 'Realism and moralism in political theory', in Williams 2005a, 1–17.

Williams, Bernard, 2005c. 'From freedom to liberty: the construction of a political value', in Williams 2005a, 75–96.

Williams, Bernard, 2005d. 'In the beginning was the deed', in Williams 2005a, 18–28.

Williams, Bernard, 2005e 'The idea of equality', in Williams 2005a, 97–114.

Williams, Bernard, 2005f. 'Modernity and the substance of ethical life', in Williams 2005a, 40–51.

Williams, Bernard, 2005g. 'The liberalism of fear', in Williams 2005a, 52–61.

Williams, Bernard, 2011. *Ethics and the Limits of Philosophy*. London: Routledge.

8   Realistic Idealism

David Schmidtz

1   Theorizing for a Reason

Is moral philosophy more foundational than social philosophy? Is the question of how to live more fundamental than the question of how to live *in a community*? Are we getting down to philosophical foundations when we set aside contingencies regarding the communities in which political animals live, and proceed as if we were pure rational wills?

I see no reason to say yes to any of these questions.

To recover a measure of relevance to questions that practitioners need to answer – questions about how to live *as social beings* – theorizing about how to live together might take its cue less from moral philosophy and more from political economy. We can go beyond thought experiments. We can ask which principles have a history of being the organizing principles of flourishing communities. Let's say that realism studies the human condition as it is, while idealism studies the human condition as it should be.[1] Thus characterized, realism and idealism are distinct but compatible projects.

Realistic idealism, one of the many possible forms of idealism, studies what should be in light of a sober assessment of what could be, here and now. It aims to identify real possibilities, then ask whether an ideal response is among those possibilities. Realistically, it need not be. An ideal response is a best response, and intuitively something more: we call the best available response ideal only if we accept some fairly strong version of the thought that we could not have done better. Suppose we say Plan A is ideal, then find that Plan A is no solution at all – maybe it is infeasible because a key ingredient is missing. When we switch to our actual best response, Plan B, we do so with regret about a solution that *seemed* within reach and that *would* have been better. If we also restock the missing ingredient so that Plan A will be a real option next time, that implies that Plan B is merely best under the circumstances, not ideal.

---

[1] See also Robert Jubb's chapter on realism in this volume, and Sleat (2013).

Realistically, not all problems have solutions, let alone ideal solutions. Sometimes studying a problem helps us see what would solve it. Sometimes we learn that the best we can do is mitigate. To introduce the main bits of advice given in this chapter:

(a) **Start with problems**. We were taught to see sound theory as grounding sound practice and therefore as needing to come first. In practice, theories are answers; questions come first.

(b) **Start with diversity**. We need to coordinate on terms of engagement that are apt even among people who do not agree that those terms are apt. Theorizing does not help. We navigate the terrain of respect for separate persons with a compass far older than any theory.

(c) **Start with injustice, not justice**. In the real world, we have no vision of 'peak justice' in mind when deciding how to act. When deciding which car to try to drive home at the end of the day, we never consult the theory of justice we spent all day perfecting, except in self-mockery. Theory is not what teaches us how to avoid triggering people's sense of injustice.

Finally, if I had a bit of meta-advice about *how to handle my advice*, it would be: **proceed with caution**. Some of my advice will survive the test of time and turn out to be good advice, but there is no substitute for exercising your own judgement, being sceptical of contemporary theorizing about morality and justice, and taking your cue from the world rather than from the literature.

2   We Are Political Animals

One enduring feature of the human condition is that we are, after all, political animals. (1) We are decision-makers. (2) We are decision-makers who want and need to live together. (3) As decision-makers, we respond to circumstances. (4) As social beings, we respond to the circumstance *that we live among decision-makers* – other political animals who treat our choices as part of their circumstances and respond accordingly.

Social theory done well is theory about a world of separate persons – separate not only in an aspirational Kantian moral sense, but in a straightforward descriptive sense that each person is a locus of agency. People decide for themselves. We choose well only if we choose with a view to what we thereby give others a reason to do in response – that is, only if we do not take others for granted, do not treat them as pawns, and do not treat them as if they have a duty to be gripped by whatever vision is gripping us at the moment. If we are not theorizing along those lines, then we are not theorizing about politics.

Consider how the mundane observation that we are political animals implies a need to take a slightly but importantly different approach to moral theory (as developed in Schmidtz 2016; the following subsection is an overture for the argument set out in that essay).

2.1   Solipsism in Theory

(a) Kantians regard 'What can be universalized?' as a foundational question. People interpret that as a rough equivalent of 'what if everyone did that?' The subtle but crucial piece missing from this informal rendering: moral questions are questions for political animals living in a social world, which means a strategic world. The actual problem moral agents face is not a question of what maxim they could will everyone to follow. In a strategic world, interpreting universalizability in solipsistic terms – imagining a choice between everyone cooperating and everyone declining to cooperate – is not universalizable. It is a test that is blind to the strategically pivotal difference between reciprocating and unconditional cooperating. A strategic deontology acknowledges that we cannot universalize ignoring the fact that the exercise's point is to identify maxims fit for members of *a kingdom of players* – beings who decide for themselves.

Therefore, in a strategic world, imagining yourself unilaterally making *the* choice between everyone cooperating and everyone defecting is nothing like imagining yourself choosing for everyone in situations *relevantly like yours*. The *essence* of your situation is that you are *not* choosing for everyone.

So, my proposal is: treat strategic deontology as an alternative to 'act-deontology' and envision a choice among strategies, not actions. Maxims like 'I should cooperate' versus 'I should free-ride' miss the moral core of your alternatives. Instead, describe your alternative maxims as 'I should encourage partners to cooperate' versus 'I should encourage partners to free-ride.' Now you see that what is properly universalizable is acting so as to teach your partners to grasp their place in a kingdom of ends and thereby mature in the direction of moral worth. Teach them to cooperate.[2]

(b) We might observe, similarly, that Peter Singer's interpretation of the principle of utility – that we should sacrifice to a point of marginal disutility – is not straightforward. What I call parametric utilitarianism rests on an *empirical* premise: picking the act with the highest utility is like

---

[2] I do not suppose this move solves all of deontology's puzzles. It does, however, address some 'indeterminacy of description' problems in articulating a maxim's proper form as the subject of the universalizability test.

picking the outcome with the highest utility.[3] Given that supposition, the only thing to consider is which of our two options, give versus don't give, has more utility. If giving has more, then give. *Keep* giving until not giving would have more utility.

But the essence of a strategic world is that it does not give us that supposition. It is not an a priori truth that the *action* with the highest number leads to the *outcome* with the highest number, and in strategic situations it is a howling non sequitur. The numbers that *count* are not numbers attached to available *acts*, but numbers attached to possible *outcomes*, where outcomes are consequences not of particular acts, but of *patterns* of cooperation. In a strategic world, someone who cares about consequences aims to *induce a response*. *If* the ideal response is cooperative, then an ideal move is a move apt to induce that cooperative response. If consequences matter, then being moral in a strategic world is about *inducing* cooperative responses, not per se *choosing* them. That means being moral involves knowing when to walk away from the act with the highest number. **In strategic situations, if you want the best outcome for all, don't worry about other people's payoffs; worry about their strategies.**

Scottish Enlightenment theorists focused on the nature and source of the wealth of nations. They cared enough about consequences to study what has a history of actually working. They observed that prosperous societies are places where traders build partnerships around principles of reciprocity. It mattered to them that, in our world, actions have more than one consequence, more than the intended consequence, and the consequence you don't see coming will matter. The kind of act-utilitarianism Peter Singer incarnated circa 1972 is remarkably inattentive to what has any robust history of good consequences. It is useless not because it is obsessed with consequences, but because it largely ignores them.[4]

When moral theory conceives our world in solipsistic terms, practitioners living in a strategic world have to ignore it, because real morality requires people to make choices apt for the strategic world they actually

---

[3] In the terms of a Prisoner's Dilemma payoff matrix, the empirical premise I am warning against is the assumption that choosing a row ('cooperate') is the same thing as choosing a cell in the matrix ('mutual cooperation'). In a strategic world, it is nothing of the kind. One unilaterally chooses an act, a row, not as a way of unilaterally *choosing* an outcome, a cell, but rather as a way of *working towards* an outcome.

[4] Amartya Sen identifies himself as within the tradition of Adam Smith. Sen earned his Nobel Prize for his work on twentieth-century famines, showing that not one was caused by lack of food. Famine is caused by eroding rights, not eroding soil. When local farmers lose the right to choose what to grow or where to sell it, they lose everything, and that is when people starve. This is what Scottish Enlightenment theorists studied: *consequences* (that is, long-term cause and effect) not imagined best responses to potted thought experiments.

face.[5] To summarize an argument only hinted at here, the premise that moral problems are first of all political problems yields a landscape of moral theory somewhat unlike – relevantly unlike – what we see in our ethics textbooks today.

2.2   Political Animals Live in a Strategic World

Rawls says his assumption that bargainers choose for a closed society 'is a considerable abstraction, justified only because it enables us to focus on certain main questions free from distracting details' (1993: 12). In principle, this could be a legitimate move. As Alan Hamlin observes in his chapter in this volume, a map of the London Underground sets aside nearly everything about London, even distances and scale, so as to distil the one kind of information that the map's users seek to glean from it, namely the sequences of stops making up the network's lines.

Yet it is easy to slide from ignoring for clarity's sake to ignoring *with prejudice*: setting details aside not because they don't affect the answer, but precisely because they do (see also Hope 2010: 135). Although we must set aside distracting details and focus on the problem, one thing we must never set aside as a detail is *the problem*. Suppose an asteroid were about to collide with Earth. What would be an ideal response? Hypothesis: we first ask what would be right under ideal conditions. Leading our list of ideal conditions: ideally, there is no asteroid about to collide with Earth.

Having noted that ideally there is no asteroid, we respond in one of two ways. Either (1) we strive to make it true that there is no asteroid, or (2) we do what would be ideal if there were no asteroid. The latter overlooks what *should be* an obvious difference between doing what *is* ideal as opposed to doing what *would be* ideal under counterfactual conditions.

I say this should be an obvious point. Clearly it is no such thing, for overlooking the difference is a repeatedly observed blunder. Tucson's city government once sought to manage traffic flows by designating inner lanes of major roads as one-way lanes toward the city centre during the morning rush. During the evening rush, the same lanes reversed and became one-way lanes *from* the city centre. At off-peak times, inner lanes reverted to being left-turn lanes. In a world of ideal drivers, it might have solved the problem. In Tucson, with its daily influx of elderly drivers not necessarily quick to adapt to novel conventions, where one indecisive driver is enough to create a dangerous mess, the system was a recipe for traffic jams, accidents, and road rage.

---

[5] Singer himself is increasingly aware of such strategic considerations. See also Schmidtz (2015).

In effect, traffic managers set aside the problem. Or, instead of tackling a real problem, traffic managers solved an idealized problem. Their job was to optimize traffic flow, but they chose instead to do what *would* optimize traffic flow *if* drivers were ideal. **Beware of idealized problems.** In general, doing what would be ideal – if only the problem were the ideal problem! – is not a way of being a serious idealist.

Here is the kind of idealism that realistic idealists scorn: 'My solution is a hammer; therefore, the problem *ideally* would be a nail. Reality is not a nail, obviously, so no one is saying my hammer is a *real* solution. Still, I just proved that the ideal problem is a nail! Therefore, impractical though my hammer may be in the real world, it remains an *ideal.*'

By contrast, to a realistic idealist, saying a traffic management system would work for ideal drivers says nothing in its favour *even as an ideal.* An ideal traffic *manager* works with an accurate picture of the real problem.

Some idealizations approximate reality, so some ideal solutions are approximate solutions to real problems. Tucson traffic managers blundered into misconceiving their ideal solution as an approximate solution to a real problem. That I am not alone but instead live in a strategic world of separate agents who decide for themselves is not a distracting detail. If a proposal stipulates that people will not react to our intervention in the way human beings *do* react, then the intervention is not an approximate solution, or even a real response. If Rawls is right to say 'an important feature of a conception of justice is that it should generate its own support' (1999b: 119), then a serious investigator does not set aside whether a conception of justice actually has that feature. A serious investigator *checks.*

2.3   Solipsism as a Snapshot of Justice

There is a literature on whether Rawls was warranted in assuming ideal bargainers would fully comply with principles of justice. But consider how much greater a stretch it is to assume ideal bargainers not only take their own compliance but the compliance of *others* as given. Once we cross that line, we are no longer checking to see whether a conception has the key feature of being able to generate its own support. Instead, we are imagining what it would be like not to need to check – not to have a political problem. In different words, once we cross that line, we are no longer stipulating simply that ideal bargainers are honest; we also are stipulating that they are clueless about the human condition's core feature: that what people need from each other more than anything is to create conditions under which they can afford to trust each other.

G. A. Cohen's objection to Rawls is that

[I]f we assume, following Rawls, that individuals are motivated to comply with justice, then the need to trade off equality and well-being disappears. It only arises in the first place because talented people demand incentive payments to become more productive. But people who are motivated to realize justice fully would not demand incentive payments but rather increase productivity without them. (Hamlin and Stemplowska 2012: 57, paraphrasing Cohen 2008)

Perhaps Cohen thought that people motivated by justice would not demand incentive payments. But even if that were true, the fact remains that even unshakably motivated Rawlsian bargainers would demand motivating incentives for *the people they represent*. Rawlsian contractors have a tough assignment: they are contracting on behalf of people other than themselves. Rawls can stipulate that *bargainers* are whatever bargainers need to be to get Rawls's desired solution, but bargainers can't stipulate the character of human psychology. By assumption, Rawlsian bargainers know human psychology. Therefore, their moral motivation does not blind them to the reality of what motivates the classes of people they represent. They know that the psychology of citizens at large is exactly what it is. (See also James 2012: chap. 4.)

It is a mistake to think we are imagining what *is* ideal when we imagine what *would* be ideal if compliance were something we got for free, rather than being the precarious achievement that it is. We are supposed to be theorizing about how to form a community, hold it together and make it worth holding together. (Let's not confuse this with talking about policy as opposed to theory. To say political theory is theory about what holds communities together and makes them worth holding together is not to propose a policy; it is to identify political theory's subject matter.) Setting aside compliance problems goes astray not because it bears on ideals, but because it *fails* to bear on problems. To say 'ideally we would not have compliance problems' is like saying 'ideally we would not need to drive defensively.' It is a remark about a world whose problems are not like ours. We have a history of solving compliance problems, but there is no recognizable rendering of the human condition on which we do not *have* compliance problems.

To set aside that we live amongst agents – beings who decide for themselves whether to comply – is to set aside the defining problem of political theory. If an institution is ideal in a given setting, it is by virtue of what it leads people to do in that setting. **Keep this in mind: what isn't an ideal incentive structure isn't an ideal institution.** Whenever we choose an incentive structure, we choose the compliance problem that goes with it (Schmidtz 2011a).

2.4   Sometimes, Ignoring Feasibility also Ignores Desirability

When we ask whether we are looking at an ideal campground, we can ignore ravines standing between us and that supremely desirable campground. I agree with Estlund (2008: 269) and Cohen (2009: 10) that ravines bear on whether getting there is feasible, but not on whether getting there would be desirable. Further and crucially, the cost of getting there can affect whether *striving* to get there is desirable, but not whether *being* there is desirable.

But here is the key. In the imagined case, I agree that to ignore ravines is to ignore questions of feasibility, and that we can ignore feasibility and still be discussing an ideal. Yet we abandon anything recognizably ideal if we ignore whether a campground is *suitable as a place to camp*. To ignore what will befall us if we get there is to ignore not whether getting there is *feasible* but whether *being* there is *desirable*.

In a Carens Market, to use Estlund's (and Cohen's) example, we imagine everyone being taxed in such a way that everyone ends up with equal disposable income after taxes. Despite this, by hypothesis, we also imagine everyone working hard to maximize *gross* income. Estlund uses the example to stress: 'So the fact, if it is one, that we shouldn't institute the Carens Market because people won't comply with it, doesn't refute the theory' that people *should* comply (2011: 217). Estlund adds, 'it is doubtful that the content of social justice is sensitive in this way to untoward motivational features of people' (2011: 227).

But we choose how to conceive of justice, and whether we see human motivation as 'untoward' turns on whether the thing we want to *call* justice characteristically induces untoward behaviour. If we see that what we want to call justice has *that* characteristic feature, that is reason to stop calling it justice, or at least to stop calling it *ideal*. If it predictably would realize our worst potentials as human beings, the relevant lesson is not that the Carens Market is altogether infeasible, but that as an aspiration it is altogether unworthy.[6] It does not solve a problem; it solves an

---

[6] We can say, the *true* ideal here is not bare instituting, but rather a conjunction of instituting and complying. So, the actual Carens ideal is a conjunction of 'make sure work doesn't pay' and 'workers keep acting as if it does'. To Estlund, the fact that we should not implement the first conjunct when the second is false has no bearing on whether the conjunction as a whole is ideal – even if, in our strategic world, instituting the first conjunct is a paradigm of what *renders* the second one false. All sides seem to agree on this much: (1) The Carens incentive structure by itself is not ideal. (2) At best, it *would be* ideal only if we

idealized problem. The lesson is not that we have no way to get there, but that we have no reason to want to.

Some idealists think ignoring compliance problems is ignoring something analogous to whether a campground is *reachable*. Not so. Ignoring what an incentive structure would drive people to do is like ignoring whether a campground would be terrible.

2.5 *When Institutions Turn People into Monsters, Blame the Institutions*

Estlund is correct when he says 'that a standard won't be met might count against people's behavior rather than against the standard' (2011: 209). For example, we may predict that students will fail our exam, without blaming our exam. That point of agreement notwithstanding, the fact remains that responsible reflection on a predictably bad outcome begins with the role our standards play in bringing it about. That students predictably misread double negations is not a defect in our exam, but littering our exam with double negations is.

Of his utopian theory and its postulation of unrealistic standards, Estlund says:

People could be good, they just aren't. Their failures are avoidable and blameworthy, but they are also entirely to be expected as a matter of fact. So far, there is no discernible defect in the theory, I believe. For all we have said, the standards to which it holds people might be sound and true. The fact that people will not live up to them even though they could is a defect of the people, not of the theory. (2008: 264)[7]

Be that as it may, if we give people a system that trips them up, and don't *want* to trip them up, then we don't celebrate our ability to trip them up by saying, 'People could be good at avoiding the trap I set for them; they just aren't. That my system turns a normal human trait into a fatal flaw is entirely to be expected, but that is a defect of the people, not the system.'

Note: saying there is no *discernible* defect is not the same as saying there is no defect. If we want to discern whether our ideal is worth a try, then we will not treat our *tools for discerning defects* as distracting details. Yet, when

could assume workers will comply. But (3) if we can safely assume anything about worker compliance, it is the opposite.
What else needs to be said? Perhaps this: anything we have reason to regard as ideal surely has at least some potential not to be catastrophically misleading as a basis for practical proposals. There is no such potential in alleged ideals like '*when work stops paying, workers keep acting as if it does*'.
[7] By 'discernible defect' Estlund has something like blatant self-contradiction in mind. Being unfit for people as they are evidently is not a discernible defect, but is instead a defect of the people.

we set aside whether our vision has a robust history of being a hideous response to the human condition, we are working to make sure our vision has no *discernible* defect, while doing nothing to make sure it has no defect.

I may imagine how ideal it would be to move my pawn to K4, but if I fail to anticipate my partner's response, then my so-called imagination is, to chess players, the paradigm of failed imagination. It takes imagination to be a realist. The player who anticipates what can go wrong is the one whose imagination other chess players have reason to admire. Imagining what *would* be ideal in a parametric world is no substitute for being able to imagine what *is* ideal in a strategic world.

Estlund speaks of 'motivational features that are themselves moral defects'. Yet only some institutions elicit predictably defective behaviour, whereas other institutions are exactly right as responses to characteristically human motivational features. If sexism were an underlying propensity, switched on or off by institutional settings, then we have a duty to choose institutions that switch it off. If we choose institutions that switch sexism on, it is our choice of institutions that is reprehensible, not human nature. When a theorist conceives of justice as answering to a *vision* rather than to *people*, the defect is not in the people. If our vision is poisonous for people as they are, the right response is to stop blaming people for being ill equipped to survive what we want to give them, and to start wanting something else.

Crucially, it is false that people 'just aren't good'. How good people are is variable, sensitive to how their institutional structure handles their separateness as decision-makers. When it comes to fostering society as a cooperative venture, it is misleading to say people are not good. Rather, people are not *as* good (not as cooperative, not as benevolent, not as trusting) when operating within frameworks that make free-riding pay.

Pablo Gilabert says, 'It is part of the job of political philosophy to keep ambitious ideals clear and visible, and to criticize a political culture when it becomes complacent and superficial' (2015: ms). I agree. Yet the phrase 'ivory tower' designates philosophy that is complacent and superficial, not ambitious. Insisting on tracking evolving reality is one way – I suspect there is no other – to keep ambitious ideals clear and visible.

It was not an ambitious ideal that drove G. A. Cohen's (2003) retreat into 'feasibility is philosophically irrelevant' mode, as communism fell apart before his eyes. If you are discouraged and hate to admit that your case for communism's economic superiority has been tested and found wanting, then you lean towards a particular kind of idealism. By contrast, **if you want to avoid complacency, don't judge people according to whether they fit your vision. Judge your vision according to whether it fits them.**

2.6   Realism and Conservatism

Judging your vision according to whether it is a competent response to the
human condition is not a way of being conservative. Starting from here is
a way of *starting*, not a way of *staying*, so realism is an orientation towards
progress, not a form of conservatism. To a realist, reality is not what needs
justifying so much as what needs *improving*.

Note that the relevant notion of feasibility here is dynamic; what can't
be done today may one day be within reach. It's *realistic* to anticipate that
the ceiling of possibility will someday look very different from how it looks
today. In 1789, William Wilberforce arguably had no way to muster the
votes to abolish England's slave trade, yet it manifestly was feasible to
work towards a day when England would have the will to abolish it.
We can be biased in an unrealistically conservative as well as an unrealistically radical direction. We underestimate prospects for change at least as
often as we overestimate them.[8]

3   We Are Diverse

Theorizing about how political animals should live could start by observing the extent of disagreement and diversity in human society. One
implication of diversity: diversity is only one of many places to start, and
where we start matters.

Consider how idiosyncratic and incompatible our individual visions of
perfection are, thus how unfit they are to be a blueprint for a community.
Part of the essence of toleration, of mature adulthood and of being fit to
live in a community at all is acknowledging that our personal visions do
not obligate others – not even if we are so gripped by confirmation bias
that we can talk ourselves into believing that our visions cannot reasonably be rejected.

The most primordial political fact of all is the fact that I am not alone.
I live among beings who decide for themselves. I may feel that people
cannot reasonably reject my deepest convictions about justice. But
they can, and they know it. This fact makes politics what it is, and justice
what it is.

Honestly taking the fact of diversity into account comes down to
grappling with a question like this: 'what terms of engagement are

[8] Was Wilberforce overconfident in the justness of his cause? I think not, but that may be the
wrong question. As I understand, Wilberforce's opponents were overconfident in the
justness of their cause, as majorities usually are. They talk themselves into feeling right-
eous when they bully those with minority views. To complicate things, majorities are not
always wrong, and may even be right most of the time. But when they are wrong, and are
holding back progress, they will be the last to know.

appropriate for people who do not even agree on which terms of engage-ment are appropriate?' The question is not cute. It is the crux of the human condition. Rushing to treat our own intuitions about perfect justice as if our intuitions were rationally compelling would be a paradigmatic way of failing to rise to the level of seriousness that justice demands.

3.1   Thinking We Should Be on the Same Page Is a Problem

Theorists sometimes assume they have high standards (even when others can see that they don't), and console themselves with the thought that human nature is too imperfect to live up to their high standards. In truth, the problem is not that other people cannot live up to 'high' standards. The simple reality is that there typically is no reason why they should. People have visions of their own. Liberalism is the insight that this is not a problem.

Some theories make it seem important that we cannot reach consensus on destinations. It is not. What matters is that under favourable circum-stances we coordinate on norms of traffic management. We have no history of being able to agree on who has the superior destination. We have a robust history of being able to agree on who has the right of way.

Freedom of religion is an example of the latter; we reached consensus not on what to believe, but on who gets to decide. You need not decide whether my choice of religion is a good choice. You need only decide whether it is *my* choice. People saw that they could ignore the most colonial and brutal premises of their own religions and philosophies. What won the day was not a religion so much as people deciding that religion didn't have to come up. There is no good reason not to let everyone decide for themselves.

What grew in the soil of religious freedom was more general than religious toleration. What flourished was liberalism: the idea that we need not presume to involve ourselves in running other people's lives. Our greatest triumphs in learning to live together stem not from agreeing on what is correct, but from agreeing to let people decide for themselves. Freedom of speech has a similar point: *not* to get more speech or to promote anointed versions of 'diversity', but to stop presuming to decide as a society.

When discussion is *not* needed, that fact constitutes success in specify-ing terms of engagement. We make progress by defining jurisdictions that respect people who want and need to share the road, but neither want nor need to share (or even justify) a destination. No one must accept being relegated to a category of persons whose destination is less important.

Thriving communities minimize our need to justify our destination to others. Indeed, the utility of a traffic management system largely lies in people not needing to justify themselves. We need not stop at intersections to justify our destinations. We stop only because it is someone else's turn. Underlying a healthy society is a logic of coordination rather than unified agency. In a healthy society, people's movements constitute a flow of traffic that moves smoothly, by virtue of people reaching consensus not on what their destinations should be so much as on who has the right of way. No one needs to agree about that. It is enough that we simply expect the people around us to adjust their expectations to fit with what they think others expect of them.

Ideally, we want to be able to co-exist with all of our neighbours, not only the ideal ones. Realistic idealism aims to identify what, if anything, is observably enabling people to thrive under actual conditions, not merely ideal ones. When disagreement is inevitable, our worthy ideal is to make disagreement non-threatening – to *make it safe to disagree.* **Aim not to minimize disagreement but to minimize the need for agreement.** The ideal of a mature political animal is not to win debates, but to avoid needing to win. Realistic idealism does not delude us into thinking other people should be on the same page as we are, and therefore avoids cursing us with the appearance of a mandate to bully those who see things differently.

Is there any alternative to consensus as a political aspiration? Is there a *realistic* ideal? Perhaps it would be something like *balance of power.* When people do not feel that they can safely abuse those with different views and values, society makes progress.[9]

It is (a not quite realistic) ideal that political power be justified to all citizens. No one expects total victory on this front any more than we expect a war on poverty to culminate in a poverty rate of zero. Respecting this ideal in practice involves minimizing how unjustified a regime's exercise of power is. One legitimate way to do that is to minimize the cost of exit (Pennington 2017). That is hardly a total victory, but approximate success marks a society as genuinely liberal. Being 100 per cent justified is not realistic, but it is entirely realistic that exit be a non-appalling option for any citizen appalled to be subject to a given regime.

---

[9] Of course, liberal politics does not simply leave things where they were. It manages traffic (dictating that people get to choose their own religion, for example). It does not treat all destinations as equally valuable. It does try to make sure no one (apart from dangerous criminals) is left facing a light that never turns green.

4   Justice Is Not a Peak

John Rawls arguably was the most influential social philosopher of the twentieth century. His greatest work opens with the thought that 'justice is the first virtue of institutions' (1999a: 3), from which we infer that a theorist's main task is to articulate principles of justice. Rawls's sentence resonates. It is lyrical, poetic, compelling.

But it is not right. Historically, we make progress when we acknowledge that justice is *not* the first virtue. The first virtue of social institutions is that they enable us to be neighbours. In practice, the first thing we need from social institutions is a settled framework of mutual expectation that keeps the peace well enough to foster conditions that enable society to be, in the most rudimentary and non-theory-laden sense, a cooperative venture for mutual benefit.[10]

Institutions with this virtue make it safe for us to show up and become a community, contributing goods and services in reasonable expectation of reciprocation. They set up society to become the cooperative venture that Rawls wants it to be. They lay a foundation for a solidarity that frees us to think about what is fair – starting from here.

When we settle disputes, we don't get resolution by deciding that our vision has a right to be colonial, and that we can condescendingly dismiss rival visions as unreasonable. Instead, real resolution starts by aiming for real resolution. To be in the grip of a vision – *any* vision – is problematic. What we need is not to envision, but to listen. That is, we need politics.

4.1   *Peaks Are Not Real, but Pits Are*

We each have our own theories and visions about the nature of justice: perfect justice. But our respective visions of perfect justice are too personal and idiosyncratic to be a basis for moral life in a social world. It is implausible that justice is *any* of our idiosyncratic peaks. A vision is not the kind of thing that could ever be good at managing traffic among diverse people.

Justice in practice arguably has no essence, which may be why we still lack an uncontroversial articulation of such essence. We would need to have an ideal in mind if there were a destination such that arriving at that summit is just, while arriving anywhere else is not. Yet there is another way of looking at it: justice is not a specific place (or distribution) we need to get to, and it is not a property, except insofar as it consists of an absence of properties that make for injustice. Specifying the essence of justice has turned out to be like specifying the essence of 'non-circle'. The closest we

---

[10] This is how I read Williams (2005).

come is to say that justice is (essentially) absence of injustice. If we some-
how were to rid ourselves of all the grinding, vicious, overreaching meddling and bullying in the world, justice would simply be the opportunity to
thrive in peace that was left over. There is no problem to solve unless
people are in one of those pits. Something needs to be done – we need to
be somewhere other than where we are – when, but only when, our
situation has features that make for injustice.

A noteworthy virtue of this perspective is that defining justice primarily
in terms of 'Thou shalt nots' (and thereby making justice revolve around
an absence of properties that make for injustice) treats justice as *limiting*
what we can do with other people's lives rather than as *dictating* what we
can do with our own. Justice so conceived leaves moral agents with room
to live lives of their own, which is how justice has to be in order to be taken
seriously as a practical guide to living well.

Pits of injustice are not theoretical visions, but real horrors. Justice on
the ground is about avoiding the pits of slavery, persecution, and sub-
jugation that lead to famine. Flourishing societies give people room to
avoid the pits, pursuing their own personal peaks in their own way, ideally
at no one else's expense.[11] The peak metaphor misrepresents that crucial
aspect of reality. Oppression and misery are real. Conceptions of justice
representing justice as a peak are theoretical constructs. Resources we
spend wrestling society towards our imaginary peak and away from someone else's are wasted. Insisting that justice is a peak, more specifically *our*
peak, is not what gets us out of the pits.

To be sure, there is such a thing as climbing. My objective here is not to
debunk climbing, but to reflect on what climbing is. When societies
climb, it is not towards a *peak*. When we climb towards a more just
society, we climb towards an expanding, not a converging, frontier of
possibility – an open rather than truncated future.

4.2   Conflict Management

Theorists treat justice as more foundational than conflict-resolving rules
of practice, yet judges and other conflict management practitioners need
to do the opposite. When judges ignore theorizing about what *would be* an

---

[11] Our personal peaks will of course have positive content, and may have to do with, for
example, reciprocity, equality, need, or desert. I wrote on such things before (Schmidtz
2006), but did not then doubt that justice has an essence. Moreover, I do not currently
believe we can altogether dispense with these positive elements of justice. We may
exaggerate how compelling our own personal peaks can be to others, and thus may
exaggerate how central a place they can hold as organizing principles for a diverse polis,
but they might for all that remain in some way meaningful and relevant. Honestly, I do
not know.

ideal response to ideal conditions, they are doing the right thing. Their role is to resolve conflict.

Judges play a role in enabling communities to climb, but see that climbing begins from where we are. It is natural but thoughtless to think a judge's job is to dream about how to do a reset from day one and rebuild society from the ground up according to a vision of justice. If you buy a house in the United States, you do a title search. The point is not to ascertain whether ideals of distributive justice single you out as having the most weighty claim, but simply to uncover any active dispute over title, or any unsettled dispute within the past forty years or so. If nothing turns up, we treat the deed as valid. No one needs reminding that there are no primordially clean land titles. Ascertaining that no one has disputed a title in forty years is not a way of giving up on justice; it is a way of getting on with the kind of justice that can ground society as a cooperative venture. To philosophers, forty years seems arbitrary, but it is property's role that dictates what works as a foundation for cooperative society. To coin a phrase, **foundation follows function**. Judges try to formulate simple rules, in a spirit of equality before the law, that enable litigants to get on with their lives, knowing how to avoid or minimize future conflict.

Property rights, including rights of self-ownership, are essentially rights to say no. The right to say no makes it safe to come to market and contribute to the community, thereby promoting trade, thereby promoting progress. When people have a right to say no and to withdraw, then they can afford *not* to withdraw. They can afford to trust each other. They can afford to live in close proximity and to produce, trade, and prosper without fear.

However, a right to say no is not a weapon of mass destruction. The operating idea is having a right to decline to be involved in a transaction, *not* to forbid transactions among others. Consider a case (see Schmidtz 2011b). In *Hinman v. Pacific Air Transport* (1936), a landowner sues an airline for trespass, asserting a right to stop airlines from flying over his property. The court's predicament: because a right to say no grounds a system of property that in turn grounds cooperation among self-owners, it was imperative not to repudiate the right to say no. On the other hand, much of property's point is to facilitate commercial traffic. Ruling that landowners can veto air transport is a red light that would gridlock traffic, not facilitate it. In *Hinman*, a property system had come to be inadequately specified relative to newly emerging forms of commercial traffic. The plaintiff's interpretation of our right to say no implied a right to gridlock air traffic, so the edges of our right to say no needed clarifying.

In *Hinman*, Judge Haney ruled that the right to say no does not extend to the heavens, but only so high as a landowner's actual use. Navigation easements subsequently were interpreted as allowing federal governments to allocate airspace above 500 feet for transportation purposes. The verdict made the system a better solution to a particular problem confronting Judge Haney's court, leaving us with a system of rights that we could *afford*.

If Hinman had a right to veto peaceful cooperation, he would have a right to veto progress. If Hinman makes demands of people to whom he is of no use, and works to be someone whom society would be better off without, then Hinman's neighbours will ignore him as best they can and seek out contributors: partners less intent on making demands and more intent on having something to offer.[12]

Property's purpose in managing commercial traffic (the purpose at stake in *Hinman*) has to condition the contours of what we call justice, not the other way around. Taking justice seriously involves seeing justice as something that comes second, not first, because taking justice seriously involves seeing justice as something a society can afford to take seriously.[13]

From a mediator's perspective, the test of theory is how it works in practice, and in practice there is no progress without negotiation and compromise, aiming for what everyone can live with. It is one thing to win. It is another thing to get a result about which no one feels triumphant but to which all can adjust without feeling sacrificed on the altar of a vision they do not (and no one honestly expects them to) share.

Judges have to play fair with the cards they are dealt. Judges can theorize about cards they ideally would have been dealt, and such theorizing is not necessarily irrelevant. But the relevance of such theorizing stems from its implications regarding how best to play their actual cards. While a philosopher's job involves reflecting on how the world ought to be in the grand scheme of things, actual governance is the art of compromise in a world that is not a blank canvas. The practical relevance of political philosophy depends on how well we take our cue from effective conflict mediators.

---

[12] See Harrison Frye, 'A Different Camping Trip: Offers, Demands, and Incentives' (presentation at Chapman University, 10 July 2015) for the idea that there is a fine line between an offer (to bring a particular service to market for a price) and what others perceive as a demand (when they want the service but resent having to pay).

[13] We cannot afford to think of justice in terms that will render it obsolete as a response to tomorrow's problems. See Rosenberg (2016).

Some questions have no answers until judges sort out what will help current and potential litigants in particular circumstances to stay out of court. After judges settle a dispute, citizens go forward not with personal visions of justice, but with validated mutual expectations about what to count as their due. Judges get it right when they settle it – when they establish mutual expectations that leave everyone with a basis for moving on.

Effective judges know this. To them, having personal convictions about fairness is not good enough. Judges aim higher, and thereby settle disputes in a way that philosophers and their theories almost never do. Philosophers spend their days convincing themselves that they have enough evidence for their view to justify ignoring the evidence against. Judges spend their days giving litigants a way to get on with their lives.

I have never been employed as a mediator, but after playing football in high school, I coached and served as a referee. Our task as referees was to interpret and apply the rules. With responsibility came power. With power came a measure of discretion. Our calls could determine a game's outcome. Crucially, it was not our place to *prefer* a particular outcome. Favouring a team would have been corrupt. Neither had we any right to prefer games ending in a *tie*. That too would have been incompatible with the unobtrusive impartiality that defines successful refereeing. We had a duty not to aim for *any* outcome, not even an equal one. It was not our place to win. Our aim was to let the players play, and let their futures be of their own making.

4.3   Corruption

Benjamin Barber notes Rawls's lack of realism in a stinging remark: 'When political terms do occasionally appear, they appear in startlingly naive and abstract ways, as if Rawls not only believed that a theory of justice must condition political reality, but that political reality could be regarded as little more than a precipitate of the theory of justice' (1989: 310). Robert Paul Wolff's criticism is equally sharp. He sees in Rawls 'no conception of the generation, deployment, limitations, or problems of political power'.

It would require very considerable political power to enforce the sorts of wage rates, tax policies, transfer payments, and job regulation called for by the difference principle. The men and women who apply the principle, make the calculations, and issue the redistribution orders will be the most powerful persons in the society, be they econometricians, elected representatives, or philosopher-kings.

How are they to acquire this power? How will they protect and enlarge it once they have it? Whose interests will they serve? (1977: 202)

It is indeed startling to see the work of the twentieth century's most influential political philosopher described as 'startlingly naive'.[14] And yet, upon reflection, it is amazing that there is no contemporary philosophical literature on the idea that power corrupts.

Imagine concentrated power in the hands of the worst ruler in living memory. Assume what you know to be true: namely, concentrated political power actually does fall into the hands of people like that. This has an important implication. **When formulating theories about what is politically ideal, ask 'ideally, how much power would be wielded by people like *that*?' and not 'ideally, how much power would be wielded by ideal rulers?'** Which of these questions is a genuine question about the human condition?

One theoretical bottom line is this. The fact that power corrupts bears on how much power we have reason to want there to be. When we ask how much good *an ideal ruler* could do with absolute power, we obscure this. We are working on an idealized problem, and gravitating towards endorsing as much power as it takes to realize our vision of true justice. Yet, among actual corruptible human beings, we ought to regard the raw power to ram any vision of true justice down people's throats as the paradigm of what true justice forbids.

Ideal theory done well cannot be a question of how much power ideally would be wielded by ideal rulers. Ideal theory done well has to be a question about how much power ideally would be wielded by the sort of human being who actually ends up acquiring power in human societies as we know them (Schmidtz 2015).

---

[14] It would be naïve indeed to suppose for example that, for the sake of fairness, university resources should be distributed among departments in whatever manner is to the greatest advantage of the least advantaged department. However, what Rawls actually says is: the principle applies only to the basic structure. We could simply stipulate this, or we could argue that the Principle more broadly applied often would fail self-inspection. For example, would it be to the greatest advantage of the least advantaged to treat rules of university budgeting as mere summary rules that answer case by case to the Difference Principle? (Would we distribute grades so as to be to the greatest advantage of the least advantaged student?) By the lights of the Difference Principle itself, ignoring empirical aspects of such questions is precisely what we have no right to do when evaluating society's basic structure and when evaluating the proper scope of the Difference Principle's application. If this is Rawls's view, then his view has none of the naïveté that Barber and Wolff find in the Difference Principle. The Difference Principle informs one and only one practice: namely the practice of *judging the fairness* of society's basic structure.

5   Conclusion

This chapter offers several conjectures about what it takes to make theorizing about political animals worthwhile. Formulated as practical advice, my conjectures are:

(a) **Theorize about players, not pawns.** We are political animals living in a strategic world. To theorize about which institutions are realistically ideal for political animals, we need to theorize about which *incentive structures* are ideal.

(b) **Theorize about ideals, but beware of *starting* with ideals.** From what I observe, theorizing in actual practice spirals between our articulating of problems and of solutions. Introspectively, it will seem true that before we were reasoning about the one, there was a previous stage of reasoning about the other. (See also Philp 2012.) Inevitably, it will feel right to ask 'to theorize about x, don't you need some conception of y?' Perhaps observation inevitably is theory-laden. (That very thought is so obviously a theory-laden observation.) However, it is just as true that some theories (including some ideal theories) are *observation* laden, and those are the theories we have reason to take seriously. Those are the theories that began life as responses to something real.

(c) **Avoid solving idealized problems.** More generally, theorizing about what *would be* ideal if reality were no constraint is a variation on the idealist theme, but not a realistic one. Realistic idealism works in the space of *educated* guesses about how the world works and how the world could work.

(d) **Set aside details and focus on what you see as a problem's essence.** Acknowledge that you exercise judgment when you set aside details. Even if you do not beg the question, others will think you did. When you simplify, beware of the impulse to simplify with prejudice by setting aside, as a 'distraction', what reveals that your solution is not ideal.

(e) **Acknowledge that your reasons for seeing the world as you do are not compelling.** Theorize about a world of people who do not see it your way, and who are perfectly aware that there is no reason why they should. Societies thrive not when they minimize disagreement so much as when they minimize the need for agreement.

(f) **Question the platitude that justice is the first virtue of social institutions.** In practice, what a theorist calls justice will be that theorist's personal vision. But in a world of people who see things differently, the first virtue of social institutions is that they curb the hunger to impose a vision. To do that, institutions need to manage traffic in such a way as to minimize conflict and to resolve conflict effectively when it does occur.

Social structures that make it easier to resolve and avoid conflict go a long way towards fostering society as cooperative venture. To the extent that a society is such a venture, it is responding well to the human condition. People are learning to trust each other far enough, and to adjust their expectations far enough, to constitute themselves as a kingdom of ends.

Over-specialized theorists will rush to get to more familiar ground by pointing out ways in which a society can be thriving yet not just. Of course! What suffices to resolve conflict is not guaranteed to be fair. Nevertheless, a resolution that stops the fighting will tend to do so partly by virtue of resonating with what seems fair enough at the time. Some societies have a primary, towering liberal virtue – the virtue of letting people pursue hopes and dreams of their own, in ways that make them appreciate each other as neighbours. Those societies are not guaranteed to be just, yet those are the societies that have a chance to be just.

Acknowledgements

My work on this chapter was supported by a grant from the John Templeton Foundation. Opinions expressed here are mine and do not necessarily reflect views of the John Templeton Foundation. Adrian Blau's advice was illuminating and helpful at every turn. The chapter also benefited from comments by Sameer Bajaj, Harrison Frye, Michael Huemer, Ellen Mease, Richard Miller, Jacob Monaghan, Joshua Ramey, and Danny Shahar.

References

Barber, Benjamin, 1989. *The Conquest of Politics*. Princeton, NJ: Princeton University Press.
Cohen, G. A., 2003. 'Facts and principles', *Philosophy and Public Affairs* 31: 211–45.
Cohen, G. A., 2008. *Rescuing Justice and Equality*. Cambridge, MA: Harvard University Press.
Cohen, G. A., 2009. *Why Not Socialism?* Princeton, NJ: Princeton University Press.
Estlund, David, 2008. *Democratic Authority*. Princeton, NJ: Princeton University Press.
Estlund, David, 2011. 'Human nature and the limits (if any) of political philosophy', *Philosophy & Public Affairs* 39: 207–37.
Estlund, David, 2014. 'Utopophobia', *Philosophy & Public Affairs* 42: 113–34.

Gilabert, Pablo, 2015. 'Justice and feasibility: a dynamic approach', in Kevin Vallier and Michael Weber, eds., *Political Utopia: Contemporary Debates*. Oxford University Press.

Hamlin, Alan and Zofia Stemplowska, 2012. 'Theory, ideal theory, and the theory of ideals', *Political Studies* 10: 48–62.

Hope, Simon, 2010. 'The circumstances of justice', *Hume Studies* 36: 125–48.

James, Aaron, 2012. *Fairness in Practice*. Oxford University Press.

Mason, Andrew, 2010. 'Rawlsian theory and the circumstances of politics', *Political Theory* 38: 658–83.

Pennington, Mark, 2017. 'Robust political economy and the priority of the right to exit', *Social Philosophy & Policy* 34: forthcoming.

Philp, Mark, 2012. 'Realism without illusions', *Political Theory* 40: 629–49.

Rawls, John, 1955. 'Two concepts of rules', *Philosophical Review* 64: 3–32.

Rawls, John, 1993. *Political Liberalism*. New York: Columbia University Press.

Rawls, John, 1999a. *A Theory of Justice*. Cambridge, MA: Harvard University Press.

Rawls, John, 1999b. *Law of Peoples*. Cambridge, MA: Harvard University Press.

Rosenberg, Alexander. (2016). 'On the Very Idea of Ideal Theory in Political Philosophy,' *Social Philosophy & Policy* 33: 53–75.

Schmidtz, David, 2011a. 'Nonideal theory: what it is and what it needs to be', *Ethics* 121: 772–96.

Schmidtz, David, 2011b. 'Property', in George Klosko, ed., *Oxford Handbook of the History of Political Philosophy*, Oxford University Press, 599–610.

Schmidtz, David, 2015. 'Corruption', in Subramanian Rangan, ed., *Performance and Progress: Essays on Capitalism, Business, and Society*. Oxford University Press, 49–64.

Schmidtz, David. 2006. *Elements of Justice*. Cambridge University Press.

Schmidtz, David, 2016. 'After solipsism', *Oxford Studies in Normative Ethics* 6: 145–65.

Singer, Peter, 1972. 'Famine, affluence, and morality', *Philosophy and Public Affairs* 1, 229–43.

Sleat, Matt, 2013. *Liberal Realism*. Manchester University Press.

Smith, Adam, 1984. *Theory of Moral Sentiments*. Indianapolis, IN: Liberty Fund.

Williams, Bernard, 2005. *In the Beginning Was the Deed*. Princeton, NJ: Princeton University Press.

Wolff, Robert, 1977. *Understanding Rawls: A Reconstruction and a Critique*. Princeton, NJ: Princeton University Press.

9   Conceptual Analysis

Johan Olsthoorn

1   Introduction

Concepts are the constituents of thoughts – the basic building blocks of whatever propositions we form. Conceptual analysis is the philosophical study of those building blocks. It is one of the more powerful tools philosophers and political theorists have at their disposal; indeed, for much of the twentieth century, philosophy in the Anglophone world was all but equated with doing conceptual analysis (Miller 1983: 35–9; Wolff 2013: 797–801).

Analytical philosophy values above all rigour in argumentation and clarity in thinking. The former is supported by logic, the latter by conceptual analysis. '[T]he very excellence of analysis', writes John Stuart Mill, 'is that it ... enables us mentally to separate ideas which have only casually clung together' (Mill 1989: 114). Besides elucidating and disambiguating complex ideas, conceptual analysis helps us to sharpen our thinking by refining and enriching our vocabulary, structuring our theories and guiding moral judgement. Furthermore, conceptual analysis diminishes risk of miscommunication by improving our grasp of language and of the ideas we seek to express with it.

The term 'analysis' has more than one sense, and so does 'conceptual analysis'. 'Analysis' can mean 'the resolution or breaking up of a complex whole into its basic elements or constituent parts' (*Oxford English Dictionary*). Conceptual analysis, so understood, aims to elucidate complex notions by breaking them up into their simpler component parts. Legal theorists have sought to clarify the enigmatic concept of property by reducing it to a bundle of analytically separable rights to a resource – rights to possess, use, manage, transfer, etc. (Honoré 1987: 165–79; cf. Penner 1996). Social and political theorists, similarly, have attempted to translate statements about complex phenomena such as corporate personalities (e.g. the nation or the state) into more lucid ones about the individuals comprising those personalities.

153

In a wider sense, 'analysis' means 'a detailed examination or study of something so as to determine its nature, structure, or essential features' (*OED*). Conceptual analysis, so understood, is the systematic study of concepts. This study can take at least four forms: (1) finding a proper definition for a given term (what does 'justice' mean?); (2) hunting for theoretically relevant conceptual distinctions (is there a conceptual difference between 'justice' and 'what the state should do'?); (3) exploring conceptual connections between different concepts (does being governed by a legitimate authority entail a general duty to obey?); and (4) studying conceptual change (does Locke's conception of property differ from modern accounts?).

This chapter offers concrete advice on how to do conceptual analysis in political theory. I begin by outlining a straightforward and hopefully helpful way of thinking about terms, principles, concepts and conceptions (Section 2). I then discuss various kinds of conceptual analysis, together with ways of doing them, and offer recommendations for concept formation (Section 3). Section 4 reiterates three prominent worries about the very possibility of analysing political and value-laden concepts like 'justice', 'equality' and 'liberty'. These worries, I argue, are exaggerated, but they do suggest tips to avoid common pitfalls. Next, I explore to what extent an analysis of political concepts can help us solve normative problems (Section 5). The final section provides practical recommendations for interpreting conceptualizations of political notions advanced in the literature. How should we determine what exactly Rawls meant by 'justice' and Locke by 'property'? While the recommendations offered in this section apply to any interpretive venture, they may be especially valuable when studying the history of political philosophy (Section 6).

2   Concepts

This section explains what concepts are and what they are not by distinguishing concepts from terms (2.1) and from conceptions, principles and criteria of application (2.2). It also explains what conceptual connections are and what conceptual change consists in (2.3).

2.1   Concepts and Terms

To be free to do something, e.g. to drive a car, consists in not being liable to interference by other people, so the Right says. No, the Left responds, to be *really* free to do something also requires having the means or resources to do it. According to the Right, everyone with a valid driver's licence is free to drive a car. According to the Left, access to a car is needed as well. Lacking resources is a way of lacking freedom; it is not just an impediment to using your 'formal' freedom. The poor are less free than the rich merely by being poor (Cohen 2011a; Van Parijs 1995: 21–4; cf. Carter 2011).

This debate in political theory, and perhaps others as well, may strike you as merely terminological. The Right calls one thing 'freedom', the Left another. Potato, potato; let's talk substance instead. When are disputes merely verbal? When we are doing political theory, we want our contributions to go beyond verbal bickering. How do we ensure that our arguments are substantive?

First of all, we should **distinguish terms and concepts**. Terms are words that express or denote concepts. They are common verbal signs that allow us to convey ideas to each other. Concepts are the basic ideas that give sense to a term or expression. (Terms that express or denote no concepts are meaningless.)[1] Terms and concepts should be kept distinct because no one-on-one relationship obtains between the two (Oppenheim 1981: 3–4). Synonyms – multiple terms for the same concept – are a familiar feature of languages. Think of 'liberty' and 'freedom'. (Synonyms often have different linguistic roots, e.g. 'liberty' is of Latin origin while 'freedom' is Germanic.) Conversely, the same term may habitually be used to express more than one concept (homonyms). Often the context clarifies which sense the speaker has in mind – whether 'bank' refers to the sloping margin of a river or to a kind of financial institution. But sometimes conceptual differences are too small for the context to settle the matter. Philosophical reflection is then called for. Isaiah Berlin (2002), for instance, argued that there are two concepts of liberty. He used two catchy labels to distinguish them: 'negative' and 'positive' liberty.

Once we understand the difference between terms and concepts – the former are labels for the latter – we recognize that disagreements can be merely semantic in two ways. First, we could agree on the nature of the underlying concept while disagreeing about the appropriate label for it. According to Hobbes, 'monarchy' and 'tyranny' make for a distinction without a difference. Both terms, he contends, express the same concept: a commonwealth in which sovereignty is held by one individual. They differ only in tone: 'tyranny' denotes a monarchy 'misliked' (*Leviathan* 19.2). Debates about appropriate labels are not pointless: labels can have great rhetorical effect, as this example shows. Still, settling

---

[1] Not every word is a term. Some words, including connectives like 'and', 'neither' and 'either', are not used to express concepts. They serve a merely syntactical function and hence lack semantic meaning.

on a label rarely constitutes a substantive contribution to theory. **Rather than criticizing people for using a term other than in your preferred sense, try to engage their underlying ideas and arguments.**

Second, we could be using the same label to express distinct concepts. The Right has in mind 'absence of humanly imposed constraints' when talking about liberty; the Left thinks lacking resources compromises freedom as well. Are these distinct ideas? Hayek thought so, warning against the 'confusion of liberty as power with liberty in its original meaning', as it would 'inevitably lead to the identification of liberty with wealth' (1960: 17). If Hayek is right, then the quibble between the Left and the Right is merely terminological: the two camps are arguing about distinct concepts incidentally both branded 'freedom'. While substantive disagreement is possible over the *value* of each concept (using *normative* arguments), the current dispute can be resolved by simply introducing new labels, e.g. by calling the first idea 'negative liberty' and the second 'liberty as power'.

Multivalent terms (homonyms) are a major source of ambiguity. Their existence seems a shortcoming of a language – a common system of signs the goal of which is to enable and facilitate both communication and reflection. Shouldn't languages have as many markers as there are concepts? Alas, this is impossible: the number of concepts is infinite. To see why, more needs to be said about what concepts are. Philosophers and cognitive scientists have proposed numerous theories about what kind of thing a concept is and about how concepts relate to other concepts and to language more generally. I shall refrain from summarizing or evaluating these debates here (for overviews, see Margolis and Laurence 1999, 2014). What I shall do is offer a way of thinking about concepts that strikes me as particularly helpful for explaining the role of conceptual analysis in political theory.

Concepts serve a classificatory purpose: they group together individual objects, both real and ideational, under a common mental heading. Cognitive scientists typically describe concepts as mental representations of categories (classes of objects in the world) (e.g. Murphy 2002: 5). Concepts, so understood, are indispensable tools for navigating the world. Possessing a concept helps you understand and respond appropriately to any new entity of the corresponding category that you may encounter. Since we understand individual objects, people and events through concepts, concepts have been called 'the glue that holds our mental world together' (Murphy 2002: 1). Philosophers tend to see concepts less as mental representations ('internal ideas') than as the shared, abstract and non-subjective classifications expressed by language. We can use and understand language by virtue of sharing concepts. As the constituents of thoughts ('mental sentences'), concepts are also the building blocks of whatever propositions we form. 'Concepts are to complete thoughts, roughly speaking, as words are to sentences' (Dummett 2010: 19).

Objects can be classified in infinitely many ways, each classification corresponding to a concept. How elaborate a system of classifications (a conceptual scheme) we require is determined functionally. Communication among certain alternative music fans would be severely restrained without words to express the different auditory experiences of 'death metal', 'deathcore' and 'Gothenburg death metal'. For others, one overarching category suffices: 'noise'. The concepts we cast to capture and classify objects can be ever more fine-grained. Some may find it useful to distinguish between 'deathcore' and 'grinding deathcore'. Adding the category 'bluesy deathcore' is unhelpful as there is no such thing in the world today. The notion is conceptually open, however: it is no oxymoron. Indeed, music may develop in such a way that need for this term arises. The set of objects falling under a concept is called its *extension*. Thus, the extension of the concept 'death metal' consists of all the objects in the world properly called 'death metal'. Note that mental associations prompted by that word (such as 'Slayer', 'leather jackets' and 'anger') are not part of the concept of death metal; these are instead called its *connotations*.

As representations of categories, concepts are not the kind of things that can be true or false (in the jargon, concepts are not truth-apt). Calling the concept 'liberty' true or false makes no sense. Rather, concepts give sense to statements that can be true or false ('propositions'). Concepts can be functionally better or worse, however: they can serve our practical, theoretical and communicative goals more or less effectively. Moreover, concepts can be incoherent. The concept 'justified slavery', for instance, is incoherent: as a violation of basic human rights, slavery is never justifiable. Observe that only composite concepts can be incoherent, as one part has to conflict with another part. It is possible for concepts to be coherent yet to have no real-world application. Think of the concept 'unicorn'. *Homo economicus* – the rational man of classical economics – is arguably another instance of a concept that cannot be rightly predicated of anything existing in the world. Concepts without real-world referents need not be meaningless or without practical import. They can function as ideals, serve theoretical purposes and even have predictive power. Concepts can also be vague or indeterminate: when they have no clear boundaries of application (Section 3.2). 'Elite' is an example of a vague concept: the boundaries of the set of individuals on which 'elite' can truthfully be predicated are intrinsically unclear, even if the dimension of assessment is settled (i.e. elite skier, social elite). **Incoherent concepts are unacceptable; vague concepts should be treated with care.** Further desiderata of concepts are discussed in Section 3.5.

While concepts themselves have no propositional content and are hence not truth-apt, claims about how language is ordinarily used – about what words 'mean' – can of course be true or false. While nothing is amiss with the concept 'minimalist electronic music', the assertion that it captures the ordinary meaning of 'death metal' is patently false. **While nothing stops you from forming new concepts, giving a new sense to existing words is permissible only if the audience understands and accepts it.** The meaning of words is socially determined. 'A language, as a social institution, is external to any individual speaker. The meanings of its words are not subjectively associated with them: they are objectively constituted by the common practice of speaking the language' (Dummett 2010: 83). Disputes are rendered merely verbal the moment one disputant glosses a term in a sense not accepted by her opponent: each then uses the same label to refer to different concepts. Hobbes was notorious for such semantic shenanigans:

> Mr *Hobs* is very dexterous, in Confuting others, by putting a new Sense upon their words, rehearsed by himself; different from what the same Words signifie with other men. And therefore, if You shall have occasion to speak of *Chalk*; he'l tell You that by *Chalk*, he means *Cheese*; and then, if he can prove that what You say of *Chalk*, is not true of *Cheese*; he reckons himself to have gotten a great Victory. (Wallis 1662: 154)

Let us return to the debate we started with, about the meaning of 'liberty'. Suppose (linguistic intuitions may differ at this point) that both the Left and the Right use the term 'liberty' correctly, i.e. in accordance with common usage. In other words, neither is guilty of 'conceptual stretching' – applying terms to things beyond their normal usage (Gerring 1999: 360; Sartori 1970: 1033–46). This suggests that the term 'liberty' is equivocal – used to express two distinct concepts. We can check whether that is really so by **examining whether either concept is reducible to the other.** According to G. A. Cohen, 'lack of money induces lack of freedom, *even if we accept the identification of freedom with absence of interference*' (2011a: 174–5). Poverty, he insists, quoting Berlin, is *not* like 'a kind of disease which prevented me from buying bread … as lameness prevents me from running'. Such inabilities 'would not naturally be described as a lack of freedom' (Berlin 2002: 170; cf. Van Parijs 1995: 23–4). 'Money structures freedom' since property arrangements, unlike physical inabilities, are social relationships of exclusion and constraint (Cohen 2011a: 175). Property relations are essentially coercive and thus freedom-depriving. People too poor to buy a ticket are not free to board a train; anyone doing so would be quickly forced out. Notice that Cohen makes a *conceptual claim* – 'a claim about how certain concepts [here "lacking money" and "freedom"] are connected with one another' (2011a: 168) – premised on a claim about the coercive nature of 'property'. His argument involves no normative statements, grounded in principles. Which brings us to the distinction between concepts and principles.

2.2   Concepts, Conceptions, Principles and Criteria of Application

We use normative or evaluative concepts like 'just', 'true' and 'beautiful' to express propositions about reasons for action, belief and feeling (Skorupski 2010, 2012).[2] Normative concepts are accompanied by normative principles – 'general statements about right and wrong' (Cohen 2011b: 227). To call a person 'just', for instance, is to express a kind of moral approval of her and to assert that she has met a certain norm or standard: that of being just. The technical term for that norm is 'principle'. Normative concepts often require many different principles, each appropriate for particular situations, actions or agents. Examples of principles of justice are: 'valid covenants should be kept', 'from each according to her ability, to each according to her need', and 'social and economic inequalities are justifiable only if they are to the greatest benefit of the least-advantaged members of society'. The principles mentioned are principles *of justice*, rather than of prudence or etiquette, since the wrong involved in their violation is 'injustice'. (On principles more generally, see List and Valentini 2016: 535–6.)

People may agree on the general meaning of a normative concept while defending mutually incompatible principles of it. For instance, I might consider the correct principle of distributive justice to be 'the social surplus should be divided according to *need*', while you favour instead the principle 'the social surplus should be divided according to *effort*'. Both of us would then agree that distributive justice expresses the idea of a fair societal division of resources. But each of us endorses a different standard to determine whether resources are in fact distributed fairly.

Rawls (1999a: 5) has introduced the terms 'concept' and 'conception' in political theory to flag this distinction. Concepts, on Rawls's account, are broader and less specific than conceptions. Conceptions are

---

[2] Philosophers sometimes distinguish between evaluative terms (used to express approval or disapproval) and normative ones (used to prescribe or proscribe actions). I shall call 'normative' any term used to express propositions about reasons for action, belief or feeling, thus collapsing the distinction between evaluative and normative.

interpretations of concepts developed by adding specifying principles and criteria. Let 'distributive justice' be the concept of 'a moral norm governing allocations of benefits and burdens within a society'. As it stands, this idea is too general to be applicable: principles are needed to spell out which distributions are just and which not. The same concept can be interpreted (fleshed out, operationalized) differently, depending on which principle of distributive justice we endorse (allocation according to need, effort, etc.). As Rawls puts it, '[t]o develop a concept of justice into a conception of it is to elaborate these requisite principles and standards' (2005: 14 n). Multiple mutually incompatible conceptions may be possible of the same concept. Widespread disagreement over what justice demands is therefore compatible with agreement on what the concept of justice consists in. The latter, Rawls suggests, is found in the accord amidst all the discord – 'by the role which these different sets of principles, these different conceptions, have in common' (Rawls 1999a: 5).

Rawls's discussion would have been clearer had he managed to **distinguish explicitly between principles and criteria of application**. Endorsement of the same principle of justice by no means guarantees agreement about which distributions are just and unjust. For we may well employ different standards to determine whether an object meets a principle or falls under a concept, and hence whether the corresponding term should be applied to it. Criteria of application, as such standards are called, are non-semantic (not part of the meaning of a word). They instead function as bridges between concepts and objects in the world (Martinich 2014: 388). Imagine we both favour the same need-based principle of distributive justice and agree on the meaning of 'need'. Moral disagreement would persist if you would judge enjoying annual paid vacations a human need, while I would consider them at most desirable. Insofar as our criteria of what counts as 'need' differ, we will apply the same concept to different objects in the world. Which criteria of application are best depends on the context and on the purposes of the speaker and audience.

Rawls's use of the distinction is further confusing insofar as it suggests that conceptions of normative notions like justice and fairness are some kind of concepts. They are not. Rival conceptions of justice are created through the addition of at least some normative principles. The concept vs. conception distinction is profitably used to explain a kind of *linguistic* disagreement. Suppose we agree that courtesy is a matter of respect but that you maintain that respect must be deserved while I think it is owed more or less automatically. Each of us thinks our own interpretation of the concept best captures the meaning of 'courtesy', the way the term is used in everyday life (Dworkin 1986: 70–2). Rawls, however, uses the distinction primarily to explain *moral* disagreement – for instance, disagreement over what is just. But when I claim that justice forbids inequalities that disadvantage the worst off, I don't just make a *linguistic* claim about how the term 'unjust' is ordinarily used. I also advance a *normative* claim about what I think is morally indefensible. Such normative propositions cannot be validated by pointing to linguistic practices. They require normative argument. Normative propositions, and the principles they are based on, can be true or false.[3] If a proposed principle of justice fails to adequately reflect our considered moral judgements, then this evinces that the principle is incorrect (see Knight's chapter on reflective equilibrium in this volume). Principles, unlike concepts, are truth-apt. Conceptions of normative concepts are therefore also truth-apt. They differ in this respect from conceptions of non-normative notions like courtesy. The latter cannot be false *qua* conceptions (although they can fail to capture the ordinary meaning of the corresponding term).

2.3   Conceptual Connections and Conceptual Change

Concepts are not self-standing entities: 'concepts always appear in clusters that are mutually defining, sustaining and, for that matter, constraining' (Freeden 2005: 125). Some conceptual clusters exist by virtue of robust patterns of associations: many people seem disposed to associate 'banker' with social irresponsibility, for one reason or another. Philosophically more important are *conceptual* connections – links to other concepts entailed by the concept itself, following logically from the internal structure of the concept. The concept of a claim-right, for instance, entails the concept 'obligation'. My claim-right against you (with respect to *x*) logically implies that you have an obligation to me (with respect to *x*) (Hohfeld 1923: 36–8; Wenar 2013). Conceptual entailments allow us to make conceptual claims (claims that purport to be true by virtue of the meaning of terms).

Concepts, we have seen, can be articulated in competing ways. Rival conceptions often weave a different web of conceptual connections around the same concept through the addition of different principles and criteria of application, each with its own conceptual implications. To conceptualize 'liberty' as 'non-domination' is to forge a conceptual

---

[3] Most analytical political theorists labour on the assumption that there is such a thing as justice, and that the theories we develop articulate this ideal for better or worse (proponents of a non-cognitivist metaethics will disagree). Those political theorists may, in turn, disagree over whether 'justice' is a mind-dependent moral property. On moral (anti-) realism and moral (non-)cognitivism, see Joyce (2015).

link between 'liberty' and 'arbitrary power' through the idea of 'non-domination' (Pettit 1997: 51–79; 2012: 26–74). 'Liberty as the absence of interference' entails no such link. On the non-domination conception of liberty, to know whether an individual is free requires exploring whether she is subject to an arbitrary or uncontrolled power. This requirement is a conceptual one: it follows logically from conceptualizing freedom in this way. Proponents of rival conceptions are spared this requirement – though possibly at the cost of linguistic and theoretical plausibility (Section 3.3).

The way a concept is linked to other concepts is not static and unalterable: connections between concepts can be rearranged and change over time. Even as entrenched a conceptual relation as that between claim-rights and obligations is plausibly conceived differently. Building on his interest theory of rights, Joseph Raz (1984) argues that claim-rights are interests deemed sufficiently important to justify holding others under a correlative duty (barring conflicting considerations). On this conception, claim-rights do not simply have corresponding obligations in others: rather, they are the justificatory grounds for these obligations.

Conceptual change in political theory consists not in changing conceptions, but in alterations to the internal structure of the concept itself. Rival conceptions of normative concepts gain and lose prominence over time. The Rawlsian conception of justice as fairness seems more popular today than the utilitarian conception of justice as efficiency (Section 3.4). Such changing fates do not necessarily imply conceptual change: they may merely reflect the shifting popularity of the normative principles accompanying different conceptions. Conceptual change has occurred whenever the concept itself has changed. Such change usually manifests itself in a rearrangement of the cluster of concepts in which the concept is embedded and through which it is understood.

For example, in the early modern period distributive justice was generally regarded as (1) a virtue of individuals, (2) regulating the division of common goods (including spoils of war and political jobs) (3) according to merit. Today, we tend to think of distributive justice as (1) a virtue of social institutions, (2) regulating, among other things, societal divisions of resources, (3) to which people have a right (Fleischacker 2004: 1–16). Early modern philosophers did not simply defend alternative conceptions of the modern concept of distributive justice. Rather, they conceptualized distributive justice itself differently. Most of them followed Hugo Grotius (1583–1645) in holding that distributive justice dealt with 'merit' or 'worthiness', rather than with rights (*De Iure Belli*, 1.1.7–8). Distributive justice did not endow individuals with (morally) enforceable titles (2.22.16).

Grotius would thus reject the modern conceptual connection between distributive justice and rights, favouring instead a linkage with 'worthiness'. Insofar as the idea of justice is conceived differently, judgements about what is just and unjust will inevitably vary, even if moral judgements stay constant.

3 Conceptual Analysis

This section explains how to elucidate complex concepts by identifying and clarifying their simpler component parts (3.1); how to determine the extension of a concept (3.2); how to explore and expose conceptual connections between different concepts (3.3); and how to discover possibly relevant conceptual distinctions through disambiguation (3.4). The section concludes with recommendations for concept formation (3.5).

3.1 Conceptual Analysis as Resolution

The term 'analysis' is of Greek origin, meaning 'breaking up' or 'unfastening'. Its antinomy is 'synthesis', meaning 'composition' or 'putting together'. Conceptual analysis, in this sense, is a method for elucidating complex concepts by breaking them up into their simpler and more comprehensible constituent parts (Beaney 2015; Jackson 1998, 2001). Locke described the process of analysis as follows:

Justice is a Word in every Man's Mouth, but most commonly with a very undetermined loose signification: Which will always be so, unless a Man has in his Mind a distinct comprehension of the component parts, that complex *Idea* consists of; and if it be decompounded, must be able to resolve it still on, till he at last comes to the simple *Ideas*, that make it up. (*Essay Concerning Human Understanding* 3.11.9)

Suppose we think of justice as 'obeying the law'. Our idea of justice will then be 'confused and imperfect', Locke claims, unless we have a clear idea of what 'law' and 'obedience' mean. **To clarify the meaning of a complex notion, explain the meaning of each term in its definition. Avoid circularity:** Locke's reductive analysis of 'justice' would not be very informative were he to define laws as 'just precepts' (Martinich 2005: 103–4).

Elucidating composite notions by explaining the meaning of their constituent concepts, and their conjunction, is an excellent way of providing conceptual clarification. A good example in political theory is Carter's (2004) analysis of the composite concept of 'freedom of choice'. He first defines 'choice' and 'freedom' and then constructs a definition of 'freedom of choice' out of the two former definitions. Note that the analysis of a composite notion requires explaining not only the meaning of its constituent parts, but also of the relationship in which they stand.

3.2   Conceptual Analysis as Extensional Analysis

In a wider sense, 'analysis' signifies any 'detailed examination or study of something so as to determine its nature, structure, or essential features'. The classical type of conceptual analysis, so understood, searches for an encompassing definition of a term by trying to identify the set of conditions that are individually necessary and jointly sufficient for the concept to apply (the concept's 'defining conditions'). Call this approach 'Extensional Analysis'. Extensional Analysis aims to arrive at a definition that accurately picks out all instances of a concept and only those. It thus aims to settle the meaning of a term by determining its extension (what it properly applies to). This way of doing conceptual analysis used to be extremely popular. It requires little else but imagination, some intelligence and a fine armchair – although to be persuasive, one also needs linguistic intuitions properly attuned to those of the wider language community.

Extensional Analysis starts by proposing a tentative definition of the concept you are studying. For this method, a definition ideally takes the following form: **first specify the general class to which the thing to be defined belongs and then state the specific differences that mark it off from other species of that same general kind.** (This is known as a *differentiating*, or *per genus et differentiam*, definition.) For example, distributive justice is 'a moral norm [*genus*] that governs divisions of benefits and burdens [*species*]'. Distributive justice as social justice, then, could be defined as 'a moral norm [*genus*] that governs the division of benefits and burdens [*species*] within a society [*subspecies*]'. **To test whether your initial definition accurately captures the individually necessary and jointly sufficient conditions for the concept to apply, try to come up with counterexamples.** The counterexamples should be cases that are both disqualified as instances of the concept by the definition at hand and intuitively plausible instantiations of the concept. **If you deem the counterexample successful, tweak and reformulate the definition to accommodate it. Continue this process until you have identified the defining conditions of the concept.** As in the empirical sciences, the definition arrived at is only provisionally correct: it remains liable to falsification by future counterexamples.

Suppose we define liberty as 'absence of interference'. Is this definition of 'liberty' adequate? Well, what does it mean to ask this question? On the current approach, we are asking whether the definition accurately picks out all and only those instances we deem to fall under the concept (its extension). Does the proposed definition of liberty succeed in doing so? Republicans think not, persuaded by the following counterexample. Suppose we are ruled by an absolute monarch who has the power to incarcerate us with a twist of her finger. Yet as it happens, her fingers keep still: we are left alone to do as we like. On the proposed definition of liberty we are 'free' as long as the monarch does not actually interfere with us. This cannot be right, republicans claim. The proposed definition of liberty they consider too loose: it identifies individuals as 'free' whom many of us are disposed to believe are not really so. Absence of interference might be a necessary condition for liberty; it is not, the counterexample suggests, a sufficient one.

A familiar objection to this style of conceptual analysis is that it wrongly assumes that concepts have an essence: a common conceptual core. Wittgenstein has argued convincingly that we have no reason to expect all instantiations of a concept to share a unique set of common features that definitions can mark out. Think of all the proceedings we call 'games'. Is there any feature common to board games, Olympic games, drinking games and war games? What binds different instances of what we call 'games' together is perhaps better characterized as 'family resemblances': 'a complicated network of similarities overlapping and criss-crossing' (*Philosophical Investigations* §66–7). No definition or short paraphrase will make sense for all instantiations of such 'family resemblance' concepts. The best we can do is *describe* the sundry uses of such concepts.

The idea of 'cluster concepts' develops this idea further (Connolly 1983: 14f.). Pointing out that all attempts to specify the individually necessary and jointly sufficient conditions for the concept 'nation' have hitherto failed, Yael Tamir argues that 'nation' is best regarded as a cluster concept. '[I]n order to count as a nation a group has to have a "sufficient number" of certain characteristics', such as common history, destiny, language, territory, religion and ethnicity (Tamir 1993: 65). Groups may thus qualify as nations by virtue of meeting different criteria.

A second objection Wittgenstein advanced against Extensional Analysis is that it has trouble dealing with irredeemably vague concepts. The boundaries of application of vague concepts are indeterminate, such that they have borderlines cases. Consider the concept 'tall'. A woman who is 1.90 meters in height is certainly 'tall', whereas a 1.60-meter woman is not (at least not in our day and age). But can 'tall' truthfully be predicated on a woman 1.75 meters in height? We can *stipulate* a criterion – any person at least x centimetres in height shall be called 'tall' – but any such criterion will strike us as somewhat arbitrary, precisely because the concept 'tallness' itself has 'blurred edges' (*Philosophical Investigations* §71). It has been argued that all language is vague; every proposition would have a certain degree of vagueness (Russell 1923).

A shortcoming common to both this objection and to Extensional Analysis generally is that they overlook the fact that '[t]he criterion for the correct application of a word is not the same as the meaning of the word' (Martinich 2014: 385). Criteria of application are context-dependent and non-semantic: they can change while the meaning of a term stays the same (Section 2.2). Thus, while the meaning of 'tall' has stayed constant, general improvements in health mean that the threshold for counting as 'tall' has shifted upwards since 1800. Likewise, the criteria of application for 'cruel and unusual punishment' have arguably altered since the US Bill of Rights was ratified, without concomitant conceptual change. Definitions aim to capture the meaning of a term as precisely as possible. But whether it is acceptable to use a word to refer to an object in the world also depends on non-semantic criteria of application, shared by conversational partners (Martinich 2014: 388).[4] Which criteria are reasonable depends on the situation: whether some activity qualifies as 'cruel punishment' will depend on what we think the point of the prohibition is. The take-home lesson is to **provide clear, precise and plausible definitions as well as operational criteria of application.** In political theory, the latter will usually depend on wider theoretical considerations (Section 4.3).

These criticisms suggest that proponents of classical Extensional Analysis have set themselves too ambitious a research programme (Schroeter 2004). The same is suggested by their conspicuous failure to produce uncontroversial definitions. Imagining counterexamples may certainly help us improve our definitions. But the definitions arrived at do not suffice to determine, in turn, which objects in the world count as instantiations of a concept. That requires both definitions and non-semantic criteria of application. However, even if the definitions it arrives at can never succeed in independently capturing *each and every* plausible instance of a concept, Extensional Analysis remains a highly useful method to sharpen our definitions and to elucidate the ordinary meaning

---

[4] Words *denote* (mean something), speakers *refer* to things (Donnellan 1966). A speaker may legitimately use any word to refer to any object provided the audience understands and accepts it, without changing the semantic meaning of the word.

of terms. Indeed, as Section 6 argues, even in interpretive ventures a method resembling Extensional Analysis comes in handy.

3.3   Conceptual Connections

Political theories are systems of political concepts and conceptions (Gaus 2000: 43). Progress in political theory consists in part in the rational rearrangement of political concepts like justice, liberty and equality. How we arrange political concepts is partly informed by our moral and theoretical convictions. Political theories will take different shapes depending on whether we give normative priority to social equality or to individual liberty. Other arrangements are conceptually required: if we conceptualize 'liberty' as 'non-domination', then our theory of liberty must explain the concept of 'being subject to an arbitrary or uncontrolled power' on pain of incompleteness. Conceptual analysis aids arrangements of political concepts, and thus construction of political theories, by exploring conceptual connections between notions.

Philosophical arguments often involve conceptual claims – claims that purport to be analytically true, i.e. true by virtue of the meaning of terms. Classical natural law theorists regard it as analytically true that we have a moral duty to obey any valid law we are subject to. For they define law as 'a just precept capable of morally binding subjects'. According to Francisco Suárez (1548–1617), whenever legislators 'prescribe that which is unjust, such a precept is not law, inasmuch as it lacks the force or validity necessary to impose a binding obligation' (*De Legibus* 1.9.4). Legal positivists reject such strict conceptual connections between law, justice and moral obligation. In the words of John Austin (1998: 184): 'The existence of law is one thing; its merit or demerit another. Whether it be or be not is one enquiry; whether it be or be not conformable to an assumed standard, is a different enquiry' (cf. Gardner 2001: 199). For natural law theorists, to ask whether we should obey a valid law is to misunderstand the meaning of 'law'. For legal positivists, this question *is* conceptually open: establishing that a norm is legally valid in no way settles the question of whether we are morally obliged to obey it. Keeping these two questions distinct is a virtue of legal positivism – although if natural law theorists are right, it does so on pain of misconstruing the concept of law.

Competing theories set out different conceptual arrangements. What qualifies as a conceptual claim on one theory may therefore not do so on another. **Remember that whether a proposition expresses a conceptual claim is determined as much by our linguistic practices as by our theoretical convictions.** This holds true in particular

for political theory since it mainly studies theoretical concepts
(Section 4.3). **Conceptual claims in political theory are best
regarded as conditionals.** *If* we define slavery as the condition of having
no civil rights, *then* it follows that citizenship and slavery are incompatible
and that wage slavery is an oxymoron. Were we to define slavery differently, then this might not follow (cf. Pateman 1988: 146–52).

Notice that Suárez requires no further *normative* argument to show that
we ought to obey valid law: on his account, this is true by definition.
Whether a proposition expresses a normative or a conceptual claim
greatly affects its truth-conditions. Consider Rawls's well-known formula
'justice as fairness'. The expression is ambiguous: Rawls could be read as
voicing either a *conceptual* or a *substantive* objection against utilitarianism
(as it happens, he does both). On the first reading, Rawls is saying that
utilitarians like Bentham and Sidgwick failed to grasp the meaning of the
term 'justice'. They think of justice as 'a kind of efficiency' whereas in fact
justice means fairness (Rawls 1999b: 64). On the second interpretation,
Rawls articulates a substantive argument against utilitarianism.
Conceiving of justice as efficiency is wrong because it leads to normatively
undesirable outcomes and/or because it is informed by an unsatisfactory
theory of justice. Thus, Rawls objects that the utilitarian conception of
justice cannot account for our basic moral intuition that 'slavery is always
[i.e. categorically] unjust' (1999b: 67). This argument, in turn, strengthens his claim that 'justice' is best understood as meaning fairness.

**Avoid conceptualizing notions in such a way that controver-
sial claims become true by definition.** The first reason is pragmatic:
we shouldn't unnecessarily hamper our thinking about complex ideas
like law and justice by discarding certain views or foreclosing certain
questions by definitional fiat. A second reason is normative: one reason
why we should value justice is because we value fairness and because
fairness requires justice. Were we to define justice as fairness, then we
would trivialize one reason for valuing justice (Carter 2011: 491;
Lovett 2012: 142–4).

3.4   Conceptual Analysis as Disambiguation

Conceptual analysis is an indispensable tool for conceptual refinement, in
turn required for clarity in thinking. Many words are multivalent: used to
express multiple analytically distinct concepts. Whether a term is in fact
multivalent depends on our actual language use and implicit linguistic
commitments. Conceptual analysis helps us to achieve conceptual refinement by disambiguating existing terms and recognizing possibly relevant
conceptual distinctions.

Consider whether the conceptual distinctions you are making are sufficiently fine-grained for your argument. Many political terms, including 'liberty' and 'justice', arguably refer to multiple distinct concepts, albeit ones that share sundry features. Sometimes it makes no difference to an argument whether such a term is understood one way or another. Sometimes it does: your argument about the value of liberty may be valid only on the assumption that we think of liberty as self-realization and not as absence of interference. **Whenever your argument hinges on a particular sense of a term, you should state this explicitly and carefully check your argument for equivocation.** If you think your argument about X holds regardless of how we interpret X, then stating this explicitly is generally good practice.

To clarify in which sense you are using a multivalent word, simply stipulate a definition: 'this paper takes "liberty" to mean ... '. Such definitions are called *declarative* or *stipulative*. They are used to indicate which of a variety of recognized senses of a term you have in mind. As long as the stipulated definition is a common one, you do not need to justify your choice – although **you should make sure that the chosen definition meets your argumentative needs and ambitions**. Declarative definitions are functionally distinct from *differentiating* ones (Section 3.2). Differentiating definitions *do* need to be argued for, as they aim to settle the extension of a concept by determining the concept's differentiating properties. Various other kinds of definitions exist, each serving a separate function (for an overview, see Sartori 1984: 29–34).

How can you see whether an existing term is ambiguous? If you always try to express yourself in as precise a manner as you can, then you will probably encounter ambiguities in passing. A more proactive step is to check a good dictionary like the *Oxford English Dictionary* – although dictionaries are generally less helpful for technical terms. **Minimize your use of overly general terms.** As Tocqueville observed, '[a]n abstract word is like a box with a false bottom: you put into it the ideas you want and take them out again unobserved' (*Democracy in America* 2.1.16). **If you insist on employing highly abstract terms like 'positivism', 'universalism', 'neutrality' and 'relativism', consider adding an adjective to specify what you're talking about** (e.g. moral relativism, epistemic relativism, relativism about perspectives).

Another practical tip is to **think about what the term's opposite(s) are**. 'Good' is used in both a purely evaluative and a moral sense, as we immediately recognize once we consider its antonyms ('bad' and 'evil'). Pateman (1988) has shown that many classical social contract theorists equivocated over the meaning of 'civil'. Where they first opposed the civil to the natural condition, 'after the original pact, the term "civil" shifts and is used to refer not to the whole of "civil society" but to one of its parts' – namely the public realm, from which women were considered excluded (1988: 11). Through this equivocation, contract theorists like Locke and Kant could simultaneously grant and deny women a place in civil society (1988: 55). Pateman's conceptual analysis reveals how the natural/civil antinomy seeped into the private/public one, thus expressing and legitimizing sexist prejudices.

Finally, you could explore the concept's internal structure – the links to other concepts that it presupposes. If diverse usages of the same term entail different conceptual linkages, then the term probably expresses multiple concepts. For instance, I believe that two irreducibly distinct concepts of justice are found in modern political philosophy. What we may call 'ordinary justice' expresses a moral norm ordering agents to respect moral rights (on pain of injustice). The rights it regulates, including human rights, are logically *prior* to justice. Ordinary justice does not deal with the distribution of rights (human rights are not distributed; we have them by virtue of being human). Distributive justice, by contrast, is a moral norm allocating rights, e.g. to a share of societal wealth. Individuals have these rights *by virtue of* distributive justice – i.e. because a particular distribution is fair. Rights are thus logically *posterior* to distributive justice. Ordinary justice and distributive justice implicate the concept of rights in divergent ways, which strongly suggests that they are distinct concepts. My point here is not to convince you that political theorists unwittingly employ two distinct concepts of justice, but to illustrate a method for disambiguation.

3.5   Conceptual Design

Sometimes we seek conceptual refinement, not by exploring the meaning of existing words, but by introducing new concepts altogether. Concepts, we have seen, are really only categories used to make sense of the world. Like fishing nets, these categories can be ever more fine-grained – and at times we need finer conceptual meshes to adequately incorporate our arguments and to properly channel our moral judgements.

Political theorists often find themselves wanting to refer to a particular set of objects lacking a common label. Suppose you believe that a prominent argument in the literature about rights of non-economic refugees actually applies not only to 'refugees facing persecution', but also to 'refugees facing systematic marginalization'. The distinction between the two kinds of refugees is not discovered by disambiguating an existing term (the meaning of 'refugee' remains constant), but by showing that an *argument* is unclear about the set of individuals it properly applies to. As a result, the argument may have hitherto unrecognized implications. The concept 'refugees facing persecution or systematic marginalization' constitutes a newly formed category – and may warrant an appropriate label.

Social scientists have written extensively on rules for good concept formation/design (e.g. Outhwaite 2010; Sartori 1970, 1984). Gerring (1999: 367) offers nine 'criteria of conceptual goodness'. Ironically, his list is itself conceptually confused – some criteria apply to the *name* chosen, others to the *concept* formed. The most important rule Gerring offers is to **introduce new concepts only when you need them for your arguments or theories**. Compare Mill's (1974: 668) advice: 'we should possess a name wherever one is needed; wherever there is anything to be designated by it, which it is of importance to express.'

Concepts cannot be true or false, but they can be incoherent, arbitrary, ad hoc, obscure and indeterminate. **New concepts should not be internally incoherent or arbitrary**. Arbitrary concepts group together disparate and apparently unconnected properties, as in the concept 'bluesy deathcore'. The latter concept is also ad hoc: relevant only to this particular argument and to nothing else – another vice in concept formation. **Newly introduced concepts should be independently intelligible**. It should be possible to explain what the concept refers to without invoking your theory. Finally, **the extension of concepts should ideally be determinate**, such that it can be known to which objects in the world, real or ideational, it applies. New terms ideally express analytically distinct concepts.

Suppose you have formed a new concept, discovered by disambiguating existing terms or suggested by your theory or arguments. This prompts a choice of labels – terms that clearly and precisely flag concepts and distinctions. You could either invent a new word ('neologism') or give an additional new meaning to an existing one ('neovalent'). This subsection concludes by offering some guidelines for how to choose appropriate labels, drawing on Sartori (1970, 1984) and Gerring (1999).

Terms you choose are ideally:

1. **Clear, short and memorable**. 'Positive' and 'negative' liberty are short and memorable labels; alas, they are not very clear. Some labels are neither clear, nor short, nor memorable. Jeremy Bentham had a particular talent in coming up with them: 'archetypation', 'phraseoplerosis', 'chrestomathia' (1838–43: vol. 8, 126, 247). Avoid acronyms. Introducing catchy names for relevant distinctions is as near a guarantee for citation fame as there is.

2. **In line with common parlance**. The meaning of technical terms inevitably departs somewhat from that of their everyday counterparts and cognates. 'Liberal' expresses a different concept for political theorists than for laypeople. Still, to convey what kind of thing a newly postulated neologism or neovalent refers to, **abide as far as possible by linguistic familiarity**. Thus, call a new system to improve education, well, anything other than 'chrestomathia'.
3. **Original.** Nearly every research field appears to have a distinction signposted by the names 'internalism' and 'externalism'. Some fields have several. Multiplication of the same set of technical labels is a common cause of confusion and miscommunication across disciplines and subfields.

4   Analysing Political Concepts

It is sometimes claimed that analysing value-laden political concepts like 'equality', 'justice' and 'democracy' is impossible. People disagree deeply about what is just and unjust, what democratic and what not. How can we then determine uncontroversially what the concepts of justice and democracy mean? Given widespread moral disagreement and conflicting political interests, how should we settle the criteria of application of terms used to express moral (dis)approval? This section discusses three worries that have been raised with respect to the analysis of political concepts. They concern the evaluative nature of many political concepts (4.1); their allegedly 'essentially contested' nature (4.2); and their theoretical background and ideological use (4.3). None of these difficulties, I shall argue, is insurmountable. They do reveal, however, that studying political concepts requires special handling.

4.1   *Essentially and Non-essentially Evaluative Concepts*

The word 'value-laden' is ambiguous (Carter 2015). One group of value-laden terms expresses *essentially* evaluative or normative concepts (recall that I treat 'evaluative' and 'normative' as interchangeable). 'Good', 'justice', 'reasonableness' and 'fairness' are all essentially evaluative concepts: using these concepts *necessarily* involves evaluation. To apply any of these concepts to an object is to evaluate it positively: anyone who sincerely declares 'this just arrangement is wrong' does not know what justice means. Another group comprises terms that are not intrinsically evaluative but whose normal use does have evaluative implications. Examples of such *non-essentially* evaluative concepts are 'freedom', 'democracy', 'charity', 'law', 'public interest' and 'equality': they are frequently used normatively, but have sufficient descriptive content to not necessarily involve commendation or disparagement. It is intelligible, albeit uncommon, to call acts of charity morally wrong or to reject freedom categorically. Non-essentially evaluative concepts like 'freedom' are evaluative not because of any feature of the concept, but because of the normative commitments of the persons using them (Carter 2015: 284). Thus, the concept 'equality' expresses a value for egalitarians, but not for malign tyrants. (Egalitarians who morally disapprove of equal distributions are not necessarily *conceptually* confused, although they do hold incoherent normative beliefs.) The widespread negative emotional connotations of 'banker' are likewise due to speakers' normative commitments; the term can actually be used purely descriptively.[5]

The distinction between essentially and non-essentially evaluative concepts helps you keep conceptual analysis and normative theorizing distinct. Oppenheim (1981) advocates rendering political concepts suitable for empirical inquiry by treating them as descriptive concepts, i.e. by defining 'equality' and 'freedom' in a non-evaluative manner. This requires a degree of reconstruction: separating the descriptive from the evaluative function of political concepts by creating purely descriptive definitions. This separation is possible only for non-essentially evaluative concepts. Definitions are purely descriptive (non-moralized, value-free) whenever they do not contain any evaluative terms (Carter 2015: 284). Before outlining the advantages of non-moralized definitions, I address Dworkin's objection that non-normative analyses of political concepts are impossible: studying political concepts would be ethical all the way down (2011: 166–70).

Dworkin's rejection of Oppenheim's methodological project is informed by the true claim that few political concepts are *value-neutral*: nearly all are ordinarily used to express values (Section 4.3). But since non-essentially evaluative concepts like 'freedom' and 'equality' express values not of themselves but because of the normative commitments of speakers using these concepts, they *can* be defined in a value-free manner. To proffer a *value-free* definition (a definition without evaluative terms) does not, however, make a concept *value-neutral*: for liberals, 'freedom' is valuable however we define it. But again, this positive evaluation is not part of the concept of freedom, but follows from the normative commitments of liberals. In sum, *pace* Dworkin, non-essentially evaluative

---

[5] Bernard Williams's (1985: 129–30) distinction between 'thin' ethical concepts (which lack descriptive content) and 'thick' ones (which have both evaluative and descriptive components) captures roughly the same idea more obscurely: 'thickness' and 'thinness' are matters of degree, whereas 'essentially' and 'non-essentially' are not (Carter 2015: 287–9; cf. Dworkin 2011: 180–4; Scheffler 1987: 417–21).

concepts like 'equality' and 'freedom' can be defined in a value-free manner, essentially evaluative concepts like 'justice' cannot.

Avoid moralized definitions of political concepts for at least four reasons. (1) As Oppenheim argues (1981: 1), scientific dialogue is facilitated by the creation of a common vocabulary of operational concepts that theorists can subscribe to regardless of their normative presuppositions and persuasions. (2) Moralized definitions cause confusion insofar as they portray moral disagreements as purely linguistic ones (disagreements over the meaning of terms). (3) Moralized definitions may render controversial questions true by definition. By defining 'law' as 'morally binding precepts', natural law theorists like Suárez settled the disputed question 'should we obey the law?' by definitional fiat. Keeping the questions of 'what is law' and 'what is the moral quality of law' distinct is methodologically preferable: to conflate them is to blur the distinction between conceptual analysis and normative theorizing (Section 3.3). (4) Finally, moralized definitions provide controversial criteria for application. Consider the moralized account of equality advanced by von Leyden (1963: 67): 'The true opposite of equality is arbitrary, i.e. unjustifiable or inequitable treatment.' By defining one controversial term ('equality') by another ('inequitable'), von Leyden drastically diminishes the possibility of agreement on what counts as (un)equal. We may agree that a relation is unequal while disagreeing about whether the inequality is such that it renders the relation unjustifiable. Moreover, we might deem the relation unjustifiable for another reason than its inequality (e.g. because it is exploitative). (We may agree that something *is* valuable or justified, while disagreeing about *what makes* it so.)

What about essentially evaluative concepts like justice and fairness? It seems conceptually impossible to define such concepts purely descriptively: to use these concepts is to make a claim about how the world should be. If so, then given widespread moral disagreement, any attempt to determine the extension of the concept of justice (the set of objects in the world properly called 'just') will be controversial. This suggests that studying concepts like 'justice' and 'fairness' will inevitably be a normative endeavour, requiring normative arguments.

The worry strikes me as sound. But it does not follow that conceptual analysis is altogether powerless with respect to essentially evaluative concepts. The objection really applies only to Extensional Analysis (Section 3.2). Other kinds of conceptual analysis, such as disambiguating equivocal terms and hunting for conceptual connections, are not impeded by a concept's essentially evaluative nature. We can elucidate what it means to call something just (i.e. what kind of claim we are making) while disagreeing over which things in the world are just

(Miller 1983: 40–1). While people strongly disagree over what the proper criteria are for institutions to qualify as just (i.e. over the *standards* of justice), disagreement over what makes something count as a standard of *justice* (rather than of prudence, good taste or efficiency) is unlikely to run as deep. This is because recognizing a norm as a norm of justice requires no normative judgement itself. We can recognize that 'divide the social surplus according to need' is a principle of justice by reflecting on what the principle aims to achieve (a fair distribution of societal resources). We do not in addition need to morally evaluate whether the principle succeeds, in our view, in capturing the true criteria for a fair distribution, such that it successfully identifies all fair distributions and only those. This discussion suggests that the extension of concepts like 'justice' is ambiguous. It could either consist of everything in the world that meets the standards of justice. Or it could consist of all these standards, principles and norms themselves. **When analysing essentially evaluative concepts like justice, do not conflate the set of objects it evaluates positively with the set of evaluative standards that fall under the concept.**

An analysis of essentially evaluative concepts can take two forms. First, **reflection on linguistic use may reveal that essentially evaluative terms are systematically used to refer to distinct kinds of objects**. As Aristotle observed long ago, 'justice and injustice are spoken of in more than one way, but because the different senses of each are close to one another, their homonymy passes unnoticed' (2000: 81–2). According to Aristotle, 'justice' is used to refer to several different ideas: (1) justice of persons and (2) of actions; (3) justice as the whole of other-regarding morality vs. (4) justice as a special virtue; (5) distributive justice; (6) corrective justice; and (7) justice in exchange. Each constitutes a distinct concept falling under the umbrella notion of justice. Disambiguating 'justice' in this way is illuminating even amidst intractable disagreement over which things in the world are just and unjust.

Second, we can **explore the basic conceptual structure of justice by identifying the elements of justice and their conceptual linkages**. These elements constitute linguistic criteria for counting as an instance of justice. An excellent example is Mill's analysis of the elements of justice in *Utilitarianism* (Gaus 2000: 182–5). After summarizing the various ways in which 'justice' is used, Mill identifies a number of elements common to each of these usages. **This requires analysing conceptually related notions** like 'rights', 'desert', 'duty' and 'impartiality'. Justice, Mill claims, essentially deals with *rights* (whether moral or legal) (Mill 1969: 241–2). 'Impartiality' is implicated in justice only insofar as it is required by 'the more general obligation of giving to every one his right'

(1969: 243). **Try to identify those elements that mark it off from 'neighbouring' concepts.** How does justice differ from related concepts like 'morality' and 'expediency'? Unlike expediency, Mill contends, justice and morality govern duties – things that 'may be *exacted* from a person, as one exacts a debt', whether by penal sanctions or moral blame (1969: 246). Justice, in turn, differs from morality in dealing exclusively with duties with correlative claim-rights: 'Justice implies something which it is not only right to do, and wrong not to do, but which some individual person can claim from us as his moral right.' By contrast, while we have a duty to act benevolently, '[n]o one has a moral right to our generosity or beneficence' (1969: 247). Observe that Mill's analysis is reconstructive: in everyday language, we do not always distinguish as clearly between justice and morality. **Conceptual clarification often requires a degree of reconstruction** (for a defence, see Oppenheim 1981: 177–202). The merits of reconstructive analyses nevertheless depend primarily on their linguistic plausibility, not on their conformity to reflectively endorsed normative judgements.

4.2   Essentially Contested Concepts

W. B. Gallie has introduced the idea of 'essentially contested concepts': 'concepts the proper use of which inevitably involves endless disputes about their proper uses on the part of their users' (1956: 169). Many political concepts have been claimed to be essentially contested, including 'distributive justice' (Gallie 1956: 187), 'power' (Connolly 1983: 97–9, 213–25; Lukes 1974: 26–7), 'the rule of law' (Waldron 2002) and 'democracy' (Gallie 1956: 183–7; List 2011). Disagreement over the proper application of essentially contested concepts does not simply reflect conflicting normative judgements. Rather, conflict is inevitable because of features of the concept itself – 'features which render contests incapable of being rationally settled' even absent moral disagreement (Swanton 1985: 183).

What makes a concept essentially contested? Consider the concept 'democracy'. As any essentially contested concept, 'democratic' is an evaluative notion that expresses an internally complex, variously describable and peculiar 'open' achievement. People disagree not just over which institutions are democratic, but also over the proper criteria for counting as 'democratic'. Some things, we agree, are paradigmatically 'democratic'. An example is our collective, unanimous and informed decision, arrived at by secret ballot and reflecting our true preferences, to go to Eve & Adam's for a pint. However, we may reasonably disagree about *which features* make that exemplary decision procedure quintessentially democratic. For there is 'no one clearly definable general use of ["democratic"] which can be set up as the correct or standard use' (Gallie 1956: 168).

The idea of essentially contested concepts suggests that describing a political concept by listing uncontroversial instances of it may not suffice as an explanation. For we might still disagree about *what makes* these undoubtedly democratic decision procedures 'democratic'. Compare the construction and development of political ideologies: while almost all political theorists agree that Locke and Mill are canonical liberal thinkers, which features of their thought are distinctively liberal is disputed (Bell 2014). It is therefore commendable to **state explicitly the criteria that make something count as an instance of that concept on your account.** This advice makes sense even if the idea of essentially contestedness does not. As Swanton (1985: 827) has argued, '[a]ttractive though the essential contestedness hypothesis is as a solution to the problem of intractable dispute in political and moral theory, the hypothesis has not yet been adequately defended.'

4.3   Value-Neutrality and Ideology

Conceptualizations of political notions are rarely value-neutral: their use 'may imply the superiority of any one of a set of contrasting substantive ethical points of view' (Carter 2015: 285). Understanding 'freedom' as the 'absence of humanly imposed constraints' favours liberals and libertarians; conceptualizing it as 'self-realization' is conducive to communitarians like Taylor (1985). Similarly, thinking of rights in a proprietary sense (as things we own and can possibly dispose of) befits contractarian theories more than viewing them as basic interests that warrant societal protection. A low degree of value-neutrality renders conceptualizations contested: liberals and communitarians each favour the definition of freedom that best fits their own theoretical commitments and ambitions. **The more value-neutral you can make a definition, the higher the chance it will be acceptable to political theorists of different normative persuasions** (Carter 2015: 297). Complete value-neutrality, though, seems impossible to attain in political theory. What does this mean for the relation between conceptual analysis and normative theory?

Conceptual analysis may reveal that one contested conceptualization chimes better with our linguistic practices. However compelling the communitarian arguments that we should value 'self-realization' rather than 'the absence of humanly imposed constraints', such normative arguments cannot prove that the word 'freedom' must be taken to mean 'self-realization'. The meaning of language being socially determined, we cannot unilaterally give a new sense to existing terms: definitions must bear fidelity to linguistic practices (Section 1.1).

Linguistic practices may be unclear, however, or too variegated to settle the matter. Conceptual analysis then requires reconstruction. Which reconstruction (conceptualization) of a notion is preferable will depend partly on its theoretical plausibility. But how plausible a political theory is will, in turn, rest on its normative claims and predictions. Normative considerations will thus indirectly inform our decisions to conceptualize a notion one way or another. Does it make sense to talk about our initial rights of moral control over ourselves in terms of self-ownership? The answer depends, in part, on the theoretical implications of conceiving the moral relation to our body and person in this way, including on the success of resulting theories in capturing and guiding moral judgement (Section 5).

We should thus **attend to the wider political theories within which concepts are articulated.** Rival political theories arrange and conceptualize political concepts differently. Insofar as particular conceptualizations are ultimately preferred on normative grounds, studying political notions involves theory formation. How to best think of the idea of self-ownership, freedom or citizenship may itself depend on linguistic as well as on wider normative and theoretical considerations. Conceptual analysis and normative theorizing are therefore often intertwined in practice. This renders it all the more important to be clear about whether your arguments are normative or conceptual in nature. **State explicitly whether you are favouring a particular conceptualization for normative/theoretical reasons or on linguistic grounds.**

The recognition that conceptualizations of political concepts are rarely value-neutral has inspired the thought that how we use and think of political concepts is itself a contested political act: political theory would be 'political' both in subject matter and in nature. How concepts of race and gender, democracy and freedom are understood and figure in public discourse indeed has tremendous socio-political consequences. Political concepts are commonly used to express and (re)produce relations of power and subordination. Critical theorists scrutinize political discourses, including political theories, in search for recurring (associative) patterns with oppressive or emancipatory effects for different groups. Such discourse analysis belongs to the study of ideologies, however, rather than to conceptual analysis proper (on ideological analysis, see Freeden 1996, and Leader Maynard's chapter in this volume).

Although conceptualizations of political concepts are rarely value-free and practically contested, this in no way spells doom for conceptual analysis. On the contrary, conceptual analysis greatly benefits discourse analysis (Freeden 2005: 124). For instance, we can **use conceptual analysis to help us recognize ideological interpretations of concepts by separating the logical core of a concept from theoretical additions.** Take the concept of 'race'. The term is frequently used to express the idea that historically and geographically related people have a shared essence that makes them morally, culturally or intellectually superior or inferior. Hardimon (2003) has argued that the ordinary concept of race, which marks out groups of humans with shared ancestry by relevant visible physical features, is not itself essentialist. Its 'logical core' does not, therefore, 'provide a rationale for racism, slavery, colonialism, or genocide' (2003: 453). Only so-called racialist conceptions of race, which attribute a shared and evaluable essence to racial groups, do so.

5   Normative Implications

What follows normatively from a successful analysis of concepts? Conceptual analysis, I shall argue, is no substitute for normative argument. It does, however, have important *indirect* implications for normative theorizing. Concepts frame our theories and guide moral judgement. They can also have a distorting effect, however – rendering certain lines of argument salient while side-lining others.

Normative arguments, and moral judgements generally, need conceptual guidance. **Conceptual analysis helps normative judgements target the right propositions, such that they don't spill over into adjacent conceptual territory** (where they don't hold true). Mill notes that proponents of *laissez-faire* often make arguments 'far outstretching the special application made of them' (*Principles* 5.11.1). *Laissez-faire* advocates object not to government intervention as such, but to *coercive* government intervention. Their arguments against government meddling do not challenge 'unauthoritative' state interventions, such as the public provision of goods the government considers too important to entrust solely to the care of the market. **To avoid argumentative spillover, consider what is at stake normatively.**

Another example is found in Cohen's article 'How to do political philosophy' (2011b: 227). Cohen urges political theorists not to conflate the following three questions:
1. What is justice?
2. What should the state do?
3. Which social states of affairs ought to be brought about?
Even if justice is 'the first virtue of social institutions' (Rawls 1999: 3), it does not follow, Cohen argues, that the concept 'what the state should do' is equivalent to 'justice'. Justice is the *primary* but not the *only* virtue of

social institutions – we also evaluate institutions in terms of their efficiency, provision of security and material welfare, securement of privacy, etc. **Do not blend concepts together just because they all signify things we value.** 'Everything is what it is: liberty is liberty, not equality or fairness or justice or culture, or human happiness or a quiet conscience' (Berlin 2002: 172). Furthermore, we could coherently deem an egalitarian division of resources the morally optimal state of affairs without wanting a coercive entity like the state to bring this about (e.g. because of the *way* the state would do so or because we refuse it the requisite powers). Thus, the claim that it is not the business of the state to redistribute resources does not imply that justice requires no redistribution. Conceptual analysis helps prevent such argumentative sliding, thus channelling or blunting the force of particular arguments.

Remember that concepts can be coherent but still theoretically unwarranted. Does it make sense to conceptualize rights to autonomy and bodily integrity as 'self-ownership'? On Locke's account, 'property' refers to exclusive rights both 'in their Persons as well as Goods' (*Second Treatise* §173). This broad conception of property is out of step with modern linguistic sensibilities; most people, I suspect, would consider 'self-ownership' a metaphor. Contemporary Lockeans may nonetheless have good *theoretical* reason to depart from ordinary language at this point. They claim that we morally control our body and our person in the same way as we morally control material resources belonging to us. It does not follow that the concepts 'self-ownership' and 'property rights in things' are structurally identical. They are evidently not: property rights in things are acquired rights, while the right in one's person is held by virtue of being human. Whether the broad Lockean conception of 'property' is acceptable depends in part on whether the conceptual differences between rights in one's person and rights to material resources are theoretically significant. A theory that treats two different things alike (by subsuming them under one category) may well fail with respect to one of them or to both. Differences in the logical structure of the two rights may imply that what is true of one is false of the other.

Kant rejected the notion of 'self-ownership': 'Man cannot dispose over himself, because he is not a thing. He is not his own property' (1997: 157). While we may sell our house, we are not entitled, according to Kant, to sell ourselves or parts of our body. Why not? Kant replies that the notion of self-ownership is internally contradictory: 'it is impossible, of course, to be at once a thing and a person, a proprietor and a property at the same time' (ibid.). Cohen accuses Kant of 'trying to pull a normative rabbit out of a conceptual hat' here (1995: 212). Kant does not show why the concept of self-ownership is incoherent, i.e. why it is logically impossible for persons to own themselves. Even if he did succeed in showing this, it is better to **let moral judgements and arguments rather than conceptual *legerdemain* do the normative weightlifting.** Thus if we believe, like Kant, that prostitution is morally unacceptable, then we should put forth normative arguments in support rather than claiming that it is conceptually impossible for persons to commodify their body.

Do not mistake the conceptual possibility of a notion with the actual existence or normative desirability of what it denotes. Proving a concept to be coherent is one thing; proving that it has real-world application and/or denotes something normatively desirable is something else. Proponents of the concept of self-ownership should do more than dislodge the Kantian objection of incoherency. They should also show that it is morally true that we own ourselves, e.g. by appealing to the widespread intuition that 'we – and not others – are morally in charge of our bodies and persons', and by showing that other property rules like trusteeship or guardianship cannot satisfactorily account for that intuition (Vallentyne, Steiner and Otsuka 2005: 208). As Cohen puts it: 'the concept of self-ownership is not identical with the thesis of self-ownership: the latter might be false, while the former, being a concept, cannot be false' (Cohen 1995: 209).

When analysing evaluative concepts, separate the questions 'what is *X*' and 'what makes *X* morally valuable/objectionable'. A conceptual analysis of racism cannot by itself explain what is morally objectionable about racism: normative judgement is needed as well. However, the more refined our grasp of this concept, the easier it becomes to determine which features make racism wrong. Conversely, if our analysis focuses exclusively on those features of racism we deem morally objectionable, then, constricted by our moral judgements, we are in danger of arriving at an impoverished account of racism.

Section 2.2 pointed out that conceptions of normative notions generally include normative principles. Consequently, **disputes over rival normative conceptions cannot normally be settled by conceptual arguments alone.** Normative arguments are needed as well. Take Galston's (1995) distinction between conceptions of liberalism based on 'autonomy' and 'diversity'. Galston does not argue that one of these conceptions captures more accurately the 'true meaning' of liberalism – wisely, as the dispute is not solely about *linguistic* intuitions. Instead he argues that the diversity conception better captures what we (ought to) find valuable in liberalism.

Do not mistake relabelling a concept for a normative argument. Since freedom is ethically valuable, it is morally significant whether lacking resources is a way of being unfree. C. L. Stevenson has called redefinitions that do nothing else but redeploy emotionally charged words 'persuasive definitions'. A persuasive definition 'gives a new conceptual meaning to a familiar word without substantially changing its emotive meaning, and which is used with the conscious or unconscious purpose of changing, by this means, the direction of people's interests' (Stevenson 1938: 331).[6] Hobbes masterfully understood the nature and use of rhetorical redescriptions (Skinner 1996: 316–26, 338–43). He argued, for instance, that the amount of freedom citizens have is determined solely by the stringency of the law, and not at all by the nature of their political regime (democratic, dictatorial, etc.). Having a voice in who governs you is not part of the Hobbesian concept of liberty (*Leviathan* 21.6–9).

Rhetorical redescriptions risk being merely semantic. It does not follow that they are ineffectual. **Adopting a particular conceptualization can make certain arguments and considerations salient, while side-lining others.** As Anne Phillips acutely notes:

> thinking of oneself as in a relationship of ownership to one's body does *not* commit one, in some inevitable chain of consequences, to supporting the commodification of the body and promoting markets in bodily services and parts. What it does do, however, is skew the kinds of arguments that become available when societies are considering policies on body matters. Property claims make the individual property owners the centre of attention and establish their preferences and choices as the predominant concerns. (Phillips 2013: 142–3)

How we present an idea – including, as Stevenson reminds us, what we call it – can distort normative theorizing by obscuring relevant considerations and increasing the salience of others.

Critical theorists have been especially attentive to the argumentative biases prevailing conceptualizations of political notions have given rise to, biases often favouring the socio-political status quo. One way to criticize existing conceptualizations is by constructing 'a genealogy of concepts' – unearthing the contingency of and ideological prejudices implicit in modern conceptualizations by tracing their history. While it goes beyond the scope of this chapter to discuss this method exhaustively, the final section will outline a key element of it.

---

[6] Stevenson opts for the term 'emotive meaning' because of his non-cognitivist metaethics. His point applies to evaluative notions generally and does not depend on a particular metaethical position.

6   Analysing Conceptualizations

As political philosophers, we do not just analyse political concepts themselves, as if they were free-floating entities ('what is justice?'). We also try to understand, if only preliminarily, how people have *conceptualized* these notions ('what did Rawls mean by justice?'). This section provides concrete advice on how to best reconstruct conceptualizations advanced in the literature. My advice, partly modelled on Extensional Analysis (Section 3.2), may be especially welcome when studying the history of political philosophy. Today's theorists usually try to advance conceptualizations that match our linguistic intuitions (indeed, they are well-advised to do so!), rendering the task of figuring out what they mean with a term comparatively easy. This task becomes harder the further we go back in history. The conceptual landscape has changed dramatically since Locke wrote the *Two Treatises*. As a result, his notion of 'property' may well depart significantly from ours. Reading historical texts is, in many ways, an exercise in translation.

How can we best reconstruct conceptualizations advanced in political texts? The first and perhaps most important tip is to **read with an open mind**. Do not simply assume that what Locke meant by 'property' is the same as what you think it means. This also holds for contemporary texts: G. A. Cohen's conception of 'justice' may well be miles apart from what you and I think the term signifies. **Do not read into the text what is not there.** In *Leviathan*, Hobbes declares that '[t]he notions of Right and Wrong, Justice and Injustice have ... no place' in the condition of 'warre of every man against every man', as it exists outside the state (*Leviathan* 13.13). Hans Morgenthau, doyen of the realist school in international relations theory, consequently attributes to Hobbes the 'extreme dictum' that 'the state creates morality as well as law and that there is neither morality nor law outside the state' (Morgenthau 1952: 34). But Hobbes is speaking only about justice. Justice and morality ('natural law') are not the same thing for Hobbes; indeed, natural law exists and is to a limited extent operative outside the state (Olsthoorn 2015: 20). The distinction between justice and morality may be irrelevant for Morgenthau's purposes; it is not for Hobbes.

Read the text, as far as possible, in the original language. This advice should not be taken to extremes: if your Latin is as rusty as mine, reading modern editions is likely to be vastly more profitable than sweating over the original. **Remember that you are reading a translation (when doing so).** Even critical editions may translate terms in a misleading or inconsistent manner. Cross-checking the original can save you much time and confusion. I have spent ages trying to make sense of Hobbes's comment that 'by natural *law*, one is oneself the judge' (*De Cive* 1.9) – only to discover eventually that Tuck and Silverthorne (1998) had mistranslated the original Latin: 'by natural *right*' (*jure naturali*). (For Hobbes, 'right' and 'law' are opposites – e.g. *De Cive* 14.3; *Leviathan* 14.3, 26.44.)

Stick as far as possible to the original terms. Substituting your own terms is potentially distorting. Translation inevitably leads to loss or change of meaning. Even if terms have roughly the same extension – i.e. when they refer to the same objects – their meaning may differ. What early moderns called 'natural law' picks out roughly the same objects as our 'morality', but the conceptual linkages of the two notions differ considerably. To highlight one salient difference, early modern natural laws are moral norms applying to us by virtue of the kind of beings we are. Modern 'morality' lacks such an explicit grounding in human nature. While substituting your own terms increases the risk of overlooking conceptual changes, sticking to the original terms is no panacea: serious historical research is needed to recover lost connotations and conceptual connections of notions like 'natural law'. **If you are using an original term whose meaning has changed over time, then describe its meaning in present-day terms as well as you can.**

Be attentive to unexpected usages of the term. We are inclined to think of 'property' as a general term for rules governing access to and control of material resources (Waldron 1988: 31). Undiscerning readers of the *Second Treatise* may assume that Locke was primarily concerned with safeguarding citizens' existing rights to material resources against the State. But Locke uses the term 'property' in a far more expansive manner as including 'Lives, Liberties, and Estates' (*Second Treatise* §123). Such unexpected usages – lives as property? – should be red flags, indicators of conceptual change.

What is the best way to systematically reconstruct what a particular philosopher meant by a term? A good first step is to **collect explicit definitions and descriptions.** Locke declares that it is of the nature of property 'that *without a Man's own consent* it *cannot be taken from him*' (*Second Treatise* §193). Notice that this is not, strictly speaking, a definition, but rather a description of an essential feature of Lockean property. Elsewhere, Locke writes: 'the *Idea* of *Property*, being a right to any thing' (*Essay Concerning Human Understanding* 4.3.18). We may formulate a provisional definition: 'property is the exclusive moral control over a material or immaterial object.' To further improve the definition, **consider assembling contextual evidence**. The *Oxford English Dictionary* often lists earliest possible usages of senses of a term still in vogue. Specialized etymological dictionaries provide more detailed information. When bogged down by an odd usage of a term, it is worthwhile to look at contemporary translations; the translator's choice is rarely authoritative but potentially revealing. **Reading contemporary writers, especially critics, is often illuminating as well.** Conceptualizations may be taken over from earlier thinkers. Critics frequently challenge innovative conceptualizations, clarifying along the way how they depart from standard accounts in the period.

The next step is to **look for other occurrences of the term, and check whether they match the provisional definition.** Indexes are handy; word searching a digital edition of a text is more convenient still. Does the way in which the term is used in the context make sense on the proposed definition? If not, reformulate the definition. Conversely, reflect whether on the proposed definition certain things would count as 'property', and then check whether Locke indeed calls them so. The aim is to arrive at a description of Locke's conception of property that accurately captures its defining conditions. Notice that this method follows roughly the same format as conceptual analysis as Extensional Analysis, outlined in Section 3.2. A main difference between interpretative and systematic analysis – that is, between analysing conceptualizations and analysing concepts – is the criterion of application. When doing conceptual analysis, we use our own linguistic intuitions and theoretical convictions to determine whether the case at hand is best regarded as an instantiation of the concept. When analysing conceptualizations, we use textual passages to determine their meaning and extension.

This leads to a second difference: inconsistent or incurably ambiguous usages and incoherent conceptualizations are real possibilities in interpretative ventures. Philosophers are, alas, fallible creatures. They may not always strictly adhere to their own definitions, and their conceptualizations may fall short of the ideals of clarity and coherency (Skinner 2002: 67–72). **Do not assume perfect terminological consistency.** Terminological inconsistencies can have various causes, including shoddy thinking. Inconsistencies are especially prone to occur when an author advances a novel conceptualization – historically and philosophically the more interesting cases. **Be aware that a term may be used in more than one sense.** Locke employs 'property' both in a narrow sense (as rights to material resources) and in a broad sense (as anything a person may exclusively call her own, including life, liberty, chastity and material goods) (Olivecrona 1975). Every instance of property in its narrow sense is an instance of its broader sense; the reverse is not true. It is worthwhile to **explore whether the apparent ambiguity can be resolved at**

a higher level by searching for a general definition that encapsulates both senses of the term.

Check for theoretical consistency. Like a real scientist, try to falsify your provisional definition by analysing whether it can fulfil the theoretical role it is supposed to fulfil. Are Locke's arguments about property logically valid on the proposed definition? If they are, then this is evidence that your definition is correct. It does not follow that your definition is *in*correct if they are not: the problem might be Locke's rather than yours. Tests for theoretical consistency are also possible across thinkers. Early modern philosophers generally argued that people are naturally equal *because* they are born free. 'Freedom' was understood as 'being your own master'. If everyone is by nature their own master, then there are no natural inequalities of hierarchy (of rule and subjection). Thus conceptualized, 'natural freedom' *implies* 'natural equality'. We can check the soundness of this interpretation by examining whether any early modern philosopher rejected natural equality *despite* holding that humans are born free.

My final piece of advice is to **be wary of interpretive charity.** Rawls is a well-known proponent of this principle: 'to present each writer's thought in what I took to be its strongest form'. Not, he clarified, 'what to my mind they should have said, but what they did say, supported by what I viewed as the most reasonable interpretation of their text' (Rawls 2007: xiii, also 52; cf. Frazer 2010). If we take 'reasonable' to mean avoiding attributing flagrant inconsistencies and non sequiturs to an author, few would object: if an argument found in 'the classics' is logically invalid on your reading, consider it a sign of misinterpretation. Rawls goes further, however: we should interpret a thinker's arguments and doctrines in the way that makes most sense to us – in its intellectually strongest form, the most plausible reading the text can bear. If you are mining the classics for insights to solve today's philosophical quandaries, then this is an excellent principle of interpretation. **If you are trying to uncover the historical meaning of a text, then you should interpret conceptualizations in the historically most plausible way, rather than the way we nowadays would think most reasonable.** Otherwise we risk forgoing from the outset a major benefit of historical research: unearthing radically different ways of conceptualizing familiar notions that reveal the contingency and tacit assumptions of their modern counterparts.

7   Conclusion

This chapter has provided a range of advice, from the obvious to the controversial, on how to do conceptual analysis in political theory. Rather than reiterating my main recommendations, I will conclude by highlighting two methodological assumptions underlying my advice. Throughout this chapter I have argued that **we should not conflate two key tools political theorists have at our disposal: conceptual analysis and normative theorizing**. What does the difference between the two reside in? Conceptual analysis, I have assumed, is essentially linguistic analysis: it consists in scrutinizing, systematizing and developing the classifications implicit in ordinary linguistic practices. Normative theorizing, by contrast, consists in the construction of arguments and theories based on normative rather than conceptual considerations. Conceptual analysis and normative theorizing thus come with different felicity conditions and burdens of proof.

The second presupposition is that we should **conduct conceptual analysis independently of normative theorizing**. This view is controversial with respect to the many political concepts normally used prescriptively rather than descriptively. I have argued that conceptually analysing concepts that express or are normally used to express values is possible, but requires special care. In particular, it requires distinguishing between the objects in the world to which an evaluative notion applies (which always involves normative judgement) and the evaluative norms or standards falling under that concept (whose nature can be analysed conceptually).

Acknowledgements

Donald Bello Hutt, Adrian Blau, Benjamin De Mesel, Alex Douglas, Robin Douglass, Cressida Gaukroger, Siba Harb, Michael Jewkes and especially A. P. Martinich provided very helpful comments on previous versions of this chapter. I would also like to thank the KU Leuven research group in political philosophy (RIPPLE) for a stimulating discussion of an earlier draft.

References

Aristotle, 2000. *Nicomachean Ethics*, ed. Roger Crisp. Cambridge: Cambridge University Press.
Austin, John, 1998. *The Province of Jurisprudence Determined*. Indianapolis, IN: Hackett.
Beaney, Michael, 2015. 'Analysis', in Edward Zalta, ed., *The Stanford Encyclopedia of Philosophy*, http://plato.stanford.edu/archives/spr2015/entries/analysis. Accessed 1 September 2015.
Bell, Duncan, 2014. 'What is liberalism?', *Political Theory* 42: 682–715.

Bentham, Jeremy, 1838–43. *The Works of Jeremy Bentham*, 11 vols., ed. J. Bowring. Edinburgh: W. Tait.

Berlin, Isaiah, 2002. *Liberty: Incorporating Four Essays on Liberty*. Oxford University Press.

Carter, Ian, 2004. 'Choice, freedom, and freedom of choice', *Social Choice and Welfare* 22, 61–81.

Carter, Ian, 2011. 'The myth of "merely formal freedom"', *The Journal of Political Philosophy* 19, 486–95.

Carter, Ian, 2015. 'Value-freeness and value-neutrality in the analysis of political concepts', *Oxford Studies in Political Philosophy* 1: 279–306.

Cohen, G. A., 1995. *Self-Ownership, Freedom, and Equality*. Cambridge University Press.

Cohen, G. A., 2011a. 'Freedom and money', in *On the Currency of Egalitarian Justice, and Other Essays in Political Philosophy*. Princeton, NJ: Princeton University Press, 166–92.

Cohen, G. A., 2011b. 'How to do political philosophy', in *On the Currency of Egalitarian Justice, and Other Essays in Political Philosophy*. Princeton, NJ: Princeton University Press, 225–35.

Connolly, William, 1983. *The Terms of Political Discourse*. 2nd edition. Oxford: Martin Robinson.

Donnellan, Keith, 1966. 'Reference and definite descriptions', *The Philosophical Review* 75, 281–304.

Dummett, Michael, 2010. *The Nature and Future of Philosophy*. New York: Columbia University Press.

Dworkin, Ronald, 1986. *Law's Empire*. Cambridge, MA: Belknap Press.

Dworkin, Ronald, 2011. *Justice for Hedgehogs*. Cambridge, MA: Belknap Press.

Fleischacker, Samuel, 2004. *A Short History of Distributive Justice*. Cambridge, MA: Harvard University Press.

Frazer, Michael, 2010. 'The modest professor: interpretive charity and interpretive humility in John Rawls's Lectures on the History of Political Philosophy', *European Journal of Political Theory* 9, 218–26.

Freeden, Michael, 1996. *Ideologies and Political Theory: A Conceptual Approach*. Oxford: Clarendon Press.

Freeden, Michael, 2005. 'What should the "political" in political theory explore?', *The Journal of Political Philosophy* 13, 113–34.

Gallie, W. B., 1956. 'Essentially contested concepts', *Proceedings of the Aristotelian Society* 56, 167–98.

Galston, William, 1995. 'Two concepts of liberalism', *Ethics* 105, 516–34.

Gardner, John, 2001. 'Legal positivism: 5½ myths', *American Journal of Jurisprudence* 46: 199–227.

Gaus, Gerald, 2000. *Political Concepts and Political Theories*. Boulder, CO: Westview Press.

Gerring, John, 1999. 'What makes a concept good? A criterial framework for understanding concept formation in the social sciences', *Polity* 31, 357–93.

Grotius, Hugo, 2005. *The Rights of War and Peace*, ed. Richard Tuck. Indianapolis, IN: Liberty Fund.

Hardimon, Michael, 2003. 'The ordinary concept of race', *The Journal of Philosophy* 100, 437–55.

Hayek, F. A., 1960. *The Constitution of Liberty*. London: Routledge & Kegan Paul.

Hobbes, Thomas, 1998. *On the Citizen*, ed. Richard Tuck, tr. Michael Silverthorne. Cambridge University Press.

Hobbes, Thomas, 2012, *Leviathan*, ed. Noel Malcolm. Oxford: Clarendon Press.

Hohfeld, Wesley Newcomb, 1923. *Fundamental Legal Conceptions as Applied in Judicial Reasoning and other Legal Essays*. New Haven, CT: Yale University Press.

Honoré, Tony, 1987. *Making Law Bind: Essays Legal and Philosophical*. Oxford: Clarendon Press, 161–92.

Jackson, Frank, 1998. *From Metaphysics to Ethics: A Defence of Conceptual Analysis*. Oxford: Clarendon Press.

Jackson, Frank, 2001. 'Précis of *from Metaphysics to Ethics*', *Philosophy and Phenomenological Research* 62: 617–24.

Joyce, Richard, 2015. 'Moral anti-realism', in Edward Zalta, ed., *The Stanford Encyclopedia of Philosophy*, http://plato.stanford.edu/archives/sum2015/entries/moral-anti-realism. Accessed 20 August 2015.

Kant, Immanuel, 1997. *Lectures on Ethics*, ed. Peter Heath and J. B. Schneewind, tr. Peter Heath. Cambridge University Press.

List, Christian, 2011. 'The logical space of democracy', *Philosophy and Public Affairs* 39: 262–97.

List, Christian and Laura Valentini 2016. 'The methodology of political theory', in Herman Cappelen, Tamar Szabó Gendler and John Hawthorne, eds., *The Oxford Handbook of Philosophical Methodology*. Oxford University Press, 525–53.

Locke, John, 1975. *An Essay Concerning Human Understanding*, ed. P. H. Nidditch. Oxford: Clarendon Press.

Locke, John, 1988. *Two Treatises of Government*, ed. Peter Laslett. Cambridge University Press.

Lovett, Frank, 2012. 'What counts as arbitrary power?', *Journal of Political Power* 5: 137–52.

Lukes, Steven, 1974. *Power: A Radical View*. London: Macmillan.

Margolis, Eric and Stephen Laurence, 1999. 'Concepts and cognitive science', in Eric Margolis and Stephen Laurence, eds., *Concepts: Core Readings*. Cambridge, MA: MIT Press, 3–81.

Margolis, Eric and Stephen Laurence, 2014. 'Concepts', in Edward Zalta, ed., *The Stanford Encyclopedia of Philosophy*, http://plato.stanford.edu/archives/spr2014/entries/concepts. Accessed 10 July 2015.

Martinich, A. P., 2005. *Philosophical Writing: An Introduction*. 3rd edition. Malden, MA: Blackwell Publishing.

Martinich, A. P., 2014. 'Political theory and linguistic criteria in Han Feizi's Philosophy', *Dao* 13: 379–93.

Mill, John Stuart, 1965. *Collected Works of John Stuart Mill, Volumes II and III*, ed. J. M. Robson. University of Toronto Press.

Mill, John Stuart, 1969. *Collected Works of John Stuart Mill, Volume X*, ed. J. M. Robson. University of Toronto Press.

Mill, John Stuart, 1974. *Collected Works of John Stuart Mill, Volumes VII and VIII*, ed. J. M. Robson. University of Toronto Press.

Mill, John Stuart, 1989. *Autobiography*, ed. J. M. Robson. London: Penguin.

Miller, David, 1983. 'Linguistic philosophy and political theory', in David Miller and Larry Siedentop, eds., *The Nature of Political Theory*. Oxford: Clarendon Press, 35–51.

Morgenthau, Hans, 1952. *American Foreign Policy: A Critical Examination*. London: Methuen & Co.

Murphy, Gregory, 2002. *The Big Book of Concepts*. Cambridge, MA: MIT Press.

Olivecrona, Karl, 1975. 'The term "property" in Locke's Two Treatises of Government', *Archiv für Rechts- und Sozialphilosophie* 61, 109–15.

Olsthoorn, Johan, 2015. 'Why justice and injustice have no place outside the Hobbesian state', *European Journal of Political Theory* 14: 19–36.

Oppenheim, Felix, 1981. *Political Concepts: A Reconstruction*. Oxford: Basil Blackwell.

Outhwaite, William, 2010. *Concept Formation in Social Science*. London: Routledge.

Pateman, Carole, 1988. *The Sexual Contract*. Cambridge: Polity Press.

Penner, J. E., 1996. 'The "bundle of rights" picture of property', *University of Los Angeles Law Review* 43, 711–820.

Pettit, Philip, 1997. *Republicanism. A Theory of Freedom and Government*. Oxford: Clarendon Press.

Pettit, Philip, 2012. *On the People's Terms. A Republican Theory and Model of Democracy*. Cambridge University Press.

Phillips, Anne, 2013. *Our Bodies, Whose Property?* Princeton, NJ: Princeton University Press.

Rawls, John, 1999a. *A Theory of Justice*. Revised edition. Cambridge, MA: Belknap Press.

Rawls, John, 1999b. *Collected Papers*, ed. Samuel Freeman. Cambridge, MA: Harvard University Press, 47–72.

Rawls, John, 2001. *Justice as Fairness: A Restatement*. Cambridge, MA: Belknap Press.

Rawls, John, 2005. *Political Liberalism*. Expanded edition. New York: Columbia University Press.

Rawls, John, 2007. *Lectures on the History of Political Philosophy*. Cambridge, MA: Harvard University Press.

Raz, Joseph, 1984. 'On the nature of rights', *Mind* 93: 194–214.

Russell, Bertrand, 1923. 'Vagueness', *Australasian Journal of Psychology and Philosophy* 1, 84–92.

Sartori, Giovanni, 1970. 'Concept misformation in comparative politics', *American Political Science Review* 64: 1033–53.

Sartori, Giovanni, 1984. *Social Science Concepts: A Systematic Analysis*. Beverly Hills, CA: SAGE Publications.

Scheffler, Samuel, 1987. 'Morality through thick and thin: a critical notice of Ethics and the Limits of Philosophy', *The Philosophical Review* 96, 411–34.

Schroeter, Laura, 2004. 'The limits of conceptual analysis', *Pacific Philosophical Quarterly* 85: 425–53.

Skinner, Quentin, 1996. *Reason and Rhetoric in the Philosophy of Hobbes*. Cambridge University Press.

Skinner, Quentin, 2002. *Visions of Politics, Volume I: Regarding Method*. Cambridge University Press.

Skorupski, John, 2010. *The Domain of Reasons*. Oxford University Press.

Skorupski, John, 2012. 'Précis of The Domain of Reasons', *Philosophy and Phenomenological Research* 85: 174–84.

Stevenson, Charles Leslie, 1938. 'Persuasive definitions', *Mind* 47: 331–50.

Suárez, Francisco, 2015. *Selections from Three Works*, ed. Thomas Pink. Indianapolis, IN: Liberty Fund.

Swanton, Christine, 1985. 'On the "essential contestedness" of political concepts', *Ethics* 95, 811–27.

Tamir, Yael, 1993. *Liberal Nationalism*. Princeton, NJ: Princeton University Press.

Taylor, Charles, 1985. *The Human Sciences: Philosophical Papers II*. Cambridge University Press.

de Tocqueville, Alexis, 2003. *Democracy in America and Two Essays on America*, ed. Isaac Kramnick. London: Penguin.

Vallentyne, Peter, Hillel Steiner and Michael Otsuka, 2005. 'Why left-libertarianism is not incoherent, indeterminate, or irrelevant: a reply to Fried', *Philosophy and Public Affairs* 33: 201–15.

Van Parijs, Philippe, 1995. *Real Freedom for All: What (If Anything) Can Justify Capitalism?* Oxford: Clarendon Press.

Von Leyden, Wolfgang, 1963. 'On justifying inequality', *Political Studies* 11: 56–70.

Waldron, Jeremy, 1988. *The Right to Private Property*. Oxford: Clarendon Press.

Waldron, Jeremy, 2002. 'Is the rule of law an essentially contested concept (in Florida)?', *Law and Philosophy* 21: 137–64.

Wallis, John, 1662. *Hobbius Heauton-timorumenos, or a Consideration of Mr Hobbes His Dialogues*. Oxford: A. & L. Lichfield.

Wenar, Leif, 2013. 'The nature of claim-rights', *Ethics* 123, 202–29.

Williams, Bernard, 1985. *Ethics and the Limits of Philosophy*. Cambridge, MA: Harvard University Press.

Wittgenstein, Ludwig, 2009. *Philosophical Investigations*, 4th edition, ed. and tr. P. M. S. Hacker and Joachim Schulte. Oxford: Wiley-Blackwell.

Wolff, Jonathan, 2013. 'Analytic political philosophy', in *The Oxford Handbook of the History of Analytic Philosophy*, ed. Michael Beaney. Oxford University Press, 795–822.

10   Positive Political Theory

Alan Hamlin

1   Introduction

This chapter is organized around two questions: what is positive political theory, and how can it be used effectively to address research questions? While positive political theory may apply in any substantive area of politics, these questions will be addressed in the context of the analysis of democratic institutions and political behaviour and, specifically, the study of referendums, elections and voting.

The next section locates positive political theory relative to its normative counterpart and indicates the range of positions that exist within positive political theory. Section 3 provides an extended example of positive political theory in the setting of the analysis of democratic elections, so as to develop a more detailed understanding of the component elements of any exercise in positive political theory. Section 4 offers a 'how-to' guide for the development of positive political analysis. While no such guide can guarantee success, the claim is that detailed, systematic and explicit consideration of the processes involved in constructing and using positive political theories can only enhance political debate. Section 5 illustrates the 'how-to' guide by using its principles as a guide to reading two journal articles.

2   What Is Positive Political Theory?

Political theory, particularly when described as political philosophy, is often taken to be essentially normative. While it is certainly true that normative analysis – including both the investigation of normative principles such as justice, well-being or rights and the evaluation and justification of particular social and political institutions and practices – is central to the overall ambition of political theory, normative analysis does not exhaust political theory.

The study of politics must also be concerned with explaining and understanding social and political institutions and practices and the political behaviour of individuals within those institutions and practices. Indeed, the tasks of explaining and understanding might be argued to be logically prior to the tasks of evaluating and justifying; if we cannot say (to some degree of approximation) how a particular institution operates, how can we evaluate that institution? It might be logically possible to offer a fully deontic justification of an institution that does not depend on an evaluation of its workings and the outcomes arising, but most normative approaches would place at least some weight on those outcomes, or the behaviour arising within the institution.

Explanation and understanding cannot simply be a matter of description or direct empirical observation. This is obvious when we seek to understand an institution that does not currently exist (perhaps to consider bringing it into existence), but it is equally true where an institution exists. However detailed our description of an institution's operation, we cannot fully explain or understand it, as our observations are limited to the particular circumstances that we happen to have experienced. A full explanation and understanding would also offer a counterfactual account of the institution's operation in other circumstances.

Positive political theory is that part of political theory that attempts to fill the gap between description and normative analysis, providing us with explanations of political phenomena and behaviour that are both crucial to our understanding of politics and essential to our normative discussion. Whenever we offer an account of any political event or institution, we are engaging in positive political theory. The ubiquity of positive political theory sometimes renders it invisible, in much the same way that Monsieur Jourdain fails to see that he normally speaks in prose (in Moliere's 'Le Bourgeois Gentilhomme'). We can hardly engage in any political discussion without invoking elements of some positive political theory, but we often fail to recognize that fact, or the implications and limitations of the particular theory that we are invoking. A main theme of this chapter is that our discussions would be improved if the underlying positive political theory component were more explicit.

The use of positive political theory should not be confused with a commitment to positivism. This is not the place to engage with the wider debate on positivism (Gordon 1993; Kincaid 1998), but it is worth pointing out that one can take any of a variety of non-positivist views in the philosophy of social science without undermining the significance of what I refer to as positive political theory. Theories may be Marxist (or post-Marxist), structuralist (or post-structuralist), feminist (or post-feminist) or embody any of a wide variety of further commitments but still form part of positive political theory in the sense that I intend it.

Similarly, theories may draw on anthropology, economics, psychology, sociology or other disciplines while maintaining their essentially political character.

If positive political theory is not necessarily 'positivist', we should also note that it need not refrain from all use of normative terms and ideas. Many positive models in politics will involve assumptions about the motivations of political agents, and many of the motivations studied are 'normative' in character: we might, for example, study the behaviour of individuals motivated by considerations of 'justice', or by considerations derived from a broader morality. While the motivations under consideration are normative, our study can still be positive if our focus is on understanding the behaviour of individuals with the specified motivation rather than evaluating or justifying that motivation. In this way, elements of our study can be recognized as normative in themselves, but still taken as the object of positive study: a piece of positive political theory can include reference to normative terms and concepts provided that the reference is of an appropriate kind.

Having identified positive political theory in this very expansive way, I should note that the phrase 'positive political theory' is often used more narrowly, sometimes to mean 'formal political theory', sometimes to mean 'rational choice political theory' and sometimes to mean 'game-theoretic approaches to politics'. I will comment on each of these usages.

Formal political theory identifies that sub-class of political theory that is expressed in the style of theorems and lemmas using the tools of mathematics or formal logic. The defining feature of formal political theory is simply its mathematical or logical formality rather than the topic that the theory addresses, the particular nature of the assumptions made within the theory, or whether the theory is positive or normative in character. Formal political theory is often, but not always, linked to detailed statistical modelling (Riker and Ordeshook 1973; Forbes 2004).

Rational choice political theory identifies the sub-class of political theory that takes as foundational the assumption that individuals act rationally. Within this class we may find both formal and informal theories, and both positive and normative discussion, although it is certainly the case that much rational choice political theory is relatively formal and positive in its orientation (Satz and Ferejohn 1994; Shepsle and Bonchek 1997; Austen-Smith and Banks 2000; Hindmoor 2006). For critical discussion of the rational choice approach, see Green and Shapiro (1994), Friedman (1996) and Hindmoor (2011). For more details, see Kogelmann and Gaus's chapter in this volume.

Game-theoretic political theory, also discussed in Kogelmann and Gaus's chapter in this volume, is a subset of rational choice political theory. Game-theoretic accounts not only take individuals to be rational in a particular sense, but the situation under study is taken to constitute a 'game' in the sense that it is the strategic interaction between rational individuals that is emphasized (Ordeshook 1986; Austen-Smith and Banks 2005). While it is possible to discuss game-theoretic political theory in a relatively informal way, game theoretic analysis is built on formal foundations. But game-theoretic approaches to politics are not the only possible intersection of formal methods and rational choice: it is possible to identify formal, rational choice models that are not game theoretic.

If formal, rational choice and game-theoretic approaches are only subsets of positive political theory, why are they sometimes claimed to occupy the whole of the territory? In part this is simply a matter of prominence: there can be little doubt that the literature that uses the language of positive political theory most explicitly is closely associated with approaches that combine formality, rationality and game theory in various combinations. But, to revert to the analogy with prose, just because some prose speakers proclaim that they speak in prose, it does not follow that they are the only prose speakers. Informal positive political theory, by the very fact that it is informal, tends to be much less self-aware than its formal cousin, but whenever a writer makes any claim about the behaviour of individuals or social groups in political settings, or the characteristics of a particular political institution, or makes a prediction about political events, he or she will normally be relying on some understanding of underlying forces or patterns of causality that merits the use of the term 'positive political theory'. Of course, many such 'theories' are largely implicit, and some may be such that any attempt to make them explicit would reveal them to be little more than prejudice or opinion. But moving from the implicit to the explicit and improving theories (however we might define 'improving') is not necessarily the same as formalizing those theories (in the sense of presenting them in mathematical form) or rendering them within the framework of rational choice or game theory. A positive political theory may be useful, revealing and insightful while being informal and making no significant reference to rational choice; just as a formal, rational choice or game-theoretic theory may also be useful, revealing and insightful.

So, what are the essential elements of a positive political theory? Here there is no clear, universally accepted answer, but it seems relatively uncontentious to begin with the idea of a model. Initially we might think of a model as a limited representation of some element of reality. It is important that the representation of reality is limited, since the reason we create models is that reality is too complex to be studied in its raw form. But it is also important to consider how a model's representation of reality is limited. There are three key elements here: abstraction, simplification and idealization. Abstraction is the idea that we manage some aspects of the complexity of the real world by ignoring them; that is, by leaving them out of the model altogether. Clearly, we would like to abstract from those aspects of reality that we think unimportant, but often we may need to abstract from some potentially important areas in order to focus our attention on others. Simplification is the idea that, even when we include an aspect of reality in our model we will typically need to include only some of its features. Again, we would like to focus on the most salient or significant features, but we will often have to sacrifice features of interest in order to focus our study. Idealization is the idea that in modelling some feature of the real world we may need to represent that feature in a rather stylized or 'pure' form, rather than the messy and complicated forms exhibited in the real world.

A simple illustrative example of a model from outside of the social sciences may help. Consider the London underground map. This is a model. It abstracts from many aspects of real-world London, completely ignoring streets and features such as parks or buildings in order to focus on the layout of the underground network. It simplifies the depiction of the underground network, so that, for example, the map is not to scale and does not depict the real geographical relationship between underground stations. It also idealizes the network to present a graphically striking image relying on colours and design features that do not correspond to the underlying reality.

This example suggests an important point: models are created for a purpose; they are good models to the extent that they serve their purpose well. In particular, good, useful models do not need to be 'realistic' in any general or complete sense; indeed most good models will abstract from, simplify and idealize reality to such an extent that they are clearly 'unrealistic'. Of course, a good model will retain some connection to the real world; but that connection may be highly stylized, so that the relationship between the model and the real world is less like a detailed photograph and more like a caricature that captures one or two key features of reality in a simplified (even exaggerated) form while ignoring everything else.

The general point here is that a model is to be judged by its usefulness rather than by any direct appeal to its realism (or the realism of its assumptions). And this in turn suggests that one might want many different models of essentially the same piece of reality, with each model aiming to capture a different aspect of that reality: just as one might want many different maps of London in addition to the underground map, each serving a rather different function, so one might want a variety of models of a political election, each focusing on a different aspect of the complex whole. Rather than these different models being rivals, they may complement each other, so that each model contributes to our more general understanding.

In moving from models such as the London underground map to models and theories in the social sciences, we need to address two complications: one concerned with a further aspect of the make-up of political models, the other with the idea of 'usefulness'.

So far, a model has been identified as an abstract, simplified and idealized representation of a part of reality. But most models in politics involve another feature, one not shared by the London underground map. This is some animating idea that adds a structure of causality to the model. It is at this point that a model becomes the carrier of a particular theory (Elster 1989; Van Evera 1997). For example, in the study of voting behaviour, an animating idea might be that a particular individual's voting behaviour is explained in part by the social group of which he or she is a member and in part by the extent of that individual's interactions with members of other social groups (Zuckerman et al. 1994; Abrams et al. 2011). A completely different idea of voters' motivation is that voters vote for the candidate they find most physically attractive (Berggren et al. 2009). Many other ideas with at least some plausibility are possible, but, whichever idea is selected, the same principles relate to the specification of an animating idea or causal theory as relate to the basic construction of the model: principles of abstraction, simplification and idealization.

The mere fact that just one or two of the wide range of possible motivational or causal ideas are selected in any particular study is sufficient to demonstrate the principle of abstraction in this context. The motivations of real individuals are hugely complex, both in the sense that any single individual is likely to display a wide range of different motivations and in the sense that different individuals are likely to display different motivations; but a theory must place some limits on the degree of complexity it admits, and most theories will focus attention on a very small subset of potential motivating or causal influences. Similarly, theories will generally need to simplify the form of the particular motivations under consideration, perhaps by restricting the degree of variation across individuals, or by imposing a particular and somewhat arbitrary definition on what features are considered relevant. Finally, theories will typically idealize the motivation of the individuals by taking extreme or pure cases, which might entail making unrealistic assumptions about such matters as the extent to which individuals have access to relevant information, or the extent to which they are consistent in their behaviour.

A basic model provides a setting in which we can isolate key aspects of reality, but without an animating idea or theory such a model is passive: it does not generate any particular understanding of the ways in which these key aspects interact to produce outcomes. This should not be taken to imply that such basic models are not valuable or useful. A basic model will be useful if it frames and addresses a research question in a way that is helpful: just as the underground map can help one to navigate across London, so a basic political model can help one to navigate the literature on a particular political question. But it is the addition of an animating idea or causal theory that transforms the model into an active tool for political investigation.

The second complication relates to the idea of 'usefulness'. While the idea of the usefulness of a basic model such as a map is easy to understand, it is more difficult to be precise about the 'usefulness' of a more animated theory in politics. The general ambition of most models and theories is to contribute to our understanding of some political phenomenon; but how can we tell if a model is indeed useful in this way, and how can we combine the insights offered by different models? Part, but only part, of the answer lies in the relationship between theoretical models and empirical work (whether quantitative or qualitative).

One way in which a theory may be useful is in its ability to explain or predict observed empirical patterns. For example, a theory that sets out to explain differences between different voting systems might be expected to cast at least some light on the patterns of results thrown up by those voting systems in the real world, and perhaps even make some predictions about future results. While this seems reasonable, it may also be difficult to achieve in practice. It is unlikely that direct empirical observation of two or more voting systems operating in otherwise identical environments is possible, so that empirical data will always be at least somewhat difficult to interpret. In some cases relevant data simply may not exist, but the issue goes rather deeper than this. Until we identify relevant models and theories, we do not even know what data may be relevant, and so what data to collect. If a theory tells us that some factor X may be important in explaining a political phenomenon, then this may persuade us to collect data on X so as to be able to 'test' the theory or at least to investigate the relationship in more detail. But notice that the data are already 'theory-laden' in the sense that we are sensitized to that particular view of the world because of the particular theory adopted. Had we adopted a different theory, one positing a relationship between Y and the political phenomenon in question, we might have gathered other data and reached other conclusions. We must avoid the trap of thinking that there is some pre-theoretic stock of 'data' that speaks for itself in guiding our choice of theories.

Even if this trap is avoided, empirical relevance is not the only sort of 'usefulness' that a model might achieve. A model will often serve to focus attention on the linkages between research questions and the way in which the exploration of an issue can be extended. In this way, a model can influence the course of development of a literature, suggesting connections and further developments that might not have been recognized in the absence of the model. If in constructing our basic model we recognize explicitly that we are abstracting from some potentially relevant factor, this will focus attention on the question of extending the model to incorporate that factor in more developed models. Different models will suggest different developmental paths, and this is another way in which a variety of modelling approaches can be complementary. Models are not just static objects; models develop over time with many authors contributing to the model in different ways. Each development throws up new challenges and criticisms, and these will in turn provoke further work both within the same model and in other models as researchers react to each other's arguments. In this way, the variety of models employed by political analysts may be thought of as a network of pathways that criss-cross the territory of politics. Each pathway may claim something distinctive, but it is the growth of the network that reflects the real range and depth of political research.

3   An Extended Example

At this point it is useful to provide an example, to illustrate the various points made. The example begins with an extremely simple model of a referendum in the broadly rational choice tradition, and shows some of the ways in which that model has developed over time. While our focus here is on the positive theory, note that the ultimate goal here, as is almost always the case, is normative – we study referendums and elections not just to understand them, but so as to be able to improve the design and performance of our political institutions. Yet the normative concern for improvement requires a relatively detailed positive understanding.

In keeping with the ideas of abstraction, simplification and idealization, we will begin by identifying the minimal necessary ingredients for a positive model of a referendum: a set of voters, some issue over which the voters disagree, two alternative policy positions with respect to that issue, and a voting rule. A referendum, in this simple model

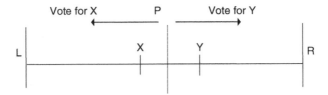

Figure 10.1: The basic Downsian model

world, is simply the choice of one of the policy positions by the set of voters acting through the voting rule. To be specific, and to idealize features of any real-world referendum, assume that the voting rule is simple majority voting (note that with just two alternatives, almost all plausible voting rules converge on simple majority voting) and that the issue at stake can be described as choosing a point along a left-right spectrum. Left-right here does not need to carry any particular political significance; it might, for example, be the level of public spending on a particular activity, or the tax rate to impose in a particular context. Assume also that each individual voter identifies an ideal point on the spectrum at issue and would like the outcome to be as close as possible to that ideal point. This adds an element of motivation to the individuals in the model and is what makes this a model in the broadly rational choice tradition: we assume that each individual acts in the way that she believes will contribute to bringing about the best available outcome seen from her own perspective. This does not amount to an assumption of self-interest. The individual may choose her ideal point because she believes it to be in the public interest, or because she believes it is morally best, or for any other reason. All that 'rationality' requires here is that the individual identifies a relevant ideal point and acts so as to bring about the closest possible approximation to that ideal. This is essentially the model of democratic decision-making introduced by Downs (1957) and may be illustrated diagrammatically.

In Figure 10.1, the L-R line represents the policy issue at stake, with points along the line representing different possible positions that might be chosen. X and Y are the two specific policy positions that are 'candidates' in this referendum, and the voters may be thought of as spread along the L-R line with each voter positioned at his or her ideal point. If we define point P to be the point halfway between X and Y, and we assume that everyone votes (note the idealization here), it should be clear that all voters whose ideal points lie to the left of P will vote for X and all those to the right of P will vote for Y. Given the simple majority voting rule, X will win if a majority of voters lie to the left of P, Y will win if a majority of voters lie to the right of P.

So far this model does nothing more than articulate the idea of majority voting in a simple setting. To animate the model further we might add another element. Consider the strategic choice of X and Y on the assumption that these policy positions are chosen by political parties whose choice is guided by the desire to maximize the probability of their proposal winning the referendum. Note that we are here introducing a second element of motivation, and again we are making that motivation as simple and stark as possible, even though this may be unrealistic.

If, in the initial position depicted by Figure 10.1, X would win the election, the political party controlling Y would face an incentive to shift Y leftward. By doing so, the position of point P will move to the left, more voters will support Y and fewer will support X. But similarly, the party controlling X will face an incentive to move rightward, so increasing its vote, and reducing its rivals. This suggests that the two party platforms will converge under competitive pressure; but where might this process stop? One aspect of the answer is that in the absence of any further argument, there is nothing to stop the two platforms converging to a single point, so that we might expect the two parties to offer the same policy.

But this is only half the answer. Imagine that both parties offer policy Y in Figure 10.1, and that more than half of the voters' ideal points lie to the left of Y. It is straightforward to argue that each party now faces an incentive to move leftward. If either party succeeds in positioning itself just to the left of its rival, it will win the referendum. But if both parties face this same incentive, we might expect both to react (one of the simplifying features of the model is that the two parties are essentially identical). Similarly, if both parties chose a policy platform such that the majority of voters' ideal points were to the right of that policy, then both would face an incentive to move rightward. So the model tells us not only that the two parties will converge on the same policy, but that there is a unique policy point at which the two parties will settle: the policy that is the ideal point of the median voter, the point at which exactly half of the voters' ideal points lie to the left and half lie to the right. This is the 'Median Voter Theorem' that says that in a two-candidate contest of the type described, both candidates will offer a policy platform aimed at the median voter's ideal point.

This is a very simple model, and its simplicity generates both a clarity of argument and a range of suggestions for further work. And these two things are closely related. It is precisely because we can see the mechanics of the model clearly, and understand the forces at work, that we can pinpoint important limitations of the model and identify further research questions. A series of questions interrogates the robustness of the model. What would be the impact of relaxing the assumption that all citizens vote? What would be the impact of introducing a third political party? What would be the impact of assuming that political parties had 'ideal policies' of their own that tempered their motivation to win the vote at all costs? What would be the impact of allowing the vote to operate on more than one political issue (so that it becomes a model of an election rather than a single-issue referendum)? How might we compare different voting system in this framework? How might the model be reformulated to capture the idea of electing representatives rather than making direct policy choices?

Some of these questions are relatively simple to address, others require considerable detailed work, but all of these questions, and many more, have been explored in the literature that has developed since Downs (reviewed in Mueller 2003). For example, the issue of abstention opens up the question of identifying the factors influencing turnout (Aldrich 1993; Blais 2000; Bendor et al. 2003). One possibility is that voters abstain when they are essentially indifferent across the alternatives on offer; another possibility is that voters abstain when the policy platforms are too far from their own ideal points (voter alienation). These possibilities have different implications. If political parties converge on identical policy platforms, and individual citizens abstain when they are essentially indifferent between the platforms on offer, the theory will generate predictions of low turnout. One branch of the literature introduces the idea that individuals might participate in the vote out of a sense of civic duty, even if they still vote for whichever platform is closer to their ideal (Riker and Ordeshook 1968; Ferejohn and Fiorina 1974). This opens up the idea that the factors that drive turnout may be rather different from the factors that drive which option to vote for.

A second example relates to animating individual voters. The initial idea in play here is just that individuals vote instrumentally to bring about whichever outcome they see as 'best' regardless of exactly how they define 'best'. But perhaps voting behaviour might be modelled differently: in terms of habitual voting, retrospective voting or expressive voting. The idea of habitual voting could be incorporated by assuming that an individual's vote in any particular election is partly determined by his or her votes at earlier elections (Fowler 2006). This might allow parties to pursue non-convergent platforms if they felt that their habitual vote was secure. The idea of retrospective voting is that voters may be backward-looking when choosing how to vote, rewarding good (or punishing bad) behaviour by parties in previous periods, rather than focusing on their proposals for the future. This idea engages with the idea of an incumbency effect (Fiorina 1981; Krehbiel and Wright 1983; Ferejohn 1986; Fiorina et al. 2003). The idea of expressive voting is that individuals may vote to express some aspect of their identity, beliefs or personality rather than voting to bring about a particular outcome, and that this is particularly likely in large elections where an individual is extremely unlikely to be instrumentally significant in determining the outcome of the election (Brennan and Lomasky 1993; Brennan and Hamlin 1998; Hamlin and Jennings 2011).

A third example focuses on the role of political parties (Duverger 1965; Panebianco 1988; Strøm 1990). In the original model, parties are sketched as independent agents who seek only to win elections, and this immediately raises questions relating to the structural relationship between political parties and their members who are themselves also citizens and voters, and further questions relating to the mechanisms and processes by which parties choose their policy platforms. Extensions to the model develop a number of aspects of political parties including: allowing individual citizens to stand as candidates (Besley and Coate 1997); viewing political parties as operating to extend political credibility over time (Brennan and Kliemt 1994); discussing the decision of individuals to join political parties (Hamlin and Jennings 2004); and discussing the internal choice of party leaders and the relationship between leaders and policy platforms (Ware 1992; Hamlin and Jennings 2007).

These examples serve to illustrate the genealogy of models: the way in which models and theories develop over generations of academic debate; and the diversity of the resultant 'family tree'. Understanding how a particular model fits into the broader landscape of such family trees is an important part of appreciating both the richness and the limitations of that family of models.

4   How to Do Positive Political Theory

While this extended example has provided a view of some of the general issues that arise in building, developing, understanding and using a positive political model/theory, it is now time to make explicit some of the lessons that have been implicit in the past two sections.

In practice it will often be the case that a model or theory is adapted from the existing literature (as suggested by our extended example) rather than designed from scratch. But whether you are attempting to build a model from scratch, adapt a model from the literature, or simply

Table 10.1: *Essential elements of a model of a referendum*

Essential Structures	Inessential Structures
Citizens/Voters	Any group structure of individual voters
An issue	Multiple issues
Two policy options/political parties	Multiple options/candidates
Voting rule	Other institutional features (representation, repeat elections, etc.)
	Etc.

understand a model in the literature, it is sensible to approach the exercise in much the same way. The remainder of this section will identify a series of steps that provide a guide to positive modelling.

The starting point should be to **identify your research area and basic research question in their simplest possible forms.** Begin by simply listing the major structural features of the research area that you believe are essential in any model that could possibly address your research question, and separately list those that might be excluded at this initial stage even if their inclusion might seem desirable. The idea is to **sketch the ingredients for the simplest possible model at this stage.** In terms of our example of the Downsian model, the essential elements of the model are listed in Table 10.1, as are at least some of the more obvious structural features that might be seen as optional extras.

The structures that you see as essential will depend on the precise focus of your research question. If the intention is to study the impact of campaigning on referendum outcomes, then the simplest specification of the essential structures to include in the model will be rather more complex than that shown here since you will need to include at least some features of campaigning. The point, however, is to arrive at the simplest list of ingredients that offer the possibility of modelling the area of your concern.

The next step is to **sketch the basic relationships among the identified ingredients of the model**. For example, many models in the area of electoral politics include both 'citizens/voters' and 'political parties' as structural features, but models will differ in the focus they wish to place on the relationship between these elements of the model. In some cases we may wish to simplify and idealize our view of political parties. In other cases, it may be essential to the intended purpose of the model to consider the internal structure of political parties and the way in which their policy platforms emerge (for a variety of approaches, see the papers

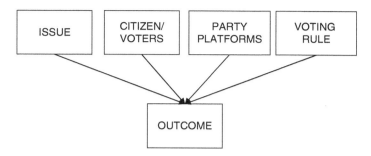

Figure 10.2: Schematic outline of basic Downsian model

collected in Müller and Strøm 1999). Clearly, the structure of the relationship in the model will be quite different in the two cases. It may be useful to transform the simple list of the type illustrated by Table 10.1 into a diagram of the form of Figure 10.2, which shows the basic structure of the relationships that are key to the model in its simplest form. The items along the top row are the basic inputs of the model, as specified in Table 10.1. The only item that is actually determined within the model is the outcome of the referendum, and that is seen as influenced by all of the independently specified features of the model, as indicated by the arrows. As is clear from Figure 10.2, the structure of the basic Downsian model is particularly simple, with a direct relationship between each of the basic features and the single outcome, and with no complicating features such as interactions among the features, or feedback from one part of the model to another.

A slightly more complicated version of the model, allowing citizens to abstain depending on the voting rule and their view of the platforms adopted by the parties, might be sketched as in Figure 10.3. Note that party platforms and the voting rule now have two effects on the final outcome: a direct effect, as in the simple model, and an indirect effect via citizens' decisions to vote or abstain.

At this stage we have a basic, passive model, comparable to the London underground map. It offers a simple guide to the research area under investigation that allows us to consider the various possible linkages between the identified features. It also suggests ways in which we might extend and complicate the model to include features that we might believe to be important (if not absolutely essential).

At this stage it is worthwhile to **reflect on your proposed approach to further study and the purposes that you want your model to serve**. One purpose common to most pieces of research is to provide

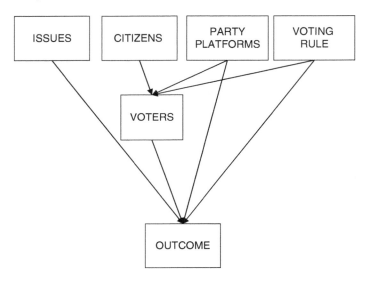

Figure 10.3: Schematic outline of Downsian model with possible abstention

a structure for reviewing the literature. A basic model of the type constructed so far can be valuable as a way of thinking about and comparing alternative accounts of referenda in the literature or in general political debate. Each account should be capable of being analysed in terms of our basic schematic structure, by means of a series of simple questions. How does the account specify each of the ingredients of the model? What assumptions are made, explicitly or implicitly, about the set of voters, or the number and nature of political parties and the way in which they set their policy platforms? What are the properties of the outcome of the referendum in the account under consideration, and how do these properties follow from the assumptions made? But beyond framing a literature review, the purposes of a model will vary from case to case. For example, if the intended study is empirical and quantitative, the model will provide the first step towards specifying the key variables and data requirements. If the intended study is qualitative and interview-based, the model will suggest key questions that should be asked and the nature of the relationships that should be probed. If the intended study is to develop a normative discussion of some aspect of institutional design, the model will suggest the key connections between behaviour and institutional arrangements that will need to feature in that normative account. But whatever the original intention, the design of the underlying positive model will play a key role, ensuring that you **move back and forth between considering the features of the basic positive model and the intended purpose of the proposed research in an iterative and flexible process.**

The next step is to **animate the model and be explicit about motivational and causal aspects of the model**. In the case of the basic Downsian model we noted two such aspects: the assumed motivation of the voters in deciding how to vote and the assumed motivation of the political parties in setting their platforms. Clearly many other motivational assumptions are possible even within this very simple structure. At this early stage, motivations and causal forces should be as explicit and as simple as possible. One way of thinking about this is to consider each of the arrows in a figure such as Figure 10.2 or 10.3, and draft a clear statement of the nature of the relationship represented by that arrow. The exercise of drafting such an explicit statement will almost always bring three points to the fore. The first is that apparently simple statements of a causal or motivational relationship often leave open a considerable range of interpretation, so that detailed thought is required to construct a clear, explicit statement of the relationship you have in mind. The second is the requirement for some degree of coherence or consistency as between the various relationships within the model. The third is that there are almost always many quite different ways of identifying a particular relationship, each of which carries at least some degree of plausibility, so that many different, but related, theoretical models could be constructed.

The first point is an example of the role of theory construction in the process of conceptual clarification. By setting yourself the task of thinking explicitly about the relationship between two parts of your model and specifying that relationship as clearly and concisely as possible, you should **think carefully and clearly about the concepts involved**. Constructing and understanding your model, albeit a simplified, abstract and idealized model, involves considerable investment in the ideas and concepts that are basic to your research. At this point the style and formality of a theory or model may come under scrutiny. As your understanding of the model and its component parts deepens, you will need to **find a means of communicating the nature of the model to others that reflects its structure and the detailed specification that you have decided on**. There is no uniform answer to how best to present a theory/model, but you should at least **be aware of a variety of options and make a conscious choice of presentational strategy that fits with the overall research plan**. It may be that an entirely textual approach is appropriate, in other cases the use of a diagram or flow chart or other device may be helpful, and in still other cases a greater degree of formalism may be appropriate. But whatever style is adopted, the underlying aim is clarity of communication, discussion and analysis.

The second point can be read at a variety of levels. At one level we might **ask whether the motivational elements of the theory/model fit together coherently**. In the simple Downsian model this is easily achieved since the only two motivational elements of the model relate to two distinct groups of agents (individual voters and political parties). But in other cases there may be some tension. For example, imagine that we are constructing a model that involves individuals voting and those same individuals making a decision on where to live, as might be the case if we are interested in differences between political constituencies or regions (Tiebout 1956). And imagine that we specify the motivations guiding the location decision in terms of maximizing some notion of self-interest, but at the same time specify the motivations guiding the voting decision in terms of some notion of the public interest. This raises the question of how we are conceiving of the individual overall. The tension between self-interest and public interest should force us to think about the underlying model of the individual and her decision making (Buchanan 1984). Such tension is potentially creative, can help to focus on issues that were not immediately apparent and can help to develop interesting ideas. A benefit of explicit and detailed modelling/theorizing is that it can both reveal such tensions and help to ensure that they contribute positively to the overall analysis.

The next step is to **consider a range of variations on the theme of the basic model.** Recognition that there is no uniquely privileged theory/model in relation to any particular research issue, and that there are many potential models that can claim to be of significant interest, may at first sight sound like a problem. But a theme of this chapter has been that a 'good' model is a useful model, and there are many ways to be useful; but just because there are many good/useful models in any area of politics this does not imply that all models are good/useful.

Once a theory/model has been constructed, that theory/model should be reconsidered by explicitly viewing variations. Here the general rule is simple enough: **vary one aspect of the theory/model at a time in order to consider the impact on the model overall**. If a particular variation makes little or no difference to the model, this provides a basis for a simple generalization of the model; if, on the other hand, a variation does make a significant difference to the overall model, you have found a potentially interesting feature that can be incorporated into your analysis.

Performing such a 'sensitivity analysis' – exploring the sensitivity of a model to changes in the specification of its component parts – deepens understanding of the model and helps to identify which of the assumptions embedded in the model are merely simplifying and which are vital to the model's conclusions. In the simple Downsian model, it might have been thought that the nature of the distribution of voters' ideal points along the L-R spectrum would play an important role in determining the way in which political parties would choose their platforms, and whether those platforms would converge. But the sensitivity analysis performed by Downs revealed that the precise distribution of voters makes no difference at all, so that he did not need to make any assumption about it. All that matters is that the distribution has a median, and this is true of all well-defined distributions in a single dimension. In this way the sensitivity analysis does two things. It generalizes the model (rather than being a model that applies only when the distribution of voters is of some particular form, it is a model that applies to all one-dimensional distributions). And it points to a key feature, the existence of a median that provides the basis for further investigation, since distributions in more than one dimension (i.e. models with more than one political issue being decided) do not generally have a median.

It is inherent in the nature of a model that no useful model can incorporate all potentially relevant aspects of reality. Thus the fact that a theory/model has limitations, in the sense that it is sensitive to some changes in its basic assumptions, is inevitable and is not in itself a criticism of the theory/model. **Explicitly recognize the limitations of your model/theory** – it can only enhance its usefulness. Sensitivity analysis can help to improve the theory/model by pointing to the areas where extensions to the model promise significant results.

A final step is to **consider zooming in and zooming out on your proposed model**. A particular way of varying a theory/model in order to understand its properties and develop them to greatest advantage might be termed zooming in or zooming out. Any particular model operates at a particular level of detail: it might be a relatively 'macro' model focused on the big picture, it might be a relatively 'micro' model focused on specific details within that picture, or it might operate in the middle ground of a 'meso' model. But whatever the level of the model, it can be very useful to **explore what, if anything, the model says in relation to other levels**. We can test out the general plausibility of the model and, as with other forms of sensitivity analysis, distinguish the important from the trivial, by taking a micro model and zooming out to the macro level, asking questions like 'what would be the implications if the assumptions of this model where applied more generally?'; or by taking a macro model and zooming in to more specific details, asking questions like 'what would my general model say about some particular case study?'.

5   Application

This approach to developing and using positive political theory is intended to provide a flexible structure for thinking about a wide variety of political questions and issues. Clearly it needs to be fine-tuned and adapted to fit any specific purpose. While it has been presented as a way of approaching research, it can also provide a way of reading the literature and, to illustrate its use in this way, this section considers two articles in the general area of democracy and voting that are published in the same issue of *The British Journal of Political Science*.

Before turning to these articles, one important point should be stressed. There is a crucial difference between the work done in a research project and the report of that work in a final document. In some contexts (a PhD thesis or monograph) it may be both appropriate and important for the final document to explicitly display almost all of the process of research – the consideration of variations on a theme, the zooming in and zooming out and so on. In other contexts, such as a journal article, the final document will typically focus on a relatively small part of the overall research, presenting just the key message and argument. Much of the research process will be implicit in the way the article refers and relates to the literature and in the way in which claims and results are framed.

With this thought in mind, consider two recent articles that relate to models of democratic behaviour. One is theoretical and normative, while the other is empirical but, despite this difference, I will point up the extent to which both depend on underlying positive political theory and how the approach outlined earlier helps us to read these articles and understand the broader research programmes of which they form part.

The more theoretical article, by Annabelle Lever (2010a), is focused on the normative question 'should voting be compulsory?' (See also Hill 2010; Lever 2010b.) Lever is clear from the outset that her approach requires consideration of the differential impacts of compulsory and voluntary voting systems, so that a positive account of each system is a required input to the normative debate. Lever identifies a general chain of argument in support of compulsory voting that proceeds through a series of steps: voluntary voting results in low turnout, low turnout normally implies unequal turnout across social groups, unequal turnout reinforces social disadvantage, therefore compulsory voting addresses social disadvantage. Furthermore, compulsory voting carries a range of further benefits over and above those that depend on increased turnout. Finally, compulsory voting carries no significant costs and does not threaten liberty, in large part because not voting is seen as a form of free-riding. She then criticizes each link in this chain of argument and develops her own sceptical view of compulsory voting.

While the explicit focus of the article is normative, there are clear indications of the underlying positive structure and equally clear, if implicit, indications of the use of the principles outlined previously. The article does not explicitly lay out the underlying model of the behaviour of voters, the relationship between the decision to vote and other socio-political variables (particularly those associated with disadvantage), or the significance of the act of voting relative to other political acts in representative democracies, but it is clear that these factors are crucial parts of the argument, and equally clear that they have to be viewed as parts of an overall, integrated model of political behaviour. This reliance on an underlying model can be read into the references cited, but is also visible in the argument developed. For example, the discussion of the view of non-voting as a free-rider problem is necessarily embedded in a game-theoretic understanding of electoral behaviour. Similarly, the discussion of the possibility that the argument for compulsory voting might depend in part on other features of the voting system (e.g. whether a first-past-the-post or a proportional representation system is in place) provides an example of recognizing the additional factors that might be included in any model and thinking in terms of variations on a theme. As already mentioned, an article-length discussion will not usually display all the features of the underlying analysis, but in reading such an article we should make the effort to consider the range of sensitivity analysis and the forms of zooming in and out in relation to the model that might be appropriate.

Any comprehensive answer to the question 'should voting be compulsory?' necessarily involves the development of a range of positive political models alongside an understanding of a range of normative considerations. Such a task identifies a major research programme. Lever's article contributes to that programme, but locating and evaluating that contribution require much more than an internal reading of the article itself. The understanding of positive political theory developed earlier provides both a way to add value to the reading of such an article, and a way to think about the wider research programme.

In the second, more empirical article, Jeffrey Timmons (2010) also directly addresses an explicitly stated research question: 'does democracy reduce economic inequality?' While much of the focus is empirical in the sense that Timmons is concerned with issues such as the country samples utilized in various studies, the time period studied and the empirical methodology employed, there is also a significant focus on identifying arguments that lead us to expect that democracy may be causally related to economic inequality, and these arise from positive political models. For example, the median voter model together with an empirical observation to the effect that the distribution of income or wealth is skewed (so that the median voter's income/wealth lies below the mean income/wealth level) generates an argument that a programme of redistribution from rich to poor can be expected to find majority support. Similarly, one might argue that models that stress that democratic support for expenditure on public goods such as education or health might be expected to benefit the relatively poor more than the relatively rich.

But, as Timmons points out, the links between these positive models and the available empirical data are relatively weak. The median voter model suggests that post-tax and benefit income may be more equally distributed than pre-tax and benefit income in democracies, and that democracies may be expected to engage in redistribution to the extent that the original distribution is skewed. But neither of these claims translates into the much wider claim that democracies will display either more or less economic inequality than non-democracies. Considerations of this sort help us to see that the apparently simple question 'does democracy reduce economic inequality?' hides a range of further questions that in turn require more detailed modelling. Such considerations will interest normative political theorists too.

This article also reveals a further relationship between positive political models and quantitative empirical work. As stressed previously, a key part of the process of developing positive political models and theories involves the ideas of abstraction, simplification and idealization. And one key point here was the importance of being explicit about the abstractions, simplifications and idealizations involved in any model. When we turn to quantitative empirical work, we need to specify not only the key variables of interest (measures of economic inequality and measures of democracy in this case), but also the control variables that might be expected to influence economic inequality independently of the postulated effects of the variable we are really interested in (democracy). The link from the process of abstraction, simplification and idealization to the specification of control variables should be clear. In a theoretical model we can usefully abstract from an issue, but in a quantitative analysis we should control for the potential impact of that issue. So, being explicit about the issues we abstract from in our theoretical work helps us to identify the variables we will need to control for when we turn to quantitative work.

By considering a range of different positive models, Timmons exemplifies the idea of searching across models and considering variations on a theme. But the mismatch between the rather narrowly focused models considered and the broadly specified empirical investigation might suggest that the theoretical models are rather 'zoomed in' on the study of micro issues that arise within a democracy, while empirical work has been rather 'zoomed out' on the macro questions that arise in comparing democracies with non-democracies. This in itself points to useful directions for further work on both the theoretical and empirical fronts.

6   Conclusion

No 'how-to' guide to the practice of positive political theorizing can guarantee that the theories/models generated will be useful, valuable and interesting. But the steps outlined in the previous sections capture and spell out the benefits of thinking carefully and explicitly about the positive theory/model element of any political analysis.

Early in this chapter I suggested that positive political theory had some of the characteristics of prose, in that we use it all the time without always being conscious of that fact. This is a metaphor that extends a little further: just as the explicit study of grammar, syntax and punctuation can improve our prose, whether as readers or writers, so the explicit study of the more detailed structure of positive political theories and models and the motivating and causal forces that they analyse can improve our political debate and understanding, as both readers and writers. Just as there are no perfect prose sentences, there are no perfect positive political theories/models. But there are ways in which we can clarify meaning and develop greater understanding, both in our prose and in our political analysis.

References

Abrams, Samuel, Torben Iversen and David Soskice, 2011. 'Informal social networks and rational voting', *British Journal of Political Science* 41, 229–57.
Aldrich, John, 1993. 'Rational choice and turnout', *American Journal of Political Science* 37, 246–78.
Austen-Smith, David, and James Banks, 2000. *Positive Political Theory I: Collective Preference*. Ann Arbor: University of Michigan Press.

Austen-Smith, David and James Banks, 2005. *Positive Political Theory II: Strategy and Structure*. Ann Arbor: University of Michigan Press.

Bendor, Jonathan, Daniel Diermeier and Michael Ting, 2003. 'A behavioral model of turnout', *American Political Science Review* 97, 261–80.

Berggren, Niclas, Henrik Jordahl and Panu Poutvaara, 2009. 'The looks of a winner: beauty and electoral success', *Journal of Public Economics* 94, 8–15.

Besley, Timothy and Stephen Coate, 1997. 'An economic model of representative democracy', *Quarterly Journal of Economics* 112, 85–114.

Blais, Andre, 2000. *To Vote or Not To Vote? The Merits and Limits of Rational Choice Theory*. University of Pittsburgh Press.

Brennan, Geoffrey and Alan Hamlin, 1998. 'Expressive voting and electoral equilibrium', *Public Choice* 95, 149–75.

Brennan, Geoffrey and Hartmut Kliemt, 1994. 'Finite lives and social institutions', *Kyklos* 47, 551–71.

Brennan, Geoffrey and Loren Lomasky, 1993. *Democracy and Decision*. Cambridge University Press.

Buchanan, James, 1984. 'Politics without romance: a sketch of positive public choice theory and its normative implications', in James Buchanan and Robert Tollison, eds., *The Theory of Public Choice II*. Ann Arbor: University of Michigan Press, 11–22.

Downs, Anthony, 1957. *An Economic Theory of Democracy*. New York: Harper & Row.

Duverger, Maurice, 1965. *Political Parties: Their Organization and Activity in the Modern State*. London: Wiley.

Elster, Jon, 1989. *Nuts and Bolts for the Social Sciences*. Cambridge University Press.

Ferejohn, John, 1986. 'Incumbent performance and electoral control', *Public Choice* 50, 5–25.

Ferejohn, John and Morris Fiorina, 1974. 'The paradox of not voting: a decision theoretic analysis', *American Political Science Review* 68, 525–36.

Fiorina, Morris, 1981. *Retrospective Voting in American National Elections*. New Haven, CT: Yale University Press.

Fiorina, Morris, Samuel Abrams and Jeremy Pope, 2003. 'The 2000 US presidential election: can retrospective voting be saved?', *British Journal of Political Science* 33, 163–87.

Forbes, Donald, 2004. 'Positive political theory', in Gerald Gaus and Chandran Kukathas, eds., *Handbook of Political Theory*. London: Sage Publications, 57–72.

Fowler, James, 2006. 'Habitual voting and behavioral turnout', *Journal of Politics* 68, 335–44.

Friedman, Jeffrey, ed., 1996. *The Rational Choice Controversy: Economic Models of Politics Reconsidered*. New Haven, CT: Yale University Press.

Gordon, Scott, 1993. *The History and Philosophy of Social Science*. London: Routledge.

Green, Donald and Ian Shapiro, 1994. *Pathologies of Rational Choice Theory: A Critique of Applications in Political Science*. New Haven, CT: Yale University Press.

Hamlin, Alan and Colin Jennings, 2004. 'Group formation and political conflict: instrumental and expressive approaches', *Public Choice* 118, 413–35.

Hamlin, Alan and Colin Jennings, 2007. 'Leadership and conflict', *Journal of Economic Behavior and Organization* 64, 49–68.

Hamlin, Alan and Colin Jennings, 2011. 'Expressive political behaviour: foundations, scope and implications', *British Journal of Political Science* 41, 645–70.

Hill, Lisa, 2010. 'On the justifiability of compulsory voting: reply to Lever', *British Journal of Political Science* 40, 917–23.

Hindmoor, Andrew, 2006. *Rational Choice*. London: Palgrave.

Hindmoor, Andrew, 2011. '"Major combat operations have ended"? Arguing about rational choice', *British Journal of Political Science* 41, 191–210.

Kincaid, Harold, 1998. 'Positivism in the social sciences', in Edward Craig, ed., *The Routledge Encyclopedia of Philosophy*. London: Routledge, 558–61.

Krehbiel, Keith and John Wright, 1983. 'The incumbency effect in congressional elections: a test of two explanations', *American Journal of Political Science* 27, 140–57.

Lever, Annabelle, 2010a. 'Compulsory voting: a critical perspective', *British Journal of Political Science* 40, 897–915.

Lever, Annabelle, 2010b. 'Democracy and voting: a response to Lisa Hill', *British Journal of Political Science* 40, 925–9.

Mueller, Dennis, 2003. *Public Choice III*. Cambridge University Press.

Müller, Wolfgang and Kaare Strøm, eds., 1999. *Policy, Office, or Votes? How Political Parties in Western Europe Make Hard Decisions*. Cambridge University Press.

Ordeshook, Peter, 1986. *Game Theory and Political Theory: An Introduction*. Cambridge University Press.

Panebianco, Angelo, 1988. *Political Parties: Organization and Power*. Cambridge University Press.

Riker, William and Peter Ordeshook, 1968. 'A theory of the calculus of voting', *American Political Science Review* 62, 25–42.

Riker, William and Peter Ordeshook, 1973. *An Introduction to Positive Political Theory*. Englewood Cliffs, NJ: Prentice Hall.

Satz, Debra and John Ferejohn, 1994. 'Rational choice and social theory', *The Journal of Philosophy* 91, 71–87.

Shepsle, Kenneth and Mark Bonchek, 1997. *Analyzing Politics: Rationality, Behavior and Institutions*. New York: Norton.

Strøm, Kaare, 1990. 'A behavioral theory of competitive political parties', *American Journal of Political Science* 34, 565–98.

Tiebout, Charles, 1956. 'A pure theory of local expenditures', *The Journal of Political Economy* 64, 416–24.

Timmons, Jeffrey, 2010. 'Does democracy reduce economic inequality?', *British Journal of Political Science* 40, 741–57.

Van Evera, Stephen, 1997. *Guide to Methods for Students of Political Science*. Ithaca, NY: Cornell University Press.

Ware, Alan, 1992. 'Activist-leader relations and the structure of political parties: "exchange" models and vote-seeking behaviour in parties', *British Journal of Political Science* 22, 71–92.

Zuckerman, Alan, Nicholas Valentino and Ezra Zuckerman, 1994. 'A structural theory of vote choice: social and political networks and electoral flows in Britain and the United States', *The Journal of Politics* 56, 1008–33.

11 Rational Choice Theory

Brian Kogelmann and Gerald Gaus

1 Introduction

'The theory of justice is a part, perhaps the most significant part, of the theory of rational choice', writes John Rawls (1999a: 15). In linking the theory of justice to rational choice Rawls both continued an intellectual tradition and began a new one. He continued an intellectual tradition in the sense that rational choice theory was first formally introduced in von John von Neumann's and Oscar Morgenstern's *Theory of Games and Economic Behavior* (1944), which launched a research agenda that continues to this day. Rawls, James M. Buchanan (1962; see Thrasher and Gaus forthcoming), and John Harsanyi (1953, 1955) led the way in applying the idea of rational choice to the derivation of moral and political principles; a later generation of political theorists applied game theoretic analysis to a wide variety of problems of social interactions (e.g. Hampton 1986; Sugden 1986; Binmore 2005). David Gauthier's *Morals by Agreement* (1986) was perhaps the most sustained and resolute attempt to apply models of utility maximization and decision theory to the derivation of social morality. Yet, despite the fact that some of the most respected political theorists of the past fifty years extensively employed the tools of rational choice theory, confusion still reigns about what these tools presuppose and how they are to be applied. Many reject the entire approach by a common refrain that 'rational choice assumes that people are selfish', and since that is false, the entire line of analysis can be dismissed; a slightly more sophisticated (but still misplaced) dismissal insists that rational choice is about 'preferences', but political philosophers are interested in 'reasons', so again the entire approach can be set aside asserting that rational choice theory assumes selfishness, denying that people are selfish, and dismissing rational choice accordingly. A fundamental aim of this chapter is to explain just what the tools of rational choice theory are – and what presuppositions they make – and to provide some guidance for those wishing to follow in Rawls's footsteps, showing how rational choice theory can be applied to some of the fundamental issues of moral and political theory.

But even for those who do not want to explicitly engage in the contractarian project and thus follow in Rawls's footsteps, there are still important reasons to learn the basics of rational choice theory. First, one cannot properly engage with those who do explicitly rely on rational choice theory without understanding its basics. As just one example, arguing that parties in Rawls's original position would not choose the difference principle is fruitless unless one further engages with how Rawls defines the original position – given the tools of rational choice theory Rawls relies on, and given how the choice problem is defined, the *only* rational choice is the difference principle. Second, even if one does not want to primarily use rational choice theory in one's theorizing, knowledge of the theory can open up avenues of research to lend a supporting role. As an example, even though a deliberative democrat's core normative theory does not rely on rational choice in the way that Rawls's does, knowledge of the theory can help one engage, say, in the social scientific institutional design literature that could be relevant for the democrat's project.

In Section 2 we explain preferences and utility functions as well as parametric and strategic choice. Section 3 sketches the dispute about whether rational choice is an adequate mode of explanation, while Section 4 highlights the way in which rational choice theory is a normative theory, and how it has been employed in normative political philosophy. Section 5 seeks to draw our observations together in a checklist of decisions for those who would employ rational choice methods in their own work.

2   What Is Rational Choice Theory?

2.1   Preferences and Utility Functions

Rational choice is, at bottom, a theory of preference maximization. Many think of preferences as non-relational tastes or desires – having a preference for something is simply liking or desiring that thing. On this common view, to say that Alf has a preference for mangos means that Alf has a taste or desire for mangos; thus to say that he maximizes his preferences is just to say that he maximizes his pleasures or desire satisfaction. It is thus very common – for both defenders and critics – to see rational choice theory as inherently bound up with a Hobbesian or Benthamite psychology (Plamenatz 1973: 20–7, 149–59; Kliemt 2009: 46ff. Sen 2009: 178–83). While such an

Table: 11.1

	μ function A	μ function B	μ function C
Mangos	3	10	1,000
Bananas	2	5	99
Apples	1	0	1

understanding of preferences is perhaps colloquially natural, rational choice theory always understands preferences as comparative or relational, and they have no necessary connection to desires or pleasure. The core of rational choice theory is the primitive conception of a preference as a binary relation, of the form 'x is preferred to y' ($x\succ y$). This is emphatically *not* a comparison of the strengths of two preferences, that for x and for y. It is literally incoherent in decision theory to claim one simply 'prefers mangos' – a preference *is* a binary comparison.

Perhaps the best understanding of preferences is as deliberative rankings over states of affairs. When Alf deliberatively ranks (x), the state of affairs in which he eats a mango over (y), the state of affairs in which he eats a banana, we say that Alf prefers mangos to bananas ($x\succ y$). Note that we can leave entirely open the considerations Alf employed to arrive at this ranking: these could have been self-interest, desire satisfaction, or his conception of virtue ('The brave eat mangos, while only cowards eat bananas!'). Utility theory is a way to *represent consistent choice*, not the foundation of those choices. If Alf employs some deliberative criteria such that he ranks x above y for the purposes of choice, then we can represent this as $x\succ y$; it is critical to realize that he does *not* rank x above y *because* he prefers x to y.

These preferences over states of affairs, combined with further information, can be used to generate preferences over actions (say, α and β). Thus in rational choice theory we can map preferences over 'outcomes' (x, y) to preferences over actions (α, β), which, at least as a first approximation, can be understood as simply routes to states of affairs. Does Alf prefer grocery shopping at (α) Joseph's or (β) Caputo's? That depends on his information. If Alf knows that Joseph's has only mangos (x) and Caputo's has only bananas (y), then since $x\succ y$, $α\succ β$ – he will prefer shopping at Joseph's to shopping at Caputo's.

From an individual's preferences we can derive an *ordinal utility function*. Let us consider preferences over three fruits: mangos (x), bananas (y), and apples (z). An ordinal utility function is a numerical representation of a person's preferences, examples of which are illustrated in Table 11.1. We can derive an ordinal utility function for any individual so long as the individual's preferences satisfy the following axioms.

1. Preferences are *complete*. For any two states of affairs x and y, either $x \succeq y$, $y \succeq x$ or, we can say, Alf is indifferent between x and y ($x \sim y$). We can define indifference in terms of what might be called the true primitive preference relation, 'at least as good as'. If Alf is indifferent between x and y ($x \sim y$), we can say that x is at least as good as y ($x \succeq y$) and y is at least as good as x ($y \succeq x$). We can also define 'strict preference' ($x \succ y$) in terms of this more fundamental binary relation 'at least as good as': $x \succ y$ implies x$\succeq$y and $\neg(y \succeq x)$.[1]

2. Strict preferences are *asymmetric*. $x \succ y$ implies $\neg(y \succ x)$. Indifference is, however, *symmetric*: ($x \sim y$) implies ($y \sim x$).

3. The true primitive preference is *reflexive*. Alf must hold that state of affairs x is at least as good as itself ($x \succeq x$).

4. Preferences must be *transitive*. If Alf prefers x to y and y to z, then Alf must prefer x to z ($x \succ y$ & $y \succ z$ implies $x \succ z$).

Note that the numbers used to rank options in Alf's ordinal utility function tell us very little. All an ordinal utility function implies is that higher-numbered states of affairs are more preferred than lower-numbered states of affairs. Turning back to Table 11.1, utility function A contains the same information as utility function B which contains the same information as utility function C. They all tell us that Alf prefers mangos to bananas to apples, nothing more. Thus ordinal utility information can be limiting. As we shall see, when modeling rational choice under risk and uncertainty, we require information about (to put the matter rather roughly) the 'distances between preferences'. We need to know more than the fact that Alf prefers mangos to bananas – we must know (again, very roughly) how much more he prefers mangos to bananas. This brings us to *cardinal utility functions*, which contain such information. We can take any ordinal utility function and derive a cardinal utility function so long as preferences satisfy a few more axioms:[2]

5. *Continuity*. Assume again that for Alf mangos (x) are preferred to bananas (y), and bananas are preferred to apples (z), so $x \succ y$, $y \succ z$. There must exist some lottery where Alf has a p chance of winning his most preferred option (x) and a $1-p$ chance of receiving his least preferred option (z), such that Alf is indifferent between playing that

---

[1] Read '$\neg$' as 'not'.

[2] For simplicity's sake, we state these in terms of the strict preference relation. A more general statement would use the 'at least as good' relation. The intuitive ideas are clearer with strict preference.

lottery and receiving his middle option (y) for sure. So if such a lottery is $L(x,z)$, we can say that for Alf $[L(x,z)] \sim y$.

6. *Better Prizes.* When Alf is confronted with two lotteries, L_1 and L_2, which (*i*) have the same probabilities over outcomes (for example, 0.8 chance of the prize in the first position, and so 0.2 chance of the prize in the second position), (*ii*) the second position has the same prize in both L_1 and L_2, and (*iii*) in the first position, L_1's prize is preferred by Alf to L_2's, Alf must prefer playing lottery L_1 to lottery L_2 ($L_1 \succ L_2$).

7. *Better Chances.* When Alf is confronted with two lotteries, L_1 and L_2, where (*i*) L_1 and L_2 have the same prizes in both positions (x and y, where $x \succ y$) and (*ii*) L_1 has a higher chance (say 0.8) of winning x than L_2 (say 0.6), Alf must prefer playing lottery L_1 to lottery L_2 ($L_1 \succ L_2$).

8. *Reduction of Compound Lotteries.* Alf's preferences over compound lotteries (where the prize of a lottery is another lottery) must be reducible to a simple lottery between prizes. Thus the value of winning a lottery as a prize can be entirely reduced to the chances of receiving the prizes it offers – there is no additional preference simply for winning lottery tickets (say, the thrill of lotteries).

If Alf's preferences obey these axioms, we can derive a cardinal utility function in the following manner, originally proposed by von Neumann and Morgenstern (1944: ch. 3). Consider Alf's ordinal utility function, represented in Table 11.1. We take Alf's most preferred option, x, and assign it an arbitrary value, say 1. We then take Alf's least preferred option, z, and assign it an arbitrary value, say 0. We then take an option in between (y) and compare Alf's preference between that option and a lottery between x and z. We manipulate the probability of the lottery until Alf is indifferent between that lottery and the middling option under consideration (the Continuity axiom guarantees there will be such lottery). Suppose Alf is indifferent between y and a lottery with $p = 0.6$ chance of winning x and, so, a $1-p$ (0.4) chance of z (the probabilities in the lottery must sum to 1). Because indifference obtains at this specific probability, we assign a numerical value of 0.6 to the state of affairs in which Alf receives y, a banana. Alf's new cardinal utility function, representing how much more he prefers certain outcomes to others, is shown in Table 11.2.

Just how we are to understand this information is disputed. On a *very* strict interpretation, all we have found out is something about Alf's propensity to engage in certain sorts of risks; on a somewhat – but not terribly – looser interpretation we have found out something about the ratios of the differences between the utility of x, y, and z, which can be further interpreted as information about the relative intensity of Alf's three preferences. It is important that our (1, 0.6, 0) utility scale is simply

Table: 11.2

	μ function
Mangos	1
Bananas	0.6
Apples	0

a representation as to how Alf views the relative choice worthiness of the options; he does not 'seek' utility, much less to maximize it. He seeks mangos, bananas, and apples. To understand his actions as maximizing utility is to say that his consistent choices can be numerically represented so that they maximize a function. It is also critical to realize that the only information we have obtained is a representation of the ratios of the differences between the three options. There are an infinite number of utility functions that represent this information. Cardinal utility functions are thus only unique up to a linear transformation (which preserves this ratio information). If we call the utility function we have derived U, then any alternative utility function U', where $U' = aU + b$ (where a is a positive real number and b is any real number), contains the same information. We can readily see why these utility functions are not interpersonally comparable: it makes little sense to simply add the utility functions of Alf and Betty, when each of their functions is equally well described in an infinite number of ways, with very different numbers.

2.2   Parametric Choice

After characterizing an agent's utility function we can go on to examine what sorts of choices rational agents make. The basic idea behind rational choice theory is that choosers *maximize expected utility*. Since utility, as we have seen, is simply a numerical representation of an agent's preferences, maximizing expected utility means that a rational agent maximizes the satisfaction of her preferences. Although this sounds straightforward – and it is, in certain contexts – maximizing one's preferences can be quite complex once we start examining choice under risk and uncertainty.

Let us first consider rational *parametric* choice. When an agent chooses parametrically, it is assumed that the choices that the agent makes do not influence the parameters of other actors' choices (i.e., do not influence their preferences over outcomes) and vice versa. Their combined choices can affect her options (for example, the combined choices of other consumers determines prices), but when she acts, she takes all this as fixed and beyond her control. As far as the chooser is concerned, she has a fixed preference ordering and confronts a set of outcomes mapped onto a set of actions correlated with those outcomes. This is opposed to *strategic* choice, examined in the next section. We can understand decision theory as the study of rational parametric choice, game theory the study of rational strategic choice.

In the simplest case of rational choice, the individual is choosing under certainty. Here Betty not only knows her orderings of outcomes ($x \succeq y \succeq z$) – an assumption we make throughout – but also that she knows with certainty that, say, action α produces x, action β produces y, and action γ produces z. Given this, she has no problem ordering her action options $\alpha \succeq \beta \succeq \gamma$, and so as a rational utility maximizer she chooses α out of the set of options (α, β, γ). But we do not always choose under certainty. Sometimes we choose under *risk*. When we are choosing under risk, the outcomes of our action options are not certain, but we do know the probability of different outcomes resulting from our choice act. Suppose Alf faces the option between action α (choosing covered fruit bowl A) and β (covered fruit bowl B). Bowl A might contain a mango or it might contain an apple – Alf does not know which. Bowl B might contain a mango or it might contain a banana. Once again Alf does not know which. Alf does know, however, that if bowl A is chosen, then there is a 0.5 chance of getting a mango and a 0.5 chance of getting an apple. Alf also knows that if bowl B is chosen, then there is a 0.25 chance of getting a mango and a 0.75 chance of getting a banana. Because Alf knows the probabilities that each action will produce different outcomes, Alf is choosing under risk. How does a rational person choose in risky situations?

In such situations, rational agents use an *expected utility calculus*. With an expected utility calculus, agents multiply the probability an action that will produce an outcome by the utility one assigns to that outcome. We assume that Alf knows all the possible outcomes that each action will produce. Suppose Alf has a von Neumann and Morgenstern cardinal function over outcomes as depicted in Table 11.2. With this cardinal utility function, Alf's expected utility calculus goes like this:

α: choosing bowl A: $0.5(1) + 0.5(0) = 0.5$

β: choosing bowl B: $0.25(1) + 0.75(0.6) = 0.7$

Since the expected utility of α (choosing bowl A) is 0.5 and since the expected utility of β (choosing bowl B) is 0.7, Alf chooses what is the best prospect for maximizing his preferences, which is β. Notice that this does not ensure that, in the end, he will have achieved the highest level of preference satisfaction: if he did choose α *and* it turned out to have the mango while β produced the banana, α would have given him the best outcome. The point of expected utility is that, at the time of choice, β offers the *best prospects* for satisfying his preferences.

It is sometimes thought that any set of cardinal numbers is sufficient for expected utility calculations, as we can multiply cardinal numbers by probabilities (you can't multiply ordinal utilities). This is too simple. Our von Neumann–Morgenstern cardinal utility functions possess *the expected utility property*, as they take account of Alf's attitude toward risk. Recall that von Neumann–Morgenstern functions are generated through preferences over lotteries, thus they include information about how Alf weighs the attractiveness of an outcome and the risk of failing to achieve it. Suppose that instead of employing the von Neumann–Morgenstern procedure, we asked Alf to rate, on a scale of 0 to 1, simply how much he liked mangos, bananas, and apples, and he reports 1, 0.6, and 0 (this *looks* just like Table 11.2). If we then multiplied, say, this type of 'cardinal utility' of 1 for mangos times a 0.5 probability that α will produce a mango, we would get the *expected value* of α, but not its expected utility, for Alf could be very reluctant to take a 0.5 chance of his worst outcome (an apple) in order to get a 0.5 chance of his best; so to him the utility of α could be far less than 0.5. But our von Neumann–Morgenstern procedure already factored in this information. Only in the special case in which people are *risk-neutral* (they are neither risk prone nor risk averse) will expected value be equivalent to expected utility.

Choice under *uncertainty* is a messier and more complex affair. Like choice under risk, when choosing under uncertainty, one does not know the outcome of one's act of choice. But unlike choice under risk, one also does not know the probabilities that an action will yield the various possible outcomes. Following R. Duncan Luce and Howard Raiffa (1957: 278), we note that the idea of uncertainty is vague. With choice under risk, we know with objective certainty the relevant probabilities that α will produce various outcomes (0.5 of x, 0.5 of z). What happens, though, if we are not certain about the relevant probabilities but more or less have a reasonable guess as to what the probabilities are? Is this choice under uncertainty? Technically speaking, it is. Instead of having two categories, risk and uncertainty, it is more helpful to think of uncertainty as coming in degrees. Though we do not know the probabilities of outcomes occurring, our credence in what the relevant probabilities are can be more or less founded. At one end of the spectrum is choice under risk, where we know the probabilities of any given action option (so that this sums to 1 for each act), and on the other end of the spectrum is choice under radical uncertainty, where we cannot even begin to intelligently guess the relevant probabilities over outcomes.

Most relevant for political theory is choice under radical uncertainty. As we shall see later on, one of the central debates in twentieth-century political theory largely revolved around what rational choice requires when one faces such uncertainty. Suppose, as before, that Alf must choose between α and β (on the basis of their associated fruit bowls). But unlike before, Alf has absolutely no basis for assigning probabilities as to which fruit the respective bowls might contain. In such a situation how does Alf choose rationally? It is here that rational choice theory turns more into an art than a deductive system. Although it is relatively straightforward how rational persons choose under risk, and somewhat less certain under uncertainty, it is by no means obvious how rational agents should choose when faced with radical uncertainty. Consider two different ways in which one might approach such choices, outlining the costs associated with the different methods.

(*i*) When facing radical uncertainty one might simply try to extend the choice procedure used in decision under risk – that is, one might employ an expected utility calculus. But an expected utility calculus requires that we assign probabilities to outcomes and, by hypothesis, when facing radical uncertainty, there is no educated basis for assigning such probabilities. In such cases the *Laplacean principle of indifference* says to assign equal probability to all possible outcomes occurring, reflecting indifference to these outcomes occurring. Continuing our example, using this Laplacean principle, Alf would assign an equal probability of α yielding a mango and an apple, and to β an equal probability of it giving him a mango and a banana. From there Alf performs his expected utility calculus as he did with choice under risk, so $\alpha = 0.5(1) + 0.5(0)$; $\beta = 0.5(1) + 0.5(0.6)$, again yielding the choice of β.

The Laplacean principle of indifference is controversial. Ken Binmore (2009: 129) points out the ambiguity present in assigning equal probability to different outcomes occurring. Suppose Alf attends a three-horse race between α, β, and γ, but has no basis for assigning probability as to which horse will win. Is the Laplacean principle of indifference to be applied to the question (*a*) 'which horse will win?' or (*b*) 'will α win or not win?', 'will β win or not win?', 'will γ win or not win?'. If the first, the Laplacean principle says Alf should assign each horse a ⅓ probability of winning (so that Alf is indifferent between which horse wins). If the second, the principle says to assign each horse a ½ probability of winning and ½ probability of not winning (so that Alf is indifferent between each horse winning and not winning).

(*ii*) Another way of choosing under radical uncertainty is by using the maximin decision rule. The maximin decision rule eschews the use of

	Prize 1	Prize 2
L_1	0	n
L_2	$1/n$	1

Figure 11.1: Rawls's problem for maximin

probabilities; it instructs one to examine each action option (α, β, γ) and identify for each its worst possible outcome (say α_W, β_W, and γ_W). Looking only at these 'minimum payoffs' for each action one is to select the highest among *them* (hence one should 'maximize the minimum'). Like the Laplacean principle of indifference, there are many criticisms of the maximin decision rule, most of which offer examples in which its application seems irrational. Suppose, following Rawls (1999: 136), one is faced with a choice between lottery L_1 and lottery L_2 whose probabilities are unknown. Suppose further the payoffs for L_1 and L_2 are in dollars (and that preferences are monotonic over money). This decision problem is shown in Figure 11.1.

Maximin says to choose L_2 because L_2 guarantees a minimum payoff of $1/n$ while the minimum payoff for L_1 is 0. And when n is small (say, $1, $2, or $3), this does not seem to be an unreasonable choice. But suppose n is quite large, perhaps $1,000,000. In this case, there does seem something irrational about choosing L_2 and thus something irrational about the maximin decision rule in general.

2.3   Strategic Choice

When choosing parametrically, the decisions of others are a fixed background; one does not have to include in one's deliberations the different things they might do. In such cases of parametric choice, maximizing one's preferences is relatively straightforward, at least until we get to choice under uncertainty. But many times the actions of agents affect each other's decisions. This is strategic choice, which is studied by *game theory*. Roughly, a game is defined by (*i*) a set of players, (*ii*) a set of strategies for each player, (*iii*) the information available to the players, and (*iv*) a set of payoffs for each player which is defined by her preference ordering (ordinal or cardinal) which are mapped onto her strategies. Change any of these and you change the game.

Game theorists originally focused on zero-sum games, interactions of *pure conflict*. Whatever one player wins the other player loses. To see this, consider Figure 11.2, which is the classic game *Matching Pennies*.

Betty

		Heads α	Tails β
Alf	Heads α	1 −1	−1 1
	Tails β	−1 1	1 −1

Figure 11.2: *Matching Pennies*

By convention, Row's (Alf's) payoffs are in the bottom left of each cell, Column's (Betty's) in the upper right. Note that the gains and losses in every cell equal 0; any gain must come from the other player, so we have a *zero-sum game*. John von Neumann (1928) proved that all zero-sum games with finite strategies have equilibrium solutions. That is, there is a rational course of action in all such games. Relating back to decision under uncertainty in parametric choice, the equilibrium solution for zero-sum games is to play one's maximin strategy – *to maximize one's minimum*. If both players maximize their minimums, then neither player can gain from unilaterally changing her strategy. If we accept that the equilibrium solution concept models rationality, then, when playing zero-sum games, it is rational to maximin.

Though the theory of games was first developed in zero-sum form, it was quickly realized that zero-sum games are of limited applicability for understanding most strategic interactions. Rarely are we locked into total conflict; we often find ourselves in situations where we are competing *and* cooperating. Consider, for example, Luce and Raiffa's (1957: 90–1) politically incorrect 'Battle of the Sexes' game. In this game, Alf and Betty wish to go out with each other on a Friday evening; the worst thing for each would be to not go out together. However, Alf would prefer a date at the prizefights, Betty at the ballet. Figure 11.3 gives an example of the game, using cardinal utility.

So we have two players, Alf and Betty, and each has the same two 'pure' strategies, {Alf α, Alf β}, {Betty α, Betty β}. We suppose that each knows the information set **S**: they know each other's utilities and what strategies are open to the other, each has knowledge of the other's rationality, and they know that each must choose without knowing what the other has chosen. Moreover they each know **S'**: each knows that the other knows all the facts in **S**. And indeed they know **S''**: each knows that the others know all the facts in **S'**. The *common knowledge assumption* is assumed to be iterative – we can go on with higher and higher levels, where each knows what the facts were at the previous level.

Betty

		Go to Fights α	Go to Ballet β
Alf	Go to Fights α	1 2	0 0
	Go to Ballet β	0 0	2 1

Figure 11.3: The 'Battle of the Sexes' in cardinal utility

If Alf goes to the fights, then Betty, given her own preferences, will do best by also going to the fights; if Betty goes to the ballet, Alf will do best by also going to the ballet. Neither knows what the other is doing, but they wish to coordinate. So this is a game of cooperation. Yet it is also a game of conflict: they disagree about the best outcome. The central concept in game theory is that of *Nash equilibrium*. We can think of the Nash equilibrium as the solution to a game insofar as when two players are playing their equilibrium strategies each has made his/her best response to the move of the other player, and so neither player has any incentive to unilaterally change his/her strategy. The strategic interaction, we might say, can come to rest there. In the 'Battle of the Sexes' game, there are *two* Nash equilibria in pure strategies: both play α or both play β. Players can also play a 'mixed strategy', which is a probability distribution over their pure strategies. In Figure 11.2's game, this would mean Alf would play α with a p probability and β with a $1-p$ probability. This game has a Nash equilibrium in mixed strategies in which Alf plays α with a probability of ⅔ (and so β with a probability of ⅓) and Betty plays β with a probability of ⅔. At this point, no adjustment to the probability that they play each of their pure strategies will allow a player to unilaterally improve her expected payoffs. John Nash (1950a, 1951), in a fundamental theorem of game theory, showed that all games in cardinal utility with finite strategies have at least one equilibrium (sometimes only a mixed equilibrium). Note that this theorem, because it requires mixed strategies, depends on the expected utility property.

We should note a more general solution concept, *correlated equilibrium* (Aumann 1987), which includes the Nash solution. Its attractions are manifest in the game of Chicken:

Chevy

		Swerve α	Don't Swerve β
Ford	Swerve α	5 5	10 0
	Don't Swerve β	0 10	−5 −5

Figure 11.4: Chicken in cardinal utility

Suppose that every Saturday and Sunday, two teenagers, one driving a Chevy and the other a Ford, drive toward each other with the pedal to the metal, and the first one to swerve is 'chicken'. So the options are between swerving (α) and not swerving (β). The best result is to keep driving straight while the other swerves: the other chickened; you didn't. If both swerve, neither crashes; if neither swerves, they crash. In this game, the two 'pure equilibria' are (Ford α, Chevy β) and (Ford β; Chevy α). There is a mixed Nash equilibrium where each swerves half the time, but this has the unfortunate result that ¼ of the time they crash! Now consider a game where we add a strategy: on Saturdays Chevy swerves, on Sundays Ford swerves. The game will not be terribly exciting, but they will never crash, and each will have an expected payoff of 5, as good as one could do against a rational opponent. But note that we seemed to have changed the game: we have expanded the strategy set to include a correlating device (the day and the make of car).

At least in their simpler forms, Chicken and the 'Battle of the Sexes' raise problems when we understand strategic rational choice as requiring agents to play their equilibrium strategies. For in these games there are *multiple* equilibria. What, then, do rational players do? Which equilibrium do they play? Unfortunately there is no definitive good answer. People have tried many ways to select one equilibrium from multiple Nash equilibria. The oldest way of solving the equilibrium selection problem is to a priori theorize about what rationality requires when faced with multiple equilibria. This is known as 'equilibrium refinement' and was pursued to its fullest by John Harsanyi and Reinhard Selten (1988). Some refinements seem plausible: for instance, if one equilibrium strictly dominates another (i.e., is better for *all* parties), then perhaps that equilibrium is more rational. At best, this is a rather limited refinement. As we proceed, we encounter deep controversy – no satisfactory account has been given to refine all games down to a unique equilibrium.

Others have employed evolutionary accounts explaining why some equilibria are selected over others: though a pair of strategies might be in equilibrium for a one-shot game, such a pair of strategies might no longer be in equilibrium if the game is continually repeated (the opposite is also true). Notable here is Brian Skyrms's (1996, 2004) work. In contrast, Thomas Schelling (1960: 57) emphasized the role of *salience* or the sheer obviousness of a solution in certain contexts. For example, when two parties are asked to split up a sum of money, they will often split it right down the middle, even though there are many possible splits. Or if two parties are asked to meet at some place in Paris, they will usually go to the Eiffel Tower because it is such a large, obvious landmark. Of course, there can be multiple salient equilibria. Moreover, differing methods of equilibrium selection can conflict. Strict dominance as a plausible refinement technique can conflict with Schelling's salience – sometimes the salient equilibrium will be dominated by a non-salient equilibrium. Though there have been many proposals of how to select among multiple equilibria, a current limitation in the theory of games is that it cannot tell us which equilibrium rational players select.

One final area of strategic choice relevant for political theory is bargaining games. Implicitly we have been examining *non-cooperative* game theory, which assumes that choices among strategies are not binding. One follows a Nash equilibrium not because it is the solution to a game, but because, given the move of the other, it is one's best available move. In *cooperative* game theory, choices among strategies are assumed to be binding by some external enforcement mechanism. The most famous case of a cooperative solution that is not in equilibrium is the Prisoner's Dilemma. The story is normally told in terms of prisoners getting caught and seeking to minimize jail time, but all games are really about utility. Figure 11.5 gives the Prisoner's Dilemma in terms of cardinal utility.

If Betty plays α, Alf will get x if he plays α, and 1 if he plays β; since $1 > x$, he should then play β. If Betty plays β, Alf gets 0 if he plays α, and y if he plays β; since $y > 0$, he should again play β. 'Confessing' (β) is thus his *dominant strategy*: no matter what Betty does, Alf does best if he plays β. And it can clearly be seen that Betty will reason in exactly the same way. So (β,β) is the sole Nash equilibrium. Yet the outcome of y/y is worse for each than the x/x outcome. The x/x is a cooperative outcome that is not in equilibrium; as a non-cooperative game there is only one solution to the Prisoner's Dilemma: *confess!* Such games can, however, form the basis of binding agreements that yield a cooperative surplus. Faced with such bargains, one might ask what distribution of surplus rational players will

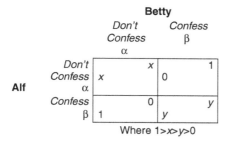

Figure 11.5: The general form of the Prisoner's Dilemma in cardinal utility

settle on. The status of bargaining theory is unsettled. There are several competing bargaining theories. Nash's (1950b) bargaining solution has the widest support. And Ariel Rubenstein (1982) appeared to put cooperative bargaining theory on a firmer footing by clearly showing how it can be derived from non-cooperative game theory. Yet Luce and Raiffa's (1957: 119–20) worry remains – that such bargaining solutions, though intellectually interesting, do not seem to model what purely rational players would select in actual bargains. And some worry that the very axioms of bargaining theory go beyond rationality to include some criteria of fairness (Thrasher 2014).

3   Is Rational Choice Theory Unrealistic?

3.1   People Aren't Always Rational

It should be manifest that rational choice theory idealizes: agents are generally understood to know all their options, rank them, and usually in a way that provides a cardinal scale. They are then assumed to be thoroughly consistent choosers, always seeking to maximize the satisfaction of their preferences. The most common refrain is that, since people are not thoroughly rational, these are wildly unrealistic assumptions, and so undermine the usefulness of rational choice theory. If people aren't rational, why care about rational choice?

One version of this common refrain simply points out that people are not *always* rational: they do not always act as rational choice theory predicts. First, we need to be clear about what rational choice theory does *not* predict: it does not predict that people will always be self-interested, or that they seek to maximize the satisfaction of their desires, or that moral considerations never move them. These are matters about the nature of the deliberation that determine a person's rankings – they concern the basis on which Alf determines whether state of affairs x is to be ranked above y. As we have stressed, rational choice theory is not committed to any account about the basis of rankings. Recall also that preferences are not desires, but rankings of outcomes, which determine preferences over actions. This is important. Many experimenters, for example, believe that they have shown that people cooperate in Prisoner's Dilemmas. In experiments in which people are confronted with situations that *mimic* Figure 11.5, where the payoffs are monetary and players are awarded sums of money where the size of the monetary payoffs is exactly correlated with the utility payoff schedule in Figure 11.5, we can observe people cooperating – an action that, for all players, is dominated by confessing. However, unless the players rank the outcomes *only* in terms of their monetary payoffs – unless their preferences are *only* over amounts of money, and thus, for example, have no concern with fairness or simply not being a jerk – we cannot say that the players are actually in a Prisoner's Dilemma interaction, so rational choice theory does not predict that they will defect.

Nevertheless, even when we are more careful, there is dispute over whether rational choice theory is a good predictor. Perhaps the most comprehensive critique of rational choice theory as a predictive tool is Ian Shapiro and Donald Green's (1996) *Pathologies of Rational Choice Theory* (see also Amadae 2015), though there have been equally comprehensive defenses of rational choice theory as a predictive tool (see, for instance, the debate in Friedman 1996). Rational choice theory is a *model* of human action: like all models, we build a simplified world so that we can better understand some salient dynamics, and get some predictive leverage in some contexts. As Michael Wesiberg (2007) notes: '[w]hen faced with ... complexity, theorists can employ one of several strategies: They can try to include as much complexity as possible in their theoretical representations. They can make strategic decisions about which aspects of a phenomenon can be legitimately excluded from a representation. Or they can model, studying a complex phenomenon in the real world by first constructing and then studying a model of the phenomenon.' These models abstract from the complexity of reality to analyze the interactions among key elements. In some contexts, the models may abstract from too much of the complexity to give adequate understanding of the phenomena, but in other contexts they can be enlightening and accurate. In social science, no model or theory explains most of the variance of interestingly complex phenomena, but this does not mean the model is without predictive and explanatory power.

Rational choice models do rather well in a variety of cases, especially where we can make accurate suppositions as to what people's utility functions look like, the information sets they have, and the actions open to them. Thus experiments have confirmed that various sorts of auction behavior and trading behavior conform to the predictions of rational choice theory (Plott 1986; Smith 2000). On the other hand, when people have complex and heterogeneous utility functions, when the options are not well understood, or, more radically, when they act out of strong emotions, rational choice theory is not apt to explain things well (Schwartz 2002; Bosman, Sutter, and Van Winden 2005).

3.2   Rationality and Intelligibility

A more radical rejection of rational choice theory insists that rationality is a 'folk concept', not a scientific one. While most of us, as normal 'folk', think in terms of preferences, options, and choices, some argue a 'true' scientific theory would be purely causal, and so would explain human actions in terms of psychological or biochemical processes. Hartmut Kleimt advances what might be understood as a 'compatibilist' reply: 'humans are citizens of two worlds, a lower "material" world and a higher one of reason' (2009: 16). On this compatibilist approach, we can understand humans both in simply causal terms and in purposive ways – as agents with preferences – who seek to secure their most favored outcome. Some suggest that we only rely on rational choice models because our causal models are underdeveloped, so perhaps someday we can do without rational choice theory. But this seems wrong. Humans understand each other through 'mind reading': the actions of another are not really intelligible to me until I see how, if *I* thought what she believes and *I* cared for what she cared for, *I* would have done what she did. Making others intelligible to us is closely bound to seeing them as rational: rational action makes sense to us (Rosenberg 1995). True, sometimes it is intelligible to us why people are not rational: we can understand all too well why someone who is drunk accepts a dangerous and silly dare. But usually, when we are confronted by simply irrational behavior, we do not understand what it is really all about. To understand the behavior of another is to see it as intelligible, and to see it is rational is to render it intelligible.

4   Rational Choice as a Normative Theory

Herbert Gintis (2009: chs. 1, 12) boldly conjectures that game theory's axioms of consistent choice express, at the deepest level, the ingredients of evolutionary success. It is indeed striking how powerful, in the guise of 'evolutionary game theory', the tools of game theory have proven in modeling natural selection (for classic statements, see Hamilton 1964; Trivers 1971; Smith 1975). If the basic idea of consistent choosers who maximize their satisfaction of their goals is foundational to selected behavior in humans and non-humans alike, we might hypothesize that creatures like us – who are conscious of their agency – cannot help but see these axioms as normative: as not simply explaining what they do, but guiding what they *should* do. In a secular world where the gods no longer seem to speak to and guide us, can we have any deeper guide than our most basic axioms of successful agency, on which perhaps our entire evolutionary past hinges? Thus is the crux of Gauthier's (1991) case for what he calls 'contractarianism': the only truly solid foundation for thinking about what we ought to do that our naturalistic and scientific age has left us are the consistency axioms at the root of successful agency. If we have any hope of identifying normative principles for our post-metaphysical world – a world shorn of faith in God's plan for us, or invisible normative properties that instruct us what to do – they must be solidly grounded in rational choice.

Contractarianism in moral and political theory seeks to show that moral and political principles or rules can be the result of an agreement between rational parties and, further, that compliance with these principles or rules is rational. When deriving normative principles, contractarians appeal to what rational parties would agree to, which is just to say what rational choice requires in strategic interaction. This can be seen informally in the case of Hobbes when he argues that rational parties, engaged in a war of all against all in the state of nature, would agree to enter the social contract, where each gives up her right to all things in exchange for security from the sovereign (1994: chs. 13, 16). Contemporary contractarians go further than examining the informal logic of what rational parties would agree to. Gauthier (1986), for instance, employs game theoretic bargaining models to examine what moral principles rational parties would agree on. He ends up developing his own bargaining solution, the principle of minimax relative concession, which is an offshoot of the Kalai-Smorodinsky (1975) bargaining solution. Most contractarians – including Gauthier at one point in his career – opt for the alternative, Nash bargaining solution (1950b). But the critical idea was that this bargain would simply be a rational bargain: the only normativity is the normativity of rationality.

Just as we had to define Alf's utility function before examining what a rational Alf would choose, contractarian approaches to moral and political theory also require that we give content to utility functions.

Before showing that rationality leads to certain normative principles, we must have some account of what people's preferences are. Hobbes (1994: ch. 11) does this when he posits in all mankind 'a perpetual and restless desire for power after power, that ceaseth only in death'. Gauthier (1986: 87) also does this when he insists that utility functions be non-tuistic, or not other-regarding. This means that the satisfaction of one's preferences cannot rely on other people's preferences being satisfied. Excluded by non-tuism is the mother who only prefers to see her children's preferences satisfied. The reason Gauthier excludes such preferences is an attempt to avoid his theory admitting solutions based on adaptive preference formation under domination: for example, Amartya Sen (2009: 166–7, 285–6) notes how in some areas Indian women's understandings of what they want and how well they are doing are fundamentally shaped by their acceptance of the normality of gender bias.

Contractarians such as Hobbes and Gauthier are the purest examples of the project of building moral and political principles on the normativity of rational choice. Rawls's famous social contract theory also seeks to base the normative appeal of its conclusions on the normativity of rational choice. At the outset of *A Theory of Justice* Rawls (1999a: 15–16) insists that

one conception of justice is more reasonable than another, or justifiable with respect to it, if rational persons in the initial situation would choose its principles over those of the other for the role of justice. Conceptions of justice are to be ranked by their acceptability to persons so circumstanced. Understood in this way the question of justification is settled by working out a problem of deliberation: we have to ascertain which principles it would be rational to adopt given the contractual situation. This connects the theory of justice with the theory of rational choice.

And thus the importance of our opening quote from Rawls (1999a: 15): 'The theory of justice is a part, perhaps the most significant part, of the theory of rational choice.'

Rawls, however, insists that the choice of moral principles is not simply governed by the 'rational', but also the 'reasonable' – a concern with fair cooperation (1993: 48ff). One way to model this is to select principles behind a veil of ignorance, in which parties have drastically restricted information sets, including information as to who they are, and what their utility functions look like (Harsanyi 1955; Gaus and Thrasher 2015). This restriction on information forces parties to choose fairly: hence non-tuistic parties, i.e., choosers only concerned with maximizing their own goals, are forced (via ignorance) to consider how the goals of *each* fare, since once the veil is lifted, one may end up being any of these people.

A rather more straightforward route, perhaps, is simply to build concerns with fairness or morality into the utility functions of the choosers (Gaus 2011: ch. 5). Again, it is crucial to stress that rational choice theory does not tell us what a person's preferences are. The more one stresses the 'reasonable' over the 'rational', the more one is insisting that the selection of principles must not only suppose utility maximizers, but those with certain substantive moral concerns.

5   Decisions to Be Made When Using Decision Theory

We have tried to stress the complexities of rational choice theory, and have tried to alert readers to the pitfalls of widespread misconceptions. We can apply these lessons to thinking about how a researcher might contemplate using a rational choice framework in her own work in political theory.

It may sound terribly simple, but **the first step is to be clear whether you are using rational choice theory as an explanatory, predictive, or normative model**. These can be surprisingly easy to run together. Think of Hobbesian political theory: part of Hobbes's famous argument is how people will act in the state of nature (an explanatory project) and the next part is a normative contract: what would be a rational agreement to leave the state of nature? These raise vastly different issues. The explanatory part of the project has been advanced by game theoretic modeling concerning the ease with which conflict can erupt in a state of nature (Vanderschraaf 2006; Chung 2015). The specification of the contract is normative: what constitutes a rational bargain? This leads to the sorts of concerns Gauthier and Rawls have investigated. Confusion between these two projects can lead to errors. In offering an empirical analysis of the state of nature, Hobbesians are not saying that this is what persons *ought* to do – in fact, the Hobbesian project is driven by a desire to show how alleviating one's self from such a state is consistent with rational choice. And in offering normative analyses of the social contract, theorists are not trying to describe anything that has happened, or necessarily will. Instead, they are trying to model the reasons we have to obey certain authority relations via a rational choice analysis.

Be clear about whether the problem is parametric or strategic. Even the best political theorists can make this mistake. Rawls (1999a: 11) said that we should understand the derivation of the theory of justice as the result of a 'fair agreement or bargain', suggesting that he wanted to model a strategic rather than parametric choice problem in the original position. But later on Rawls (1999a: 120) insists that, due to the normalization of the parties' interests, we can *really* understand choice in the original position 'from the standpoint of one person selected at random', suggesting a parametric rather than strategic choice problem. This can lead to confusion. Consider, for instance, Rawls's (1999a: 132–3) continual insistence that we can think of the two principles of justice as 'those a person would choose for the design of a society in which his enemy is to assign him his place.' If Rawls models the original position as a parametric choice problem, then such remarks conjure up the maximin choice principle under uncertainty – which, as we have seen, is riddled with controversy. But suppose Rawls models the original position as a strategic choice problem rather than a parametric one. Then, if the game is zero-sum, we have seen that the maximin choice *is the uniquely rational solution to the game*, and thus not subject to controversy. Whether the original position is parametric rather than strategic is thus highly relevant in terms of its plausibility as a rational choice model. We end up following the standard way of understanding the original position in the literature as a parametric choice problem rather than a strategic choice problem, though, again, Rawls's language could be clearer on this point.

The really hard step is to determine the utility functions of the parties. And how utility functions are defined can have tremendous relevance for the plausibility of a rational choice model, regardless of whether the model is normative or explanatory. Consider again Gauthier's normative contractarian project. As we mentioned, Gauthier defines utility functions by requiring preferences be non-tuistic so that his bargain is not the result of preference adaptation under domination. Such stipulation, though, is not without controversy. Donald Hubin (1991) argues that excluding tuistic preferences means that rational persons with such preferences will not find it rational to comply with the resulting bargain. After all, if the bargain was derived from a non-tuistic utility function, but a rational person has a tuistic utility function, then it is hard to see why it is rational for the other-regarding person to obey constraints derived specifically for persons who are not other-regarding. And from the explanatory side, Jean Hampton (1986: 75) argues that, given one interpretation of how Hobbes defines utility functions of actors in the state of nature, there would actually be no conflict in the state of nature at all. If people really were rational actors who only cared only about self-preservation, then the iterated context of the state of nature would allow for cooperation. No need for the sovereign after all!

You should now decide whether to represent these preferences ordinarily or cardinally. For some simple games (such as the Prisoner's Dilemma), an ordinal representation will be sufficient; but if risk or uncertainty is involved, we have seen, a cardinal representation is likely to be required.

Your next decision is: what are the actor's information sets? Do they know everything, or only a little? And if one is modeling strategic interaction, one must decide if what the parties know is the same, or if some parties know more than others. This latter difference can be crucial, again for both normative and explanatory rational choice models. On the normative side, we again turn to contractarianism. One common assumption in bargaining theory is the assumption that parties are 'symmetric' – that they have the same strategies available to them, the same bargaining ability, and, importantly, the same information sets. This assumption was originally introduced by Nash (1950b), but is common in many bargaining models, including Gauthier (1986). Yet as John Thrasher (2014) shows, this assumption can often be at odds with the contractarian project – it amounts to importing fairness criteria into the terms of the bargain, when really what the contractarian is trying to do is *derive* fairness criteria *from* the bargain itself. For the reason the symmetry assumption is often introduced is because once we admit things like asymmetric information sets into the bargain, the resulting distribution might not be so intuitively attractive when compared to the symmetrical case. And from an explanatory standpoint, Zachary Ernst (2005) forcefully argues that many explanatory models of the evolution of conventions and fairness norms obscure more than they reveal when they assume symmetry across parties, of which symmetrical information sets is one such part. These sorts of considerations are highly relevant when determining the information sets of the parties – symmetrical information might be clean and easy, but possibly problematic.

If you decide that you are concerned with a strategic choice, you will need to learn a bit of game theory. There are a number of good introductory texts (e.g., Maschler, Solan, and Zamir 2013). **Do not be too quick to focus on a particular game before you have determined the preferences and the information sets of the parties.** Games are defined by the preferences, information sets, and strategies of the players. It is all too common for even postgraduate students (and, alas, professors!) to get fascinated by a game such as the Prisoner's Dilemma or Chicken, and then to try to find ways to apply it, often forcing a case or situation into an inappropriate game. Once one has made the previous decisions on our list, one can fruitfully think about game theoretic representations.

A last lesson: **when using rational choice theory, especially in normative contexts, it is critical to realize its limits.** Often our disputes are not about what a rational person would do, but about the correct preferences to ascribe to people, or the conditions for fair bargains. Understanding moral and political principles as an object of choice among rational choosers can clarify their basis, but we must be very careful not to reduce all these to disputes about rationality. Even experts can believe that their dispute is about rationality, rather than the proper content of an agent's concerns. A good example of this is the Rawls-Harsanyi debate. Harsanyi (1953, 1955) and Rawls pursued very similar contract-based normative projects, reducing the problem of moral justification to one of rational choice behind the veil of ignorance. *Contra* Rawls, however, Harsanyi believed that rational parties choosing behind a veil of ignorance would select average utilitarianism rather than Rawls's two principles of justice. At first blush the dispute between Rawls and Harsanyi reduced to an argument about rational choice under uncertainty. Rawls thought rational parties, when faced with radical uncertainty, ought to adopt the maximin decision rule. Harsanyi thought rational parties, when faced with radical uncertainty, ought to adopt the Laplacean principle of indifference. The debate continued after both parties published their seminal social contract contributions. Harsanyi (1974) continued to point out the irrationality of the maximin decision rule, while Rawls (1999b: 225–31) continued defending it.

Recent analysis of the Rawls-Harsanyi dispute, though, suggests that the disagreement between the two cannot merely be reduced to a debate about rational choice. Michael Moehler (2013) argues that Rawls's and Harsanyi's disagreement over what rationality requires *itself* reduces to a philosophical dispute about which moral values should be modeled in the choice situation, and thus which moral values are important. Rawls wanted to model *impartiality* in the original position. Harsanyi was especially concerned with modeling *impersonality*. While impartiality merely requires that agents do not unjustifiably favor their own interests in making decisions, impersonality requires agents to make decisions only on the basis of the common interest. This inclusion of impersonality, which Rawls (1999a: 24) rejected, *required* Harsanyi to use the Laplacean principle of indifference. And as Rawls (2001: 97–100) notes later on, the use of maximin reasoning in the original position ultimately comes down to a moral, not a rational choice. The putative debate between Rawls and Harsanyi over the nature of rational choice theory reduces to a disagreement over what is to be valued – impartiality versus impersonality. This is an object lesson. **Rational choice theory by no means replaces philosophical analysis. Remember always that it is a tool, and like all tools, is effective only when it is used to perform its proper tasks in its proper ways.**

References

Amadae, S. M., 2015. *Prisoners of Reason: Game Theory and Neoliberal Political Economy*. Cambridge University Press.

Aumann, Robert, 1987. 'Correlated equilibrium as an expression of Bayesian rationality', *Econometrica* 55: 1–18.

Binmore, Ken, 2005. *Natural Justice*. Oxford University Press.

Binmore, Ken, 2009. *Rational Decisions*. Princeton, NJ: Princeton University Press.

Bosman, Ronald, Matthias Sutter, and Frans van Winden, 2005. 'The impact of real effort and emotions in the power-to-take game', *Journal of Economic Psychology* 26, 407–29.

Buchanan, James and Gordon Tullock, 2004. *The Calculus of Consent: The Logical Foundations of Constitutional Democracy*. Indianapolis, IN: Liberty Fund.

Chung, Hun, 2015. 'Hobbes's state of nature: a modern Bayesian game-theoretic analysis', *Journal of the American Philosophical Association* 1, 485–508.

Ernst, Zachary, 2005. 'A plea for asymmetric games', *Journal of Philosophy* 102: 109–25.

Friedman, Jeffrey, ed., 1996. *The Rational Choice Controversy: Economic Models of Politics Reconsidered*. New Haven, CT: Yale University Press.

Gaus, Gerald, 2011. *The Order of Public Reason*. Cambridge: Cambridge University Press.

Gaus, Gerald and John Thrasher, 2015. 'Rational choice and the original position: the (many) models of Rawls and Harsanyi', in Timothy Hinton, ed., *The Original Position*. Cambridge, MA: Harvard University Press, 39–58.

Gauthier, David, 1986. *Morals by Agreement*. Oxford: Clarendon Press.

Gauthier, David, 1991. 'Why contractarianism?', in Peter Vallentyne, ed., *Contractarianism and Rational Choice*. Cambridge University Press, 15–30.

Gintis, Herbert, 2009. *The Bounds of Reasons: Game Theory and the Unification of the Behavioral Sciences*. Princeton, NJ: Princeton University Press.

Hamilton, W. D., 1964. 'The genetical evolution of social behaviour I', *Journal of Theoretical Biology*, 7: 1–16.

Hampton, Jean, 1986. *Hobbes and the Social Contract Tradition*. Cambridge University Press.

Harsanyi, John, 1953. 'Cardinal utility in welfare economics and in the theory of risk-taking', *Journal of Political Economy* 61: 434–5.

Harsanyi, John, 1955. 'Cardinal welfare, individualistic ethics and interpersonal comparisons of utility', *Journal of Political Economy* 63: 309–21.

Harsanyi, John, 1974. 'Can the maximin principle serve as the basis for morality?', *American Political Science Review* 69: 594–606.

Harsanyi, John and Reinhard Selten, 1988. *A General Theory of Equilibrium Selection in Games*. Cambridge, MA: MIT Press.

Hobbes, Thomas, 1994. *Leviathan*, ed. Edwin Curley. Indianapolis, IN: Hackett Publishing.

Hubin, Donald, 1991. 'Non-tuism', *Canadian Journal of Philosophy* 21: 441–68.

Kalai, Ehud and Meir Smorodinsky, 1975. 'Other solutions to Nash's bargaining problem', *Econometrica* 43: 513–18.

Kliemt, Hartmut, 2009. *Philosophy and Economics I: Methods and Models.* Munich: Oldenbourg.

Luce, Duncan and Howard Raiffa, 1957. *Games and Decisions.* New York: Dover Publications.

Maschler, Michael, Eilon Solan, and Shmuel Zamir, 2013. *Game Theory.* Cambridge University Press.

Moehler, Michael, 2013. 'Contractarian ethics and Harsanyi's two justifications of utilitarianism', *Politics, Philosophy, and Economics* 12: 24–47.

Nash, John, 1950a. 'Equilibrium points in n-person games', *Proceedings of the National Academy of Sciences of the United States of America* 36: 48–49.

Nash, John, 1950b. 'The bargaining problem', *Econometrica* 18: 155–62.

Nash, John, 1951. 'Non-cooperative games', *Annals of Mathematics* 54: 286–95.

Plamenatz, John, 1973. *Democracy and Illusion.* London: Longman.

Plott, Charles, 1996. 'Rational choice in experimental markets', in Robin Hogarth and Melvin Reder, eds., *Rational Choice: The Contrast between Economics and Psychology.* Chicago, IL: University of Chicago Press, 117–43.

Rawls, John, 1993. *Political Liberalism.* New York: Columbia University Press.

Rawls, John, 1999a. *A Theory of Justice*, Revised Edition. Cambridge, MA: Harvard University Press.

Rawls, John, 1999b. *Collected Papers.* Cambridge, MA: Harvard University Press.

Rawls, John, 2001. *Justice as Fairness: A Restatement.* Cambridge, MA: Harvard University Press.

Rosenberg, Alexander, 1995. *Philosophy of Social Science*, 2nd edition. Boulder, CO: Westview.

Rubinstein, Ariel, 1982. 'Perfect equilibrium in a bargaining model', *Econometrica* 50, 97–110.

Schelling, Thomas, 1960. *The Strategy of Conflict.* Cambridge, MA: Harvard University Press.

Schwartz, Norbert, 2002. 'Feelings as information: moods influence judgments and processing strategies', in Thomas Gilovich, Dale Griffin, and Daniel Kahneman, eds., *Heuristics and Biases: The Psychology of Intuitive Judgments.* Cambridge University Press, 534–47.

Sen, Amartya, 2009. *The Idea of Justice.* Cambridge, MA: Harvard University Press.

Shapiro, Ian and Donald Green, 1996. *Pathologies of Rational Choice: A Critique of Applications in Political Science.* New Haven, CT: Yale University Press.

Skyrms, Brian, 1996. *Evolution of the Social Contract.* Cambridge University Press.

Skyrms, Brian, 2004. *The Stag Hunt and the Evolution of Social Structure.* Cambridge University Press.

Smith, John Maynard, 1975. *The Theory of Evolution*, 3rd edition. New York: Penguin.

Smith, Vernon, 2002. *Bargaining and Market Behavior: Essays in Experimental Economics.* Cambridge University Press.

Sugden, Robert, 1986. *The Economics of Rights, Cooperation and Welfare*. Oxford: Blackwell.

Thrasher, John, 2014. 'Uniqueness and symmetry in bargaining theories of justice', *Philosophical Studies* 167: 683–99.

Thrasher, John and Gerald Gaus, forthcoming. 'James Buchanan and Gordon Tullock, *Calculus of Consent*', in Jacob Levy, ed., *The Oxford Handbook of Classics in Contemporary Political Theory*. Oxford University Press.

Trivers, Robert, 1971. 'The evolution of reciprocal altruism', *The Quarterly Review of Biology* 66: 35–57.

Vanderschraaf, Peter, 2006. 'War or peace? A dynamical analysis of anarchy', *Economics and Philosophy* 22: 243–79.

von Neumann, John, 1928. 'Zur Theorie der Gesellschaftsspiele', *Mathematische Annalen* 100: 295–320.

von Neumann, John and Oscar Morgenstern, 1944. *The Theory of Games and Economic Behavior*. Princeton, NJ: Princeton University Press.

Weisberg, Michael, 2007. 'Who is a modeler?', *British Journal for Philosophy of Science* 58, 207–33.

12   Interpreting Texts

Adrian Blau

1   Introduction: Meanings and Understandings

There are three main ways of interpreting texts, based on three kinds of understanding and three equivalent kinds of meaning: (1) what authors mean, which is empirical; (2) what the ideas mean, which is philosophical; and (3) what one or both of these mean to the reader – how you or I feel when we read a text – which is aesthetic.

Aesthetic interpretation is primarily the province of literature departments. Of course, what texts mean to those of us in other departments can still influence what we study. Rousseau has made me cry, because of the beauty and passion of his writing. Habermas has made me cry, for other reasons. Such reactions can influence our empirical and philosophical understanding. And we do sometimes study the effects authors had or tried to have on their readers, for example through their rhetoric. But what texts mean to us is not usually our academic focus, and I discuss it no further.

By contrast, philosophical interpretation – what the ideas mean – is very significant for us. Not that you would know it from our methodological literature, which mainly emphasizes empirical issues, especially what authors mean. Yet both kinds of meaning matter when interpreting texts, because they involve different kinds of understanding. If you read Mill's *On Liberty* and understand exactly what he meant by every word he used, you have understood something very important. But you understand his writing better if you also spot his ambiguities, contradictions, successes and failures. Unfortunately, the best methodological writings about textual interpretation – those by Quentin Skinner (2002a) – say almost nothing about the second kind of meaning and understanding, and hence imply that the first can always be achieved on its own.

I seek to connect these two kinds of meaning and these two kinds of understanding. A piece of research typically prioritizes one of the two, but almost always handles both. They are not alternatives: we usually need one to find the other. That fundamental point has not, I believe, been made in previous methodological discussions.

Equally unfortunately, most methodological writings give the wrong impression by talking about different 'approaches' or 'schools of thought', like contextualism, Straussianism, Marxism and so on. These categories have some value, and I cover them later. But mental categories can limit our thoughts and actions, and I believe this has happened here: most commentators imply that these categories are very different without adding that there are principles of good interpretation that apply to *all* of us (see especially Pocock 1971: 6–11; Rorty 1984: 49; Dunn 1996: 19; Ball 2004: 19; Richter 2009: 7–11; Schulz and Weiss 2010: 284–8). Despite some marked differences in our interpretive aims, there is or should be much overlap in our interpretive methods. Silence about these core principles has not prevented excellent interpretations, but has permitted more dubious scholarship than otherwise.

This chapter's main aim is to make explicit these core principles of good interpretation. You will find relevant principles in every section of this chapter, even in sections you might think do not apply to you.

Three brief caveats. First, my examples are mostly historical, but the principles also fit contemporary texts. Second, my examples mainly come from well-known Western authors, like Machiavelli and Rousseau, but the principles also apply to less well-known Western authors, and to authors in other cultures. (See also the chapters in this volume by Leader Maynard on ideological analysis, and by Ackerly and Bajpai on comparative political thought.) Third, and most important, although I cover both empirical interpretation (e.g. what Locke meant by 'property') and philosophical interpretation (e.g. how well Locke's defence of property works), and although I link the two more than other commentators do, most of my how-to guidance involves empirical interpretation, including using philosophical interpretation as part of empirical interpretation. Other chapters in this volume will help more for readers primarily interested in philosophical interpretation in itself (especially the chapters by Knight on reflective equilibrium, and Brownlee and Stemplowska on thought experiments). But you should still read this chapter to the extent that you want to get historical or contemporary authors right. And Olsthoorn's chapter (especially Section 6) will help for both empirical and philosophical interpretation.

Section 2 summarizes contextualism: despite its crucially important focus on history and context, there are other secrets to contextualists' success, and pitfalls we must all beware. Section 3 addresses *Begriffsgeschichte*, conceptual history and genealogy, which combine textual and/or contextual analysis with conceptual comparison. Section 4, the most important section, considers reconstruction, which is sometimes seen as purely philosophical, but which we all do – even historians. Section 5 questions the usefulness of treating perspectives like feminism or Marxism as if they are 'approaches'. Rather, they provide hypotheses and distinctions that help us see things that other scholars overlook, and these 'approaches' are far more numerous than we usually think. Nor is 'reading between the lines' exclusively a Straussian tool, Section 6 argues. Section 7 then offers further general principles of good interpretation that apply to all of us – whatever categories, approaches or schools of thought we identify with.

2   Contextualism

Contextualism is often called the 'Cambridge School' approach, albeit misleadingly (Skinner 2012: 16–17). Contextualism has dominated methodological debates about textual interpretation for half a century. And contextualists have essentially won the battle, both through their theoretical arguments and the high quality of actual contextual research. Although their theoretical arguments sometimes remain controversial, the core idea is widely accepted: place texts in their historical contexts. Even scholars who do not themselves do historical research usually consult such publications, to make misinterpretation less likely.

Contextualism has a long history (e.g. Allen 1928: xvii–xx), but started its upsurge in the late 1940s and flowered in the 1960s, with the theoretical ideas and substantive interpretations of writers like Peter Laslett, John Pocock, Quentin Skinner and John Dunn (Pocock 2006: 37–9). Given diversity within and between these writers and their followers (Boucher 1985: 151–272; Skinner 2012: 16–17), I focus mainly on Skinner, who I see as the supreme methodologist in our field. I have learned much from his methodological writings, but even more from his substantive interpretations, which I find methodologically richer and more impressive. By contrast, Mark Bevir only tackles Skinner's methodological writings (1999: 40–50, 327) and thus overlooks some of Skinner's most important methodological lessons (see also Stuurman 2000: 319; Skinner 2002a: 178–9). Treating Skinner as a practitioner, not just a theorist, lets me sidestep his speech-act theorizing, which is essentially separate to contextual analysis (Hutton 2014: 927), and which I address elsewhere.[1]

---

[1] Adrian Blau, 'Extended meaning and understanding in the history of ideas' (working paper, 2016).

Although Skinner does not say so, and although most commentators emphasize his contextualism, the foundation of Skinner's success is actually close *textual* analysis. Indeed, he has taught history of political thought to graduate students like this, such as eight weeks of close reading of *Leviathan* in Cambridge. The first principle of contextualism, and all sensible interpretation, is thus: **read texts carefully.**

This requires us to **read passages in their textual contexts.** Consider Hobbes's comment that 'the Thoughts, are to the Desires, as Scouts, and Spies, to range abroad, and find the way to the things desired' (Hobbes 1991: 8.16, 53). Although this does not mention 'reason', many scholars seem to equate 'thoughts' and 'reason', and treat Hobbes as implying that reason is instrumental to the passions, or even the slave of the passions. But in the context of the chapter as a whole, this comment is surely not about reason: Hobbes is merely saying that our thoughts jump to what we desire. If I like baseball and see a big stick, my mind might think: 'could I hit a baseball with that?' (Blau 2016: 201–2).

We cannot always read much of an author's output: inevitably, we sometimes dip in, especially for authors who are not central to our work. Being corrected on such grounds is an occupational hazard. But ideally, we should **read an author's texts widely**, to avoid overlooking important passages elsewhere in the text and in other texts. Book 2 chapter 3 of Rousseau's *Social Contract* makes more sense alongside book 4 chapter 1, casting light on how Rousseau may have understood the general will (which is not to say that this is what Rousseau had in mind). 'Non-political' texts might also be relevant: Rousseau's *Emile*, ostensibly about education, might also be read into these passages (e.g. Rousseau 1979a: book 4, p. 286): perhaps morally pure people can look inside themselves and intuit the general will. That said, the draft of the *Social Contract* implies that intuitionism is inappropriate in modern society (Rousseau 1997a: 1.2.6–14, 154–7). Yet the exclusion of these passages from the final version must give us pause for thought. **You never know when to read different ideas/texts into each other and when they are not consistent. Consider different options.**

Textual analysis alone is never enough: a key contextualist contribution is to **place texts in their linguistic contexts by reading other texts from the similar time/place, or by reading the work of scholars who have done this.** This can let us understand words we no longer use, like *dehort* (dissuade). It helps us spot 'false friends' – words that look familiar but whose meanings once differed, like *prejudice* (pre-judgement, not bias), or *force*, which in eighteenth-century French had a sense of strength/energy that might not be recoverable from merely textual analysis of Rousseau's 'forced to be free' (Mason 1995: 135–6).

Placing texts in their linguistic contexts also helps us infer intentions and indicates originality. Machiavelli uses *fortuna* conventionally but *virtù* unconventionally, dramatically undercutting the orthodoxies of his day (Skinner 1981: 24–31, 34–47). If we only read the 'canon' of great thinkers – Aristotle, Locke, Marx and others – we will miss part of what made these texts so ground-breaking. For some scholars, contextualism has had 'a hugely negative impact' by making the study of past thinkers 'merely antiquarian', even 'frivolous' (Kelly 2006: 48). But it can be wonderfully exciting to see how authors interacted with, built on or subtly knifed their lesser-known contemporaries, who can be wonderfully exciting in themselves.

We should thus **place texts in their intellectual contexts – political, philosophical and so on.** We can understand much of Hobbes's *Leviathan* when simply read as an abstract account of citizens' rights and duties, but when we also see it in its civil war political context and its anti-Aristotelian philosophical context, we understand more of it, we understand parts of it differently, and we understand parts of it better. That philosophical context, note, involves both Aristotle himself and Hobbes's contemporaries, whose use of Aristotle Hobbes saw as dangerous, indeed as one cause of the civil war: Hobbes's political and philosophical contexts overlap. Incidentally, Hobbes's 'Aristotle' is not our 'Aristotle': we may need to consult the 1598 English translation of Aristotle's *Politics* that Hobbes used, not a modern edition.

Placing texts in their contexts may not solve our problems. For example, contextualism shows what notions of virtue Machiavelli was probably challenging and why, but to uncover his own conception(s), we must think through his arguments and examples philosophically, and see what fits. Section 4 discusses this in more detail. Indeed, this chapter frequently stresses the need to **combine empirical and philosophical analysis**. Contextualists often do this brilliantly, but it is not covered in their methodological writings. For example, Dunn's (1967) analysis of Locke on consent powerfully combines historical and philosophical reasoning; but in his methodological discussion of the interdependency of historical and philosophical interpretation (1968: 85–8), he does not say that to uncover what authors mean, we may need to analyse their arguments philosophically, not just contextually. Worse, some historians explicitly disdain philosophical analysis (e.g. Laslett 1988: 81–90; for criticisms of Laslett, see Waldron 2002: 50–2, 62, 68, 190–1).

Even when contexts give an answer about authors' meanings or motives, do not assume that the answer is complete. Consider Rousseau's claim that a man can be forced to obey the law and still be free (Rousseau 1997a: 1.7.8, 53). Rousseau's justification is unclear.

Helena Rosenblatt suggests that Rousseau, like many opponents of the Genevan government, implies a traditional Christian/Calvinist view of freedom. 'Just like abiding by God's will makes men free in Christian thought, abiding by the general will makes citizens free in Rousseau's thought' (Rosenblatt 1997: 255–6; also 246–7). This explanation looks right, but it is not enough: it may not fit Rousseau's ensuing comment that forcing someone to obey the general will makes him free by protecting him from dependence on other people. Why that should be so requires us to think through Rousseau's ideas philosophically.

Skinner does this kind of philosophizing expertly in arguing that Hobbes changes his account of liberty for contextual *and* philosophical reasons (2008: 24, 45, 108, 132–8). But Skinner underplays the political-economic and theological contexts, which imply somewhat different conclusions (Whatmore 2006: 121–5). **More than one context may be relevant.** Note, indeed, that I have been referring to contex*t*s, plural.

Remember that historical parallels can be coincidental. According to Richard Tuck, Hobbes was responding to a form of scepticism (1993: 285–7, 293–8, 304–7, 316). Most commentators, though, explain the parallels differently (see Zagorin 1993: 512–18 for more details). No evidence, including contextual evidence, is conclusive: the same evidence can always be read differently.

Such points have not been adequately theorized by contextualists, who have trumpeted the value of historical interpretation without saying much about how to do it well (Green 2015: 436). The starting point, as Section 7 argues, is to place hypotheses, inference and evidence centre stage. Historians who doubt this should consider what happens when one 'knows' the answer and just seeks evidence that fits it, as with Leo Strauss (Blau 2012).

Contextualization can even help with recent authors. We understand Rawls better by placing him in his philosophical and political contexts (see, respectively, Wolff 2013; Forrester 2014). But we can still understand much of Rawls acontextually – just as with *some* historical passages. **Contextual analysis usually helps, but it is not always necessary, and is often insufficient.**

I have treated contextualism as seeking to recover authors' meanings and motives, through textual, contextual and philosophical analysis (although the last of these is rarely noted). But it is unfair to complain that 'contextualist methodology . . . reduces the point of political theory to historical questions of authorial intention and meaning' (Kelly 2007: 11). For some historians and many political theorists and philosophers, recovering authorial intentions and meanings is at least partly aimed at other things, including normative arguments, as we will now see.

3   *Begriffsgeschichte*, Conceptual History and Genealogy

Begriffsgeschichte, the 'history of concepts', is usually associated with Reinhart Koselleck, who co-led the *Geschichtliche Grundbegriffe* (in English: *Basic Concepts in History*), a multi-volume, 7,000-page analysis of more than 100 social and political concepts, published in German between 1972 and 1997. This enterprise was so big, requiring so many years and so many authors, that I do not cover it here. (For more information, see Olsen 2012: chapter 4. For much more detail on the *Geschichtliche Grundbegriffe* and *Begriffsgeschichte*, see Richter 1995, especially pp. 124–42 on similarities and differences between *Begriffsgeschichte* and contextualism.)

I focus instead on the smaller-scale version of *Begriffsgeschichte*: conceptual history, or genealogy. I treat the terms as equivalent: Skinner now calls his conceptual history of the state a genealogy of the state (Skinner 1989, 2009). *Genealogy*, a Rousseauian term (Griswold 2016: 277), is for most scholars associated with Nietzsche, whose genealogical approach is actually wider than that of historians like Skinner (Lane 2012: 75–82). (For a comparison of the ideas of genealogy in Nietzsche and Foucault, see Prado 2006: 76–81.)

Conceptual history has long been practised informally, but it arrived self-consciously in the Anglo-American mainstream with Terence Ball, James Farr and Russell Hanson's edited book *Political Innovation and Conceptual Change* (1989). Each chapter takes a concept, like corruption or patriotism, and examines different conceptions of that concept over time and sometimes place. (For the concept/conception distinction – i.e. a general idea, and particular versions of that idea – see Rawls 1971: 5, and Olsthoorn's chapter in this volume, Section 2.2.) For example, Peter Euben (1989) discusses changing senses of 'corruption', from physical decay, through the lack of civic virtue in the body politic, to the much narrower notion that dominates today. (For a partial critique of Euben, see Blau 2009: 614–16. For a book-length conceptual history of corruption, see Buchan and Hill 2014.)

Conceptual history has two parts: primarily empirical and primarily conceptual. The primarily empirical part will typically include textual, contextual and philosophical analysis; the aim is to recover authors' own understandings of their terms (Skinner 2002a: 50). But because the aim is comparison, rather than understanding a single author, case selection needs extra attention. The ideal – taking all possible cases – is impractical, especially in a single chapter or article. **Be conscious, and perhaps explicit, about how your case selection may affect your conclusions,** such as whether your claims are limited to a particular time, place or language (e.g. Skinner 2009: 325). **You may need to consider words not used, as well as words used**, as with Josiah Ober's analysis of 'democracy' and similar terms in ancient Greece (2008: 5, 7). And **distinguish the word from the idea** (see Olsthoorn's chapter in this volume, Section 2.1).

The primarily conceptual part of the analysis involves conceptual comparison: we stand back and compare authors' understandings, e.g. asking how similarly Bentham and Mill saw 'utility'. **Careful conceptual analysis is vital**, as with Skinner's fine-grained genealogy of liberty (2003: 22). By contrast, Isaiah Berlin's (1969) confused and confusing conceptual analysis undermines his conceptual history of liberty (for a critique, see Cohen 1960). Conceptual history is not just history: it is also conceptual – philosophical. Olsthoorn's chapter in this volume has many other tips to help rigorous conceptual analysis in conceptual history.

Anachronistic conceptualizations may help, especially when comparing authors who used different terms. Anachronism is dangerous: it can infect our efforts to recover authors' meanings (Skinner 2002a: 49–51). For example, James Mill's 'middle rank' does not mean 'middle class' (Ball 1992: xx–xxi). But if handled carefully, using appropriately fine-grained distinctions, and preferably not until you have first recovered authors' meanings, anachronism lets us apply conceptual frameworks that usefully highlight similarities and differences between authors. For example, Rousseau's *Considerations on the Government of Poland* recommends that citizens elect deputies every six weeks, on an explicit set of instructions, divergence from which would see deputies being executed (Rousseau 1997b: 7.14–19, 201–3). This is an extreme example of the so-called mandate or delegate conception of representation (Pitkin 1967: 145–7). Rousseau did not use these terms: he even denies that this is 'representation' (1997a: 3.15.5–6, 114). But what he says amounts to how *we* use these terms. If we are to compare notions of representation over time, we will almost certainly have to apply such anachronisms. So, **first try to work out what authors meant, then see how well this fits your own conceptualization or an existing one**.

Conceptual history is interesting and important, not only historically and politically, but also normatively: we see why some conceptions won out, how new and old conceptions often differ, and how old conceptions might revive contemporary discussions, as with Skinner's revealing conceptual histories of freedom and the state (Skinner 2003, 2009). **Be attentive to the normative implications of your interpretations**.

4   Reconstruction

Reconstruction means testing and potentially supplying, supplementing, modifying or removing presuppositions, definitions, links between comments/ideas and steps in arguments, as with Skinner's analysis of Hobbes on representation (2002b: 177–208), John Gray's account of Mill on happiness (1996: 70–85) and A. J. Simmons's testing of Locke's moral theory (1992: 14–67). Note that these scholars are, respectively, a historian, a political theorist and a philosopher.

Reconstruction is often seen as a special, philosophical technique (e.g. Rorty 1984: 49–53), but everyone reconstructs, simply to understand what is said or written. Some degree and some kind of reconstruction are inseparable from the very nature of interpretation, and necessary to the understanding of our texts. Again, compartmentalizing approaches into different categories has led us to overlook key unifying ideas.

Simplifying somewhat, I distinguish between three kinds of reconstruction:

(a) empirical reconstruction – trying to work out what authors meant;
(b) systematic reconstruction – linking authors' ideas, making implicit distinctions explicit, assessing consistency and so on, whether or not authors themselves saw these things;
(c) adaptive reconstruction – altering what authors wrote and perhaps what they intended.

These are not alternatives. We almost always do all three simultaneously, to greater or lesser extents. Even the simplest empirical reconstructions add, subtract or amend words. Even the most extreme adaptive reconstructions make some assumptions about what authors meant. And we typically interpret authors with some kind of systematic reconstruction, e.g. reading one idea into another even when the author does not specify a link. (Strictly speaking, systematic reconstruction is not a separate category, but a mix of empirical and adaptive reconstruction where we might be agnostic about the extent to which authors were conscious of the systematization we offer.)

Some historians, including Skinner (1964), worry about systematic and adaptive reconstruction. My point is that we cannot avoid doing either, so we should learn to do them well – as, indeed, with Skinner's virtuoso systematic reconstruction of Hobbes's views on the state and representation (2002b: 177–208), including carefully worded adaptations of Hobbes's views (2002c: 190; see likewise 2002b: 217, 235). A key message of this section, and of this chapter, is thus that thinking philosophically helps us reconstruct what authors meant, even if some scholars baulk at altering or 'improving' the authors they study.

I will start with the most minimal kinds of reconstruction that we all do, every day. All communication involves resolving ambiguities and filling in gaps: we cannot say everything we want to say (Searle 1978). If you ask, 'Did you have a good day?', you presumably mean, 'Did you have a good day [today]?', not, 'Did you have a good day [five weeks after you were born]?'. Likewise, when Sidgwick (1981: ix) writes that he has made 'numerous alterations and additions' in preparing the second edition of *The Methods of Ethics*, he presumably means 'numerous alterations and additions [to this book]', not 'numerous alterations and additions [to my trousers]', even though that is logically consistent with what he wrote, and might have been a better use of his time.

During conversations, our brains reconstruct such comments in a flash. When we read, the process is often slower and more conscious. For example, Mill writes: 'As it is useful that while mankind are imperfect there should be different opinions, so is it that there should be different experiments of living' (1989: 3.1, p. 57). Is Mill commending experiments of living only while mankind is imperfect, or even once perfected? The latter, it turns out, fits better with what Mill later says about individuality and self-development. Of course, 'fits better' does not signify that he meant this, or even that he was clear in his own head. We can easily over-interpret authors and make them more consistent than they were: no author is fully consistent (Skinner 2002a: 67–72). But **thinking through the implications of ideas, and probing their consistency with other things they said or implied, gives us evidence about what authors *might* have meant.** Contextual analysis is all well and good – and it is very, very good – but it goes hand in hand with more philosophical analysis, even merely of the kind that probes consistency.

Another use of consistency involves testing authors' definitions, or testing possible definitions where authors do not provide them. For example, Machiavelli never defines *virtú*, and contextual analysis only tells us what Machiavelli was reacting against, not how he understood the term. It takes a more philosophical cast of mind to stand back from the text and reconstruct what Machiavelli means when he discusses *virtú*: he generally means 'those qualities, whether moral or otherwise ... most conducive to military and political success' (Skinner 2002a: 48).

This is not to imply that a single notion must fit a term. C. G. Prado (2006: 81–103) finds five kinds of truth in Foucault's many writings. It does not really matter how aware Foucault was of this: these ideas are there, and we understand Foucault better by systematizing his comments more neatly. Indeed, we should do this even if Foucault emphatically insisted that he only had one notion of truth. We never fully control what we say or write. Mill's 'one very simple principle' (1989: 1.9, 13) turns out to be neither one nor very simple. We understand Mill better by distinguishing between what he says he will do, and what he does do. We should **be careful about taking authors at face value**: to say that we must recover authors' motives in order to understand what they mean (Skinner 2002a: 103–7) should not mean that we are bound by those intentions (Skinner 2002a: 110–11).

A more complex example involves an apparent error in *On Liberty*. Mill emphatically argues that you can do as you like, even harm yourself or cause offence, provided you do not harm others (especially 1989: 1.9, 13; 2.44, 54–5). But suddenly Mill says, briefly and without justification, that you cannot do self-harming things in public if they cause offence (1989: 5.7, 98). This seems like an astonishing about-turn. To understand what actions Mill thought permissible, we must think through these passages and see if this apparent contradiction is resolvable. This could imply a different notion of harm or offence than we had assumed, potentially entailing a significant reinterpretation. If we cannot find such a resolution, we might want to disregard this passing comment (as recommended by Gray 1996: 102). We might still *explain* why Mill wrote it, e.g. to protect himself from objections of libertinism, but we risk misunderstanding Mill if we treat this apparently incidental passage as his considered view of harm. **When you find an apparent contradiction, consider how (if at all) to resolve it – including the possibility that it is not a contradiction at all.**

A still more complex example involves Hobbes's ambiguous references in *De Cive* to 'the dictates of right reason' (1998: e.g. 2.2, 34; 15.4, 173). Does he mean that reason forces our passions to obey, or merely that it tells us what we should do even if our passions then disregard this? Or has he not fully thought this issue through? (See Blau 2016.)

In effect, simply to understand one phrase we may need to reconstruct Hobbes's account of reason, the passions, deliberation and their interconnections – quite an enterprise. It is thus problematic that contextualists encourage us to place texts in their contexts without addressing the value of thinking through texts philosophically. Both matter.

This example actually has two even trickier dimensions. First, although Hobbes's other writings might help us interpret these comments in *De Cive*, his account of reason might have changed over time (Skinner 1996: 298–437). Understanding the *De Cive* passages may involve tackling this much bigger issue. Second, and even worse, our judgement of the change-over-time thesis itself rests partly on how we read the comments about reason and the passions in *De Cive* and elsewhere. In other words, the thesis that informs our interpretation of individual comments itself depends on how we read those comments. Many scholars describe such situations as 'hermeneutic circles'. I argue elsewhere that the language and literature of hypotheses is more precise and practical than the language and literature of hermeneutics (Blau 2015b). We read Hobbes's comments, alongside contextual evidence, to see which hypothesis – that Hobbes's account changed, or stayed fairly constant – best fits the evidence, what evidence does not fit or remains unclear and what this implies for the hypotheses overall. (There are other hypotheses, of course, including Hobbes being unclear or confused. See Blau 2016: 213–14.) Such analysis is never conclusive, but no empirical analysis is conclusive. The best approach is to **be aware of interdependent interpretations and consider different hypotheses**.

Our assessment of authors' consistency helps our interpretations. For example, Rousseau states that freedom is linked to the general will, but leaves the nature of the link unclear (e.g. 1997a: 1.7.8, 53; 4.2.8, 124). We are more likely to reconstruct the nature of this link in a way that also fits Rousseau's other ideas if we read him as a rigorous, systematic philosopher than if we read him as a polemicist focusing more on politics than philosophy, or an erratic rhetorician who would say anything that sounded good. As with Hobbes's alleged change over time, these interpretations are interdependent: whether we find a workable link between freedom and the general will may affect how hard we seek links in other places in Rousseau. Again, **understanding even one or a few comments may require more systematic reconstruction**.

Sometimes such systematic reconstructions are a key aim, rather than merely a means to uncover meaning. Consider John Gray's (1995) systematic reconstruction of Isaiah Berlin's liberalism. He collects Berlin's arguments in one place, clarifies key ideas (e.g. freedom) and shows their links and underpinnings, such as Berlin's agonism and value-pluralism. Gray tries to stay true to Berlin, but is clearer and more compelling. To the extent that Gray's reconstruction is right, we understand Berlin better than by reading Berlin alone. Gray's reconstruction also lets him identify weaknesses in Berlin's position, resolving which might require significant changes (1995: 2, 143, 151–68). To the extent that this adaptive reconstruction is right, we understand Berlin even better.

I now address another book-length reconstruction – A. J. Simmons's (1992) analysis of Locke, revered by many political theorists and philosophers, but largely sidestepped by historians. One reason for this neglect, I fear, is that while historians have successfully made the case that political theorists and philosophers should address historical research, political theorists and philosophers have not made the reverse case so effectively. Another reason may be that historians dislike Simmons's adaptive reconstruction of Locke for contemporary purposes. But Simmons also does empirical and systematic reconstruction. And his techniques are often brilliant, worthy of contemplation by even the most empirical of historians, because they can help us recover the beliefs of authors we study, especially more philosophical authors.

Much of Simmons's reconstruction is fairly standard, filling gaps and resolving ambiguities by using textual, contextual and/or simple philosophical reasoning. For example, when trying to understand what Locke meant about making something one's property by mixing one's labour with it, Simmons defends his interpretation over Tully's by pointing to how Locke used certain words, by asking whether certain arguments really were historically unavailable to Locke and by looking at the implications of ideas: 'it is awfully hard to believe that Locke thought picking up an acorn to be sufficiently like God's act of creation to generate rights under the same creationist principle' inferred by Tully (Simmons 1992: 252–64; but compare Tully 1995: 114–19).

Such philosophical reasoning is straightforward. Importantly, though, Simmons's empirical and systematic reconstructions sometimes involve greater philosophical sophistication. For instance, he chooses to **separate out the different steps in an argument** of Locke's (Simmons 1992: 23) – a powerful technique that helps us probe arguments' strengths and weaknesses, missing steps, unstated assumptions and so on (see Simmons 1992: 23–36, 46). Locke does not flesh out the final step, for example, but Simmons uses what Locke wrote to get 'a good sense' of what duties Locke might have thought we had (1992: 59–67).

Another helpful technique is to **list the possible or plausible meanings of ambiguous words or ideas** (Blau 2015c: 1184–5; 2016: 213–14). This technique helps Simmons think through what Locke might have meant by such vague but important comments as the 'original community of all things' and 'enough, and as good' (1992: 237–40, 295–8). More controversially, to try to grasp what Locke might have meant by 'rights', Simmons anachronistically applies modern distinctions, from writers like Hohfeld, Hart and others (1992: 70–5, 85–94). An even more controversial anachronism is Simmons's rule-consequentialist interpretation of Locke's moral theory that 'fit[s] ... Locke's most firmly entrenched positions' (but not everything he wrote), lets us 'make sense of some central but puzzling passages in the *Second Treatise*', and is thus Simmons's 'best guess' at Locke's 'undoubtedly inchoate' intentions (1992: 46–59). **Anachronistic analysis is dangerous and needs considerable care, but it can**

potentially help us see what authors meant or were getting at, by showing us interpretive possibilities that we might have missed.

Perhaps unsurprisingly, inventive and sophisticated philosophers like Locke often need to be read philosophically if we are to grasp their meanings, link their ideas and so on. Just as political theorists and philosophers should think historically, or at least consult historical scholarship, so too historians should think philosophically, or at least consult philosophical scholarship. Most political theorists and philosophers would now take seriously contextually driven hypotheses of what Locke meant by 'property' or 'rights': I think more historians should place greater weight on philosophically driven hypotheses too.

I wonder if it is revealing that Dunn uses a visual metaphor when arguing that historians, political theorists and philosophers can all 'see' deeper structural features of Locke if they 'look closely' (2005: 442–4). Dunn is arguing, rightly, that no disciplinary approach need stop us from grasping Locke's ideas. But thinking through authors' ideas, or robust contextual analysis, obviously takes conscious effort. Even the terms I often use in this chapter – 'uncovering' or 'recovering' authorial beliefs and meanings, following Skinner's (2002a) terminology – does not capture the hard reasoning often needed for empirical and systematic reconstruction (exemplified superbly by Dunn himself – e.g. Dunn 1967: 156–82).

I now turn to the aspect of Simmons's book that is most controversial, at least for historians: his attempt to improve Locke with a 'revised Lockean account' of such things as the natural right to punish (1992: 121–40, 161–6). Indeed, one of Simmons's aims is to uncover 'not Locke's own theory ... but the best version of that theory – a theory close enough to Locke's to be considered "Lockean", but improved by certain departures from the letter of Locke's theory' (1992: 4; emphasis removed). Most importantly, his Lockean theory of rights drops Locke's theological foundations (1992: 3, 10–11, 153–66, 177–204, 343–54). Simmons is explicit that his adaptations 'capture some of the spirit' of Locke's moral theory, but are not 'fully consistent' with it: 'God is too much at the center of Locke's work for such secular, Kantian arguments to capture its essence' (1992: 44, 46).

But what is the 'best' version of an author's theory, or at least, a 'better' version? Historians will probably seek answers that the author could have accepted (e.g. Dunn 1967: 166–8), but need not deny that other answers are legitimate (e.g. Dunn 1969: 214–16). Political theorists and philosophers can also opt for answers that the author could have accepted (e.g. Martinich 2005: 101–4), but may ultimately prefer answers that many of us could accept today (e.g. Simmons 1992: 10). There will be some overlap here: most writers, past and present, would want to avoid egregious contradictions and factual or logical errors. But ultimately, historical and contemporary answers may differ markedly (Dunn 1967: 159). There is no one 'right' adaptive reconstruction.

Can we justifiably drop authors' deeply held commitments? Dunn holds that 'an extremely high proportion of Locke's arguments' have an 'intimate dependence' on his theological commitments (1969: xi). Simmons replies, in effect, that Dunn's systematic reconstruction is overly contextualized and misconstrues Locke's philosophical position: Locke actually over-determines his conclusions, intentionally and consciously making theological *and* secular arguments, which are logically separable (e.g. Simmons 1992: 10–12, 45, 101–2, 254, 354). But if Dunn is right and Simmons is wrong, would secularizing Locke still be permissible? Similarly, though not identically, should we drop republicans' gender assumptions when appropriating republican liberty for contemporary purposes (e.g. Pettit 1997: 138–40), even though this would have appalled most historical republicans? Do such adaptations go too far?

For some people, yes. But two caveats are crucial here. First, the adaptations look less radical once we accept that we cannot understand authors without altering what they said, that we must sometimes make choices when authors are inconsistent, and that we often want to impose more clarity on authors than they themselves managed, as I argued previously. Second, even leaving aside contemporary applications of historical ideas, it is intellectually interesting and important to see how well authors' arguments work, to what extent they were on the right track and how fundamental their problems are – whether Locke's ambiguities, gaps, contradictions and errors can be corrected within his system or not, say.

We should try not to depict such alterations as if they are true to the author. Unfortunately, this is quite common, as with caricatures of Hobbes by many international relations scholars (criticized by Malcolm 2002: 432–56). By contrast, Gray is explicitly agnostic about whether his reconstruction of Mill on happiness is what Mill intended (1996: 70–86). When discussing Hobbes's account of representation, similarly, Skinner infers what Hobbes 'seems to have had in mind', and offers the 'daring' view that 'the best statement of Hobbes's theory is the one that he never explicitly gave' (2002b: 190; see also 217, 235). This is not actually too daring: we consciously or subconsciously improve on what other people say and write every time we hear or read them. But that quibble aside, Skinner's carefulness is absolutely right. **Try to be explicit, or at least implicit, when distinguishing between what authors meant, what they may have meant, what their account implies and what, in your view, they should have said.**

5   Theoretical and Normative Perspectives

I now turn to a different style of analysis. Again I question traditional depictions of the methodological issues.

Consider Susan Okin's feminist perspective, which helps her spot presuppositions and implications in many authors, including those claiming to be gender-neutral (Okin 1989: 10–13, 44–60, 80–7, 90–7). Or consider C. B. Macpherson's Marxist perspective, which leads him to infer Hobbes's conscious or unconscious assumptions about 'possessive individualism' and other capitalist traits (1962: 4–5, 26–9, 37–40, 46, 59–68, 78–80, 84–106; see Townshend 1999 for a defence of Macpherson against common complaints, and Svacek 1976 for whether Macpherson's perspective is really Marxist).

Both authors use theoretical and normative perspectives that are often presented as essentially different 'schools' or 'approaches', as with Ball's comparison of feminist, Marxist, totalitarian, psychoanalytic, Straussian and postmodernist interpretations (Ball 2004, 19–27; see also Ball 2011). I will argue, rather, that these analysts do the same thing: they use theories and norms to develop empirical hypotheses or conceptual distinctions that help us uncover assumptions and implications.

Seen like this, there are far more perspectives than are usually mentioned, even by Ball. For example, Skinner's republican perspective alerts him to ideas often neglected in Machiavelli (Skinner 1990: 300–6). John McCormick's democratic perspective highlights features in Machiavelli overlooked by republicans (2011: see especially 3, 7–11, for the critique of republican interpretations). Hayek's libertarian/classical liberal perspective uncovers more individualism in Burke than other writers saw (1948: 4–8, 13, 24). Terrell Carver's gender perspective reveals assumptions about men passed over by feminist scholars concentrating on assumptions about women (2004). David Armitage's international perspective pinpoints oft-overlooked issues in Hobbes and Locke (2013: 62–7, 79–85). Jon Elster's analytical approach, combining ideas such as methodological individualism and rational choice theory, pinpoints forgotten features of Marx (Elster 1985: see especially 3–48 on Elster's analytical tools). Martin Hollis's game-theoretic approach provides powerful insights into Hobbes, Hume, Smith, Kant and others (1998). And so on.

A contribution I find especially interesting, and worrying, is Robert Bernasconi's race/ethnicity perspective. He uncovers assumptions about race in Locke, Kant, Hegel, Mill, Nietzsche and others (2003: 14–20; 2010: 500–4, 510–11, 515–16). 'Western philosophy has been and is still largely in denial about its racism', he writes (2003: 14), challenging those of us who have missed these writers' explicit or implicit racism, or passed over it in silence in our writing and teaching.

These perspectives, then, can be incredibly powerful. They are one way we keep seeing new things in old texts. But should we depict different perspectives as different 'schools of thought' or different 'approaches'? Throughout this chapter, I have tried to ask what our interpretations really involve. And in my view, theoretical and normative perspectives boil down to approaching a text with one or more hypotheses or distinctions, and potentially seeing new things.

I am not disparaging such research: **do not underestimate the insights you can get by applying an empirical hypothesis or conceptual distinction from an existing theoretical/normative perspective or elsewhere.** In fact, you need not wholly accept a perspective to apply it. You don't have to be a republican to ask if authors uphold freedom as non-domination, a feminist to uncover authors' gender presuppositions or a poststructuralist to apply Foucault's distinction between a governmentality of *politiques* and of *économistes* (2009: 333–57). You don't have to be a Marxist to notice authors' socio-economic presuppositions. Indeed, it may help not to be a Marxist, because Marxists might be inclined towards certain conclusions, potentially infecting their interpretations.

Two related dangers thus need attention. The first is that a perspective leads you to misread a text, read too much into it or overlook relevant passages – a common problem (Ball 2004: 21–3). Arthur Melzer shows that most scholars dislike the idea of esoteric writing (i.e. writing that hides messages between the lines, for careful observers to infer – see Section 6) and thus overlook ample evidence of esotericism (2014: especially 13–24, 137–42, 299–317). Yet he himself is so keen to show Rousseau's sympathies for esotericism that he overlooks Rousseau's critical comments about esotericism (Melzer 2014: 163; Blau 2015b: 163). Such writers 'mistake an expectation for a presumption' (Bevir 1999: 147). Meanwhile, Robin Douglass (2015: 283) argues that Skinner's 'preoccupation' with Hobbes's republican context leads to misinterpretations: Skinner's reading 'conceals more than it reveals about [Hobbes's] battle with republicanism'. If one has a normative axe to grind, one often chops off key parts of texts. **Be attentive to potential theoretical/ normative biases: try to be impartial. If your perspective gives you an expectation about an author's influences or motives, it is only an expectation – a hypothesis – never a certainty.**

The second danger is becoming a mouthpiece for flawed ideas. If you can, *test* **perspectives, don't just apply them.** For example, many scholars apply Berlin's flawed distinction between negative and positive liberty without mentioning its inadequacies, thus overlooking aspects of liberty noticed by republican scholars (Pettit 1997: 17–50). Showing a perspective's shortfalls, and ideally, refining and improving it, magnifies your work's value and could expand your audience. For example, Anne Brunon-Ernst (2012) not only applies Foucault's ideas of biopolitics to Bentham, but criticizes and amends Foucault's ideas in the process.

Both dangers apply to *any* interpretation: everyone interprets everything through many lenses (Bevir 1999: 92–3; Brewer and Lambert 2001). So, **try to be aware, if you can, of perspectives that already influence your readings**. In my ongoing Hobbes work, I tried to chart all of Hobbes's practical proposals for averting a state of nature. Yet my mind-set was not attuned to international issues, and after reading Armitage's (2013) work on international perspectives, I started noticing internationally oriented proposals in Hobbes that I had previously missed. We all have such biases. Even supporting an interpretation can have this effect: part of you may want it to be right, potentially infecting your reasoning.

6   Reading Between and Outside the Lines

This chapter has regularly challenged our inherited categories. The same applies to the idea that 'reading between the lines' is an essentially different approach. Despite claims that some scholars read between the lines while others take a purely literal approach (Melzer 2014: 112–14, 207, 368), no one takes a purely literal approach, restricting herself to the actual words: all communication and all textual interpretation involves reading between the lines, as Section 4 showed. Contextualists agree. For example, *The Prince*'s attack on humanist mirror-of-princes handbooks 'cannot be discovered by attending to Machiavelli's text, since this is not a fact contained in the text' (Skinner 2002a: 143). In effect, when Machiavelli discusses *virtù*, we often insert the words 'unlike the views of my contemporaries' into his comments. Similarly, many great historical authors were religiously unorthodox, but could not say so publicly; we can sometimes read between the lines and infer what they really thought, because they cannot conceal all of their views or because they left subtle signs about their real thoughts (e.g. Schotte 2015: 65–72).

Great care is needed here: without sensible guidelines, we can easily read too much into texts, especially when asking if authors esoterically hid messages in their writings for clever readers to spot. Some authors certainly did this (Patterson 1991). But many esoteric interpretations overreach themselves, with highly questionable use of evidence (Blau 2012).

Careful readers will note that this section has not yet mentioned Leo Strauss. Those who have read between the lines may already see what I now state explicitly: we should not equate 'esoteric' and 'Straussian' interpretation. From the 1940s on, Leo Strauss and his followers made esoteric interpretations of writers like Plato, Machiavelli, Rousseau and Nietzsche. There is nothing wrong with esoteric interpretation, but much wrong with *Strauss*'s esoteric interpretation – due not to its esotericism, but to its naive and flawed methodology (Blau 2012; see also Blau 2015b for some corrections to the original argument).

Unfortunately, our methodological lexicon has clouded the real problems. We should not say that Strauss has a different hermeneutic or particular techniques of reading texts. Rather, he has *hypotheses* about the particular ways that authors hid messages, and inadequate tests of these hypotheses (Blau 2015b: 32–40). Fortunately, Melzer's wonderful practical advice (2014: 288–99, 323–4) warns Straussians not to infer esotericism too hastily. Unfortunately, Melzer's own handling of claims about esotericism may still encourage such hastiness (Blau 2015a: 162–3).

The excesses of Straussian readings have helped and hindered the cause of esoteric interpretation. They have helped it by highlighting a largely forgotten kind of writing and offering evidence of esoteric techniques. But they have hindered it through methodologically flawed over-interpretations that have given esoteric interpretation a bad name – 'Straussian'. **Esoteric interpretation, like any empirical interpretation, is only a hypothesis.** And the failure to provide fundamental principles for testing hypotheses, through a flawed focus on supposedly separate approaches, is one of the great tragedies of twentieth-century methodological writings. Readers should not think that my critiques of Straussians are aimed only at Straussians.

7   Further Core Principles of Good Practice

I have already identified certain core principles for all textual interpreters, such as reading texts both contextually and philosophically. I now summarize other core principles.

The underlying ideas are uncertainty and under-determination: **no empirical claims can be known for certain, and the same evidence can always be read differently**. We even disagree about what counts as evidence. Uncertainty and under-determination are more fundamental than 'approaches' like contextualism or Straussianism: claims about the relevance of a particular context or the use of a specific esoteric technique are only ever hypotheses, and uncertainty and under-determination are pervasive whenever hypotheses are tested. I expand on these ideas elsewhere (Blau 2011, 2012, 2015b, 2015c).

Uncertainty has two main implications. First, **be careful of overconfident claims.** Try not to talk of 'proving' anything, and where relevant, **indicate how confident you are in your interpretations.** There are differences between saying, 'Machiavelli wrote *The Prince*', which we have no good reason to doubt; 'Mill does not seem to have had a single, clear idea of harm in *On Liberty*', a plausible inference; and 'there is evidence both for Hobbes's atheism and for his being a believer, but I find the evidence for the latter stronger than for the former', a safe stance given the highly contestable evidence. **Do not see yourself as reporting facts, but as reporting your confidence in your inferences.** The inherent subjectivity of empirical research means that however stylistically ugly you find this, **you may need to put the focus on you, not on the text/author**, e.g. 'I suspect that Cicero meant P', 'Cicero could have meant P or Q, but P seems likelier' and so on (Blau 2011: 362–8).

Second, and more important, uncertainty often requires us to *test* empirical claims. Under-determination kicks in here, so **your simplest and best test of a claim is to see if it fits the evidence better than plausible alternatives.** Simplifying somewhat, you should consider what fits your interpretation and what does not, and also what fits alternative interpretations and what does not. Interpretation is comparative (Blau 2015c: 1184).

The secondary literature is usually a good source of alternative interpretations. Addressing other scholarship is not something we do as an offering to the footnote gods: we need to see if other scholars interpret ideas differently or have spotted things we have missed. Critically comparing interpretations is simultaneously defence and offence, supporting one's account by showing that it works better than the alternatives (if space permits). But your initial expectations may not endure. **Don't become attached to an interpretation because it's yours; become attached to an interpretation because you think it's better than the alternatives. The two won't always go together, unless you are staggeringly clever or astonishingly lucky.**

A powerful test is to **triangulate evidence by seeing if textual, contextual, philosophical and motivational evidence imply the same conclusions.** Textual and contextual evidence have been amply discussed earlier. Philosophical evidence refers to such things as the implications of arguments or the consistency of two ideas. Might the implications of Rousseau's comments of liberty imply his motivations – are his definitions implicitly undermining the positions of other authors?

Do the implications of his comments on civil and moral freedom help us understand which, if either, applies to 'forced to be free'?

Motivational evidence means inferences about authors' motivations, which can provide further evidence in our investigations. For example, book 1 of the *Republic* uses Socrates's style of argument, 'elenchus', but books 2–10 use Plato's own approach, 'dialectic': perhaps Plato was subtly showing Socrates's limitations (Reeve 1988: 3–24). There are other possibilities too, e.g. that the text was written at different times, and we read the *Republic* differently depending on our stance here. Note that we cannot see motivations: we only infer them from textual, contextual and/or philosophical evidence.

Ideally we want as much evidence as possible. Imagine that textual and philosophical analysis gives you a possible solution to Mill's confusing comments about offence (see Section 4). Think about seeking contextual evidence: might a controversy at the time explain Mill's comments, e.g. parliamentary debates about public drug-taking or masturbation? Finding such a link would strengthen your inference about what Mill had in mind. Not finding one would not weaken your position, as Mill might plausibly have discussed such an example anyway. Or perhaps you are a historian who has uncovered such a contextual event. If it fits philosophically with the relevant passages in Mill, your position is strengthened; if not, you might rethink. (For more on such uses of 'observable implications' to test ideas, see Blau 2012: 152; 2015b: 35–6. This draws on the hypothesis-testing approach of Van Evera 1997: 31–2.)

We do not always have the time or energy for this. Being corrected on these grounds is to be expected. My fear, though, is that our inherited disciplinary and methodological categories often constrain us: seeing ourselves as contextualists, philosophers or Straussians, say, can deflect us from important evidence. True, we all have certain skills, and while this partly reflects disciplinary training, some people just are better at concrete historical research or abstract philosophizing. Even then, we can read the expert literature from another field, consult experts or find a co-author. Ultimately, though, if someone neglects relevant evidence, others can supply it and test the argument: triangulation can be communal.

Our evidence should be visible. Some scholars follow the bad academic convention of giving page numbers only for quotations, but not ideas. This can facilitate caricatures. Yet we should not robotically give page numbers alone where there are many different editions and translations (e.g. for Rousseau's *Social Contract*). Further details are needed here. The principle is thus: **make clear what your evidence is so that others can easily follow it up and test your claims.**

Another aspect of clarity involves interpretation that is both empirical and conceptual. Strictly speaking, this is always the case (Bevir 1999: 98; Skinner 2002a: 16, 45). But sometimes conceptualization is especially important, as when we ask how 'modern' Machiavelli was or how 'liberal' Rousseau was. In such cases, conceptual clarity is vital. Harry Lesser's (1979) short article on Plato's feminism does not say what he means by 'feminism', although we could probably make some inferences from his account. Virginia Sapiro, by contrast, is much conceptually clearer when discussing Wollstonecraft's feminism (1992: 258–9). **When analysis is partly conceptual and partly empirical, try to define key terms** (see Olsthoorn's chapter in this volume, Section 3).

The terms in quotation marks in the preceding paragraph are anachronistic. Care is needed here, as Section 3 noted. For example, Michael Losonsky (2001: 53–4) talks of 'deliberative reason', 'passionate reasoning' and 'reasoned deliberation' in Hobbes. These terms misconstrue Hobbes's position (Blau 2016: 209–10). By contrast, David Wootton asks how democratic the Levellers were by applying careful conceptual distinctions to rigorous analysis of their writings (1992: 71–80).

Skinner finds such anachronisms 'pointless' (2002c: 58), but this might reflect his particular view of meaning and understanding – a purely empirical view ('the Levellers meant X') in contrast to a philosophical view ('their comments fit modern democratic criteria, which means that we can call them democrats'). Both types of meaning matter: the first lets us understand what the Levellers meant, the second lets us understand their originality and importance. Skinner's criticism of anachronisms seems to reflect his dependency on a single notion of meaning and understanding. This chapter has sought to liberate us from the dominant approach.

8   Conclusion

This chapter's key guidance can be summarized as follows: **Read widely and carefully. Think contextually and philosophically. Embrace uncertainty. See both sides. Think against yourself. Question evidence and interpretations. Test. Retest. Be open. And be open-minded.** Such how-to guidance – sometimes obvious, sometimes not – is largely absent from the existing methodological literature, because of the tendency to discuss different approaches and schools of thought without also emphasizing core principles of good interpretation. I do not mean to deride our methodological literature, and would especially encourage novice interpreters to pore over Skinner's methodological writings – but also his substantive interpretations. My final suggestion is thus: **see** methodology as something that you do not learn merely from methodological writings. Reflect also on what is good and less good in actual interpretations, and infer principles of good practice from that.

Acknowledgements

For comments and criticisms on earlier versions of this chapter, I thank Seebal Aboudounya, Richard Bourke, Emillie De Keulenaar, Robin Douglass, John-Erik Hansson, Eva Hausteiner, Johan Olsthoorn, Joanne Paul, Mustafa Rehman, Paul Sagar, Dave Schmidtz, Max Skjönsberg, Bertie Vidgen and Sarah Wilford.

References

Allen, J. W., 1928. *A History of Political Thought in the Sixteenth Century*. London: Methuen.

Armitage, David, 2013. *Foundations of Modern International Thought*. Cambridge University Press.

Ball, Terence, 1992. 'Introduction', in James Mill, *Political Writings*, ed. Terence Ball. Cambridge University Press, ix–xxviii.

Ball, Terence, 2004. 'History and the interpretation of texts', in Gerald Gaus and Chandran Kukathas, eds., *Handbook of Political Theory*. London: Sage Publications, 18–30.

Ball, Terence, 2011. 'The value of the history of political philosophy', in George Klosko, ed., *The Oxford Handbook of the History of Political Philosophy*. Oxford University Press, 47–59.

Ball, Terence, James Farr and Russell Hanson, eds., 1989. *Political Innovation and Conceptual Change*. Cambridge University Press.

Berlin, Isaiah. 1969. *Four Essays on Liberty*. Oxford University Press.

Bernasconi, Robert, 2003. 'Will the real Kant please stand up: the challenge of Enlightenment racism to the study of the history of philosophy', *Radical Philosophy* 117, 13–22.

Bernasconi, Robert, 2010. 'The philosophy of race in the nineteenth century', in Dean Moyar, ed., *The Routledge Companion to Nineteenth Century Philosophy*. London: Routledge. 498–521.

Bevir, Mark, 1999. *The Logic of the History of Ideas*. Cambridge University Press.

Blau, Adrian, 2009. 'Hobbes on corruption', *History of Political Thought* 30, 596–616.

Blau, Adrian, 2011. 'Uncertainty and the history of ideas', *History and Theory* 50, 358–72.

Blau, Adrian, 2012. 'Anti-Strauss', *The Journal of Politics* 74, 142–55.

Blau, Adrian, 2015a. 'Philosophy between the lines, or through dubious signs?', *Perspectives on Political Science* 44, 162–5.

Blau, Adrian, 2015b. 'The irrelevance of (Straussian) hermeneutics', in Winfried Schröder, ed., *Reading Between the Lines: Leo Strauss and the History of Early Modern Philosophy*. Berlin: De Gruyter, 29–55.

Blau, Adrian, 2015c. 'History of political thought as detective-work', *History of European Ideas* 41, 1178–94.

Blau, Adrian, 2016. 'Reason, deliberation and the passions', in A. P. Martinich and Kinch Hoekstra, eds., *The Oxford Handbook of Hobbes*. Oxford University Press, 195–220.

Boucher, David, 1985. *Texts in Context: Revisionist Methods for Studying the History of Ideas*. Dordrecht: Kluwer Academic Publishers.

Brewer, William and Bruce Lambert, 2001. 'The theory-ladenness of observation and the theory-ladenness of the rest of the scientific process', *Philosophy of Science* 68 supplement, 176–86.

Brunon-Ernst, Anne, 2012. *Utilitarian Biopolitics: Bentham, Foucault and Modern Power*. London: Pickering & Chatto.

Buchan, Bruce and Lisa Hill, 2014. *An Intellectual History of Political Corruption*. Basingstoke: Palgrave Macmillan.

Carver, Terrell, 2004. *Men in Political Theory*. Manchester University Press.

Cohen, Marshall, 1960. 'Berlin and the liberal tradition', *The Philosophical Quarterly* 10, 216–27.

Douglass, Robin, 2015. 'Thomas Hobbes's changing account of liberty and challenge to republicanism', *History of Political Thought* 36, 281–309.

Dunn, John, 1967. 'Consent in the political theory of John Locke', *The Historical Journal* 10, 153–82.

Dunn, John, 1968. 'The identity of the history of ideas', *Philosophy* 43, 85–104.

Dunn, John, 1969. *The Political Thought of John Locke: An Historical Account of The Argument of the 'Two Treatises of Government'*. Cambridge University Press.

Dunn, John, 1996. *The History of Political Theory and Other Essays*. Cambridge University Press.

Dunn, John, 2005. 'What history can show: Jeremy Waldron's reading of Locke's Christian politics', *The Review of Politics* 67, 433–50.

Elster, Jon, 1985. *Making Sense of Marx*. Cambridge University Press.

Euben, Peter, 1989. 'Corruption', in Terence Ball, James Farr and Russell Hanson, eds., *Political Innovation and Conceptual Change*. Cambridge University Press, 220–46.

Forrester, Katrina, 2014. 'Citizenship, war, and the origins of international ethics in American political philosophy, 1960–1975', *The Historical Journal* 57, 773–801.

Foucault, Michel, 2009. *Security, Territory, Population: Lectures at the Collège de France 1977–1978*, tr. Graham Burchell. Basingstoke: Palgrave Macmillan.

Gray, John, 1995. *Berlin*. London: Fontana Press.

Gray, John, 1996. *Mill On Liberty: A Defence*. 2nd edition. London: Routledge.

Green, Jeffrey, 2015. 'Political theory as both philosophy and history: a defense against methodological militancy', *Annual Review of Political Science* 18, 425–41.

Griswold, Charles, 2016. 'Genealogical narrative and self-knowledge in Rousseau's Discourse on the Origin and the Foundations of Inequality among Men', *History of European Ideas* 42, 276–301.

Hayek, Friedrich, 1948. *Individualism and Economic Order*. University of Chicago Press.

Hobbes, Thomas, 1991. *Leviathan*, ed. Richard Tuck. Cambridge University Press.

Hobbes, Thomas, 1998. *On the Citizen*, ed. Richard Tuck and Michael Silverthorne. Cambridge University Press.

Hollis, Martin, 1998. *Trust Within Reason*. Cambridge University Press.

Hutton, Sarah, 2014. 'Intellectual history and the history of philosophy', *History of European Ideas* 40, 925–37.

Kelly, Paul, 2006. 'Political theory – the state of the art', *Politics* 26, 47–53.

Kelly, Paul, 2007. *Locke's Second Treatise of Government: A Reader's Guide*. London: Continuum.

Lane, Melissa, 2012. 'Doing our own thinking for ourselves: on Quentin Skinner's genealogical turn', *Journal of the History of Ideas* 73, 71–82.

Laslett, Peter, 1988. 'Introduction', in John Locke, *Two Treatises of Government*, ed. Peter Laslett. Cambridge University Press, 3–126.

Lesser, Harry, 1979. 'Plato's Feminism', *Philosophy* 54, 113–17.

Losonsky, Michael, 2001. *Enlightenment and Action from Descartes to Kant: Passionate Thought*. Cambridge University Press.

Macpherson, C. B., 1962. *The Political Theory of Possessive Individualism: Hobbes to Locke*. Oxford University Press.

Malcolm, Noel, 2002. *Aspects of Hobbes*. Oxford: Oxford University Press.

Martinich, A. P., 2005. *Hobbes*. London: Routledge.

Mason, John Hope. 1995. 'Forced to be free', in Robert Wokler, ed., *Rousseau and Liberty*. Manchester University Press, 121–38.

McCormick, John, 2011. *Machiavellian Democracy*. Cambridge University Press.

Melzer, Arthur, 2014. *Philosophy Between the Lines: The Lost History of Esoteric Writing*. University of Chicago Press.

Mill, J. S., 1989. *On Liberty and Other Writings*, ed. Stefan Collini. Cambridge University Press.

Ober, Josiah, 2008. 'The original meaning of "democracy": capacity to do things, not majority rule', *Constellations* 15, 3–9.

Okin, Susan Moller, 1989. *Justice, Gender, and the Family*. New York: Basic Books.

Olsen, Niklas, 2012. *History in the Plural: An Introduction to the Work of Reinhart Koselleck*. Oxford: Bergahn Books.

Patterson, Annabel, 1991. *Censorship and Interpretation: The Conditions of Writing and Reading in Early Modern England*. 2nd edition. Madison: University of Wisconsin Press.

Pettit, Philip, 1997. *Republicanism: A Theory of Freedom and Government*. Oxford University Press.

Pitkin, Hanna, 1967. *The Concept of Representation*. Berkeley: University of California Press.

Pocock, J. G. A., 1971. *Politics, Language, and Time: Essays on Political Thought and History*. New York: Atheneum.

Pocock, J. G. A., 2006. 'Foundations and moments', in Annabel Brett and James Tully, eds., *Rethinking the Foundations of Modern Political Thought*. Cambridge University Press, 37–49.

Prado, C. G., 2006. *Searle and Foucault on Truth*. Cambridge University Press.

Rawls, John, 1971. *A Theory of Justice*. Cambridge, MA: Harvard University Press.

Reeve, C. D. C., 1988. *Philosopher-Kings: The Argument of Plato's Republic*. Princeton, NJ: Princeton University Press.

Richter, Melvin, 1995. *The History of Political and Social Concepts: A Critical Introduction*. Oxford University Press.

Richter, William, 2009. 'Introduction: the study of political thought', in William Richter, ed., *Approaches to Political Thought*. Lanham, MD: Rowman & Littlefield, 1–12.

Rorty, Richard, 1984. 'The historiography of philosophy: four genres', in Richard Rorty, J. B. Schneewind and Quentin Skinner, eds., *Philosophy in History: Essays on the Historiography of Philosophy*. Cambridge University Press, 49–75.

Rosenblatt, Helena, 1997. *Rousseau and Geneva: From 'the First Discourse to The Social Contract, 1749–1762*. Cambridge University Press.

Rousseau, Jean-Jacques, 1979. *Emile or on Education*, ed. Allan Bloom. New York: Basic Books.

Rousseau, Jean-Jacques, 1997a. 'The Social Contract,' in *The Social Contract and Other Later Political Writings*, ed. Victor Gourevitch. Cambridge University Press.

Rousseau, Jean-Jacques, 1997b. 'Considerations on the Government of Poland', in *The Social Contract and Other Later Political Writings*, ed. Victor Gourevitch. Cambridge University Press.

Sapiro, Virginia, 1992. *A Vindication of Political Virtue: The Political Theory of Mary Wollstonecraft*. University of Chicago Press.

Schotte, Dietrich, 2015. 'The virtues and vices of Leo Strauss, historian. A reassessment of Straussian hermeneutics', in Winfried Schröder, ed., *Reading Between the Lines: Leo Strauss and the History of Early Modern Philosophy*. Berlin: De Gruyter, 57–76.

Schulz, Daniel and Alexander Weiss, 2010. 'Introduction: approaches in the history of political thought', *European Political Science* 9, 283–90.

Searle, John, 1978. 'Literal meaning', *Erkenntnis* 13, 207–24.

Sidgwick, Henry, 1981. *The Methods of Ethics*. Seventh edition. Indianapolis, IN: Hackett.

Simmons, A. John, 1992. *The Lockean Theory of Rights*. Princeton, NJ: Princeton University Press.

Skinner, Quentin, 1964. 'Hobbes's "Leviathan"', *The Historical Journal* 7, 321–33.

Skinner, Quentin, 1981. *Machiavelli*. Oxford University Press.

Skinner, Quentin, 1989. 'The state', in Terence Ball, James Farr and Russell Hanson, eds., *Political Innovation and Conceptual Change*. Cambridge University Press, 90–131.

Skinner, Quentin, 1990. 'The republican ideal of political liberty', in Gisela Bock, Quentin Skinner and Maurizio Viroli, eds., *Machiavelli and Republicanism*. Cambridge University Press, 293–309.

Skinner, Quentin, 1996. *Reason and Rhetoric in the Philosophy of Hobbes*. Cambridge University Press.

Skinner, Quentin, 2002a. *Visions of Politics. Volume I: Regarding Method*. Cambridge University Press.

Skinner, Quentin, 2002b. *Visions of Politics. Volume III: Hobbes and Civil Science*. Cambridge University Press.

Skinner, Quentin, 2002c. 'Interview with Quentin Skinner', *Finnish Yearbook of Political Thought* 6, 32–63.

Skinner, Quentin, 2003. 'States and the freedom of citizens', in Quentin Skinner and Bo Stråth, eds., *States and Citizens: History, Theory, Prospects*. Cambridge University Press, 11–27.

Skinner, Quentin, 2008. *Hobbes and Republican Liberty*. Cambridge University Press.

Skinner, Quentin, 2009. 'A genealogy of the modern state', *Proceedings of the British Academy* 162, 325–70.

Skinner, Quentin, 2012. 'On politics and history: a discussion with Quentin Skinner', *Journal of Intellectual History and Political Thought* 1, 7–31.

Sreenivasan, Gopal, 2000. 'What is the General Will?', *The Philosophical Review* 109, 545–81.

Stuurman, Siep, 2000. 'On intellectual innovation and the methodology of the history of ideas', *Rethinking History* 4, 311–19.

Svacek, Victor, 1976. 'The elusive Marxism of C. B. Macpherson', *Canadian Journal of Political Science* 9, 395–422.

Townshend, Jules, 1999. 'Hobbes as possessive individualist: interrogating the C. B. Macpherson thesis', *Hobbes Studies* 12, 52–72.

Tuck, Richard, 1993. *Philosophy and Government 1572–1651*. Cambridge University Press.

Tully, James, 1995. 'Property, self-government and consent', *Canadian Journal of Political Science* 28, 105–32.

Van Evera, Stephen, 1997. *Guide to Methods for Students of Political Science*. Ithaca, NY: Cornell University Press.

Waldron, Jeremy, 2002. *God, Locke, and Equality. Christian Foundations of John Locke's Political Thought*. Cambridge University Press.

Whatmore, Richard, 2006. 'Intellectual history and the history of political thought', in Richard Whatmore and Brian Young, eds., *Palgrave Advances in Intellectual History*. Basingstoke: Palgrave Macmillan, 109–29.

Wolff, Jonathan, 2013. 'Analytic political philosophy', in Michael Beaney, ed., *The Oxford Handbook of the History of Analytic Philosophy*. Oxford University Press, 795–822.

Wootton, David, 1992. 'The Levellers', in John Dunn, ed., *Democracy: The Unfinished Journey*. Oxford University Press, 71–89.

Zagorin, Perez, 1993. 'Hobbes's Early Philosophical Development', *Journal of the History of Ideas* 54:3, 505–18.

13   Comparative Political Thought

Brooke Ackerly and Rochana Bajpai

1   Introduction

Two features characterize the emerging field of comparative political thought (CPT). The first is an interest in bringing Islamic, Indian, Chinese, African and Latin American ethical-political thought to the attention of Western audiences. The second is an interest in combining the methods of political theorists with those of historians, political scientists and anthropologists to enhance real-world relevance of political theory. This chapter provides an overview of normative-analytic, historical, interpretive and critical approaches to CPT with examples of variants within each category. It argues for a methodology-based definition of CPT, and for a non-hierarchical pluralism in which multiple vocations of political theory prevail. Recognizing the complexity of questions raised by the topic of methods in political theory generally, our aims in this chapter are first to provide an introduction to CPT, second to provide a schematic of the four methodological strands within CPT and finally to highlight the range of methods useful for CPT research, and, where these have something in common with other practices of political theory, to elaborate on how they are used in CPT. To underline, this is an argument about the variety of methodologies and methods in CPT scholarship and an appreciation of the value of this methodological pluralism for the field overall.

Political theorists have been comparing across time, authors and contexts since the field began. In the twenty-first century, given the contributions of post-colonial, feminist and queer scholars, we would expect most political theorists to attempt to be self-aware regarding the parochialism and historical elitism of some political theory. However, today, the phrase 'comparative political thought' indicates to an Anglophone audience a way to teach and practise political theory that is less Western-centric. Obviously, non-Western-centric approaches to political thought have long featured in teaching and writing *in* Asia, Africa, the Middle East and Latin America. Today, the phrase 'comparative political thought' is used to characterize political theory within the Anglo-American academy that uses methods that challenge Euro-American parochialism. The difference between contemporary CPT and cross-cultural, cross-language and cross-time comparisons of previous generations may be its self-reflective attempts to define the field and methods of CPT.

Early progenitors of CPT sought to emphasize cultural differences and incomparability. For example, British colonizers engaged with political elites in South Asia and China to interpret local political theory and cultural practice in ways that facilitated the political economy of colonial rule. The post–World War II project of identifying the universal human rights that provided the anchor commitments of the United Nations, however, sought to identify universal values that transcended cultural differences. In the post–Cold War era, the breakup of the former Yugoslavia and multinational communist regimes, the transformations in the political economies of East Asia, the ongoing tensions in the Middle East and the influence of Islamist political thought has led to the demand for political theory that does not serve imperial ends and is open to universal dimensions of humanity and yet treats differences as strengths.

Contemporary CPT reflects the incorporation within mainstream political theory of the influences of anti-colonial, anti-racist and feminist political theory (see also Gordon 2014).[1] The groundwork for the self-reflective turn in political theory embodied in CPT was laid by their criticisms of imperial and patriarchal ideologies. In particular, post-colonial and feminist criticisms of hierarchal notions of difference on the one hand, and false universalisms on the other, represented one of the profound contributions to political theory. CPT reflects a broadening of the range of intellectual resources being brought to bear on these critiques beyond the Euro-American core of political theory. It represents the motivation to develop theories and methods grounded in the historical traditions and contemporary practices of non-Western societies that transcend the frameworks of area studies, and at the same time, are not dominated by liberal theories.

How do we determine which intellectual traditions should inform contemporary comparative reflections? Should we dialogue between or among such traditions? Do we need to study multiple languages in order to participate in such dialogues? Or do we need language fluency along with deep ethnographic and historical understanding of a particular unknown conceptual terrain in order to shed light on new problems?

[1] Compare this account of the history of the field with those of Freeden (2007), Godrej (2011) and Von Vacano (2015). On the parallels between Orientalist scholarship, and comparative political theory in terms of seeking to articulate the value of non-Western scholarship for Western knowledge, see Thomas (2010).

Or, does CPT require engagement with contemporary scholars who have training, experience and imaginations developed in multiple traditions? As all of these questions suggest, many scholars today feel the need to broaden the tool-kit of political theory to include not only new languages, but also new ways of thinking about the historical epistemology of concepts. These are questions about methods.

CPT scholars use a range of methods and answer these questions differently. Methods choices depend on the researcher's ontology, epistemology and methodology. Ontology is the worldview that determines what the theorist finds to be an interesting question; epistemology is the theoretical distinction between fact and opinion and is behind a theorist's choice of methodology; methodology is the theory of how research should proceed. Methods are the specific techniques or tools for carrying out the research (Ackerly and True 2010: 9–10; 2012). Certain methods – for example the close reading of historical texts – are used by all methodologies of CPT. However, these methods are used differently depending on the specific research question and overarching methodology of the project.

In order to discuss the methodologies and methods of CPT, we have to engage, but not embrace, two suspect premises: that the field of comparative political thought is a subdiscipline with distinct methods and that delimiting those methods strengthens the field. Perhaps because comparative political thought is a relatively new field in political theory, most participants in the field have spent significant time being explicit about and defending their methods. Michael Freeden refers to 'the absence of considered approaches, and their attendant methodologies' of CPT as 'one of the great lacunae in the study of political thinking' (2007: 1). For many political theorists, explaining and defending our choice of and use of chosen methods is part of justifying our arguments (Herzog 1985; Gaus 1990; Forst 2001). We believe that a discussion of methodologies is useful in order to clarify the choices available and to defend the intellectual case for all of the methods in the field. What the field needs now is a pluralist account of those methodologies so that rather than debating which methods and approaches the field should privilege, we can build an inclusive field whose methodological attentions focus on the importance of (1) choosing the approach or approaches appropriate to the particular question at hand and (2) doing that approach well.

In this chapter we discuss a range of normative, historical, interpretive and critical approaches to comparative political thought. Not all of those who participate in the field use all of these approaches, and some CPT scholars would not recognize certain approaches as being appropriately understood as part of the field. However, we have taken a pluralist under-standing of the field and thus review a broad range and their methodological implications. To prescribe how comparative political thought should be done from the standpoint of one particular methodology or method is to truncate prematurely the scope of this emerging field. In this sense, our view of CPT is critical of non-pluralist approaches; however, we treat these approaches, like the others, as offering resources for studying certain questions.

2   What Is Comparative Political Thought?

The defining aim of comparative political thought has been to foster greater engagement with non-Western thought within mainstream political theory. The reasons for studying political thought in the Middle East, Asia, Africa and Latin America of course differ among CPT scholars. A secondary aim has been to enhance the lived-world relevance of political theory, in many cases through combining the methods of political theorists with those of political scientists, historians, anthropologists and other empirical disciplines. In their early work in CPT, Fred Dallmayr and Roxanne Euben engaged with both strands. For Dallmayr, political theorists were late in responding to the issues raised by Islamic extremism and globalization, because they neglected real-world political processes in their preoccupation with abstract theory-building (2004: 249). Euben noted that the boundaries between political theory and comparative politics were arbitrary (1999: 159).

The first aim raises a challenging set of questions: is a focus on non-Western thought *sufficient* to characterize a study as 'comparative political thought', or does it need to fulfil additional criteria to qualify as comparative inquiry, as some have argued (Freeden 2007; March 2009)? There has been a long history of centralizing the Western canon, and also of the post-colonial critique of Eurocentrism within political theory. Does bringing texts from Asia, Africa and Latin America into the canon then suffice for *comparative* inquiry in political thought? In this vein of reflection, the use of the label 'comparative political thought' simply as an account of a thinker's geographical location, independent of whether comparison in a substantive sense is engaged, appears to ghettoize non-Western political thought (March 2009).

The second aim raises another set of questions for CPT. If the *primary* definition of comparative political thought is methodological, in terms of combining methods of political theory and comparative politics for instance, is the study of non-Western political thought *necessary* for the definition of the field? In other words, does the significance of the method of comparison mean that we should drop the initial emphasis on non-Western texts as a defining feature of comparative political theory, while still recognizing that it has great value (just as some comparisons in political science are more instructive than others)? In this vein, studies that compare political thought across Western countries, for instance, would qualify as exercises in comparative political thought, as is the case in sub-disciplines like comparative literature or comparative religion (Freeden 2007; Goto-Jones 2011), as would single-country comparisons of different cases (Bajpai 2011). In interpretive and critical approaches discussed later, the initial aim of CPT of engaging with marginalized bodies of political thought takes the form of a focus less on non-Western sources than on non-elite texts and action, usually the subject of comparative politics, as the 'texts' of political theory.

To what extent should we think of both regional and comparative methods approaches to CPT as part of the same enterprise? We argue that these are both essential parts of the field. To deny the first is to divorce CPT from its animating impulse that remains relevant, that of challenging the marginalization of non-Western forms of knowledge production and transmission (Godrej 2011: 14) and potentially transforming the repertoire of concepts and methods in Western political theory (Jenco 2007). To deny the second is to ignore the pitfalls of a disciplinary division of labour between political theory and political science (e.g. Freeden 2007), as well as the politics of disciplinary boundary policing and crossing, that have always been a part of political theory as well (e.g. Wolin 1969).

The methodological meaning of the 'comparative' in CPT – the joining up the methods of political theorists and comparative analysts – is equally central to intellectual engagement with marginalized bodies of thought. In our view, the comparative enterprise seeks to challenge dominant ideologies and epistemologies and therefore cannot rely only on traditional textual resources. As such, it becomes part of the *role* of CPT to reflect on methodologies in political theory and the epistemological and ontological power dynamics these exhibit.

Within CPT, political theory has been construed broadly, to include analytical political philosophy (sometimes called 'normative' theory), history of political thought, critical theory and interpretation, the study of political ideologies and discourse analysis (Freeden 2007; March 2009). Constructing normative arguments about what it is right to pursue, advancing understanding of thinkers, texts and traditions, as well as enhancing explanations of political phenomena, all count as political theory inasmuch as they focus on concepts and arguments that are at the heart of political theory.

Like political theory, comparison too is construed widely in comparative political thought, across differences of space as well as time. Most broadly, political theory has been comparative since the time of Aristotle; indeed, some have argued that political theory is inherently comparative (Euben 1999; Freeden and Vincent 2013). Most narrowly, CPT might compare *cultural difference* between Western and non-Western thought (March 2009). However, as noted earlier, whether comparison across a Western/non-Western difference is a necessary criterion for comparative political thought is a matter of continuing debate in the field.

CPT destabilizes familiar references points within political theory. CPT questions can be disruptive and 'decolonizing' (e.g. Chan 2009; Mills 2015), seeking to displace the hegemony of Western categories and methods (Jenco 2007; Godrej 2011). They can also be transformative and constructive (e.g. Jenco 2011; Kim 2014). And CPT can be conversational or discursive, seeking to exchange insights and build new insights (e.g. Dallmayr 1999; Angle 2002; Ackerly 2005; Bajpai 2011). Some CPT scholars, trained in Western thought, have no training in the languages and political thought traditions outside of the West and have been working outside of their comfort zone for intellectual and pedagogical reasons. There are others – often academics from non-Western traditions – for whom academic training in political thought has always been cross-contextual. And there are others who have trained in one tradition but later develop research interests that require another tradition and extensive language training. Hence, the practice of CPT reflects a range of methodologies.

3   How Do We Do CPT? Four Methodological Approaches

CPT is like a family tree, with participants utilizing a broad range of methodologies drawing on a complex root system constructed out of a range of political and intellectual struggles. As the field has developed, sometimes rigorous defence of the appropriateness of one's methodology has meant privileging a particular approach. In contrast, our aim is not so much to argue for the superiority of a particular approach, but to highlight the diversity of methodologies and purposes in the field.

We distinguish four principal modes of doing CPT for heuristic purposes: normative-analytic, historical, interpretive and critical. Our intention is not to reproduce conventional disciplinary categories, but to show how these have been configured and challenged in CPT scholarship. Within each methodology, there are of course multiple practices.

In our discussion, we nuance our categorization with specific examples. Individual theorists often work in more than one mode: theorists may emphasize one methodology in one work and another approach in another work, or, indeed use multiple methodologies in a single study. Thus, our classification does not seek to label scholars, but rather to identify the diversity of methodologies that have constituted the field of CPT, and to suggest exemplary instances of each.

Distinguishing between these approaches is important for at least two reasons. First, it gives those interested in turning to CPT a sense of how to draw on their own individual strengths in political theory to become more comparative in their scholarship. Second, in the field of political theory, critical and interpretive social science approaches are often misrecognized as normative and historical approaches, respectively. We argue that these are qualitatively distinct in their epistemological and methodological implications. Interpretive social scientific and critical methodologies act in part as a check on the epistemological power of normative-analytic and historical methodologies in the field of political theory.

3.1   Normative-Analytic CPT

The first category is of CPT as a form of or as an aid to building normative-analytic theory. One strand among normative-analytic approaches is a response to the criticism that political philosophers have been insufficiently attentive to the empirical conditions needed for their recommendations to be translated into reality (see also the chapters by Jubb and by Schmidtz in this volume). CPT in this vein attempts to construct normative arguments that are sensitive to the gap between 'ideal principles and social reality' and seek to 'find a way to connect facts and norms, practical reforms and substantive ideals' (Laborde 2008: 13) (cf. Chan 2009: 5). Among scholars of non-Western political thought, normative-analytic methods are to be found in studies that compare familiar Western principles such as democracy, rule of law and human rights with the intellectual resources of non-Western traditions such as Confucianism (e.g. Ackerly 2005), or use Western terms of political philosophy – such as 'ideal' and 'non-ideal' theory – when studying non-Western traditions (see Chan 2009: Introduction; Kim 2014: chapter 1).

By way of illustration, Stephen Angle (2005) elaborates and juxtaposes the normative resources for democratic centralism in Rawls's notion of a decent society on the one hand, and in Chinese thought, on the other. His motivation is not only to find 'grounds for mutual respect' (Angle 2005:

540), but also to further the cause of practical reforms in contemporary China. Importantly, although the desired direction is of democratizing reform, Western liberal democracy is not posited as the desired end-state in Angle's account. Instead, the comparative reconstruction of the Rawlsian notion of a decent society and of Chinese ideas of democratic centralism in conversation with each other allows for the elaboration of alternative ideals that are *distinct* from traditional liberal democracy (and also from Chinese practice), and crucially, that can be accepted as legitimate by those engaged in Chinese politics. In a similar vein but with different conclusions, Daniel Bell (2000) offers controversial proposals for a democratic regime based on traditional Confucianism of rule by 'a capable and public-spirited "Confucian" intellectual elite'. Like Angle, Bell affirms 'the importance of local knowledge of cultural traditions' not only 'from the standpoint of their efficacy, but also from the point of view of revising political ideals themselves' (Bell 2000: 19, 14).

In these writings, both theorists draw on empirical knowledge of non-Western societies and institutions and seek to construct normative arguments of real-world relevance in an analytic mode. Engagement with non-Western traditions serves in both cases to enlarge the repertoire of desirable ideals. Other work by these authors demonstrate a more explicitly interpretive and even critical CPT methodology – see, for instance, Bell (2008), Angle (2012) and Kim (2014).

The connection between ideal and non-ideal theory is common among normative approaches (see also Tan 2003), but it is not the only framing of normative-analytic CPT. Andrew March in some of his writings offers a combative statement in support of certain normative-analytic approaches to non-Western thought. March argues that the ultimate aim of CPT should be to evaluate moral conflicts between distinct traditions of thought: 'comparative political thought derives its greatest sanction from the cases of principled value conflicts which matter between more or less systematic and autonomous doctrinal systems', instantiated 'in its purest form by religious or other doctrinal truth claims' (March 2009: 34, 31). The turn to non-Western religions and philosophies here is animated by a specific motivation to identify areas of moral disagreement between relatively 'autonomous systems of argumentation', and most importantly to adjudicate in instances of moral conflict, to seek '*plausible* grounds for consensus in other traditions' (March 2009: 38). This kind of normative comparative political thought, according to March, includes and subsumes what is valuable 'in the weaker form of comparative political thought, namely the "diagnostic" element of examining the contours of disagreement between traditions and the "appreciative" element of demonstrating the diversity of other traditions'.

As a rejection of the term 'comparative political thought' simply as a proxy for non-Western political thought, and as a call for thinking seriously about why and what we should *compare* as political theorists, March (2009) offers a welcome perspective. As a prescription for how CPT should be done, however, there are reasons for caution. First, the approach treats different religious traditions as developed within self-referential cultural systems. This was a feature of religious studies of the colonial era that has been debunked. March can respond by saying that his is a stylized account of religion and liberal democracy. Normative-analytic theorists, as we know, often do rely on models that are not meant to be literal descriptions of society (well-known examples include the state of nature and the original position). Nevertheless, at the very least, this needs to be much more explicit in arguments involving religious traditions, given the role of intellectual, political and economic power in defining what religion is and who its followers are. Second, perhaps deriving from its choice of religious doctrines as the units of comparison, March's definition of CPT stipulates unnecessarily demanding criteria for comparison, notably that comparison should be between units that are more or less autonomous or mutually exclusive. This relies on an idealized model of comparison of distinct objects, which has long been deconstructed in the practice of comparative social and humanities-oriented disciplines (literature, art, philosophy, religion and politics) that reject the separateness of the objects of comparison as artificial. Third, it is simply not the case that comparison in the normative-analytic mode can subsume without remainder what is valuable in historical, critical and interpretive forms of political thought (Bajpai 2011). Normative-analytic theorists have typically wielded highly reified notions of tradition and culture, whereas the central thrust of historical, interpretive and critical approaches has been to demonstrate the internal complexity and diversity of unified wholes as well as the dialogical development of traditions, cultures and ideas. As such, while the construction of normative-analytic theory is undoubtedly *one* important purpose that a comparative political theorist might pursue, to elevate its requirements as the standard for all endeavour in the field is to limit the scope of CPT.

3.2   Historical CPT

Historical CPT is by far the most prevalent approach. It comprises impressive scholarship on key non-Western thinkers, schools of thought and traditions. We distinguish historical approaches not by the time periods of the studies (e.g. prior to 1945), but by their methodologies. Historians of non-Western political thought, like their counterparts working on European thought, have offered different answers to the question of how we ought to interpret historical texts from the non-Western world, which kind of texts we should focus on, how we should define the appropriate context that is relevant for understanding texts and how the interpretations of past thinkers can instruct us about current intellectual and political problems.

What these diverse approaches share is that analysis is driven primarily by an interest in the recuperation or retrieval of lost or misunderstood meanings of concepts (e.g. *jihad*), thinkers (e.g. Islamists such as Qutb and Mawdudi) and traditions (e.g. Confucianism). Historical interpretation is of course informed by normative aims, and in some cases explanatory intentions, and we can see the family resemblance between certain normative and historical projects (Ackerly 2005). However, the central thrust of analysis undertaken is to foster greater appreciation of the intricacy and sophistication of non-Western thinkers, texts and traditions, and thereby to enrich and possibly transform the repertoire of political theory.

Historical approaches in CPT have advanced research methods in political theory in important respects. First, with regard to the sources of political thought, political theorists have conventionally focused on prestigious texts and great thinkers, whereas historians of ideas and theorists of ideology have highlighted the significance of more mundane sites of political thought – political pamphlets, propaganda pieces, politicians' speeches. Students of non-Western political thought have also suggested that an adequate appreciation of these traditions requires us to examine not just verbal knowledge articulated in texts and speech, but also knowledge that is implicit in *non-verbal* expressions of ritual, painting, music and dance (Jenco 2007), as historians of pre-modern periods have also emphasized. Indeed, games, graphics and new media technologies may 'hold expressive potentials for political ideas that a more "conventional" treatise cannot express' (Goto-Jones 2011: 107).

A second contribution of historical approaches relates to what the appropriate contexts are for comparative inquiry into non-Western thought. Theorists have offered two standpoints, one that emphasizes *resemblance*, and the other, *difference*. In the first case, scholars have located concepts and thinkers of non-Western thought in interpretive contexts familiar to students of Western political thought. This can involve, for instance, the recuperation of the histories of concepts such as democracy and civil society in Arab thought (Browers 2006), of secularism and liberal ideologies in India (Bajpai 2002, 2012). Roxanne Euben's work is a leading example of this strategy. In *Enemy in the Mirror*, she argues that 'Qutb is not a critic of modernity per se – for he views technologies and scientific achievements as desirable – but an opponent of post-Enlightenment rationalism.' She argues that the ethico-political worldview of Qutb and other Islamic fundamentalists is best understood when placed alongside Western critics of Enlightenment rationality such as Hannah Arendt, Charles Taylor and Alasdair MacIntyre (Euben 1999: 155). Reframing Islamist thought as substantively similar in its formulations to internal Western critics of modernity undermines popular stereotypes of Islamism as a foreign, extremist and archaic ideology, at the same time as serving to highlight currently marginal strands within Western political thought. More generally, the excavation of parallels between non-Western and Western thought undermines influential claims of a clash of civilizations between Islam and the West, or the 'West and the Rest'. A key challenge its practitioners face, however, is to mitigate the pitfalls of using Western conceptual frameworks for the reconstruction of non-Western thought, and thereby imposing Western categories and frames on non-Western traditions and practices (for a discussion of the pitfalls and how these can be mitigated, see Godrej 2011, chapter 2).

The second strategy addresses this risk by emphasizing *difference*. Some historians of non-Western thought have argued that global political theory requires us to work primarily from within the terms and approaches internal to non-European traditions, attempting to jettison, at least temporarily, the familiar categories of Western political theory. Leigh Jenco cogently articulates a case for deriving methods for the study of texts from within the scholarly traditions in which these are embedded (Jenco 2007: 745). Jenco points out that the 'frames of inquiry' of cross-cultural theorists have remained 'beholden to modern Western epistemological debates' (2007: 745). Proper understanding of non-Western thought requires not just linguistic knowledge and hermeneutic sensitivity, but also locating it within the distinct modes of knowledge production and transmission, and perhaps a willingness to accept 'foundational hierarchical premises of nondemocratic worldviews' as they are (Jenco 2007: 744). The emphasis on cultural distance also informs the cosmopolitan method advocated by Farah Godrej, in which the theorist first adopts the language and cultural experience associated with the intellectual and lived tradition of the text, then tries to articulate its meanings to an audience that has not undergone these existential and experiential transformations (Godrej 2011). Godrej's cosmopolitan method develops Dallmayr's dialogic approach, which similarly calls for a comparative method that entails experiential transformation and an ability to write from the lived experience of more than one tradition (Dallmayr 1999, 2004).

The emphasis on cultural difference can serve to highlight the ways in which non-Western thought can potentially extend or displace Western political theory in ethical and epistemological terms. In many cases, considerable linguistic, theoretic and ethnographic skills are required for immersion in a different tradition and the translation of its resources for Western audiences. The main pitfalls for advocates of the distancing approach involve how to avoid reinstating an East-West chasm under a different guise. The attempt to step outside Western concepts and categories poses two challenges. One is empirical: given historical cross-cultural engagement, a strong separation between so-called Western and non-Western traditions is implausible (for a response, see Godrej 2011: 14). The second is the theoretical corollary to the first: the commitment to working within a tradition reifies the boundary of the tradition *a priori*.

In fact, the tension between resemblance and difference is a productive tension *for* CPT. Instead of treating this as a problem that needs to be resolved or transcended, a fruitful stance is to treat it as a necessary quality of the field. The tension is productive methodologically because it reminds us to self-reflect on the concepts, categories and norms that define our epistemological perspective. The tension also offers multiple intellectual contexts for the reconstruction of political thought.

In both normative-analytic and historical CPT discussed thus far, the practice of comparative political thought has focused overwhelmingly on key thinkers, exemplary texts and elite intellectual traditions (see also Thomas 2010). This has served to challenge the Eurocentrism of political theory in important respects, demonstrating, for instance, that Asia, Africa, the Middle East and Latin America have produced thought that matches Western thought in terms of its sophistication and creative power, and has the capacity to extend its moral and political scope. A key substantive contribution of these approaches has been to bring metaphysics back to the study of political thought (Goto-Jones 2011). CPT scholarship demonstrates that political and metaphysical questions pursued in separate domains in post-Enlightenment thought are deeply intertwined.

Nevertheless, the focus on semi-autonomous traditions and key thinkers underestimates the field's potential to expand the frontiers of mainstream political theory. In the next two sections we outline two approaches that go beyond the traditional preoccupation of political theorists with individual thinkers and elite traditions, to engage with how these are inhabited by people in their lived practices. Whereas normative-analytic approaches and historical approaches have tended thus far to emphasize 'non-Western' sources, as well as the Western and non-Western dichotomy as the telling axis of comparison (for an exception, see Goto-Jones 2011), the other two approaches seek to break down that dichotomous construction of 'comparison' and the focus on 'traditions' that has often accompanied this.

3.3   Interpretive CPT

Interpretive theorists challenge the view shared by the other approaches, that the primary purpose of political theory is normative or prescriptive, that of advancing visions of the right or the good (Freeden and Vincent 2013). Instead, in interpretive social science writings, the political-theoretic task of conceptual reconstruction serves also to theorize real-world political processes, and to advance explanations of political outcomes (Bevir and Rhodes 2002; Bajpai 2011). Interpretive social science approaches have often been conflated with historical approaches, but these are distinct. Interpretive theorists use social scientific methods – qualitative data and qualitative methods of analysis (see Yanow and Schwartz-Shea 2013) – to provide detailed empirical accounts of meanings and 'thick description', to use Geertz's well-known term (Geertz 1973; Taylor 1985). Data sources can include constitutional and policy debates, interviews, participant observation, focus groups and ethnography. Methods of analysis can include discourse analyses of elite and colloquial texts (Bajpai 2011; Tripp 2013), as well as political ethnographies (Mahmood 2005; Wedeen 2008).

Like historical CPT scholars, interpretive social scientists too seek to reconstruct the meanings of ideas in particular contexts – what democracy, social justice, civil society mean to people in particular times and places. However, there are important differences with historical approaches. First, in interpretive CPT, the focus is not on the thought of exemplary thinkers or 'innovating ideologists' (Bajpai 2011), on the appreciation of the theoretical and political creativity of individuals such as Qutb or Gandhi. Instead, interpretive social scientists focus on what Lisa Wedeen terms meaning-making practices – discursive, rhetorical and performative. Practices pertain to what agents do, and how this interacts with language and other symbolic systems (Wedeen 2002: 714). Thought practices and meaning construction are not pursued here in the form of the ideas, beliefs or writings of individuals, as is common in historical approaches, but, rather, as embedded and framed within collective actions, both everyday and extraordinary (e.g. of compliance or protest) as characteristic of anthropological writings (Mahmood 2005; Wedeen 2008). For instance, Charles Tripp's account of ideas of political participation in the Middle East is based more on their articulation in repertoires of collective action and protest than on the writings of individuals (Tripp 2013). Tripp distinguishes conceptions of participation that derive from different types of political struggles – for a nation-state against Western rule, for '*dimuqratiyyat al-khubs* [democracy of bread]' through direct action and occupation of public spaces, and for the preservation of an Islamic community through 'observance of the *shari'a*' (Tripp 2013: 91, 95–7). Humeira Iqtidar's account of shifts in Islamist political imaginaries in Pakistan goes beyond the focus on founding ideologues such as Maududi, to examine the narratives of ordinary activists and supporters of the Jama'at-e-Islami engaged in social and humanitarian work (Iqtidar 2011).

Second, interpretive CPT can be explanatory in ways that are distinct from historical CPT. Historians of political thought have also engaged explanation, but usually in terms of explicating why ideas assumed the form that they did at a given historical moment. Occasionally, links are posited between ideas and political outcomes. For instance, Roxanne Euben's study of Sayyid Qutb pursues a 'deeper, richer, fuller account of Islamist ideas', also because demonstrating 'the intellectual coherence and depth of fundamentalist ideas makes explanations of Islamic fundamentalism more causally adequate' (1999: 156). However, in most historical approaches, the further task of identifying and establishing such links between thought and action in specific contexts remains unaddressed. By contrast, in many instances of interpretive CPT, the reconstruction of thought focusses directly on improving explanations of particular political phenomena. How are religio-political identities (e.g. being Muslim, Hindu) produced, and why do these gain salience in certain contexts, and not others? How is political compliance produced, and why do 'some political ideologies, policies, and self-policing strategies work better than others'? How do actors' perceptions of what 'democracy' and 'religion' mean affect political outcomes (Wedeen 2002: 714)? For instance, Rochana Bajpai's account of conceptions of secularism, social justice, democracy, national unity and development in India based on the practices of political argument in constitutional and legislative debates seeks to delineate the distinctive features of these concepts in India, and also to improve explanations of policies of minority rights and affirmative action at critical junctures (Bajpai 2011).

Ideational explanation here has two elements. First, our explanations of political outcomes are necessarily incomplete without a grasp of the normative resources available to actors, just as they would be without knowledge of other resources – economic, institutional – available to them (Bajpai 2011). Here, ideas or norms can serve as an explanatory variable. For example, Matthew Nelson has shown how the shift from custom to *shari'ah* radically altered the pattern of local politics in Pakistan (Nelson 2011). Second, ideational practices (e.g. debates in institutional as well as non-institutional fora) serve as a *lens* for viewing political processes, for gaining better descriptions and thereby explanations of political change, in particular of shifts in relations of power (Asad 1993; Wedeen 2002: 714). For instance, the centralization of power in a polity at a given historical moment and its decentralization at another are manifested not necessarily, or only in the nature of party competition, but also in patterns of political argument, which a conceptual analysis of policy discourse reveals (Bajpai 2011).

Interpretive approaches have the potential to advance CPT in important respects. First, the focus on *practices* as the units of analysis opens up the category of 'tradition', which has often privileged elite sources and reinforced cultural boundaries. It offers the prospect of more nuanced assessments of similarity and difference across different traditions, and over time within a tradition. Second, interpretive CPT approaches typically focus on the present, bringing attention to bear on the recent political experience of Asia, Africa, the Middle East and Latin America that has remained relatively neglected in historical and normative CPT thus far. Third, interpretive CPT extends the role of political theory *in* political science, specifically in relation to ideational explanations of political outcomes, which remain underdeveloped in social science scholarship (see Bajpai and Brown 2013).

Nevertheless, one potential problem with interpretive approaches is that in expanding the role of CPT to include political explanation that is conventionally associated with political science, it risks losing what is distinctive in political *theory*. Its advocates reply that using the tools of political theory to conceptualize and theorize political phenomena and processes enhances the real-world relevance of political theory. This latter interpretation is in keeping with the historical emergence of the discipline in which political theory served as the reflective dimension of political science, helping the field define its questions and concepts (Wolin 1969; Gunnell 2010). Furthermore, within political theory, engagement with empirical politics on the part of political theorists is a growing trend. Here, the task of political theory is not seen just in terms of providing solutions to our current moral predicaments, but also as clarifying what these are, in helping give 'form to emergent realities that otherwise remain beyond our ken' (cf. Wolin 1969; Isaac 1995; Kaufman-Osborn 2010: 668), and thereby relocating political theory within the realm of political science (Freeden 2007; Gunnell 2010).

3.4   Critical CPT

In the Marxist tradition of political theory, critical CPT connects to the 'struggles and wishes of the age' (Marx 1967). Critical CPT identifies the dissenting strands within elite traditions of political theory and the non-elite voices within the lived experience of political thought. Methodologically, critical CPT is the study of elite *and non-elite* actors, of canonical *and non-mainstream* texts, of texts *and the actions and aspirations* of those in struggle. Some of these actors can be marginalized in global politics or by local politics in struggles with elites. Globally and locally, marginalization differs whether due to race, religion, ethno-nationality, language, sexuality or perceived sexuality.

Christine Keating situates her argument about the meaning of the social contract in the context of the decolonization of India (Keating 2011). Luis Cabrera locates his argument about global citizenship in the actions of global migrants, citizens policing the borders and those engaged in humanitarian aid in the borderlands (Cabrera 2010). Brooke Ackerly draws on the insights of women's rights activists from around the world to articulate a theory of human rights from the practice of struggle for rights (Ackerly 2008). Kim places his argument about Confucian democracy and law in the context of contemporary South Korea politics over the meaning of democracy and freedom (Kim 2014).

Sometimes called *grounded political theory*, these approaches are quintessentially question-driven inquiry, framing their questions around the political struggles of non-elites, that is, those who are not privileged in their contemporary political contexts. This approach seeks to broaden the history of ideas at stake in the political struggle to include not just the ideas of the winners, but also of those who struggled for a different political practice. The actions and aspirations of those in struggle are treated as text on a par with the texts inherited by elites. It also treats activists as political theorists (Cabrera 2010; Keating 2011: 114), and applies the insights gained by studying the struggles in one context (India) to the struggles in another (Keating 2011), to make more general claims about specific concepts and their use (Ackerly 2008; Beltrán 2009; Cabrera 2010), and to challenge familiar conceptualizations.

While critical, this view entails a general claim: that it is the study of ideas and concepts that are *revealed in the struggles of politics*, not just in the ideas and concepts that emerge victorious *from those struggles*. Certain substantive universals may emerge from such inquiry. But these claims proceed with a sceptical scrutiny for the potential to false essentialisms, false universalisms and exclusions. These can be made through the intent to include or broaden the perspectives being considered. At their best, critical grounded approaches to CPT work in alliance with non-elites in political struggle; this is a methodological alliance for understanding the struggle, not an ideological alliance of researcher and political actors.

One interesting potential problem with critical approaches is that they can be mired in discursive politics. If these politics get disassociated from the underlying problem or used to silence or deny the voice of some participants in the struggle (Mackey 2005; Rothschild, Long and Fried 2005; Fricker 2007; Medina 2012), then critical CPT does not lead to political or theoretical insights more fruitful than the more elite-text-based historical approaches to CPT. The critical grounded approach requires either an empirical component or triangulation across comparative methods.

Finally, critical CPT approaches use normative, historical and interpretive methods. What distinguishes critical CPT is its authors' normative commitment to those contemporary political struggles. In the following section, we turn to the discussion of methods – specific tools – that multiple methodologies may use to effect the author's goals.

4   How to Do CPT

In a CPT project, as in other subfields of politics, methodologies and methods need to be chosen with respect to a particular question. CPT scholars often use a mixed methodology, perhaps beginning in one methodology and revising using another. In this light, it is best to think of the four CPT methodologies as providing an initial guiding framework. As with empirical social science, triangulation across methodologies and methods can be more fruitful than relying on one. The key to avoiding the potential for epistemological imperialism in political theory is to be *question*-driven, attentive to *methodological pluralism* even if your own methods tend towards one strand of the field, attentive to the potential of any *method* to be self-centric due to the building blocks of scholarship, and self-reflective about the *best execution* of the methods of your selected approach or approaches. These are 'meta-methods' if you will. Many, maybe even all of these, are or should be part of any political theory practice. Post-colonial, feminist and other critical approaches have made similar arguments. Nevertheless, we offer a CPT perspective on research practices and outline their concrete instantiation in CPT scholarship.

(a) **Start with your research question rather than methodology or method.** Several scholars have called for more question-driven research, in contrast with the emphasis on methods and models in political theory and political science (on the general point, see Isaac 1995;

Shapiro 2005). CPT joins calls in the discipline for putting the question before methods. It has the potential to enlarge research questions beyond those traditionally addressed by political theorists to include those informed by deep engagement with non-Western sources on the one hand, and empirical social science on the other.

As with other forms of political theory, a CPT question can be based on an empirical observation. These can be empirical problems (such as violence, immigration, climate change, gender oppression and poverty) that pose challenges for how we live together. Such an empirical problem can also lead to a theoretical problem that needs to be addressed before we can think about how we might address the empirical problem (and others like it). As we saw earlier, CPT scholars have addressed questions of governance, human rights, democracy and citizenship. A CPT question can also come from a new way of reading a text that comes from the reading of texts in and/or across traditions. In sum, a CPT question can be grounded in a problem (e.g. poverty), a concept (e.g. human rights) or texts (e.g. Confucian and Neo-Confucian texts). Be aware of the fact that your question will influence your methodological commitments.

(b) **Know your ontological perspective *and* be open to its revision.** By your selection of a research project, you reveal to yourself and the world the ontological perspective behind the inquiry. Some differences among theorists can be ontological, but manifest themselves methodologically. For example, Andrew March argues that the important differences across historical traditions lie in the differences in their worldviews. In fact, March has a worldview (an ontological perspective) about the differences in worldviews. By contrast, Roxanne Euben argues that by familiarizing ourselves with seeming differences in worldviews, we can gain better self-understanding and an appreciation that differences are not as different as we might have thought. She has an ontological perspective on the inter-comparability and inter-compatibility of worldviews. In *Enemy in the Mirror*, she argues that 'Qutb's work must be understood as a "dialectical response" to rationalism and Westernization', and that he is 'participating in a conversation that we, as Western students of politics, not only recognize, but in which we participate' (Euben 1999: 155).

Consider the ways in which the tensions among competing readings or interpretations and seeming 'discontinuities' or irreconcilable differences across time and geography reveal not just intra-disciplinary methodological disagreements, but ontological differences. If you are doing CPT well, you challenge yourself to revisit your ontological perspectives throughout the research process.

(c) **Know your methodology and be open to its development.**
Question-driven research is in principle methodologically plural at the
moment of inquiry. None of the methodologies discussed earlier requires
that you use just one method. Each exemplifies a particular *combination* of
methods. For instance, Euben in the example cited previously also uses
interpretive and critical methods to some extent when she situates her
reading of Qutb in the context of contemporary politics of his reception by
Sunni and Western audiences.

Likewise, the same method can be used across methodologies. For
example, historical and interpretive social scientists use textual analysis;
however, interpretivists usually try to supplement this 'with more ethnographic modes of analysis (interviews, observation, etc.) so as to give more
widespread accounts of the beliefs found among the different actors
involved in a practice'.[2]

In choosing your methodology, ask yourself what your main *purpose* in
undertaking CPT is. Is it the retrieval or recuperation of particular non-
Western thinkers or debates? If so, historical methodologies are likely to
be most appropriate. Is it to respond to contemporary challenges that
affect people across the globe (e.g. climate change) from the standpoint of
the experience of those most vulnerable in Asia and Africa? If so, critical
or normative methodologies are likely to be more suitable. Alternatively,
your main interest may be the conceptualization and theorization of new
forms of political action among elites and/or subalterns in Asia, Africa or
the Middle East, for which interpretive CPT methodologies are likely to
be most useful. Each methodology embodies a particular priority among
the methods it deploys in order to resolve conflicts and ascertain the
validity of conclusions.

(d) **Know which methods you will need and be open to multiple
methods.** Consider the possible methods and select the right combination for your question. As with other areas of research, in CPT the use of
multiple methods across different methodologies has yielded rich
insights.

For example, conceptual analysis is typically used in analytic methodologies to construct normative arguments (see Olsthoorn's chapter in
this volume and the discussion of the normative-analytic approach
earlier), including arguments about the possible kinds of desirable political change (Angle 2005; Kim 2014). However, it can also be used in
interpretive CPT, where conceptual reconstruction serves to advance
explanations of political outcomes and political change (e.g. Bajpai
2011). Interpretive CPT offers an interstitial space between political

---

[2] Mark Bevir, personal communication, May 2015.

theory and political science, where the tools of political theorists are used for improving social science explanations.

Critical comparative political theorists have analysed non-elite texts and even treated as texts the arguments that are embedded in the political actions of non-elites who are seeking alternative political arrangements. Critical CPT methods include observation of contemporary struggles (Beltrán 2009; Cabrera 2010; Clifford 2012; Forman and Cruz forthcoming), critical rereading of historical struggles (Keating 2011) and even interviews with actors in the struggle (Ackerly 2008). Sungmoon Kim's *Confucian Democracy in East Asia* utilizes historical, interpretive and critical methods and normative-analytic argument in setting out the import of his project (Kim 2014).

Be aware that the findings from different methods may conflict. Methodological location and triangulation (see later) can help with the resolution of such conflicts.

(e) **Be aware of your own boundaries.** It is important to recognize that as a comparative political theorist, you both construct and decon-struct boundaries as you work. Attentiveness to that construction and reconstruction is a feature of CPT best practice.

Consider, for example, the political and theoretical debate in the 1990s about 'Asian Values' and their (in)commensurability with political equality, individual freedom and rights. In the Asian Values debate, some partici-pants emphasized the distinctiveness of East Asian cultures (Zakaria 1994; Bell 2000). Drawing on textual analysis and cross-cultural comparison, they developed a reified dichotomy between Western and Asian traditions. Participants in that same debate challenged those readings of historical texts and offered competing interpretations of 'the' cultural tradition (Kim Dae 1994; Chan 1997). The debate revealed great differences within each of these intellectual and cultural groupings. The diversity within those broad civilizational categories – and their political import for charting possible ways of thinking about what ethical responsibility requires in the face of contemporary challenges – is obfuscated by the overgeneralized characterization of and sharp delineation between the dialogue partners.

(f) **Acquire requisite language skills.** CPT methods typically, but not necessarily, require competency in the language of the texts. Depending on the research question, the availability and quality of trans-lations and knowledge about the politics and epistemology of a text's translators, some CPT can be done without fluency.

(g) **Read texts closely and contextualize these.** All CPT makes use of close textual reading. Whether your reading is typical or a nuanced rereading, be attentive to alternative readings of the texts (see also Blau's chapter in this volume). Debates from the time period, contemporary secondary literature and political history of the context can enhance the reading. Whereas the focus in reading texts is often the substance of their arguments, CPT scholars can also read texts for their insights into how to do political theory (e.g. Jenco 2007).

(h) **Consider the broad range of available sources.** When your research question relates to broad categories – such as culture or religion – contextualize your account of any particular text or other evidence with reference to a broad range of sources. Remember (or reconsider) your ontological commitments when you identify your sources.

From a critical CPT perspective, it is especially important for you to consider the status of the authors of your texts at the time and in history. Much CPT broadens our sources, but you may not be able to include non-elite sources, those either lost to time because they did not generate texts that are available today or omitted because their texts are not considered 'theory.'

For example, in *East Meets West*, Daniel Bell broadens what counts as a text for political theory by taking the political ideas of two leaders in the Asian Values debate of the 1990s and articulating their views in the form of fictionalized characters. However, the fictionalized protagonists of the dialogue that he constructs between East and West are as elite as the political leaders on whose ideas the text is based (Bell 2000). Neither protagonist is engaged in a struggle for recognition and enjoyment of his own human rights. This is a critical CPT assessment of Bell's sources.

(i) **Pick your qualitative methods carefully.** Political practice can be a source of CPT 'text' for analysis. Michael Freeden, in his call for explicit methods for CPT, urges theorists to focus more on 'real world forms of political thinking' rather than great thinkers and texts that are unrepresentative of their contexts (2007: 2; see also Bajpai 2011). Godrej (2011) calls on CPT work to be anthropological or ethnographic. However, such work can also be qualitative without being ethnographic. For example, Ackerly (2001) looks at the human rights practices of activists to complement what they say about their work. Cabrera (2010) looks at the actions of migrants and those near and crossing borders.

Be aware too that textual and written sources also encode practices and ritual forms – the latter are not just to be found in the realm of 'behaviour'.

(j) **Attend to sources of bias.** A narrow source list can be one source of bias, but there are others. Because each methodological approach has strengths and weaknesses, be attentive to and make explicit the biases in your framing of the comparative project. For instance, does it frame Islamic, Indian or Chinese traditions in terms of their orthodox variants, or even their dominant heterodox strands? What alternative sources provide a counter-reading of the thinkers and traditions that are its focus?

Have you constructed a dichotomous juxtaposition of two readings of a text? Are there others whose nuance is lost by your heuristic? In what ways are your empirical sources limited or limiting?

(k) **Triangulate.** Even if you use only one methodological approach, use your awareness of the other methodologies to create a reflective dialogue with yourself about the possible other approaches to studying your question. Consider other approaches. What would the approach consider or recommend, why is it tempting, and why is it less suited your question? Following Goodin's advice in this volume, show your work. The standard of showing your work is more detailed in a book-length treatment. However, the excuse of space for not treating a serious criticism or alternative reading is not intellectually satisfying. Space constraints may justify not pursuing a mixed methodology approach, but again, it is a weak response to not reflecting on the insights such an approach might offer your project.

(l) **Consider co-authorship.** Given the specialization of debates within political theory, the voluminous scholarship on the Middle East, Asia, Africa and Latin America, not to speak of the desired linguistic skills, serious comparative work requires considerable time and effort. Furthermore, as we have discussed and demonstrated in our co-authorship of this chapter, behind all CPT methodologies is an epistemological commitment to broadening the scope of insights that are brought to bear on a question. No matter your skills, the scale of comparative work and the scope of insight can be broadened through co-authorship.

(m) **Be humble.** When writing from a position of privilege, and most political theorists do, humility vis-à-vis what you can know is appropriate. Many of the 'how-to' points make reference to limitations, such as limited access to historical knowledge, disproportionate access to elite texts and limited access to the lived politics of those in struggle. In addition, use humility to reflect on the privileges of being able to do this work and the intellectual obligations of this privilege.

5   Conclusions

In the twenty-first century, the field of political theory and comparative political thought is global, not in the sense that any articulation of the complex web of concepts would be globally agreed to or that such agreement should be the goal, but rather that our interlocutors in this endeavour are not predetermined by our training, experience, geography or imagination, but may come from any place, time or family of inquiry.

CPT can help us do political theory better. The field's internal discussions of methodologies and method can help its practitioners – novice and experienced – do their work better. One day the modifier 'comparative' will become associated with this time in the historical development of our discipline because in fact what we learn from how we do comparative inquiry improves how we do political theory (Dallmayr 2004; Euben 2006: see especially chapter 2; March 2009: 536–7; see also Leader Maynard's chapter in this volume). CPT enables us to deepen our reflections about what we mean by 'we' when 'we' as theorists engage in an ethical and political reflection.

Political, economic and social empirical problems with normative import are the important questions for political theorists. Because many of these recur, the history of political thought is a likely source for a wealth of reflective insights. Because these issues have been relevant in the world and over time, the historical intellectual traditions that may provide insight may come from anywhere. Because these issues are pressing now, contemporary theorists around the world should draw on each other's reflective insights in order to broaden our understanding of the web of relevant concepts and help clarify our articulations of them. The vastness of these ambitions extends beyond the capacity of any individual's life work. Therefore, political theory relevant to the significant challenges posed by these ambitious normative puzzles needs to be a collaborative enterprise. Taken together, the range of methodological forms that CPT takes enables political theory to ever improve its contributions to the study and practice of politics.

CPT methods build a shared, though not necessarily common platform across multiple domains of knowledge production. They challenge false universalisms and dominant Western stereotypes. They situate political theory in multiple contexts of resemblance and difference and expand the notion of text to include debates and action. CPT is one of the subfields in political theory that engages in constructive criticism of the ways in which political theory can perform global politics, not just write about it. CPT methods push political theory to become increasingly self-aware about that possibility.

Acknowledgements

We are grateful to participants in the London Comparative Political Thought seminar, and to Adrian Blau, Humeira Iqtidar, Leigh Jenco, Sungmoon Kim and Tejas Parasher for their comments on earlier versions.

References

Ackerly, Brooke, 2001. 'Women's human rights activists as cross-cultural theorists', *International Feminist Journal of Politics* 3, 311–46.

Ackerly, Brooke, 2005. 'Is liberalism the only way toward democracy? Confucianism and democracy', *Political Theory* 33, 547–76.

Ackerly, Brooke, 2008. *Universal Human Rights in a World of Difference*. Cambridge University Press.

Ackerly, Brooke and Jacqui True, 2010. *Doing Feminist Research in Political and Social Science*. Palgrave Macmillan.

Ackerly, Brooke and Jacqui True, 2012. 'Methods and methodologies', in Georgina Waylen, Karen Celis, Johanna Kantola and Laurel Weldon, eds., *The Oxford Handbook of Gender and Politics*. Oxford University Press, 109–33.

Angle, Stephen, 2002. *Human Rights and Chinese Thought: A Cross-cultural Inquiry*. Cambridge University Press.

Angle, Stephen, 2005. 'Decent democratic centralism', *Political Theory* 33, 518–46.

Angle, Stephen, 2012. *Contemporary Confucian Political Philosophy*. Cambridge: Polity.

Asad Talal, 1993. *Genealogies of Religion: Discipline and Reasons of Power in Christianity and Islam*. Baltimore, MD: Johns Hopkins University Press.

Bajpai, Rochana, 2002. 'The conceptual vocabularies of secularism and minority rights in India', *Journal of Political Ideologies* 7, 179–97.

Bajpai, Rochana, 2011. *Debating Difference: Group Rights and Liberal Democracy in India*. Oxford University Press.

Bajpai, Rochana, 2012. 'Liberalisms in India: a sketch', in Ben Jackson and Marc Stears, eds., *Liberalism as Ideology: Essays in Honour of Michael Freeden*. Oxford University Press, 53–76.

Bajpai, Rochana and Graham Brown, 2013. 'From ideas to hegemony: ideational change and affirmative action policy in Malaysia, 1955–2010', *Journal of Political Ideologies* 18, 257–80.

Bell, Daniel, 2000. *East Meets West: Human Rights and Democracy in East Asia*. Princeton, NJ: Princeton University Press.

Bell, Daniel, 2006. *Beyond Liberal Democracy: Political Thinking for an East Asian Context*. Princeton, NJ: Princeton University Press.

Bell, Daniel, 2008. *China's New Confucianism: Politics and Everyday Life in a Changing Society*. Princeton, NJ: Princeton University Press.

Beltrán, Cristina, 2009. 'Going public', *Political Theory* 37, 595–622.

Bevir, Mark and R. A. W. Rhodes, 2002. 'Interpretive theory', in David Marsh and Gerry Stoker, eds., *Theory and Methods in Political Science*. Basingstoke: Palgrave, 131–52.

Browers, Michaelle, 2006. *Democracy and Civil Society in Arab Political Thought: Transcultural Possibilities*. Syracuse University Press.

Cabrera, Luis, 2010. *The Practice of Global Citizenship*. Cambridge University Press.

Chan, Joseph Cho Wai, 1997. 'An alternative view', *Journal of Democracy* 8, 35–48.

Chan, Joseph Cho Wai, 2009. 'Is there a Confucian perspective on social justice?', in Takashi Shogimen and Cary Nederman, eds., *Western Political Thought in Dialogue with Asia*. Lanham, MD: Lexington Books, 261–77.

Chan, Joseph Cho Wai, 2015. *Confucian Perfectionism: A Political Philosophy for Modern Times*. Princeton, NJ: Princeton University Press.

Clifford, Stacy, 2012. 'Making disability public in deliberative democracy', *Contemporary Political Theory* 11, 211–28.

Dallmayr, Fred, ed., 1999. *Border Crossings: Toward a Comparative Political Theory*. Lanham, MD: Lexington Books.

Dallmayr, Fred, 2004. 'Beyond monologue: for a comparative political theory', *Perspectives on Politics* 2, 249–57.

Euben, Roxanne Leslie, 1999. *Enemy in the Mirror: Islamic Fundamentalism and the Limits of Modern Rationalism*. Princeton, NJ: Princeton University Press.

Euben, Roxanne Leslie, 2006. *Journeys to the Other Shore: Muslim and Western Travelers in Search of Knowledge*. Princeton, NJ: Princeton University Press.

Forman, Fonna and Teddy Cruz, forthcoming. 'Global justice at the municipal scale: the case of Medellín, Colombia', in Thomas Pogge and Luis Cabrera, eds., *Institutional Cosmopolitanism*. Oxford University Press.

Forst, Rainer, 2001. 'Towards a critical theory of transnational justice', *Metaphilosophy* 32, 160–79.

Freeden, Michael, 1996. *Ideologies and Political Theory: A Conceptual Approach*. Oxford: Clarendon Press.

Freeden, Michael, 2007. 'The comparative study of political thinking', *Journal of Political Ideologies* 12, 1–9.

Freeden, Michael and Andrew Vincent, eds., 2013. *Comparative Political Thought: Theorizing Practices*. New York: Routledge.

Fricker, Miranda, 2007. *Epistemic Injustice: Power and the Ethics of Knowing*. Oxford University Press.

Fukuyama, Francis, 1992. *The End of History and the Last Man*. New York: Free Press.

Gaus, Gerald, 1990. *Value and Justification: The Foundations of Liberal Theory*. Cambridge University Press.

Geertz, Clifford, 1973. *The Interpretation of Cultures: Selected Essays*. New York: Basic Books.

Godrej, Farah, 2011. *Cosmopolitan Political Thought: Method, Practice, Discipline*. Oxford University Press.

Gordon, Jane Anna, 2014. *Creolizing Political Theory: Reading Rousseau through Fanon*. Bronx: Fordham University Press.

Goto-Jones, Chris, 2011. 'A cosmos beyond space and area studies: toward comparative political thought as political thought', *boundary 2* 38, 87–118.

Gunnell, John, 2010. 'Professing political theory', *Political Research Quarterly* 63, 674–79.

Herzog, Don, 1985. *Without Foundations: Justification in Political Theory*. Ithaca, NY: Cornell University Press.

Huntington, Samuel, 1996. *The Clash of Civilizations and the Remaking of World Order*. New York: Simon & Schuster.

Iqtidar, Humeira, 2011 'Secularism beyond the state: the "state" and the "market" in Islamist imagination', *Modern Asian Studies* 45, 535–64.

Isaac, Jeffrey, 1995. 'The strange silence of political theory', *Political Theory* 23, 636–52.

Jenco, Leigh, 2007. '"What does heaven ever say?" A methods-centered approach to cross-cultural engagement', *American Political Science Review* 101, 741–55.

Jenco, Leigh, 2011. 'Recentering political theory: the promise of mobile locality', *Cultural Critique* 79, 27–59.

Kaufman-Osborn, Timothy, 2010. 'Political theory as profession and as subfield?', *Political Research Quarterly* 63, 655–73.

Keating, Christine, 2011. *Decolonizing Democracy: Transforming the Social Contract in India*. Pennsylvania State University Press.

Kim Dae, Jung, 1994. 'Is culture destiny: the myth of Asia's anti-democratic values', *Foreign Affairs* 73.

Kim, Sungmoon, 2014. *Confucian Democracy in East Asia: Theory and Practice*. Cambridge University Press.

Laborde, Cécile, 2008. *Critical Republicanism: The Hijab Controversy and Political Philosophy*. Oxford University Press.

Mackey, Eva, 2005. 'Universal rights in conflict: "backlash" and "benevolent resistance" to indigenous land rights', *Anthropology Today* 21, 14–20.

Mahmood, Saba, 2005. *Politics of Piety: The Islamic Revival and the Feminist Subject*. Princeton, NJ: Princeton University Press.

March, Andrew, 2009. 'What is comparative political theory?', *The Review of Politics* 71, 531–65.

Marx, Karl, 1967. *Writings of the Young Marx on Philosophy and Society*, ed. Loyd David Easton and Kurt Guddat. Garden City, NY: Doubleday.

Medina, José, 2012. *The Epistemology of Resistance: Gender and Racial Oppression, Epistemic Injustice, and Resistant Imaginations*. Oxford University Press.

Mills, Charles, 2015. 'Decolonizing Western political philosophy', *New Political Science* 37, 1–24.

Nelson, Matthew, 2011. *In the Shadow of Shari, ah: Islam, Islamic Law, and Democracy in Pakistan*. Columbia University Press.

Parel, Anthony, 2006. *Gandhi's Philosophy and the Quest for Harmony*. Cambridge University Press.

Rothschild, Cynthia, Scott Long and Susana Fried, eds., 2005. *Written Out: How Sexuality Is Used to Attack Women's Organizing*. New York: International Gay and Lesbian Human Rights Commission & The Center for Women's Global Leadership.

Shapiro, Ian, 2005. *The Flight from Reality in the Human Sciences*. Princeton University Press.

Tan, Sor-Hoon, 2003. *Confucian Democracy: A Deweyan Reconstruction*. Albany: State University of New York Press.

Taylor, Charles, 1985. *Philosophy and the Human Sciences*. Cambridge University Press.

Thomas, Megan, 2010. 'Orientalism and comparative political theory', *The Review of Politics* 72, 653–77.

Tripp, Charles, 2013. 'Acting and acting out: conceptions of political participation in the Middle East', in Michael Freeden and Andrew Vincent, eds., *Comparative Political Thought: Theorizing Practices*. New York: Routledge, 88–109.

Von Vacano, Diego, 2015. 'The scope of comparative political theory', *Annual Review of Political Science* 18, 465–80.

Wedeen, Lisa, 2002. 'Conceptualizing culture: possibilities for political science', *American Political Science Review* 96, 713–28.

Wedeen, Lisa, 2008. *Peripheral Visions: Publics, Power, and Performance in Yemen*. University of Chicago Press.

Whitehead, Laurence, 2013. 'Latin American approaches to "the political"', in Michael Freeden and Andrew Vincent, eds., *Comparative Political Thought: Theorizing Practices*. New York: Routledge, 40–59.

Wolin, Sheldon, 1969. 'Political theory as a vocation', *American Political Science Review* 63, 1062–82.

Yanow, Dvora and Peregrine Schwartz-Shea, eds., 2013. *Interpretation and Method: Empirical Research Methods and the Interpretive Turn*. Armonk, NY: M. E. Sharpe.

Zakaria, Fareed, 1994. 'Culture is destiny: a conversation with Lee Kuan Yew', *Foreign Affairs* 73, 109–26.

14   Ideological Analysis

Jonathan Leader Maynard

1   Introduction

The past two decades have seen a proliferation of academic work on ideology (Freeden et al. 2013: v). While the study of ideology is older than this (Larrain 1979; McLellan 1995), recent developments have made it increasingly appropriate to speak of 'ideology studies' or 'ideological analysis' as a distinct interdisciplinary field of research within the humanities and social sciences. Researchers of ideology have made significant methodological, theoretical and empirical advances, in disciplines as diverse as political theory (Freeden 1996), intellectual history (Tully 1983; Skinner 2002b), political psychology (Rosenberg 1988; Jost and Major 2001; Haidt et al. 2009; Jost et al. 2009a), discourse analysis (Howarth et al. 2000; Fairclough 2010), political science (Knight 2006; Carmines and D'Amico 2015), sociology (Boudon 1989) and social and cultural studies (Eagleton 1991; Hall 1996; Shelby 2003). Indeed, the biggest problem facing the contemporary study of ideology is the fragmentation of work across disciplines – one thing this chapter attempts to address (for existing interdisciplinary work, see Žižek 1994a; van Dijk 1998; Freeden 2007; Fréeden et al. 2013). But while problems and lacunae remain, ideological analysis is currently at a high point of sophistication, diversity and output (for guideline maps to such contemporary research, see Norval 2000; Leader Maynard 2013; Leader Maynard and Mildenberger 2016).

The overwhelming bulk of this work has occurred within research domains that could loosely be described as *empirical*. But that is not the focus of this chapter. I contend that ideological analysis is also important for the sort of conceptual and normative political theory covered in most chapters of this volume. Some theorists, notably the leading ideology scholar Michael Freeden, have argued for the relevance of ideological analysis to political theory by advocating a broad conceptualization of the latter: where political theory goes beyond conceptual and normative analysis to include theoretical reflection about empirical features of politics (Freeden 2005b, 2006, 2008, 2013b: especially chs. 1 and 2). There are merits to this argument, but this is also not my approach here. Instead, I'm happy to limit the scope of political theory to a normative form – though I assume that this encompasses a broad range of 'ideal' and 'non-ideal' theorizing (Valentini 2012; see too the chapters by Jubb and by Schmidtz in this volume). I will show how ideological analysis can support such normative political theory (although my discussion should be useful for those engaged in empirical work too). In Section 1, I discuss how to conceptualize ideology, before going on, in Section 2, to explain how ideological analysis can be valuable for normative political theory, arguing that political theorists need to attend to it more frequently. Finally, in the more substantive Section 3, I offer an integrative account of how to engage in rigorous ideological analysis.

At many points my comments are necessarily cursory. My objective here is to offer the most practically useful guide to engaging in ideological analysis for scholars and students. Offering the fullest justification for every piece of advice I give would make it impossible to explain that advice clearly. Instead, my bibliographical references should serve to link readers to key texts that examine the corresponding issues in more depth.

2   The Meaning of Ideology

To analyse ideology is to be concerned with two important features of human beings. First, **ideological analysis requires a recognition that different individuals, groups, institutions or societies are characterized by *distinctive idiosyncratic worldviews* that meaningfully shape their political thought and political behaviour**. To understand, explain or predict what they say, think and do, we therefore need to identify and study those worldviews. This stands in contrast to modes of political analysis that present human beings as fundamentally mentally alike – as, for example, uniform rational actors – or as overwhelmingly governed by forces that render distinctive worldviews irrelevant – like class position or a universal set of material self-interests. Second, ideological analysis reflects an awareness that we cannot simply study the role of individual 'ideas' in isolation. **To explain why human beings buy into certain ideas, and to explain how and why those ideas affect their behaviour in certain ways, we have to appreciate how those ideas operate as part of broader *systems of ideas*.** Taken on its own, for example, the way many of the materially worst-off members of liberal democracies support low spending on the sorts of social services they would benefit from, and simultaneously support tax cuts for the wealthiest, looks almost inexplicable (Jost and Hunyady 2005). Yet such a view is often just one component of a set of ideological claims regarding the historically demonstrated superiority of the small free-market state, the need to minimize taxes and state spending in order to promote (wealthy) 'job creators', the alluring promise that wealth and success are accessible to every individual who works hard and the demand to avoid dangerous 'socialist' notions that would create a slippery slope to an authoritarian, unfree society. Once this interlocking system of ideas is brought into focus, the reasons some individuals might accept such ideas become clearer.

Ideological analysis is thus concerned with the excavation and forensic examination of distinctive systems of ideas and the powerful role they play in political life. Yet ideological analysis has frequently been undermined by the infamous diversity of meanings that have been attached to the term 'ideology' (Eagleton 1991: 1–2; McLellan 1995: 1; Freeden 1996: 13, 47; van Dijk 1998: 1; Humphrey 2005: 225, 227). To remedy this problem, I offer a definition of ideology that reflects dominant contemporary usages amongst theorists of ideology – which I suggest have finally started to converge on a shared understanding (Leader Maynard and Mildenberger 2016). But regardless of whether readers find my definition amenable or not, **it is always critical to clarify what one means by 'ideology'**. And in doing so, scholars must avoid what Matthew Humphrey (2005: 299) has aptly labelled the stipulative error: justifying particular definitions (against competitors) by superficially empirical assertions about 'what ideology is', when how to classify different bits of the empirical world is precisely what is being disagreed over in conceptual disputes. Rather, **different definitions should be justified according to how functionally useful they are for research.**

This functional usefulness should be assessed with reference to three main considerations:

(a) essential features about the way ideology has been used in general academic and lay discourse – for example, it would be a drawback of a particular conception if it ended up asserting that phenomena universally seen as ideologies, like liberalism, communism or socialism, were in fact not ideologies;

(b) the functional usefulness of the conception for the *specific research project* at hand;

(c) the functional usefulness of the conception for *broader academic understanding across projects and disciplines* – highly idiosyncratic conceptions, that are liable to promote confusion or fragmentation in usage across different research communities, are undesirable.

Since (b) and (c) can pull us in opposite directions, striking a balance between them is necessary.

So there needn't be one single definition of ideology that all theorists should use. But in this chapter I follow recent trends in ideological analysis by suggesting that **political theorists should use a conception of ideology that is both broad and non-pejorative** – respectively, that it encompasses a large range of idea systems and thought practices, and that it does not assume that ideology is necessarily false, inflexible, poorly formulated or otherwise 'bad'. Such a conception is recommended by two of the most sustained conceptual investigations into ideology, by Malcolm Hamilton (1987) and John Gerring (1997), and has been favoured by many other leading theorists (Freeden 1996; van Dijk 1998: 11–12; Jost 2006; Knight 2006). Following their advice, I advocate the use of the following definition (closely resembling Hamilton's):

A political ideology is a distinctive overarching system of normative and/or reputedly factual ideas, typically shared by members of groups or organizations, which shapes their understandings of their political world and guides their political behaviour.

This definition is not so broad that *all* sets of ideas become indistinguishably ideological, but it rejects assertions (by politicians or political theorists) that certain political worldviews are 'beyond ideology' or 'not ideological but pragmatic' (see also Bell 1960; Freeden 2005a; Coote 2014). Such claims frequently suggest exceptionalism, cryptonormativity and an attempt at partisan and contestable political tactics rather than sound conceptual distinctions (Žižek 1994b; Freeden 2005a; Worsnip 2015). In this broad and non-pejorative conception, ideologies denote whatever distinctive idea systems people do in fact use to think about politics. No human being can engage in some kind of perfectly rational disembodied reflection about politics that simply 'sees the world as it is' uninfluenced by prior thinking. Instead, every individual's political thinking occurs via networks of values, meanings, narratives, theories, assumptions, concepts, expectations, exemplars, past experiences, images, stereotypes and beliefs about matters of fact already existing in their mind (Geertz 1964; Berger and Luckmann 1967; Tversky and Kahneman 1974; Wittgenstein 2001; Baurmann 2007). These networks of ideas vary, at least somewhat, from person to person, group to group and society to society, which is what makes them important objects of study. In this conception, ideology is not reprehensible, but inescapable. As Aletta Norval (2000: 316) writes: 'It is this emphasis on the ubiquity of ideology ... that is at the heart of contemporary approaches to the question of ideology.'

This broad and non-pejorative conception stands in contrast to more 'negative' or 'critical' conceptions that have been historically prominent in the study of ideology, especially in Marxist theory, but are increasingly unpopular (van Dijk 1998: 3; Leader Maynard and Mildenberger 2016). Such negative conceptions vary in the pejorative connotations they attach to ideology – ideologies might be defined as 'false consciousness', or oppression-legitimating systems, or especially fanatical or dogmatic forms of belief, or some other unfavourable mode of thought. Advocates of such conceptions of ideology frequently argued that such connotations are essential for the concept of ideology to retain any critical power and normative relevance (Larrain 1979: 15, 52, 118; Thompson 1984: 4, 12, 82; Boudon 1989: 24–30; Rosen 2000: 393–5). But this argument has consistently been offered as a non-sequitur. There is no reason why a concept needs to be *defined* pejoratively in order to be *useful* for critical or otherwise normatively evaluative work (Larrain 1979: 77; McLellan 1995: 23; Freeden 2005a: 262; Steger 2008: 4–5). As Teun van Dijk (1998: 11) argues

Does [the] more general conception of ideology take away the critical edge of the enterprise, as is sometimes suggested, or prevent ideological critique? Of course it does not. No more than that the use of the general concept of 'power' precludes a critical analysis of power *abuse*, as well as solidarity with the forms of counter-power we call resistance.

What *is* lost with a broad and non-pejorative conception of ideology is the ability to critique something *simply by labelling it ideology*. But this sort of terminological smearing is not the limit of normative critique, nor a persuasive form of it. And a key problem with pejorative conceptions of ideology is that they tend to encourage a prejudicial form of analysis. It is notable that some of the major non-Marxist figures to deploy them were, ironically, anti-Communist scholars during the Cold War. For these figures, the concept of ideology denoted 'extremist', 'totalitarian' and 'anti-modern' views outside the mainstream of Western politics. Such an understanding amounted, as Terry Eagleton (1991: 4) aptly caricatures, to the claim 'that the Soviet Union is in the grip of ideology while the United States sees things as they really are'. In these examples and others, pejorative definitions conceptually encode the sorts of normative commitments political theory is intended to render explicit and subject to interrogation and reflection.

By contrast, broad and non-pejorative conceptions allow us to conduct a more open-minded and rigorous form of analysis where, as Humphrey (2005: 237) puts it, 'ideological forms are not presupposed but emerge through careful empirical analysis of thought instantiations.' And they

also allow us to avoid high levels of fragmentation in scholarly understandings of ideology, by keeping the master concept inclusive, but
leaving room for the identification of subtypes of ideology that might be
dogmatic, irrational and so forth.

We should therefore maintain a distinction drawn by Freeden (1996:
27–8, 133; 2013b: 52–3) between *ideological analysis* (the study of real-
world ideologies) and *ideologizing* (the construction of ideologies, which
occurs partly through political theory). These two activities are always
entangled. Since we all think about politics under the influence of our
various respective ideologies, there may be no *completely* neutral social
science or analytical philosophy. But it is vital to recognize a difference
between the construction of our own concepts and normative principles,
and the efforts to find out what are or were the extant concepts and
normative principles (and other ideas) of others (Weber 2009: 145–6).
This chapter explains how to do the latter in ways that inform, support or
otherwise take a central role in the former.

I make three further remarks about the meaning of ideology. First,
**an important distinction should be drawn between what we
might call *personal ideologies*, by which I mean the particular
ideologies of individual people, and *shared ideologies*, that
describe the systems of ideas held in common by groups.**
Ideologies ultimately exist in minds (though they have emergent social
aspects too), and groups do not truly have minds, so imputing ideologies to groups represents something of a metaphorical abstraction,
though a benign and often productive one (Thagard 2010). Every
member of a group inevitably has slightly distinct ways of thinking –
slightly different personal ideologies. But scholars can and usually do
talk of shared ideologies to make generalizations about important
similarities between the personal ideologies of individuals, and to
draw attention to emergent properties of ideologies as they become
consciously identified in social discourse and embedded in institutions
and practices. There is nothing mysterious about this in and of itself
(though, of course, such generalizations can be formulated erro-
neously), and a productive analogy can be drawn with the way we
talk about languages. Just as every 'conservative' thinks in a somewhat
different way, so every speaker of 'Spanish' or 'Urdu' will speak in
a unique, idiosyncratic manner. But in both scholarly and lay talk, we
can productively talk about the language they speak in common, in
a way that generalizes about key similarities without denying individual variation (van Dijk 1998: 30). So too with ideology. And like
languages, the ideologies we talk about can involve varying levels of
generalization – from low (Al Qaeda leadership ideology, IMF

neoliberalism) to medium (Rawlsian liberalism, Stalinism) to high (socialism, conservatism). **Labelling ideological subtypes in this way is useful for retaining conceptual precision in the sorts of ideologies we are talking about.**

Second, **it is important to appreciate that ideologies are substantively rich phenomena.** It is common to talk about ideologies as defined by certain core concepts, values, political ambitions or dominant narratives. But ideologies are built from all of these and a vast array of other sorts of idea or idea cluster: identities, myths, memories, stereotypes, epistemic rules, beliefs about matters of fact, rhetorical repertoires, strategic preferences, exemplars, expectations, horizons of possibility, images, lived experiences and so forth. Human beings differ in their thinking on all of these, often in important ways that exert a powerful effect over their broader thinking and behaviour. By thinking of ideologies as complex networks of a vast array of notions, one can engage seriously with the idiosyncratic forms of thinking that characterize particular individuals and groups in the real world.

Third, while I advocate a somewhat 'cognitive' understanding of ideologies, **it is vital to recognize the inextricable relationship between ideology and discourse** (van Dijk 2013). Since it is arduous and ineffective to invent new ways of talking from scratch on every issue, ideologies are characterized by certain ways of talking, certain rhetorical repertoires and certain arguments and justifications. These are picked up and reused by individuals to engage in argument, legitimation, persuasion, sophistry and so forth. And individuals' ideologies are, in turn, shaped by the discourse of themselves and others – as new ideas are encountered in communication, engaged with and rejected or internalized. Many ideologies are also represented socially in discourse, picking up social meanings and connotations, and they may inhabit social movements and become embedded in social institutions and groups through discourses and practices (van Dijk 1998: ch. 3). Ideological analysis is thus inevitably concerned with not just how people think, but also how they talk and act.

3   Why Should Normative Political Theorists Use Ideological Analysis?

In this section I provide four main reasons to think that ideological analysis can be of deep relevance to the kind of normative political theory that is a key focus of this volume.

3.1   Evaluating Institutions and Ideologies

Perhaps most obviously, ideologies may be essential components of the operation or legitimation of various institutions and social processes that are problematic (or progressive) from a normative political theory standpoint. Put simply, ideologies have major social and political effects, and are involved in the use of social and political power. There are two key ways in which ideological analysis supports political theory in grappling with such effects.

First, **ideological analysis allows us to diagnose the normative failings of existing *political institutions* by illustrating the problematic ideologies they generate** (or, conversely, identify normatively beneficial aspects of institutions by showing the beneficial ideologies they generate). For example, diagnoses of the normative dangers of unregulated private media in emerging democracies should examine the way in which such media tend to produce nationalistic and racist political discourses (Price 2000; Mann 2005). Similarly, assessments of the value of two-party over multi-party electoral systems should consider how the former may narrow the ideological landscape of society (which could be seen as good or bad), encouraging people to coalesce into just two major ideological camps, but also incentivizing movement towards 'centrist' and away from 'extremist' ideological positions (Sartori 1976: 178–9; Evans 2002). Analysing how such outcomes are created, why they might be normatively problematic or desirable, and the normative permissibility (and efficacy) of potential political responses, will all rest on ideological analysis.

Second, **ideological analysis allows us to critique particular *ideologies* by illustrating the flawed socio-political institutions they generate or sustain** (or, conversely, identify strengths of particular ideologies by highlighting their role in desirable socio-political arrangements). For example, free-market ideologies may reproduce idealized understandings of property and markets that efface awareness of racial hierarchies in the real-world economic system (Mills 1999; Shelby 2003). But this suggestion relies on empirical claims about the impact certain ideological notions have on political thinking and, thereby, on economic and political behaviour. Such ideological analysis may include interrogation and critique of certain concepts or ideas used by political thinkers and actors (see Olsthoorn's chapter in this volume). This may reveal historically changing connotations and assumptions that are involved in particular speech acts, and shed light on the impact of different interpretations of different concepts on political outcomes (Ball et al. 1989: ix; Freeden 1996: 100–17; Skinner 2002b: 114–21, 158–74). Again, all such critique of existing systems of political thought and talk needs to be grounded in ideological analysis.

Frequently, the ideological notions that produce institutions or practices, and the ideological notions those institutions or practices produce, are simultaneously relevant. For example, evaluations of the policy of racial profiling might be concerned with the way its political rationale relies on crude racial constructs and ignorance of structural causes of crimes, *and* with how it encourages racist stereotypes of certain ethnic groups as having a propensity to criminality (Shelby 2003: 175–6). Evaluations of fee-paying schools might be concerned both with the way they entrench misconceptions of the added educational value such schools generate (if much of their superior performance is simply because they attract already high-performing students) *and* with how such misconceptions legitimate and sustain support for private schools (Swift 2003: 21–3). Most obviously, Marxist and post-Marxist traditions of normative theory have long engaged in analysis of both how ideology serves to legitimate domination, political exclusion and various other forms of political injustice *and* the way those practices reproduce the legitimating ideology (Žižek 1994b; Laclau 2007). Given the vital role ideology continues to play in the legitimation and operation of a panoply of leading political and social institutions, this form of ideological analysis (shorn of implications that ideology is always malign) ought to feature more extensively across contemporary normative political theory.

More generally, normative evaluation of the *general role of ideologies* in political life is central to many questions in political theory. Ideological diversity is a critical ingredient of a free society, and the fact that human political thought and behaviour occurs under the influence of distinctive ideologies is non-contingent and inescapable. All political theory – ideal and non-ideal alike – therefore needs to grapple with this general role of ideology. The ideological nature of human beings may pose obstacles to certain accounts of rational citizenship, deliberation in democratic discourse, solidarity in a civic community, neutrality in state institutions and fair distribution of political, communicative, epistemic and material resources. Ideological analysis is therefore relevant to the comparative normative evaluation of theories and institutions with respect to all these questions.

3.2   *Assessing Political Theory's Principles in Real-World Contexts*

The first reason for thinking that ideological analysis is relevant to political theory highlights the relevance of ideology to all sorts of normative political theorizing. But there is a further reason to think ideological analysis important to the degree that political theory moves away from ideal-type theorizing and becomes 'non-ideal' (Valentini 2012) or 'realist' (Galston 2010). In such situations, **ideological analysis is needed to assess the likely real-world effects of certain moral or political principles in practice,** and consequently their viability and normative attractiveness. Such forms of non-ideal normative political theory are concerned not just with reflection on moral rightness in some 'ultimate' sense, but the actual application of political theory to the world, and the design of political prescriptions and norms to guide policy. How real-world agents – perceiving, thinking and acting under the influence of real-world ideologies – would actually operationalize normative principles is thus a key question. As Jennifer Welsh (2010: 424) notes: 'principles, when adopted, always take on a life of their own. It is difficult to control their meaning, or to avoid their misuse.' Predicting how this 'life of their own' will unfold ought to be a critical component of the assessment of normative principles at the non-ideal level.

Ideological analysis supports these sorts of non-ideal and realist assessments in four ways. First, it may provide *contextual knowledge about actually existing ideologies in particular circumstances.* Failure to analyse the nature and power of these extant ideologies can undermine normative theorizing about the right way to approach injustice. For example, a range of left-wing terrorist groups in the 1970s and 1980s believed that a few symbolic acts of violence would expose the fragility of the capitalist order and inspire a mass revolution, and acted accordingly (Tsintsadze-Maass and Maass 2014). This legitimation of deadly political violence involved a wildly naïve failure to appreciate the power and breadth and depth of internalization of liberal, free-market ideologies in modern Western societies. A parallel problem might be thought to exist in neoconservative or neoliberal theories of why military intervention in countries to spread democracy should be legitimate. Such theories carry many flaws, but these include a fundamental blindness to the complex ideological terrain of target states, and the radicalizing ideological consequences of militarized action on both its victims and on the interveners themselves (Doris and Murphy 2007; McCauley and Moskalenko 2011). The problem is no less salient for other political strategies – one needs to know the ideological context of a proposed policy to predict the normatively relevant consequences. Normative political theorists have not been completely blind to this. Members of the International Commission on Intervention and State Sovereignty (ICISS), for example, advanced the international norm of a 'responsibility to protect' in 2001 partly in the belief that this concept would do a better job than the previous concept of 'humanitarian intervention' at reconciling competing attitudes and commitments in the extant ideologies of Western democracies, developing world states and authoritarian great powers (Evans 2011). This, it was hoped, would be more efficacious in giving 'the responsibility to protect' the force and political traction needed to save lives.

Second, ideological analysis may *reveal general tendencies in political thinking* – whether rooted in basic psychological propensities with roots in human nature, cultural dispositions or something else – which are critical in foreseeing how political ideas will play out in practice. For example, leading political psychology research on ideology demonstrates strong human tendencies towards 'system justification' and 'just-world thinking' (a predisposition to rationalize the existing political system and its consequences as just). This research also shows that humans have a preference for epistemic satisfaction, i.e. achieving a set of beliefs that seem satisfying for a range of underlying psychological motives, rather than epistemic optimization, i.e. making sure that one is actually right (Furnham 2003; Jost and Hunyady 2005). This is highly relevant for non-ideal political theory, since it problematizes any assumptions that most individuals will respond to policies as rational, contemplative actors, and reveals key psychological supports for injustice and barriers to political and social reform. Again, political thinkers have not completely eschewed this line of theorizing. John Stuart Mill's (2008) defence of free speech rested fundamentally on empirical assumptions about how political thinking evolved, progressively, in a society, and about how false or oppressive ideological notions could best be countered given the way human thinking and discourse worked. But the validity of such an account rests on claims about these real-world dynamics of ideological change – necessitating ideological analysis.

Third, partly but not solely through the first two ways, ideological analysis may provide the *methods and skills for reflecting on how a certain normative system or prescription will play out in the political thinking of real-world actors* – focusing not on logical implications of arguments and claims under rigorous philosophical analysis, but the likely forms of reasoning, assumptions and attitudes such arguments and claims might encourage in actual political practice by citizens and elites. Once again, examples of such an approach already exist. Isaiah Berlin's famous (1969) critique of 'positive liberty' did not necessarily deny any normative attractiveness to that notion in the abstract. Many of Berlin's concerns lay instead with the attitudes and assumptions positive liberty subtly encouraged, and the sorts of pernicious political programmes it could be mobilized to legitimate. In the sense I mean it here, Berlin's political theory involved a form of ideological analysis: imagining how a concept would operate in 'actual political thinking' (Freeden 2008: 197).

Fourth and finally, a range of *context-specific questions* for political theory may also arise at the non-ideal/realist level for which ideological analysis is particularly relevant (see also the chapters by Jubb and by Schmidtz in this volume). How, for example, should we know what political institutions or policies to implement in a state formerly under an ideological monopoly but now emerging into competitive party politics? Or in a society increasingly polarized across apparently irreconcilable ideological divisions? Or in a state whose unity and future stands in question in the face of nationalistic ideological groups? Or in a context where radicalizing violent ideologies appear to thrive through institutions long thought essential to free speech? To grapple with such questions in detail, political theorists need a developed understanding of how ideologies operate in these various contexts.

In all such instances, particular normative concepts or principles are being advanced in non-ideal theory because of assessments of extant ideologies, the ideological tendencies of human beings in general, how particular normative claims would work in practice as ideology or the specific ideological dynamics of real-world problems. Yet whilst I have noted that such lines of theorizing are more common than is perhaps consciously appreciated, they are often grounded on speculation by political theorists rather than rigorous, empirically grounded ideological analysis. Consider, for example, Raymond Geuss's (2003: 285–6) interesting but entirely unsubstantiated claim that Rawlsian political theory underpinned neoliberal economic policies and a rise in global inequality in the 1970s and 1980s. This could be investigated through ideological analysis. Instead, Geuss bases his argument on the mere correlation of Rawls being influential in American universities with rising inequality – a classically invalid causal inference (see also Sagar 2014). Even ICISS, Mill and Berlin, though they do rest their arguments on some sort of ideological analysis, do not deploy any rigorous or developed methodology for doing this. Consequently their conclusions are contentious: it is not clear that R2P has successfully evaded the ideological connotations of humanitarian intervention (Chandler 2004), substantial evidence exists against Mill's theories of the epistemic benefits of free speech (Edelman 1977; Vigna and Gentzkow 2010; Ipsos MORI 2014), and it is questionable whether Berlin's distinction between negative and positive liberty effectively maps onto real-world divergences in actual political thinking (see also Skinner 2002a: 238–9; Nelson 2005). More generally, normative political theorists interested in non-ideal or realist approaches have not engaged in detail with ideological analysis (Freeden 2012).

So, done in a sophisticated manner, ideological analysis could increase the solidity of the empirical assumptions on which non-ideal and realist political theory arguments rest. It could even provide empirical evidence of how particular normative concepts or principles *have* played out in practice in the past. Ideological analysis might reveal, for example, how notions of liberal toleration can encourage unintended belief in moral relativism, how claims about inheritance rights can undermine awareness of inequality in the initial distribution of resources or how arguments that the targeting of 'human shields' is permissible can encourage a cognitive slippery slope in the perception of when violence against civilians is legitimate. None of these effects definitively establishes the unacceptability of the normative beliefs or claims in question. But, *if they exist*, they may be considered relevant marks against such beliefs or claims. This form of ideological analysis of normative concepts and principles might be particularly crucial to any form of 'critical' political theory (in the broadest sense) that seeks to expose the unintended justificatory power of various normative concepts and principles.

3.3   Exposing Ideological Assumptions behind Arguments in Political Theory

Ideological analysis also **allows an interrogation of the validity of normative arguments in and of themselves by exposing their background ideological assumptions.** Sophisticated ideological analysis involves seeking out the full range of contextual, idiosyncratic notions within which individual claims are embedded, which shapes their specific meaning, and which explains their plausibility to those espousing them. Normative political theorists are very used to seeking out the principles and values that logically precede certain claims, but these may not be the only sorts of ideas or the only form of support that ideological notions lend to an argument. Revealing the beliefs about matters of fact, the narratives, the familiar stereotypes, the particular interpretations of concepts and so forth connected to a certain argument may be vital for both (a) understanding why another political theorist (including a historical thinker) considers that argument plausible, and (b) thoroughly assessing the argument's defensibility.

Perhaps the most important use of this mode of ideological analysis is that which serves to maximize a theorist's own self-critical rigour – subjecting their own political theory to ideological analysis, to unpack not just the analytical assumptions on which the argument formally rests, but the other attached notions that might explain the moral intuitions behind key claims. Ideological analysis might, for example, expose particularistic commitments rooted in certain moral worldviews, cultural perspectives or historical epochs that are wrongly presumed to reflect universal moral assumptions (which is not to presume that there can never be such universals, just that particularistic beliefs can often masquerade as them). Political theorists and philosophers are sophisticated thinkers, but not without their own ideological environments and standpoints, nor are they immune to the well-researched psychological tendencies like just-world thinking or consistency bias mentioned earlier. Rigorous political theory should critically examine those environments, standpoints and possible tendencies in analysing claims by political theorists themselves.

3.4   Encouraging Creative Political Theory

Finally, ideological analysis can be a powerful method for spurring creativity in formulating new ideas, concepts and arguments. I gently suggest that many sections of normative political theory – whilst valuable and sophisticated – are not as innovative as they could be, taking the form of seemingly interminable debates over a narrow set of basic questions between a narrow set of well-established standpoints. **Ideological analysis should be used to enable a rigorous engagement with the thought systems of other periods in history, and other cultures in our present** (see the chapter by Ackerly and Bajpai in this volume). In doing this we might discover new concepts, ideas and claims that open up unexplored political-theoretic spaces (though it is important to avoid a 'touristic' approach, where ideas seem alluringly exotic but are used anachronistically and without real understanding). When one considers all the possible (and historically existing) ideological positions that can be generated, it should be clear that contemporary political theory in predominantly Western academic institutions occupies only a small portion of the ideological universe of possibilities. Many of the potential normative positions may be unexplored for good reason – being patently incoherent, radically counterintuitive or reprehensible in light of moral commitments that we are loath to part from. But it is unlikely that contemporary political theory exhausts the plausible normative realm. The classic example of a form of such ideological analysis yielding notions of normative interest concerns 'republican liberty', which has frequently – from the nineteenth-century writings of Benjamin Constant to the contemporary work of Quentin Skinner – been rooted in an ideological excavation of earlier systems of political thought (Constant 1988; Skinner 1998). And ideological analysis may not only support such projects through the investigation of existing but temporally or culturally distant ideologies. It may also support innovative normative political theory by allowing us to schematize and map out *potential* normative positions, irrespective of whether these have been actually espoused by historical or contemporary cultures (Freeden 2013a: 118).

3.5   Summary: The Need for Ideological Analysis in Normative Political Theory

These four uses of ideological analysis suggest that **scholars doing normative political theory should take ideological analysis seriously**. This point needs wider recognition, since all four will be increasingly important enterprises as the discipline looks ahead to the rest of the twenty-first century, for two reasons. First, many of these uses of ideological analysis for normative political theory assume that one is engaging in a fairly non-ideal, empirically engaged and perhaps applied project, or at least serve that sort of political theory in more obvious ways than they serve ideal theory. Such forms of non-ideal political theory are increasingly popular, creating an increasing need for rigorous ideological analysis. This should not, though, be taken to marginalize ideal theory or obscure how my first, third and fourth uses for ideological analysis all could (and should) be deployed in ideal political theory.

Second, in the remainder of this century, political theory is inevitably going to become more internationalized and globally integrated, with deeper engagement between Western intellectual traditions and those from the many other parts of humanity's cultural heritage. This is going to be a challenging but intellectually vital process. Cross-cultural fertilization in political theory will expose divergences on issues and assumptions long thought settled within particular academies and paradigms. And it will force scholars from all nations to encounter claims, arguments, theories and political problems that they struggle to understand on a superficial examination, rooted as they are in assumptions, beliefs, ways of reasoning and contexts unfamiliar to the scholars' own ideological positions. For such engagement to be productive rather than lead to radical misunderstanding and bemusement, political theorists on both sides of cultural, ideological and theoretical divides are going to have to get better at ideological analysis, especially in my second and third senses: to properly interpret, interrogate and engage with each other's positions, and evaluate the (possibly varying) applicability of certain normative concepts and principles to diverse ideological contexts.

4   How to Do Ideological Analysis

As I noted in my introduction, a problematic feature of the developing field of ideological analysis is that work on ideology remains very fragmented across disciplines. Since these different disciplines generally display contrasting strengths and weaknesses, I suggest that if we are to get to grips with ideology, **it is vital to deploy an integrative approach** (the best cross-disciplinary compendium is provided by Freeden et al. 2013). Intellectual historians and political theorists have generated sophisticated methods for examining and conceptualizing the *content* of ideology. Political psychologists and sociologists have conducted extensive research on some of the *causes* of ideological attachment – why people internalize the ideological positions they do. Political scientists and discourse theorists, meanwhile, have studied extensively the *effects* of ideology on behaviour. Yet all three of these aspects of ideology are relevant for political theorists.

4.1   Uncovering Ideological Content

Studying ideology is fundamentally about examining how actual people think. As such, to say anything of consequence about ideology, **we need to find out something about the actual *contents* of the ideology in question**. Too often, scholars studying ideology eschew this task. Instead they presume that ideological content is familiar and uncomplicated, by reducing it to a label, or a point on a crude dimension – such as the seven-point scale from 'Extremely Conservative' to 'Extremely Liberal' used in US election surveys – which is often presumed to self-evidently denote a set of policy preferences, or normative standpoints, or value attitudes. This might be defensible for certain limited forms of correlational analysis in political science, but it is of little use to normative political theory (and most other fields). Consequently, **effective ideological analysis requires that researchers deploy methods that actually collect rich data on, and engage seriously with, real-world political thinking** (Freeden 2013b).

I suggest that there are four primary methods of collecting such data: (i) *behavioural inference* – reaching conclusions about individuals' ideologies in light of the ways they behave; (ii) *textual analysis* – examining ideas expressed in *any* forms of communication, including non-verbal works, which exist independently of the analyst; (iii) *inquiry* – the attempt to directly solicit ideas or beliefs out of individuals through questioning – including qualitative methods like interviewing and quantitative methods like surveying; and (iv) *neuroscientific methods* – the study of neurological processes in an individual's brain and wider nervous system. I will concentrate on inquiry and textual analysis, the two methods likely to be most useful for political theorists interested in real-world ideologies.

Defensible ideological analysis rests on interpreting texts and responses to inquiries rigorously and accurately – drawing plausible conclusions about individuals' thinking from the data contained therein, including non-verbal instances of communication. The deep methodology of this practice is the subject of an extensive literature and considerable debate in the discipline of hermeneutics and broader study of interpretation. It is beyond my capacity to reproduce that literature here (but see Blau's chapter in this volume, as well as Skinner 2002b; Yanow and Schwartz-Shea 2006; Wodak and Meyer 2009; Fairclough 2010). Instead I wish to list some key practical pointers on how to interpret data in order to build pictures of the ideologies of certain individuals or groups.

The most important pointer in this respect is that to generate reliable accounts of an ideology, **researchers need to avoid the cardinal hermeneutic sin of *acontextualism*.** I use this label to refer to the general tendency to assume that individuals, across cultures, spaces and times, generally hold a set of basic perceptions, beliefs, values and interests pretty close to that of the analyst, or the analyst's society (Boudon 1989: 74–80, 95–6; Skinner 2002b). The contrary fact that individuals actually hold highly diverse sets of such beliefs doesn't imply that individuals are wildly irrational, or deny that there are also commonalities in the way individuals think. But as Skinner points out: 'what is rational to believe depends in large measure on the nature of our other beliefs' and as a result, we should 'interpret specific beliefs by placing them in the context of other beliefs [and] interpret systems of belief by placing them in wider intellectual frameworks' (Skinner 2002b: 4–5). This includes asking what it is feasible to assume individuals were expressing and thinking given the intellectual resources and dominant ideological environment in which they were writing/speaking (Skinner 1974: 283, 289; Baurmann 2007).

Matters are further complicated, however, by the possibility that individuals may be engaging in dissimulation, irony, rhetoric or some other form of speech that does not sincerely reflect their views. Hence the importance of attending to not just what bearers of ideology are *saying* but what they appear to be *doing* – e.g. lobbying for support, trying to persuade, satirizing another, making the interviewer happy, saying what they 'ought' to, etc. (Tully 1983: 490–4; Skinner 2002b: 2–4; George and Bennett 2005: 99–108). **Ideological analysts must attend to the possible strategic purposes of a particular text or expression and to the intended audience.**

The obvious implication of contextualism is that ideological analysis rests in large part on gathering considerable information on the context of the ideology in question. This might be done through examining relevant historical or cultural studies, through absorbing as much of the discourse produced by the individual or group we are studying as possible, through studying primary data (i.e. other cultural products and discourse fragments) from the relevant context and so forth. The burden here could easily become unmanageable for a normative political theorist who is not primarily an ideological analyst, but interested in ideological analysis for the four reasons I listed in Section 2. But a more modest contextualism is possible, where we **take seriously underlying differences in the cultural and political environment of those we are studying and ourselves, and are aware of the necessarily tentative nature of interpretations of the thinking of others in light of uncertainty about their broader ideological assumptions derived from their social context.**

With such a hermeneutic sensitivity, researchers might proceed by **asking a series of structured questions about the ideological data (texts or interview responses) they are able to gather.** Exactly what questions researchers ask will relate to their objectives, but I shall propose a possible core list as a starting point. The speakers (or authors) being studied might be institutions, movements, political parties or other group entities, as well as specific individuals, but we should still ask **who are the actual specific individuals who have authored apparent statements of group entities as a whole, and how ideologically heterogeneous might the broader group be.**

1) What has the speaker seemed to say, and what does he or she seem to be doing in saying this?
2) What are the concepts and terms that make up the speaker's expressions, and what are the most plausible meanings of those concepts and terms the speaker would attach to them? (In interview methods, such meanings might be solicited by further questioning.)
3) What beliefs, arguments or other ideas do these concepts and terms together seem to express?
4) Are there reasons to believe that the speaker does not sincerely hold those beliefs/arguments or other ideas? On all available evidence, does it seem fair (it will never be certain) to assume that these reflect the speaker's own views? If not, why are they being said – and what might this tell us, if not about the speaker's own ideology, about the broader ideologies of others in the context in which he or she is speaking?
5) What possible ideas, not explicitly expressed by the speaker, (a) might lend comprehensibility and consonance to his or her overall ideological system and (b) might there be good reasons to believe the speaker held consciously or unconsciously?

6) What appears to be the *ideological structure* of the speaker's ideas? By this I mean the relationships between the various ideas – relationships that might be logical (presupposition, inference, entailment, etc.), semantic (connotation, inclusion, exclusion, clarification, is a subset of), emotional (attraction, antipathy, felt association), causal (producing, requiring, precluding, encouraging) or something else?

By asking these questions, a researcher can start to put together a picture of the system of ideas that constitutes an individual's ideology, *or* the part of his or her ideology relating to some particular defined question or issue. That picture might be rendered in detailed, prose description, it might be conceptualized dimensionally on a single dimension or multidimensional space (although, as I have suggested, this may oversimplify ideological content too heavily for the political theorists) or it might be visualized through a form of concept mapping, such as the Cognitive-Affective Mapping methodology developed by Paul Thagard and colleagues at the University of Waterloo (Thagard 2012). The reliability of this picture rests on the open-mindedness, free exploration and interpretive honesty of the researcher. It is all too easy for scholars, superficially deploying appropriate data collection methods, considering context, and asking the right sorts of interpretive questions, to 'see what they want to see'. Ideological analysis must **always attend to this danger of contrived, biased analysis, explicitly consider alternative interpretations and explain why they have been rejected.**

4.2   Explaining Ideological Attachment

I already mentioned the strong tendency for individuals to engage in system justification and just-world thinking: to adopt the default assumption that outcomes are fair, with individuals deserving what they get, even when evidence for this is lacking (Jost et al. 2003; Jost and Hunyady 2005). That this is often a default assumption obviously doesn't mean it is always felt – perceptions of unfairness and injustice are fundamental and widespread in human thinking. But it is just one of the pieces of evidence that shows how ideological belief formation is driven by a broad range of underlying *psychological motives* and *social processes* (both of which are deeply interrelated). Political theorists may frequently be concerned with the role of such psychological and social causes of ideology in their analysis.

   Key psychological motives driving belief formation include:
   (i) *epistemic motives* – sincere concerns with working out what is true;

(ii) *cognitive dissonance minimization* (also known as *consistency bias*) – a desire to maintain consonance between one's beliefs, and beliefs and actions, even when this involves adopting beliefs not supported by evidence;

(iii) *self-esteem motives* – the need for a sense of self-worth, social standing, superiority, belonging, recognition and life purpose;

(iv) *cognitive efficiency concerns* – the drive to avoid overly burdensome mental activities;

(v) *comprehensibility motives* – the need to find the world comprehensible, determinate and not worryingly uncertain;

(vi) *anxiety suppression* – for example, about death, ethical propriety, sexual status, the wrongness of past decisions and commitments and so forth.

This is not a comprehensive list but highlights some of the key findings in psychological research that could be of relevance in considering how political ideologies form (see, in general: Tversky and Kahneman 1974; Boudon 1989; Pinker 1998; Boudon 1999; Jost and Major 2001; Jost et al. 2009b; Kahneman 2012; Varki and Brower 2013).

Key social processes driving belief formation include:

(i) *ideational resources* – the availability of ideas, concepts or frameworks of reasoning in the discourses accessible to the individual;

(ii) *discursive saturation* – the saturation of ideas into discourse within the particular social networks or media environments in which the individual is embedded, such that those ideas appear to be 'common sense';

(iii) *epistemic dependence* – where an individual relies on certain epistemic authorities that appear credible (or that the individual lacks more credible alternatives to) for information that is difficult for them to personally verify;

(iv) *groupthink* – the tendency of individuals to adopt the beliefs, or at least the *avowed* beliefs, of the majority around them;

(v) *ideological incentivization* – the attachment of desirable material or symbolic outcomes to the adoption of a belief, or at least the *avowed* adoption of a belief;

(vi) *rhetorical presentation* – the skilful deployment of rhetorical devices and emotional appeals in communication that encourage internalization of certain ideas.

Again, this list is a tentative summary of major themes in existing research, rather than a comprehensive list (see in general: Berger and Luckmann 1967; Hardwig 1985; Boudon 1989; Simonds 1989; Fairclough 2001; Skinner 2002b; Baurmann 2007; Rydgren 2009).

These psychological and social processes that shape ideological attachment should help political theorists construct plausible pictures of the ideologies of real-world individuals, explain a wide range of just and unjust states of affairs, and assess the viability of certain political prescriptions and strategies. They are at the root of why certain sorts of legitimating practices are effective, certain key realities denied, certain human consequences of actions or policies ignored. That is not to suggest that such processes are immutable, universal or constant across individuals and societies – on the contrary, they vary and might themselves be targets of political reform by prescriptive theory. But this is just another reason to believe that political theorists should attempt to understand and analyse them.

4.3   Analysing the Effects of Ideologies

But constructing an accurate understanding of extant ideologies, and the psychological and social processes that encourage them, is unlikely to be the only activity of interest to the political theorist. **Ideological analysis should then involve an examination of** *what political and social effects these ideologies have.*

Ideologies provide cognitively necessary repertoires for *thinking* and socially comprehensible repertoires for *talking:* they enable, constrain and shape political thought and discourse. They *constitute individuals' own internalized thinking* about subjects and provide them with ideas, arguments, concepts and claims to *instrumentally use* (for a range of sincere or strategic purposes) in communication with others. The broadest effect of ideology, via both these avenues, is to provide individuals and groups with the intellectual resources used to think and talk about that world, thereby constructing their understanding of social reality (Searle 1995; Tileagă 2007: 722; Thagard 2012: 51–2). But in particular, ideologies shape individuals' conceptions of what is desirable, and what is permissible – as I term it, they *motivate* and *legitimate* certain forms of action, including the establishment and maintenance of institutions and other political arrangements.

Unpacking these effects comprehensively would take at least a book. Aiming only to generate ideas and focusing attention for researchers, I shall provide a fairly ad hoc list of particularly significant sorts of beliefs that are generated by and constitute ideologies. Ideologies contain:

(i) Notions of the *proper members of a society or group,* and conceptualizations of the borders between those proper members and others, between the in-group and the out-group. In particular, ideologies shape notions of *differential obligations owed to different categories of person* (Tajfel 1974; Opotow 1990; Huddy 2001; Tileagă 2007; Hammack 2008).

(ii) Latent assumptions or explicit judgements regarding the *prototypical, expected and proper behaviour* or characteristics of members of a society or group. In particular, ideologies determine the characteristics/attitudes/behaviour to which praise, glory and status, on the one hand, and shame, disempowerment and exclusion, on the other, are attached (Huddy 2001: 133–7, 143–5; Finlayson 2012).

(iii) Specification of *key objectives, ends and anticipated futures* towards which a society or group is aiming, and programmes of collective action for getting there (Mullins 1972: 510).

(iv) Assertion of *values* and objects, perhaps of a quasi-sacred or truly sacred nature, to which individuals and groups feel deep emotional attachment (Atran and Axelrod 2008).

(v) Identification of *key problems, threats, challenges or obstacles* to its objectives and ends that a society or group faces (van Dijk 1998: 66).

(vi) Conceptions of the relevant *'field of possibilities'* – the set of policies, strategies or institutional arrangements that are feasible, imaginable or otherwise warrant consideration. What is excluded from this field of possibilities (presented as impossible, infeasible, futile, idealistic, utopian, etc.) may be as important as what is included (Foucault 1982: 789–92; Crawford 2002: 20).

(vii) Specific *normative prohibitions and normative obligations*, for individuals, for collective actors or institutions and for a society at large (Crawford 2002; Van Dijk 2013: 74–7).

(viii) *Characterizations, whether impressionistic or detailed, of rival groups and competitors*, within or without a polity, and their objectives, characteristics, own ideologies and current activities (Shenhav 2006; Hammack 2008).

(ix) Particular *beliefs about matters of fact*, whether true or false, whether inchoate and vague or specific and dense, whether rooted in narratives and imagery or statistics and apparent evidence (Hochschild 2001).

(x) Epistemological or ontological *'meta-beliefs'* about how to determine what one should believe, for example, by affirming empirical, exegetical, faith-based or intuitionist epistemic rules (Crawford 2002: 19).

Through different configurations of such ideas, ideologies define the key political differences between individuals and groups, as well as the commonalities and unquestioned common sense on which many political arrangements rest. Critically, **political theorists must recognize that the ideas in question are often generated only unconsciously or semi-consciously, involve both explicit 'beliefs' and more latent** 'aliefs' (Gendler 2008) and might be produced by subtle rhetorical devices and discursive techniques – the classic focus of critical theorists and discourse analysts. For example, 'Critical Discourse Analysts' are interested in processes like *nominalization*, the way in which the consistent rendering of social events as nouns ('the recession', 'urban decay', 'homelessness', 'suppression of the protests') disguises the human agency responsible for such events, instead presenting them as natural, agentless, happenings or default features of the world (Billig 2008). Interrogating such discursive devices and techniques can be important to analysing how the ideas that make up ideologies are successfully disseminated, and why they lead to certain outcomes.

Via such ideas, ideologies critically shape the decision-making and the patterns of life of whole societies and particular political actors by shaping what appears desirable and legitimate – whether amongst the elites who directly make government policies or the ordinary citizens who may engage in a variety of politically salient activities to contest or reinforce them. Consequently, they have substantial political outcomes – producing or affecting the actual and possible political states of affairs that political theorists analyse, diagnose, critique, alter or recommend.

5   Conclusion

Ideological analysis is difficult, often tentative and always open to contestation and challenge. I have certainly not exhausted key methodological precepts and techniques. Nor are the many points of advice or empirical claims about human thinking that I have asserted immune from criticism. What this chapter might do, I hope, is two things: to show political theorists that ideological analysis matters to a far greater extent than is generally appreciated, and to show them how they can do it better. An expanded engagement with ideology in political theory is an exciting direction for the discipline, and suggests a panoply of potential research projects. But for it to be successful, political theorists need to draw on interdisciplinary research on ideology more thoroughly, and to reflect on how to study ideology more deeply.

References

Atran, Scott and Axelrod, Robert, 2008. 'Reframing sacred values', *Negotiation Journal* 24, 221–46.
Ball, Terence, Farr, James and Hanson, Russell L., eds., 1989. *Political Innovation and Conceptual Change.* Cambridge University Press.

Baurmann, Michael, 2007. 'Rational fundamentalism? An explanatory model of fundamentalist beliefs', *Episteme* 4, 150–66.

Bell, Daniel, 1960. *The End of Ideology: On the Exhaustion of Political Ideas in the Fifties*. Cambridge, MA: Harvard University Press.

Berger, Peter and Luckmann, Thomas, 1967. *The Social Construction of Reality*. New York: Anchor Books.

Berlin, Isaiah, 1969. *Four Essays on Liberty*. Oxford University Press.

Billig, Michael, 2008. 'The language of critical discourse analysis: the case of nominalization', *Discourse and Society* 19, 783–800.

Boudon, Raymond, 1989. *The Analysis of Ideology*. Cambridge: Polity Press.

Boudon, Raymond, 1999. 'Local vs general ideologies: a normal ingredient of political life', *Journal of Political Ideologies* 4, 141–61.

Carmines, Edward and D'Amico, Nicholas, 2015. 'The new look in political ideology research', *Annual Review of Political Science* 18, 205–16.

Chandler, David, 2004. 'The responsibility to protect? Imposing the "liberal peace"', *International Peacekeeping* 11, 59–81.

Constant, Benjamin, 1988. Biancamaria Fontana, ed., *Political Writings*. Cambridge University Press.

Coote, Anna, 2014. Who made ideology a dirty word? *The NEF Blog* [Online]. Available from: www.neweconomics.org/blog/entry/who-made-ideology-a-dirty-word. Accessed 26 May 2015.

Crawford, Neta, 2002. *Argument and Change in World Politics: Ethics, Decolonization and Humanitarian Intervention*. Cambridge University Press.

Doris, John and Murphy, Dominic, 2007. 'From My Lai to Abu Ghraib: the moral psychology of atrocity', *Midwest Studies in Philosophy* 31, 25–55.

Eagleton, Terry, 1991. *Ideology: An Introduction*. London: Verso.

Edelman, Murray, 1977. *Political Language: Words That Succeed and Policies That Fail*. New York: Academic Press.

Evans, Gareth, 2011. 'Ethnopolitical conflict: when is it right to intervene?', *Ethnopolitics* 10, 115–23.

Evans, Jocelyn, 2002. 'In defence of Sartori: party system change, voter preference distribution and other competitive incentives', *Party Politics* 8, 155–74.

Fairclough, Norman, 2001. *Language and Power*. Harlow: Pearson Education.

Fairclough, Norman, 2010. *Critical Discourse Analysis: The Critical Study of Language*. Harlow: Pearson Education.

Finlayson, Alan, 2012. 'Rhetoric and the political theory of ideologies', *Political Studies* 60, 751–67.

Foucault, Michel, 1982. 'The subject and power', *Critical Inquiry* 8, 777–95.

Freeden, Michael, 1996. *Ideologies and Political Theory: A Conceptual Approach*. Oxford University Press.

Freeden, Michael, 2005a. 'Confronting the chimera of a "post-ideological" age', *Critical Review of International Social and Political Philosophy* 8, 247–62.

Freeden, Michael, 2005b. 'What should the "political" in political theory explore?', *The Journal of Political Philosophy* 13, 113–34.

Freeden, Michael, 2006. 'Ideology and political theory', *Journal of Political Ideologies* 11, 3–22.

Freeden, Michael, ed., 2007. *The Meaning of Ideology: Cross-disciplinary Perspectives*. Oxford University Press.

Freeden, Michael, 2008. 'Thinking politically and thinking about politics: language, interpretation, and ideology', in David Leopold and Marc Stears, eds., *Political Theory: Methods and Approaches*. Oxford University Press, 196–215.

Freeden, Michael, 2012. 'Interpretative realism and prescriptive realism', *Journal of Political Ideologies* 17, 1–11.

Freeden, Michael, 2013a. 'The morphological analysis of ideology', in Michael Freeden, Lyman Tower Sargent and Marc Stears, eds., *The Oxford Handbook of Political Ideologies*. Oxford University Press, 115–37.

Freeden, Michael, 2013b. *The Political Theory of Political Thinking: The Anatomy of a Practice*. Oxford University Press.

Freeden, Michael, Lyman Tower Sargent and Marc Stears, eds., 2013. *The Oxford Handbook of Political Ideologies*. Oxford University Press.

Furnham, Adrian, 2003. 'Belief in a just world: research progress over the past decade', *Personality and Individual Differences* 34, 795–817.

Galston, William, 2010. 'Realism in political theory', *European Journal of Political Theory* 9, 385–411.

Geertz, Clifford, 1964. 'Ideology as a cultural system', in David Apter, ed., *Ideology and Discontent*. London: Free Press of Glencoe, 47–76.

Gendler, Tamar Szabó, 2008. 'Alief and belief', *The Journal of Philosophy* 105, 634–63.

George, Alexander and Andrew Bennett, 2005. *Case Studies and Theory Development in the Social Sciences*. Cambridge, MA: MIT Press.

Gerring, John, 1997. 'Ideology: a definitional analysis', *Political Research Quarterly* 50, 957–94.

Geuss, Raymond, 2003. 'Neither history nor praxis', *European Review* 11, 281–92.

Haidt, Jonathan, Jesse Graham and Craig Joseph, 2009. 'Above and below left-right: ideological narratives and moral foundations', *Psychological Inquiry* 20, 110–19.

Hall, Stuart, 1996. 'The problem of ideology: Marxism without guarantees', in David Morley and Kuan-Hsing Chen, eds., *Stuart Hall: Critical Dialogues in Cultural Studies*. London: Routledge, 24–45.

Hamilton, Malcolm, 1987. 'The elements of the concept of ideology', *Political Studies* 35, 18–38.

Hammack, Philip, 2008. 'Narrative and the cultural psychology of identity', *Personality and Social Psychology Review* 12, 222–47.

Hardwig, John, 1985. 'Epistemic dependence', *Journal of Philosophy* 82, 335–49.

Hochschild, Jennifer L., 2001. 'Where you stand depends on what you see: connections among values, perceptions of fact, and political prescriptions', in James Kuklinski, ed., *Citizens and Politics: Perspectives from Political Psychology*. Cambridge University Press, 313–40.

Howarth, David, Aletta Norval and Yannis Stavrakakis, eds., 2000. *Discourse Theory and Political Analysis: Identities, Hegemonies and Social Change.* Manchester University Press.

Huddy, Leonie, 2001. 'From social to political identity: a critical examination of social identity theory', *Political Psychology* 22, 127–56.

Humphrey, Matthew, 2005. '(De)contesting ideology: the struggle over the meaning of the struggle over meaning', *Critical Review of International Social and Political Philosophy* 8, 225–46.

Ipsos Mori. 2014. Perceptions Are Not Reality: Things the World Gets Wrong. Available: www.ipsos-mori.com/researchpublications/researcharchive/3466/Perceptions-are-not-reality-Things-the-world-gets-wrong.aspx. Accessed 9 May 2015.

Jost, John, 2006. 'The end of the end of ideology', *American Psychologist* 61, 651–70.

Jost, John, Christopher Federico and Jaime Napier, 2009a. 'Political ideology: its structure, functions and elective affinities', *Annual Review of Psychology* 60, 307–37.

Jost, John, Jack Glaser, Arie Kruglanski and Frank Sulloway, 2003. 'Political conservatism as motivated social cognition', *Psychological Bulletin* 129, 339–75.

Jost, John and Orsolya Hunyady, 2005. 'Antecedents and consequences of system-justifying ideologies', *Current Directions in Psychological Science* 14, 260–65.

Jost, John, Aaron Kay and Hulda Thorisdottir, 2009b. *Social and Psychological Bases of Ideology and System Justification.* Oxford University Press.

Jost, John and Brenda Major, 2001. *The Psychology of Legitimacy: Emerging Perspectives on Ideology, Justice and Intergroup Relations.* Cambridge University Press.

Kahneman, Daniel, 2012. *Thinking, Fast and Slow.* London: Penguin Books.

Knight, Kathleen, 2006. 'Transformations in the concept of ideology in the twentieth century', *American Political Science Review* 100, 619–26.

Laclau, Ernesto, 2007. 'Ideology and post-Marxism', in Michael Freeden, ed., *The Meaning of Ideology: Cross-disciplinary Perspectives.* Oxford University Press, 98–109.

Larrain, Jorge, 1979. *The Concept of Ideology.* London: Hutchinson and Co.

Leader Maynard, Jonathan, 2013. 'A map of the field of ideological analysis', *Journal of Political Ideologies* 18, 299–327.

Leader Maynard, Jonathan and Mildenberger, Matto, 2016. 'Convergence and divergence in the study of ideology: a critical review', *British Journal of Political Science.* FirstView early online edition.

Mann, Michael 2005. *The Dark Side of Democracy: Explaining Ethnic Cleansing.* Cambridge University Press.

Mccauley, Clark and Sophia Moskalenko, 2011. *Friction: How Radicalization Happens to Them and Us.* Oxford University Press.

Mclellan, David, 1995. *Ideology.* Buckingham: Open University Press.

Mill, John Stuart, 2008. *On Liberty and Other Essays.* Oxford University Press.

Mills, Charles, 1999. *The Racial Contract.* Ithaca, NY: Cornell University Press.

Mullins, Willard, 1972. 'On the concept of ideology in political science', *American Political Science Review* 66, 498–510.

Nelson, Eric, 2005. 'Liberty: one concept too many?', *Political Theory* 33, 58–78.

Norval, Aletta, 2000. 'The things we do with words – contemporary approaches to the analysis of ideology', *British Journal of Political Science* 30, 313–46.

Opotow, Susan, 1990. 'Moral exclusion and injustice: an introduction', *Journal of Social Issues* 46, 1–20.

Pinker, Steven, 1998. *How the Mind Works*. London: Penguin Books.

Price, Monroe, 2000. 'Information intervention: Bosnia, the Dayton accords, and the seizure of broadcasting transmitters', *Cornell International Law Journal* 33, 67–112.

Rosen, Michael, 2000. 'On voluntary servitude and the theory of ideology', *Constellations* 7, 393–407.

Rosenberg, Shawn, 1988. *Reason, Ideology and Politics*. Cambridge: Polity Press.

Rydgren, Jens, 2009. 'Beliefs', in Peter Hadström and Peter Bearman, eds., *The Oxford Handbook of Analytical Sociology*. Oxford University Press, 72–93.

Sagar, Paul, 2014. 'A broken clock', *The Oxonian Review*, 3 June. Available from: www.oxonianreview.org/wp/a-broken-clock.

Sartori, Giovanni, 1976. *Parties and Party Systems: A Framework for Analysis*. Cambridge University Press.

Searle, John, 1995. *The Construction of Social Reality*. London: Penguin.

Shelby, Tommie, 2003. 'Ideology, racism, and critical social theory', *The Philosophical Forum* 34, 153–88.

Shenhav, Shaul, 2006. 'Political narratives and political reality', *International Political Science Review* 27, 245–62.

Simonds, A. P., 1989. 'Ideological domination and the political information market', *Theory and Society* 18, 181–211.

Skinner, Quentin, 1974. 'Some problems in the analysis of political thought and action', *Political Theory* 2, 277–303.

Skinner, Quentin, 1998. *Liberty Before Liberalism*. Cambridge University Press.

Skinner, Quentin, 2002a. 'A third concept of liberty', *Proceedings of the British Academy* 117, 237–68.

Skinner, Quentin, 2002b. *Visions of Politics. Volume I: Regarding Method*. Cambridge University Press.

Steger, Manfred, 2008. *The Rise of the Global Imaginary: Political Ideologies from the French Revolution to the Global War on Terror*. Oxford University Press.

Swift, Adam, 2003. *How Not to Be a Hypocrite: School Choice for the Morally Perplexed Parent*. London: Routledge.

Tajfel, Henri, 1974. 'Social identity and intergroup behaviour', *Social Science Information* 13, 65–93.

Thagard, Paul, 2010. 'Explaining economic crises: are there collective representations?', *Episteme* 7, 266–83.

Thagard, Paul, 2012. 'Mapping minds across cultures', in Ron Sun, ed., *Grounding Social Sciences in Cognitive Sciences*. Cambridge, MA: MIT Press, 35–62.

Thompson, John, 1984. *Studies in the Theory of Ideology*. Cambridge: Polity Press.

Tileagă, Christian, 2007. 'Ideologies of moral exclusion: a critical discursive reframing of depersonalization, delegitimization and dehumanization', *British Journal of Social Psychology* 46, 717–37.

Tsintsadze-Maass, Eteri and Richard Maass, 2014. 'Groupthink and terrorist radicalization', *Terrorism and Political Violence* 26, 735–58.

Tully, James, 1983. 'The pen is a mighty sword: Quentin Skinner's analysis of politics', *British Journal of Political Science* 13, 489–509.

Tversky, Amos and Daniel Kahneman, 1974. 'Judgment under uncertainty: heuristics and biases', *Science* 185, 1124–31.

Valentini, Laura, 2012. 'Ideal vs. non-ideal theory: a conceptual map', *Philosophy Compass* 7, 654–64.

Van Dijk, Teun, 1998. *Ideology: A Multidisciplinary Approach*. London: Sage Publications.

Van Dijk, Teun, 2013. 'Ideology and discourse', in Michael Freeden, Lyman Tower Sargent and Marc Stears, eds., *The Oxford Handbook of Political Ideologies*. Oxford University Press, 175–96.

Varki, Ajit and Danny Brower, 2013. *Denial: Self-Deception, False Beliefs and the Origins of the Human Mind*. New York: Twelve.

Vigna, Stefano Della and Matthew Gentzkow, 2010. 'Persuasion: empirical evidence', *Annual Review of Economics* 2, 643–69.

Weber, Max, 2009. 'Science as a vocation', in Hans Heinrich Gerth and C. Wright Mills, eds., *From Max Weber: Essays in Sociology*. Abingdon: Routledge, 129–56.

Welsh, Jennifer, 2010. 'Implementing the "responsibility to protect": where expectations meet reality', *Ethics and International Affairs* 24, 415–30.

Wittgenstein, Ludwig, 2001. *Philosophical Investigations*. Malden, MA: Blackwell Publishing.

Wodak, Ruth and Michael Meyer, eds., 2009. *Methods of Critical Discourse Analysis*. London: SAGE Publications.

Worsnip, Alex, 2017. 'Cryptonormative judgements', *European Journal of Philosophy*.

Yanow, Dvora and Peregrine Schwartz-Shea, 2006. *Interpretation and Method: Empirical Research Methods and the Interpretive Turn*. Armonk, NY: M.E. Sharpe.

Žižek, Slavoj, ed., 1994a. *Mapping Ideology*. London: Verso.

Žižek, Slavoj, 1994b. 'The spectre of ideology', in Slavoj Žižek, ed., *Mapping Ideology*. London: Verso, 1–33.

15 How to Do a Political Theory PhD

Keith Dowding and Robert E. Goodin

The other chapters in this book describe and critique the standard methods used in analytical political theory. Here we give a few pointers, of the sort we give to our students, about doing a political theory PhD.

1 Choosing Your Topic

Choose a topic that you actually like. You're going to have to live with it for three, four or more years.

Get on with it. Don't take forever making the choice. You have only three or four years to write it, and time spent dithering over a topic eats into writing time.

What's the problem? A thesis needs to answer a question. It must address a problem; it is not simply your thoughts on a subject in which you are interested.

A thesis needs a thesis. You need to settle on more than just a topic or even a problem: a thesis needs a thesis. It has to *argue* something.

Why are others wrong? The simplest way of thinking of an answer is to consider what others have said and why they are wrong.

It's not your life's work. Every initial thesis proposal is too big and ambitious. Remember: you are not Marx, and this is not *Kapital*. If it is any good, you will get a job and write other books.

2 Organizing Your Work

Papers or monograph? The traditional thesis is a monograph – a sustained argument over six to eight chapters. Thesis by papers is now established in political science and can be transferred to political theory. But it is not an easy option. A monograph needs only a couple of original chapters; in a set of papers, each of them needs to say something original.

Bite-sized pieces. Break the thesis down into chapters and focus on one at a time. Don't spend too long on each one, but move to the next, even when you know that more work is required. Once they are all written, you can fine-tune and work on the final draft.

Plan, but not too rigidly. You will need a plan for the whole thesis from the start. But your structure and argument may well change, even radically, before the end. Don't worry. Just keep writing, and repackage later.

Reading is the enemy of writing. At the beginning you will need to read widely around the literature to get the lie of the land and situate your work within it. That done, get on with writing; don't chase up footnotes or pursue everything written on the subject. Getting your own ideas down and then seeing who has said something similar is a good way of distinguishing what you want to say from others. That way you avoid following the same ruts as the existing literature.

Let it go. Everything can be improved with a little more work, but don't let that stand in the way of submission. Plug the big holes and learn to live with the problems (though plan a response in case someone else, especially your PhD examiner, spots them).

3   Planning for Life Post-PhD

What is it for? If your aim is to enter the academic profession, writing a PhD thesis is not enough. You also need to publish, and you should be thinking about that aspect from the start.

Index

absence of interference, 165
abstract reasoning, 5
abstraction in positive political theory, 196
Ackerly, Brooke, 285
acontextualism, 313
act deontology, 133
act-utilitarianism, 134
adaptive reconstruction, 251, 254–5
Adorno, Theodor, 119
advice in analytical writing, 19–20
aesthetic interpretation, 243
agonism, 254
agreement and realistic idealism, 142–3
ambiguity of concepts, 156, 255
anachronistic conceptualizations, 250,
    255–6
analytic methodologies, 288
analytic normative theory, 93
analytical philosophy, 153
analytical political theory. *See also*
    conceptual analysis in political theory;
    political theory
    complementing and competing ideas,
        12–13
    conclusion, 13–16
    defined, 2
    historical reflections, 4–6
    how to write, 18–20
    introduction, 1–2, 6–7
    meta-ethics and, 92
    overview, 8–12
    reasons for, 3–4
    scope of, 6–8
Angle, Stephen, 276
Anglo-American political theory, 91–2, 93
anonymous Pareto principle, 76
anti-Aristotelian philosophical context, 247
anxiety suppression, 316
application approach to models, 210–13
arbitrary concepts, 171
Arendt, Hannah, 280
argumentative relevance, 33–4

Aristotle, 94–5, 105, 175
atheism, 262
attachment and ideological analysis,
    315–17
Austen, Jane, 106
authoritarian demagogue, 99
autonomy concept, 114, 181

background theories, 58, 61
Bajpai, Rochana, 283
balance of power, 143
Ball, Terence, 249
Barber, Benjamin, 148
bargaining theory, 238
Barry, Brian, 86–7
Begriffsgeschichte (history of concepts),
    249–50
behavioral inference, 312
beliefs in ideological analysis, 318
Bell, Daniel, 290
Bentham, Jeremy, 99
Berlin, Isaiah, 119, 155, 250, 254, 307
Bernasconi, Robert, 258–9
better chances, defined, 221
better prizes, defined, 221
bias concerns, 23, 36, 290–1, 310, 316
Binmore, Ken, 225
book-length reconstruction, 254–5
The British Journal of Political Science, 210
British Labour Party (BLP), 117
Buchanan, James M., 217

Cabrera, Luis, 285
Camping Trip thought experiment, 22
cardinal utility functions, 220
Carens Market example, 138
Carver, Terrell, 258
characterizations in ideological
    analysis, 318
Christiano, Thomas, 112
classical liberal perspective, 258
classification of concepts, 156–7